The
Environmental
Unconscious

The Environmental Unconscious

ECOLOGICAL
POETICS
FROM SPENSER
TO MILTON

Steven Swarbrick

UNIVERSITY OF
MINNESOTA PRESS
MINNEAPOLIS
LONDON

The University of Minnesota Press gratefully acknowledges the financial assistance provided for the publication of this book by Baruch College, CUNY.

Portions of chapters 1 and 2 are adapted from "The Life Aquatic: Liquid Poetics and the Discourse of Friendship in *The Faerie Queene*," *Spenser Studies* 30 (2015): 229–53, https://doi.org /10.7756/spst.030.014.229-53; copyright 2015 by the University of Chicago. Portions of chapter 3 are adapted from "Tempestuous Life: Ralegh's Ocean in Ruins," *Criticism* 59, no. 4 (2017): 539–63; copyright 2018 by Wayne State University Press. Portions of chapter 5 are adapted from "Milton's Queer Earth: A Geology of Exhausted Life," in *Queer Milton*, ed. David Orvis, 255–91 (New York: Palgrave Macmillan, 2018); reprinted by permission from Springer Nature.

Published by the University of Minnesota Press
111 Third Avenue South, Suite 290
Minneapolis, MN 55401-2520
http://www.upress.umn.edu

ISBN 978-1-5179-1380-9 (hc)
ISBN 978-1-5179-1381-6 (pb)

A Cataloging-in-Publication record for this book is available from the Library of Congress.

Printed in the United States of America on acid-free paper

The University of Minnesota is an equal-opportunity educator and employer.

UMP BmB 2023

To Rebecca

CONTENTS

INTRODUCTION

This book argues that four early modern poets—Edmund Spenser, Walter Ralegh, Andrew Marvell, and John Milton—advanced a poetic materialism not only at odds with the empirical science of their time but also one that challenges theoretical inclinations in the new materialisms today. The new and old materialisms both propose a return to matter in order to overcome loss. For early modern materialists like Francis Bacon, the loss was empirical knowledge;[1] now, for the new materialists, it is the loss of more-than-human lifeworlds.[2] By contrast, this book shows that Spenser, Ralegh, Marvell, and Milton used their poems to teach readers how to *enjoy* loss. Moreover, it argues that a poetry that invites us to enjoy loss is of radical importance to ecological politics today. Writing at the dawn of the Anthropocene,[3] when nature's resources seemed limitless and the risk of loss merely contingent with respect to the wealth and freedom promised by capitalism,[4] Spenser, Ralegh, Marvell, and Milton crafted an ecological poetics in which loss was no longer contingent but rather constitutive of desire. This focus on the pleasures of loss presents a new kind of materialism. Following a reading tradition running from Lucretius to Lacan, I argue that these writers invite us to read matter as structured by loss—just like poetic form.[5] By aligning matter with poetic form, these poets not only took pleasure in the dissatisfactions of the present but also resisted the promise of future gain.

Recent studies in early modern ecocriticism have devoted considerable attention to the natural historical underpinnings of early modern literature. Laurie Shannon has posited a human–animal cosmopolitics in the time of Shakespeare; Dan Brayton and Steve Mentz have each cast sails in the maritime literature of early modernity; Jonathan Goldberg, Stephen Greenblatt, and others have revealed a subrepresentational level of atomic Lucretian matter or seeds; and Phillip John Usher has extracted a subterranean awareness of early modern geomedia.[6] Although these and other ecocritical projects have done much to reveal the articulate relations that early modern materialism makes possible, they leave underexplored the disarticulating force of matter—its semiotic excess.[7] Gerrard Passannante refers to this disarticulating power as the "catastrophizing" power of materialism, leaning on the sense of *strophe* as a turning that turns the poetic imagination against itself.[8] By *not* attending to this catastrophic power, we, posthumanists, produce instead a hyperhumanism that sees matter from the perspective of the human subject alone. Rather than foregrounding materialism's explosive force, ecocriticism has become a vehicle for the humanist belief that matter and meaning must coincide.

To attend to materialism's explosive force, this book develops an environmental poetics that investigates the complex relations among new and old materialist discourses, environmental theory, and an early modern poetry pierced by lack. The writers in this study all shape their poems around objects that fail to satisfy. The truth that Spenser's Redcrosse Knight pursues is forever unclaimed, coming only in the form of a trauma enacted on trees. Likewise, Ralegh's pursuit of wealth ends disastrously in the tropics, where local ecologies disrupt his adventures. Marvell's vision of home vanishes in the time-lapse of history. And Milton's paradise proves a site of loss and contradiction. Although the poets in this study partake of the early modern fascination with material objects, evidenced by the historical rise of empiricism, colonial extraction, and aesthetic realism, the materialism they put forth is highly counterintuitive: theirs is a materialism *without* matter because it gives priority to the structuring role of the unconscious in psychic life.

Taking a page from psychoanalytic theorists like Lacan, *The Environmental Unconscious* asserts that matter, far from being immediate, knowable, or countable, houses an incognizable lack. This lack underpins the subject of ecocriticism while pinning that subject to the singular nub of their enjoyment—what Lacan calls the *sinthome*. The *sinthome* refers to the missing signifier of desire, that which is in the other *more* than the other, in the world *more* than the world, and which sustains the subject's libidinal circuit while remaining unknowable and unspeakable. A kernel of jouissance that resists symbolization, the *sinthome*, in Lee Edelman's queer reading of Lacan, "binds the subject to its constitutive libidinal career, and assures that no subject, try as it may, can ever 'get over' itself—'get over,' that is, the fixation of the drive that determines its jouissance."⁹ The *sinthome* functions as a point of attraction and bewilderment, organizing the subject's "libidinal career" while endangering the subject's illusory identity. This, then—the *sinthome* as the locus of the drive—is what the ecological subject cannot "get over"; indeed, despite its many attempts at surpassing, posthumanizing, and networking its way into harmonious accord with the web of life, where all is entangled, the ecological subject cannot surpass or entangle the obscene jouissance at its core, since this core of enjoyment paradoxically *sustains* the ecological subject as a breach or tear. Hence Lacan's rewriting of existence as ex-sistence, a formalization of the inexorable *ek-* (out) or exit from concrete reality that the *sinthome*, ever bordering on madness, names. Ingeniously, Edelman calls this mode of ex-sistence *sinthom*osexuality and aligns it with queer subjects who refuse the relentless pull of reproductive futurity. For my part, I offer the term *sinthom*oenvironmentality,¹⁰ a precursor, if you will, to Edelman's queer *sinthome* in that it pays tribute to Lacan's premodern etymology: "Sinthome is an old way of spelling what was subsequently spelt *symptôme*."¹¹ Sinthomoenvironmentality invites greater appreciation of the eco-negativity at the heart of life—a negativity that throws life into contradiction; perforates matter; haunts ecological subjectivity with its own abject enjoyment; and, what is more, gives the subject its freedom to enjoy beyond the network of objects and their relations. Desire, so conceived, has no object, and thus no relation. The eco-psychoanalysis I model in this book is radically nonobject oriented.

If this merger of eco-psychoanalysis sounds like a "strong theory," out-of-joint with the current fashion of "weak" epistemology in that it uses a universalist language to examine ideas like the split subject, the unconscious, and desire (desire as such)—it is.[12] The poets in this study exemplify a universal failure of language that could (why not?) be applied to other poets and other periods. I assemble these poets not like "the beads of a rosary," moving from one causal connection to the next, as in Walter Benjamin's metaphor of what historicism does.[13] Instead, I adopt a strong methodology of reading for exemplarity. There was a time, not long ago, when reading for exemplarity was alive and well: William Empson's *Seven Types of Ambiguity,* for example, or, in the 1990s, Joan Copjec's *Read My Desire.* The first would be impossible today. The second is a clarion call against the strictures of historicism, which Copjec links to the notion of immanence. When everything is immanent, entangled, or enmeshed, when the outside has been curtained off, Copjec argues, one thing is undoubtedly missing: desire.[14] That is because desire can only appear as a fissure in the web of life. Since Copjec's writing in 1994, the situation has only gotten worse for desiring subjects. "Always historicize!" has become the drumbeat of the humanities and environmental humanities.[15] Theories of immanence are everywhere (see my Conclusion). But as biospheric conditions continue to unravel, as the capitalist death machine continues to speed up, and as the crisis of the humanities worsens from austerity, I am convinced of nothing more than the urgency of big, symptomatic readings.[16] Today's task isn't to historicize. The task is to symptomatize. "Enjoy your symptom!" is the battle cry of psychoanalytic ecocriticism.[17]

Building on the pathbreaking ecomaterialism of medieval and early modern scholars like Jonathan Gil Harris, Karen Raber, Karl Steel, and Julian Yates,[18] and focusing on the "surplus vitality" of psychoanalytic theories of desire, as articulated by Edelman, Mari Ruti, and others,[19] this book foregrounds the compromised workings of the environmental unconscious with its intrusions and interruptions (slips of the Real) into the steady flow of life and meaning as the *poetic* underside of environmental thought. Each of my chapters reads material objects—including trees, oceans, rivers, animal dwellings, plants, and fossils—as poetic forms demanding our close reading, not because of their supposed thereness (signaling the "great outdoors" in Quinten Meillassoux's sense)[20] but because of their failure to be there. In circling endlessly around ciphered objects, these poets reveal that loss is central to the enjoyment poetry offers—and that nature offers. They offer readers an environmental poetics in which loss is not the obstacle to desire, but its aim.

Materialism's Absent Center

By aligning materialism with poetic form, this book makes a critical intervention in the "materialist turn" currently sweeping the theoretical landscape. This new wave of materialisms includes the "agential realism" of Karen Barad, the "transcorporeality" of Stacy Alaimo, the "hyperobjects" of Timothy Morton, and the "actor-network theory" of Bruno Latour.[21] I use the phrase "new materialisms" in this book as shorthand for several related discourses, including animal studies, posthumanism, and ecocriticism. The new materialisms emphasize that matter and meaning are entwined; not only that, this entwinement necessitates responsiveness to the nonhuman bodies and artifacts that make up the "human" world. The goal of the new materialisms has been to place special emphasis on relations of care and mutuality among human and nonhuman actors and to develop ways of dismantling the hegemony of the human in appreciation of a wider world of matter.

The emphasis on "matter" in new materialist philosophies, including affect theory, object-oriented ontology, cognitive literary studies, and environmental criticism, is itself a direct response to the growing concern (though it is a concern that has been growing at least since Plato) that reading, which is by definition belated and thus out-of-step with the present demand, has delayed our attention to bodies and things for long enough, and that what truly matters now is that we attend urgently, ethically, and compassionately to . . . matter, precisely. The return to matter is staged as a return to an ethics and politics of repair, one in which we, having regained the great outdoors, work to rebuild a common world. Bruno Latour's landmark essay, "Why Has Critique Run Out of Steam?," which is less a postmortem on critique than it is a kind of critique of critique, ends with exactly this call to rebuild and to multiply the commons. He asks: "What would critique do if it could be associated with *more*, not with *less*, with *multiplication*, not *subtraction*."[22] The emphasis here, as in

all Latourian-inspired criticism,[23] is to have done with linguistic re-
ductionism (the reduction of all matters to a single surface of sense)
by forging a common lifeworld. Getting real, then, is not only a materialist or scientific endeavor; it is also a matter of care and ethical
responsibility. Increasingly, the spirit of our times demands that we
stop taking the long way around by reading matter as a signifying
chain, a chain without a final destination, and instead extend our care
to the immediate, the visceral, and the literal thing. What the new
materialisms all say, without always exactly saying it, is that close attention to language is not only escapist but worse: simply beside the
point. New materialists assume that matter *must* mean. Matter must
mean because, as Karen Barad writes in the opening sentences of
Meeting the Universe Halfway, "Matter and meaning are not separate
elements. They are inextricably fused together, and no event, no matter how energetic, can tear them asunder."[24]

Yet while Barad and others define their materialism against the
deracinated materialism of the Enlightenment, which privileged the
human knower over and against the natural world, there is, on this
essential point (the fusion of matter and meaning), very little difference between Barad's materialism and that of naturalist philosopher
and early modern humanist Francis Bacon, who, though charged
with bringing about "the death of nature" and the "extirpation of
animism,"[25] sought not just to reeducate his readers about the natural world but to rediscover in the world of things the primordial
accord between matter and the senses. For Bacon, too, matter must
mean; not only human knowledge but also human salvation de-
pended on it. According to Joanna Picciotto, Bacon attributed "an
apparent design flaw—the maladaptation of human perception to
the scope of creation—to original sin."[26] Consequently, Bacon's ad-
vocacy of a new science required a new understanding of the senses.
"For created humanity," Picciotto writes, "divine worship was indistinguishable from satisfying the cognitive appetite."[27] By contrast,
the question for fallen humanity was, according to Bacon, "What is
creation *before* the fallen body and mind experience it?"[28] It is this
unique understanding of the "maladaptation" of the fallen senses to
the natural world, a view that left open the possibility of their im-
provement, that radically distinguished Bacon's reformist project

from other, like-minded reformers who shared his zeal for returning to things themselves. Earlier figures such as Paracelsus had already denounced the bookishness of humanist learning in favor of the immediacy of the first book, the Book of Nature, which he proposed revealed the imprints—or "signatures"—of the divine *verbum dei*.[29] But whereas Paracelsus imagined the divine "signatures" to be accessible to humanity's exegetical practices, Bacon demurred, arguing instead that the stable link between signatures and the divine, signs and signified, had been lost. What was left to humanity were the senses, wayward and needing reform. Bacon "worked to make visible the material causes or 'originals' of sensory experience" through a progressive "de-education" of the senses. He tried, in other words, to reclaim paradise.[30]

Centuries later, we are still searching for Bacon's paradisal object, precisely what he made the object of his scientific reforms, as did Immanuel Kant and the speculative realists after him.[31] Unlike the poets in this study, however, the turn to matter in contemporary literary and cultural criticism does not just hinge on a revival of early modern materialism (Lucretius and Spinoza, among others); it dampens early modern materialism's explosiveness: Bacon's paradisal object, Jane Bennett and Latour's reenchanted object, are both immaculate objects, both beneficiaries of the communicative ideal that matter and meaning must cohere.[32] For these thinkers, no less than Bacon, human salvation depends on it. The new materialist faith in matter ultimately redounds on the humanist subject whose place in the world is again guaranteed (and redeemed) by interconnection.

At precisely the moment when these and other thinkers turn to matter, they turn away from matter by making all things—from animals to plants to minerals—synonymous with human meaning. Far from surpassing Bacon's brand of materialism, the new materialisms repeat it unconsciously: the neovitalist reads "life" into matter in order to explain how all matter works to assemble in the making of more-than-human lifeworlds; the affect theorist reads affect (or emotion, or mood) in the immediate and recognizable sensations of the lived body; the speculative realist reads traces of the prehuman past in the most absolute of ideal objects—mathematics; and the ecocritic, together with the posthumanist, joins hands with the naïve realist by reading matter (animals, plants, and minerals) as words made flesh. At its worst, the turn to matter suggests that reading itself is beside the point; reading simply *unveils* bodies-objects-things (e.g., the brain as the answer to the problem of sense, or the animal as the answer to the problem of ethics).

What we have now more than ever is an abundance of "matters" serving, as they did for Bacon, as answers to the problem of sense. Yet for all of that, we have a dearth of any real readings. And that is because language (the operator of sense) so conceived by the new materialisms isn't materialist at all; it is Adamic.[33] Just as Adam named the first creatures, welcoming them inside the human fold, so the Baconian naturalist and new materialist meet on the same plane of human meaning: they both make the human master of his own house by endowing him with a language perfectly fitted to his environment. Consequently, we have been living for some time in the stifled terrain of what environmental philosopher Frédéric Neyrat calls "saturated immanence,"[34] when everything is brought inside the house of human meaning, and it becomes impossible, indeed mad, to think matter from without, to think the outside.[35]

In their introduction to *New Materialisms*, Diana Coole and Samantha Frost state:

> In the history of philosophy, materialism has remained a sporadic and often marginal approach. For there is an apparent paradox in thinking about matter: as soon as we do so, we seem to distance ourselves from it, and within the space that opens up, a host of immaterial things seems to emerge: language, consciousness, subjectivity, agency, mind, soul.[36]

True enough, when one sets out to think about matter, one often encounters a gap. Nevertheless, just as it would be misguided, according to the authors, to fill in that gap with matters of the "soul," I argue that it is equally misguided to fill it in with bodies-objects-things. Why? For the simple but important reason that matter, like language, is not all.[37] When one looks to matter, one encounters a minus. Indeed, there would be no thinking at all without the encounter with this minus. Without a tear in our vision of the world, there would be no consequence to our readings (and hence, no readings). Matter would simply cohere.

Lucretius to the Letter

At the heart of this problem in new materialist discourse lies a misreading of atomist poet and philosopher Lucretius, a misreading that, as I have been arguing, counterintuitively aligns contemporary new materialism more closely with Francis Bacon than their supposed inspiration. The ecocritic or the science studies scholar turns to Lucretius to show that matter "speaks" (it articulates relations among elements, as does language) with or without the human. In the epoch of the Anthropocene, in which we are compelled to envision a world without humans, the insight into nonhuman language is critical (a point I return to later). However, it also sacrifices one of the principal lessons of the linguistic turn: that language itself is implicated in a gap. Lucretius calls this gap "void." By insisting that matter and meaning are indissoluble, the new materialisms provide an abundance of significant matters. But this insistence masks a prior refusal: the refusal, namely, to grapple with matter's incompletion or the structural nonidentity of matter-language. This nonidentity is something that Lucretius insists upon.

In *De rerum natura*, Lucretius compares atoms to alphabetic letters; like letters, Lucretius argues, tropological arrangements structure the whole universe: "Now do you see the point of my previous remark," Lucretius asks, "that it makes a great difference in what combinations and positions the same elements occur and what motions they mutually pass on and take over, so that with a little reshuffling the same ones may produce forests and fires? This is just how the words themselves are formed, by a little reshuffling of the letters, when we pronounce 'forests' and 'fires' as two distinct utterances."[38] In Lucretius's analogy, the material word is no less dependent on the "combinations and positions" of atoms to make sense of reality—to make distinctions, say, between "forests" and "forest fires"—than the letters that compose the words "forests" and "fires." Both letters and atoms make sense because they are a priori gatherings: "The same elements compose sky, sea and lands, rivers and sun, crops, trees and animals, but they are moving differently and in different combinations."[39] Moreover, "The letters which denote sky, sea, earth and rivers also denote crops, trees and animals."[40] What Lucretius describes is not a world of things, but, as Jacques Lezra has argued, a world of events.[41] The whole of *De rerum natura* can be said to constitute a radical declination in the history of philosophy because it affirms that, in fact, everything is an event: happenings rather than things, becomings rather than being. It makes little difference, in this case, whether we are talking about atoms or letters since atoms and letters are composed of the same stuff.

Lucretius's comparison between atoms and letters has been at the forefront of new materialist readings.[42] Whereas the linguistic turn is said to have left the material at the wayside, the turn to matter now hails matter as sense-making in its own right: matter is said to organize, to assemble, to affect and be affected, to trigger events, to become, to possibilize and de-possibilize, to create vital networks, to democratize, to give voice, to usher in the Open, to animate, and above all, to make *live*. Matter has become a surrogate for language and matters of representation because matter—read in the Lucretian vein—is already sense-making. The signifier and the symbolic are at best redundancies, and the linguistic turn was already the material in sheep's clothing.

What the new materialisms neglect is the a-syntaxis that Lucretius builds into his philosophical system. For the new materialist, matter *makes sense*; it is geared toward relations and becomings that echo symbolic structures of meaning. In *The Environmental Unconscious,* the point is just the opposite: for it is not the case that matter as language is only sense-making; matter, as Lucretius shows, is built on a foundation of nonsense, of letters with no natural order, logic, or syntactic belonging.[43]

Despite the now ubiquitous refrain on matter's sense-making ability, the turn to matter, though it may have redressed a certain naïve anthropocentrism, has, more importantly, failed to account for the revolutionary thesis of Lucretius: that matter, a system of letters without totalization, implicates failure at every turn.[44] What is inextricable for Lucretius is not matter and meaning, but matter and void. Lucretius's poetics of matter is, strictly speaking, a poetics of the impossible. Lucretius writes: "But now to resume my task begun of weaving the web of this discourse: the nature of the universe, there-fore, as it is in itself, is made up of two things; for there are bodies, and there is void, in which these bodies are and through which they move this way and that."⁴⁵ There is something like an inaugural *décal-age* (gap) in Lucretian materialism, a scattering of bodies identical to the "elements" of his discourse:

> All through these very lines of mine you see many elements com-mon to many words, although you must confess that lines and words differ one from another both in meaning and in the sound of their soundings. So much can elements do, when nothing is changed but order; but the elements that are the beginnings of things can bring with them more kinds of variety, from which all the various things can be produced.⁴⁶

It could be said that all matter is discursive, according to Lucretius. However, the discursive is not all. Although all of being results from a chain of letters, these letters assemble around a void. The scandal of Lucretian materialism is not that it grants the same meaning-making capabilities throughout the whole universe—from stars to atoms to flora and fauna—but that it roots the negativity of language within matter itself. Matter, a system of letters etched by void, is, for Lucre-tius, the failure to communicate. By weaving void within itself, matter speaks, but it speaks endlessly of its own impossibility.

Lucretian materialism is, in this way, a perfect example of the psychoanalytic notion of the symptom. What life articulates via the various comings and goings of matter is not the "real" that the new materialisms take it for; life in all its multiplicity is the symptom, or the expression, of lack—precisely what Lucretius calls void and psychoanalysis calls the failure of full speech. Far from producing meaningful matters at every turn, the Lucretian unconscious turns matter around itself; it is the site of antiproduction in the material universe.⁴⁷ And just as psychoanalysis distinguishes between un-conscious and conscious discourse, Lucretius distinguishes between letters and things: although we speak of the latter, the former—the Lucretian unconscious—speaks us. Lucretius was the first to put na-ture's symptoms (its hysteria, slips of the tongue, compulsiveness, and forms of forgetting) on the couch—to hear the silence of another dis-course in nature's message, one altogether different from that spoken by the new materialists today.

The point Lucretius makes is that language is not only radically contingent but also shot through with negativity or lack. The ground of sense, according to Lucretius, is groundless. Consequently, the Lu-cretian universe is first and foremost a purloined universe; it is always one letter too few. Against the countless ecophilosophies that sing rapturously of life's communicative network, Lucretian materialism argues that life is at bottom the *absence* of a work. Life sings end-lessly of its own incompletion and failure of full speech. Moreover, as a symptom of the void, life's sole drive, its animating thrust, is to repeat the absence that Lucretius installs at the very center of things. The invocation of Venus at the start of *De rerum natura* supports this point.[48] Venus spurs desire, but a desire that is, according to Spenser (see my first chapter), abyssal. *The Environmental Unconscious* shifts readers' attention to this other scene, to the radically deviant, avital, and inhuman language Lucretius and the early modern poets writ-ing after him uncover in life's discourse. Matter, in this book, not only adds up, sublimating its desultory force into higher orders of mean-ing but also cracks up, in Gilles Deleuze's sense of nonsignifying relations.[49] If it is true that matter is meaning-making even without the human supplement as interpreter or gloss, it is also the case that matter endlessly falls apart through language.

Matter *thinks*, it speaks in this book—through animal cries, tree tropology, alluvial flows, inhuman architecture, and geo-logic formations—but it does so in compromised relation to an environmental unconscious that is, for us, untranslatable. These poets' materialism is akin to the psychoanalytic theory of the uncon-scious in that language there combines in a-syntactic series, leaving gaps in the reader's symbolic awareness. As in poetry, these gaps, or caesurae, though incommensurable with the manifest content of the page, give matter its structure, meaning, and flow. My readings of these poems bring void—the environmental unconscious—to bear on early modern ecocriticism.

Ecocriticism and the Environmental Unconscious

This book is, consequently, an excavation of the unconscious structures that, from the Renaissance to now, animate and constrain environmental discourse. Although the psychoanalytic theory of the unconscious may appear anachronistic to my focus on early modern poetry, it was, according to Lacan, the materialism of the early modern period, not the Freudian, that first gave rise to the theory of the unconscious. History, like trauma, works in twos in psychoanalysis. Thus it is only with René Descartes's famous formula, "*I am thinking, 'therefore I am,'*" that the subject of the unconscious becomes legible: "It is legible," says Lacan, "that thought only grounds being by knotting itself in speech where every operation goes right to the essence of language."[50] This alone establishes "for the subject a certain anchoring in being."[51] Moreover, this anchoring of being to the place of thought, which Lacan rightly reads as the place of language, links the Cartesian revolution to the Freudian one.[52] The Freudian subversion of the subject, which begins by positing a subject who is *not* at home in thought and who is, by definition, self-divided, "is unthinkable," Lacan argues, before Descartes. The Freudian unconscious is unthinkable without Descartes because Descartes's subject of science allowed Freud to see our true place in the unconscious, which thinks only where we are not.[53]

Nature, of course, is also where we are not—an insight with implications that have not yet been sufficiently attended to in ecocriticism. The term "environmental unconscious" was first introduced to ecocriticism by Lawrence Buell in 2003 to refer to preconscious or not-yet-conscious environments that go beyond human perception. According to Buell, the environmental unconscious "foreshortens" our perception, meaning that it restricts what is possible for us to know about our surroundings. A term borrowed from linear perspectivism, "foreshortening" means that our perception bars whatever surpasses its inevitable vanishing point. Beyond that point, Buell argues, lies the environmental unconscious—everything that is, for us, out of sight:

> Environmental unconscious in its negative aspect refers to the impossibility of individual or collective perception coming to full

consciousness at whatever level: observation, thought, articulation, and so forth. I do not pretend to be able to identify all the many causes of foreshortening: scientific ignorance, inattention, specialized intellectual curiosity, ethnocentricity, self-protectiveness, the conventions of language—the list is long. Yet environmental unconscious is also to be seen as potential: as a residual capacity (of individual humans, authors, texts, readers, communities) to awake to fuller apprehension of physical environment and one's interdependence with it.[54]

In Buell's perspectival metaphor, the environmental unconscious recedes from view. It can, however, return in moments of awakening. In Buell's use, the potential to wake up is precisely what makes the environmental unconscious so uplifting: vibrant matters are always just around the corner; we simply have to look. Now, it is this definition of environmental unconscious that my book quarrels with.

What is striking, above all, in Buell's definition is the extent to which it foreshortens the insights of psychoanalysis. The Freudian theory of sexuality is not on Buell's list of explanatory causes of environmental destruction: "scientific ignorance, inattention," and so on. The reason why we may imagine is that the Freudian unconscious is not simply the result of geometric foreshortening; it is not something somewhere, a space waiting to be uncovered by later readings. The unconscious is, according to Freud, incompletion itself. Let us consider what Freud says: "The interpretation of dreams is the royal road to a knowledge of the unconscious."[55] Now, what Freud discovers on the road to the unconscious should be familiar to anyone who has taught undergraduate literature: the road to the unconscious is paved with meanings. Better still: the road to the unconscious is paved with sexual meanings. In fact, there are so many ways to find (sexual) meaning within a given dream-text that one begins to wonder if the meanings themselves are not the obstacle or a screen hiding "something." Had Freud stopped at these meanings, psychoanalysis would never have matured beyond the point of reading on sight. That is, it never would have learned to read beyond sensible matter, to see the gaps in language, and to listen for silences. As it happens, psychoanalysis only becomes a science of the unconscious after it begins to see the dream-text's manifest content as a screen preventing further investigation.

Investigation into what exactly? Not the dream's meanings, for which, no doubt, there are always more just around the corner, coming-into-being, but its *failure* to mean, its impasses and contradictions. Freud's great discovery, in other words, is that the road to the unconscious is paved in meanings. We must attune ourselves, then, to the gaps in meaning, to the areas where interpretation fails and reading matter becomes synonymous with reading for silences.

Freud's lesson opens the space for a different hypothesis regarding matters of the real: this book argues that in contemporary turns to the "real" in posthumanist, new materialist, and ecocritical scholarship, the real has no place.[56] The real has no place because, as I argue, the real marks a nonplace, or rupture within being, and second, because the real that dislocates vision from within, revealing a non-place or absence where one would expect to see "x," has been screened from sight by a proliferation of new bodies-objects-things, all guaranteeing, in Buell's definition of environmental unconscious, to reanimate the dreamer. Both as a literary discipline and as a political orientation, ecocriticism grounds itself on the reader's "residual capacity . . . to awake to fuller" consciousness. Consequently, endless materialisms now crowd the field of environmental study, all seeking to deliver a plaintive message: not only that matter *means,* but that matter cannot *not* mean. Ecological reading seeks to give the lie to psychoanalytic and deconstructive navel-gazing. The story goes that while readers like Freud and Lacan problematized our structures of reference, the planet, our first and final referent, burned with extravagant neglect. Much like the burning child in Freud's *Interpretation of Dreams,* the turn to matter in literary studies demands that we wake up to reality, asking, in so many words: Can't you see we're burning?[57]

No doubt, the Earth is on fire. We live in truly catastrophic times, which is why when a climate activist such as Greta Thunberg, at the age of sixteen, says to us, "Our house is on fire," *wake up,* we do well to listen.[58] Still, I cannot help but wonder whether the demand to wake up to reality does not mask a prior wish, one altogether incompatible with the redemptive tenor of our moment; whether behind the image of the burning house, another wish does not insist itself, one more urgent, and more pressing than the last. Call me paranoid, but I see in such dreams of consciousness-raising the fulfillment of a fantasy:

not to put an end to dreaming, but to prolong it. What the environmental humanities all tell us is that we are not thinking, calculating,
self-enclosed life; according to the onto-clichés of ecocriticism, we
are, properly speaking, open, enmeshed, autopoietic life. The ecocritic
can now turn the clock back to a time before Descartes's reduction
of matter to a single surface of sense to imagine what the Marxist
ecologist Jason W. Moore calls the "web of life." "The 'web of life' is
nature as a whole: *nature* with an emphatically lowercase *n*," Moore
tells us. "This is nature as us, as inside us, as around us. It is nature
as a flow of flows."[59] Moore's shorthand for "nature as a flow of flows"
is *oikeios*. The word, we learn, has premodern roots: "the concept of
the *oikeios* goes back to Theophrastus,"[60] and in fact, much of Moore's
writing focuses on the early modern *oikeios* specifically. "Rather than
presume humanity's separation, in the recent or distant past, the
oikeios presumes that humanity has always been unified with the
rest of nature."[61]

My deceptively simple wager in this book is that this commitment
to the *oikeios* and to the network of our ecological relations makes the
ecocritic surprisingly Cartesian.[62] The ecocritical toolkit now rests
on the formula, "I connect, mesh, assemble, *therefore I am*." The "I
am" is a tautology, of course, a cliché, precisely what Descartes, to his
credit, held under extreme doubt. In the environmental humanities,
however, the cliché is raised to the level of an axiom. Across the environmental humanities, matter serves as the answer to the problem
of sense; it testifies to the ecocritic's hermeneutic powers of demysti-
fication and results in several easy-to-use formulas. To the question,
What is the source of my discontent? the ecocritic's response is the
lack of "lively matter."[63] Or: the waning of the affects.[64] Or: the forgetting of the brain's plasticity.[65] Each of these "matters" provides the
missing link in the chain of our reading. They provide the missing
ground and so give substance to our readings. The dominant view
of ecological and new materialist criticism is that matter cannot be
thought apart from its meanings, apart from the promise of an intention to mean—which is to say, from the structuring goal of futurity,
which is to survive the catastrophe of nonmeaning at any cost.

In the epoch of the Anthropocene, when so many posthumanisms
and new materialisms demand that life go on and promise a better,

newer, and more authentic human in touch with nature, animality, and the biosphere, it is all the more important to reject this demand as both a redemptive narrative akin to "reproductive futurism" (as defined by Lee Edelman),[66] and as a pastoralization of matter's internal divide. By making a countervitalistic demand, one identical to the demands of the death drive, my reading questions the imperative to survive as a turn *away* from (1) the detours and complexities of close reading, and (2) materiality as such. This book does not, then, argue against materialism. To the extent that certain thinkers privileged an undue anthropocentrism, viewing human language as unique in comparison to other semiotic systems (including lithic, chemical, atmospheric, oceanic, biological, meteorological, molecular, evolutionary, and contagious semiotic systems), this book stands in solidarity with those who read nature's figures (swarms, bird calls, animal tracks, electrical chatter, ocean currents, and geological layers) as just that: systems of the earth or, better yet, language without the human.[67]

The point I want to make is not that the current interest in materiality is wrongheaded—not at all; my goal, rather, is to theorize matter beyond the promise of the "turn," to think, that is, a version of materiality that is already *here*, in the silences of a language known to poets. Although poetic materialism does not promise "life" or "futurity," it offers something else, dare I say, something better: the encounter with a disastrous materiality that undoes the imperative to survive. At stake in this argument are the pleasures that result from repeating loss, as we saw already in the case of Lucretius, who put loss (void) at the center of his poetics. For what remains of this Introduction, I examine the broader relationship between poetry and loss and show why, with respect to ecology, a poetics that enjoys loss is vital. Above all, this book tries to uncouple the urgency of repairing the environment—a goal I hold unwaveringly—from the images of matter that have prolonged its devastation.

Poetry and the Fate of the Planet

Despite recent attempts to read lively matters in their real, unmediated sense—everything from atoms to electrical grids[68]—the turn to matter, far from exiting the discourse of human finitude (biopolitics), has paradoxically redoubled its characteristic gesture by re-creating a world in which bodies and their relations are all that there is. Alain Badiou, for one, defines our current state of new materialism in the starkest of terms. He writes: "*There are only bodies and languages.*"[69] Although it is commonly said that Badiou polemicizes with a bulldozer ("there are ONLY bodies and languages"), his thesis on "democratic materialism," by which he means "the axiom of contemporary conviction" regarding "the objective existence of bodies alone,"[70] rings true in a number of ways, especially given the current wellspring of interest in multiplying bodies and languages across the theoretical spectrum. For starters, these "matters" *only* refer to "countable" matter, according to Badiou. And that is because they signify within the world of the material given. In one such example taken from the arts, Badiou writes: "The most inventive artists—choreographers, painters, video makers—track the manifestness of bodies, of their desiring and machinic life, their intimacy and their nudity, their embraces and their ordeals. . . . They all impose upon the visible the dissection of bodies bombarded by the tumult of the universe."[71] Here, the multiplication of bodies-objects-things can be seen as symptomatic of the multiplication of language games under postmodernism. For every new body that becomes "visible," "democratic materialism" provides the language to capture its "tumult," its bare life and finitude. The result is a widespread tendency toward reading matter *at sight.* Bodies-objects-things now occupy the gaps left by the linguistic turn. The problem with this narrative of "turns," however, is that for materialist thinkers like Badiou, the gaps in language were never the problem; they were not the result of theoretical oversight—a space waiting to be filled by bodies-objects-things. For Badiou in particular, the gap was the *thing.*

Although critical of the arts, Badiou grants art, particularly poetry, the power of conditioning "truth" insofar as poetry is able to punch holes in knowledge. Badiou writes: "Art is pedagogical for the simple reason that it produces truths and because 'education' (save in its oppressive or perverted expressions) has never meant anything but this: to arrange the forms of knowledge in such a way that some truth may come to pierce a hole in them."[72] Truth in this sense does not assure happiness, meaning, or even, as Badiou clarifies, the "good." Instead, "truth," in this case, the truth of poetry, attests to the real failure of meaning where "matter" is concerned. Truth, as Badiou understands it, is "real" for the precise reason that it escapes every object-matter and marks the impossibility of "democratic maxims," the point at which language, including the language of democracy (we can extend this claim to the "democracy of objects"),[73] *no longer works,* where language ceases to *mean* and becomes Real.[74] Hence Badiou's qualifying claim: "*There are only bodies and languages, except that there are truths.*"[75]

Poetry, Badiou argues, is uniquely equipped to make truth materialize by directing us back toward loss. Why? Contemporary poet and translator Anne Carson's theory of poetic origins provides another explanation. In her argument, poetry begins with loss. Of course, this is not a novel proposition. It is downright Orphic. As the tale of Orpheus and Eurydice tells us, Orpheus makes poetry in order to redeem and forestall the disappearance of his beloved. Recent studies have made similar claims about the poetic function. In *Poetry and the Fate of the Senses,* Susan Stewart argues, "The cultural, or form-giving, work of poetry is to counter the oblivion of darkness."[76] Stewart adds: "Poetic making is an anthropomorphic project; the poet undertakes the task of recognition in time—the unending tragic Orphic task of drawing the figure of the other—the figure of the beloved . . . out of darkness."[77] This "Orphic task" has been redoubled of late by environmental criticism. In *The Mushroom at the End of the World,* anthropologist Anna Lowenhaupt Tsing writes of the importance of cultivating a poetic sensibility attuned to nature's forms. Tsing finds in poetry a means of noticing forms of living where life should not be, places destroyed or written off by capitalist exploitation.[78] Likewise, feminist philosopher of science Karen Barad says of poetry that it is a unique kind of scientific apparatus: a way of experimenting with—not on—nature's elaborate forms.[79]

As these examples illustrate, poetry has become a site for thinking about the challenges facing our world, including environmental collapse and human and nonhuman collaboration. If in Stewart's definition of cultural work, poetry begins as a fight against the darkness, its symbols producing new ideal wholes where there would otherwise be loss and oblivion, it is now the case that environmental scholars turn increasingly to poetry to redeem and restore our better nature, both in the ecological and moral sense. In this version of poetic making, poetry gathers the ruins of the past to make good on loss. Although critics such as Tsing and Barad would no doubt take exception to Stewart's characterization of poetic making as "anthropomorphic," this is but a small difference in their overall shared aesthetic orientation. We have gone from what Leo Bersani once called "the culture of redemption,"[80] which puts cultural artifacts such as poetry in the service of repair, to what I call the naturecultures of redemption, which now put all of nature's art in the service of repairing loss.[81] "A crucial assumption in the culture of redemption," Bersani writes, "is that a certain type of repetition of experience in art," including the art of reading, "repairs inherently damaged or valueless experience. . . . This may sound like an unattackable truism . . . and yet," Bersani remarks, the "catastrophes of history matter much less if they are somehow compensated for in art, and art itself gets reduced to a kind of superior patching function, is enslaved to those very materials to which it presumably imparts value."[82] The compulsion to eliminate from life what Corey McEleney calls the "futile pleasures"[83] of poetry "has led to the infinitely more dangerous idealizing of that pleasure as moral masochism," the belief that not only must matter mean, but also that any reading that suggests otherwise is—worse than futile—intolerable.[84]

Carson's theory of poetry is subtly different. Unlike the naturecultures of redemption, Carson's theory reveals a high level of ambivalence about its object. According to Carson, "A simultaneity of pleasure and pain is at issue":

> The Greek word *eros* denotes "want," "lack," "desire for that which is missing." The lover wants what he does not have. It is by definition impossible for him to have what he wants if, as soon as it is had, it is no longer wanting. This is more than wordplay. There is a dilemma within eros that has been thought crucial by thinkers from Sappho to the present day. Plato turns and returns to it. Four of his dialogues explore what it means to say that desire can only be for what is lacking, not at hand, not present, not in one's possession nor in one's being: *eros* [desire] entails *endeia* [lack]. . . . Who ever desires what is not

gone? No one. The Greeks were clear on this. They invented eros to express it.[85]

Contra Stewart and others, poetry does not simply repair loss. As Carson shows in her readings and translations of Sappho, the inaugural act of Sappho's love poetry is not repair, but repetition. The lover repeats loss so that desire can continue. What the naturecultures of redemption hold separate—loss and repair—the love poem holds together as so many incongruous shards. Cultural artifacts thus become mere detours in poetry's erotic repetition of failure. Moreover, because formal limits define poetry—generic limits and the limits of the sayable—it is especially ripe with loss. Carson translates Sappho's address to Aphrodite in "Fragment 1" to explicate poetry's constitutive relation to loss:

> But you, O blessed one,
> Smiled in your deathless face
> And asked what (now again) I have suffered and why
> (Now again) I am calling out . . .
> (Sappho, "Fragment 1," 13–16)[86]

Although "calling out" for love may be the occasion for Sappho's poem, the real interest of Carson's translation lies in the parenthetical refrain "(now again)," which subverts the speaker's desire for relation by repeating an impossible referent. The refrain repeats—silently, parenthetically—the speaker's inability to translate desire into matter. Thus, the poem's questioning and beseeching resumes "again" and "again." If "calling out" draws the object closer, "(now again)" pushes it further away, reenacting the discordant meanings of the refrain: more, no more.

In Sappho's love lyric, no object, no matter how tangible it appears, can suture the lack left by language. More forcefully still, psychoanalysis posits that every phenomenal object is a figure of this lack: all matter curves around the void left by language. Hence the radical nature of Lucretian poetics: in De rerum natura, as we have seen, something of the nature of the unconscious intervenes, allowing another language (silent, but no less present) to be heard in the fullness of our statements. Not only that, Lucretius does one better than Freud and Lacan: he treats lack as a manifestation of the unconscious *in* nonhuman language, something that psychoanalysis does not— and cannot—entertain.

Following Lucretius, what unites Spenser, Ralegh, Marvell, and Milton under the umbrella of my argument is that their poems do not turn *to* matter; if anything, they retreat from it. To the extent that their poems serve a tutelary function at all, it is, as far as the Baconian naturalist and speculative realist are concerned, a bad education, for it leads us further and further away from the matter at hand. This is not to say that their poems arrive at nothing, for they arrive at what Badiou calls "truth." By reckoning with the environmental unconscious, Spenser, Ralegh, Marvell, and Milton reveal the ideological shortcomings of returns to matter (both in its Baconian and new materialist inflections) and advance a materialism that, like all poetic structures, fails to materialize. These poets cross out ~~matter~~. Although this makes their poetry an inauspicious vehicle of environmental redress, it is precisely their departure from the hermeneutic demands of ecocriticism that makes their poetry, in my view, not only quintessentially materialist but also refreshingly orthogonal to the orthodoxies of environmental thought.

Eco-psychoanalysis

Because of its strict adherence to the idea that humans alone are contaminated by signs, psychoanalysis maintains a narrow view of semiosis, thus ruling out of court the idea that nature too is contaminated by signifiers. Jean Laplanche has done the most to radicalize the psychoanalytic view that the unconscious is structured like a language. Within Laplanche's relational model, human sexuality does not unfold unilaterally from biology; it comes from the outside. Quite simply, the unconscious is the unconscious of the other, implanted in us from birth.[87] Far from seeing language as a "prison house" (Fredric Jameson) or as "the house of being" (Martin Heidegger), Laplanche sees language as an alien form that houses the other (the unconscious) in us. Laplanche thus turns the screws on the entire metaphysical tradition that associates language with the truth of being. For instead of the house of being, language becomes a torture house: to the extent that we dwell in it, "it" puts something in us, something of the order of the "unrealized."[88]

Herein lies the essentially conflictual nature of the unconscious: not only is the "unrealized" not of the order of being; it is antagonistic to being. What makes psychoanalysis a science of the letter, that is to say, a poetics in the Lucretian sense, is that it takes as its starting point not the plurality of interests that make up the psychosexual field, but rather the *limit* to that field—matter's void. That limit is, according to psychoanalysis, sex, or the sexual.[89] What inaugurates the sexual, according to Laplanche, is the enigma of the other; we are traumatized into sexuality by "enigmatic signifiers,"[90] which not only reveal the presence of the unconscious in the other (the point of the other's inconsistency) but also install holes in the self. What Lucretius calls "void," Laplanche calls "sexuality." It is the lack installed in the body by the incompletion of sexuality's meanings that triggers the organism's indefatigable desire to repeat, and so to read, the enigma that is its own corporeality. The lover (or the poet) is really at a loss, for the truth of desire is a hole, which no object can fill.

Against the pseudo-Freudian and pop-psychoanalytic version of the unconscious, which posits all manner of sexual drives, impulses, and perversions just below the surface of sense, Laplanche returns to psychoanalytic foundations, not by hastily dismissing Freud's theory of repression, but by reading Freud's theory of repression to the letter. According to Laplanche, before there is a self who represses sexual thoughts, there is first fore-pression, or "primal repression,"[91] which produces both the self and the objects of her world. Primal repression curves the world of the self around it by implicating the world in a gap, precisely the gap inaugurated by the unconscious of the other. Freud's theory of repression crossed out sex. Sex was no longer the hidden truth of one's desire. Sex, according to Freud, was the incompletion of a reading. As a figure of the unconscious, sex became a metonymy of our unconscious investment in loss, so much so that Freud became convinced that what defines the sexual, the *only* thing that defines the sexual, is loss itself—loss and the repetition thereof.

Much of the discourse of the environmental humanities has, in recent years, followed Freud's example. As Timothy Morton argues, we no longer believe in ecology *with* nature.[92] In fact, much of what counts as ecological criticism today operates in a distinctly melancholy mode, mourning the loss of a nature that was never really ours to begin with.[93] To say that I will place the argument of this book within the discourse of the environmental humanities thus begs the overall question of what my discourse supports, or better still, suffers with regard to its "proper objects": nature, the *oikeios,* and so on. Indeed, suffering is right, for if there is one thing that ecocriticism knows about its objects, it is that "we"—the subjects of this knowledge—are forever out of place, adrift in relation to our proper home: matter. In Morton's version of "dark ecology,"[94] nature is a phantasm. We entomb it psychically as "lost" and materialize its absence as melancholic subjects.

Melancholy attitudes aside, critical orientations to loss (of species, wetlands, forests, etc.) have come with a surprising uptick in eco-euphoria. Although we may be bereft of a certain idea of nature, we are, for that reason it seems, rich in "vibrant matters," bodies, objects, and things that no longer serve under the yoke of capital N "Nature" and instead echo our greatest Ptolemaic fears: that we are *not* at the center of things and that this world, far from reflecting our wants and interests, no longer turns for us; it never did. Rather than mourn the loss of nature, the new materialisms embrace our wayward condition as salutary, cosmopolitical, indeed, queer.[95] We have all become a bit like Copernicus, adrift among the starry cosmos, discovering worlds within worlds.

Or have we? New materialist and ecocritical decenterings granted, have we not also maintained, quietly, a certain Ptolemaic fixation on the center? Although we have given up on status quo "Nature," we still turn to bodies-objects-things and turn ever more frequently in order to gain a surer hold on the matter-at-hand, be it the endless proliferation of vibrant matters or the animate, atmospheric surround.

Put differently: Is it possible that despite our melancholy attitude toward nature, that the so-called "death of nature" has amounted to very little, scarcely a sea change in our Ptolemaic habits of thought, and that, instead of becoming *unheimlich* with respect to nature and vice versa, we have become increasingly earth-bound? Could it be that the three wounds to human narcissism hailed by Freud

(Copernican, Darwinian, psychoanalytic) have not gone far enough? Laplanche suggests that the second wound, Darwin's, may be entirely misleading after all. In "The Unfinished Copernican Revolution," Laplanche writes:

> Man, believing himself to be of divine origin, an alien in the animal kingdom, learns from science that "he himself is of animal descent." Now, this place accorded to evolutionism and so-called biological humiliation, alongside the decenterings introduced by Copernicus and Freud, seems to me both ambiguous and dangerous. . . . Wrongly placed by Freud alongside the revolutions of decentering, the doctrine of evolution in fact recenters man among living things; what is more, it is drawn on dangerously by Freud to jeopardize the essence of the psychoanalytic discovery.[96]

That discovery, of course, is the discovery of the unconscious, the truth that man is decentered not only with respect to the stars but also concerning his own self-knowledge. "The discovery of the unconscious, in so far as it is precisely *not* our center, as it is an 'excentric' center"—"*Das Andere*, the other thing in us"—constitutes Freud's radical break with both geocentrism and anthropocentrism.[97] But far from upending geocentricism or anthropocentrism, evolutionism puts us, in Laplanche's words, "Solidly in place, firmly centered on the animal pyramid."[98] Although I may look outside my window and see that I am one part of a vast and complex web, I am, nonetheless, certain that this web of life supports *my* being. The unconscious, by contrast—though its messages may resemble a web—undoes the very web we depend on. The unconscious is not, and has never been, our home.

Despite recent efforts within the environmental humanities to look outside to the more-than-human world around us, we, like Ptolemy, still treat the earth as *our* place and consciousness as *our* home.[99] Hence the ubiquitous calls for consciousness-*raising*. To be sure, the aforementioned entanglements are real; we are "all connected." But the boredom elicited by such ecological refrains points to another reality beyond the given and suggests that the oft-cited entanglements are merely the attempts made by every living organism to sew together a much deeper tear in life's messy fabric.[100] Because it is true: life is a mess, or mesh, or web, or assemblage. I don't reject the terms. However, I fear they have long served as a screen preventing us from grappling with the discourse of the environmental unconscious.

The early modern poets in this book show that nature is not all. By tarrying with the Lucretian unconscious, these poets ask that we stop reading nature as adaptable, well-adjusted, and coherent and start reading it as misaligned, plaintive, and, like the text of the unconscious, enigmatic—even to nonhumans. In their poetry, there is a vehement call to read in the signifier "nature" the absence of the signified and to register in the fault lines of an impossible materialism the presence of "without." I am proposing the existence of the environmental unconscious, a proposal that cannot but leave our readings of the other (human and nonhuman) shaken. Matter in all its creative diversity attests to the perturbation at its core, where matter stops being "matter" and becomes a poetics of the incomplete.

If it is true that being Copernican today means being ex-centric with regard to thought, my claim is that ecocriticism has not yet answered its Copernican calling.[101] It has not yet begun to read the enigmatic messages coming from outside. Laplanche, for one, may have spoken too soon in his rejection of the Darwinian wound to human narcissism. Clearly, the philosopher and psychoanalyst did not think to extend the enigmatic message to the animal and vegetable kingdom. This omission accounts not only for the reticence of some theorists when it comes to the signifying capacities of nonhumans but also, and more intriguingly, for the reticence of those who do attribute language to the nonhuman world.[102] Because the posthumanities ignore the split in nature's representational schema, the return to nonhuman bodies and languages remains perilously human. It is now taken for granted in posthumanist circles that matter means, nature speaks. What has yet to be surmised is the compromised nature of the posthuman message. Although it is now unquestioned that animals, plants, and other biota make sense of their environments through signs, the fact remains that this turn to posthuman sign-making is still auto-centric; we have merely transposed *Homo loquens* to the rest of the environment: animals and plants now "speak" with the same self-certainty and presence to mind as humans. When, instead, I speak of the environmental unconscious, my point is not to repeat the banality that we have lost touch with nature. Rather, it is to say that nature is already other to itself.[103] What if, instead of providing the ultimate mother tongue (perfectly adapted to our environment), evolution proffered a mOther tongue, that is, messages with no proper signified? All of nature's flourishing would thus be driven by a gap, by a failure to translate the enigmatic message and make matter and meaning stick together.

The critical difference between the psychoanalytic theory of the unconscious and the Lucretian unconscious explicated in these pages is that both Lucretius and the early modern poets writing in his wake theorize the language of the unconscious as an ecological inscription. Where Lacan and his readers have it wrong is in assuming that human language alone falters,[104] as if to say (myopically) that humans never had, not once, in the deepness of planetary history, been confronted with the enigmatic signs of the nonhuman. As if we had never once been met with, and are not ourselves the improbable outcome of, the seductive signs of the environmental unconscious.[105] The turn to the new materialisms is no better in this regard, for although it grants nonhumans the power to signify and conceives of matter as semiotic, it makes no space for the workings of the environmental unconscious.[106] The animal speaks. Matter performs. But there is zero recognition of that *other scene*, the one that, according to Lacan, stains every speech act with the pleasure of its own undoing.

In drawing out this other scene and giving it a name—the environmental unconscious—this book intervenes in the pastoralization of Lucretius and early modern poetry. The poets in this study were not sweethearts. I do not pretend to argue that they wrote to save Mother Earth, much less our future. So much the better. For it is my contention in this book that the illusion of the civic-minded subject, whose good intentions no doubt resound in the echo chamber of full speech, stands in the way of ecocriticism far more than its ecocidal double. The latter we know. The latter is in power. The latter speaks volubly, but his words are empty. This enemy ecocriticism can and must resist. But we do not gain power by simply opposing a violence that appears elsewhere than here, in the verdures of eco-euphoria. Doing so only puts us on the same terrain of that which we resist because it masks the ecological subject's murderous commitment to full speech: to the certainty of the "I am," which resonates no less in the language of ecosophy than in ecopathy. If I communicate one thing in these pages, it is, I hope, a lack of certainty on the usefulness of our good intentions. What I offer instead of full speech, instead of the good-intentioned ego and the object matter to which it intends, are the enigmatic signs of those who know not what they do.[107]

Outline of Chapters

My first two chapters form a conceptual couplet. Chapter 1, "Sex or Matter? (Malabou after Spenser)," theorizes what I call the allegorical event—a term derived from Spenser's epic romance, *The Faerie Queene*, but related in important ways also to what materialist philosopher Catherine Malabou calls the "accident." For Spenser, accidents or events are key elements of allegorical materialism. In the invocation to Venus in book 4, Spenser figures the allegorical event as both form-giving and form-destroying. The two sides of allegory—formation and destruction—are inseparable from how Spenser views poetry and how poetry views "matter." The latter always risks becoming a "darke conceit," and poetry, consequently, becomes what Malabou calls "destructive plasticity": a demonic materialism that demolishes its own creations. The biology of the brain is Malabou's exemplary figure of destructive plasticity, which she opposes to the plasticity of sex in psychoanalysis, arguing that Freud had too much sex on the brain; he missed, therefore, according to Malabou, the dynamics of the brain itself, not only its creativity but also its destructions (we are all the outcomes of the brain's creative/destructive art). Although Malabou introduces "cerebrality" as an advance over Freud's theory of sexuality and frames destructive materialism as a "new materialism," my chapter reads the ontology of the accident vis-à-vis Spenser to show that sexuality in Spenser's poem, represented by the invocation of Venus, is already other to itself—is already allegorical (from the Greek *allos*, meaning "other"). This otherness or destructive plasticity reveals itself in Spenser's poetry not, as in Malabou's argument, by turning from sex to matter, but by reading "matter" as already sexual, and therefore unconscious to its destructive impulses.

I travel this theoretical path from Spenser to Malabou in order to prepare the way for chapter 2, "Trauma in the Age of Wood (Spenser after Malabou)," where I explore the consequences of my—and Spenser's—theoretical intervention in destructive form for a reading of book 1 of Spenser's *Faerie Queene*. There, I sharpen my analysis of the allegorical event by turning to a privileged moment in both literary and psychoanalytic history: the wounding of a living, speaking tree. Freud turns to this moment in Torquatto Tasso's epic romance, *Gerusalemme liberata* (1581), to showcase his theory of traumatic repetition. Cathy Caruth turns to it again and makes this moment the centerpiece of her theory of the traumatic event—what she calls "unclaimed experience." Neither Freud nor Caruth theorizes Tasso's tree allegory. Neither asks what it means to have a tree that not only speaks but *suffers* the allegorical event. Spenser does. By entering this psychoanalytic terrain, Spenser reframes psychoanalytic history *as* natural history. He makes psychoanalysis say something "other" than itself; that "other" is the environmental unconscious. This chapter builds on the theoretical insights of the first chapter to show that Spenser's allegorical materialism is not only a destructive materialism but also one that reads destructive plasticity at its root: as wood.

Spenser undoes hylomorphism by positing a wooden materialism that is both form-giving, as in the new materialisms, and form-destroying. From this focus on wooden materialism, we turn to bluer horizons. From wood, we enter deep. Spenser points us in this direction. In book 3 of the *Faerie Queene*, Spenser praises Ralegh, nicknamed "Ocean"; Ralegh's liquefacient verse promises (or indeed, threatens), according to Spenser, to lull the reader into "slomber of delight"—a slumber that is both vitalizing and, as I argue, avital. Chapter 3, "The Oceanic Feeling (Ralegh)," reads Ralegh's ocean ecologies in light of the blue humanities as "transcorporeal" (Alaimo). Ralegh's travel writing and verse collates human and nonhuman bodies in a state of perpetual dissolve. From his *Ocean to Cynthia* poem to his writings in the American tropics, Ralegh's transatlantic verse epitomizes Freud's idea of "the oceanic feeling," which Freud characterizes (disparagingly) as a feeling of eternity, of oneness with the world's flesh. Although Freud is cautious not to indulge in such transversal affect, Ralegh drips with it.

What is more, he plumbs the oceanic for what I call the not-all of ecological materialism. Far from returning us to the image of the One (Freud's fear), Ralegh imagines the tides of his life as a tempest, wherein human action confronts nonhuman durations—what I call ocean writing. Ralegh writes obsessively of his personal and extraterritorial failures. He makes those failures the object of his poetry—our "delight."

Chapter 4, "Architectural Anthropologies (Marvell)," returns to solid ground, but a ground that more closely resembles the torsional metaphysics of topography (the branch of geometry that considers geometric objects undergoing constant change—the square becoming a circle, the circle becoming a torus, and so on) than the timeless metaphysical objects of Plato and Euclid. Marvell's poem, *Upon Appleton House*, partakes of a long metaphysical tradition stretching from Vitruvius to Heidegger and beyond, which sees the human as both a cognizer and builder of architectural forms. Marvell enters this tradition, but only to turn it upside down. In Marvell's proto-surrealist poem, not only humans but also animals, plants, and the earth itself build. This chapter picks up an important thread from chapters 1 and 2 by reading Marvell's architectural anthropology as a strange geometry of *events*. Following Lucretius and in dialogue with Deleuze and Guattari, I show that Marvell's cryptic line, "In ev'ry figure equal man," inverts human exceptionalism by making "man"—not the measure of all things but—level *with* nonhuman measures, or meters.

Marvell focuses on figure/ground relationships—How does the ground generate the figure? How does the figure explicate the ground? Chapter 5, "Queer Life, Unearthed (Milton)," takes us underground, where the past has never been past and emerges in the form of fossil remains. This chapter radicalizes my claims about the environmental unconscious, which appears in Milton's *Paradise Lost* as a geologic unconscious. Instead of witnessing deep time as a steady evolutionary progression, Milton's *Paradise Lost* draws a jagged line through the geologic record (marked by discontinuity, rupture, and break), and so anticipates the extinction events that Elizabeth Kolbert and others outline in the present.[108] Milton reads fossil life as a tear in the universe's tidy fabric. Echoing the allegorical event in Spenser, Milton's geologic events are both form-giving—they birthed organic life—and form-*destroying*—they cut through life like so many caesurae, inter-mixing *bios* and *geos* at once. I read Milton's geologic cuts as queer for that reason, not because they promote life's furtherance but because they interrupt life with its own archive of disappearance.

Milton locates queerness in the unlivable durations of the earth. My conclusion, "Toward Wild Psychoanalysis," locates desire in the impossibility of ecocriticism itself. To say that ecocriticism is im-possible is not, in psychoanalytic discourse, a rejection, quite the opposite. The impossibility of ecocriticism makes it *desirable*, if, for that same reason, untenable.[109] In putting forth an impossible eco-criticism, my conclusion says "no" to environmentalism's big Other (the figure who demands that matter and meaning must cohere) and takes up cause with poets who found the world of matter and mean-ing *wanting*, their place in it, abyssal. Spenser, Ralegh, Marvell, and Milton desired more from life than the possible, more from sense than the sensible, and more from matter than the cliché. *The Environ-mental Unconscious* invites speculation into that something more. It asks us to enjoy what early modern poetry lacks.

PART I

Into the Wood

ONE

SEX OR MATTER?

(Malabou after Spenser)

> Psychoanalysis does, of course, start out from the vi-
> cissitudes of human beings, on which it focuses its
> investigations. What keeps it from becoming a kind of
> "psychologized" human-interest philosophy, however, is
> precisely its discovery of and insistence on the sexual as a
> factor of radical disorientation, a factor that keeps bring-
> ing into question all our representations of the entity
> called "human being."
>
> —Alenka Zupančič, *What Is Sex?*

Near the end of book 4 of *The Faerie Queene*, Edmund Spenser writes:

> O What an endlesse worke haue I in hand,
>   To count the seas abundant progeny,
>   Whose fruitfull seede farre passeth those in land,
>   And also those which wonne in th'azure sky? (4.12.1)[1]

A modesty topos, to be sure: Spenser, having just recounted the "seas
abundant progeny" in the previous canto, in what is, without doubt,
a bravura performance of the poet's genealogical cum thalassologi-
cal knowledge and poetic mastery, begins canto 12 less as a mariner
in command of the "seas abundant progeny" and more as a courtier
and lover avowing his shortcomings before the sea's inimitable "seede."

The "fruitfull seede" that most confounds Spenser's numerical qua metrical "count" is Venus, both goddess of beauty and fertility and figure for the errant sexuality of the seas:

> That *Venus* of the fomy sea was bred;
> For that the seas by her are most augmented.
> Witnesse th'exceeding fry, which there are fed,
> And wonderous sholes, which may of none be red.
> Then blame me not, if I haue err'd in count
> Of Gods, of Nymphs, of riuer yet vnred:
> For though their numbers do much more surmount,
> Yet all those same were there, which erst I did recount.
>   (4.12.2)

Venus, figure of life-giving fertility, of the sea's autoerotic *excess*, disturbs Spenser's numerical "count," and so also, for a moment, interrupts the measure or metric of his poem, exposing the errancy ("err'd") internal to both the life represented (in this case, the sea) and Spenser's own poetic making. Venus augments the seas ("the seas by her are most augmented"), meaning that she multiplies, grows, swells (the Latin *augmentare* means "to increase") the already "abundant" oceans, "th'exceeding fry," and the "wonderous sholes," which, being too many, "may of none be red." Venus multiplies life, but she also exceeds it ("their numbers do much more surmount"). If Spenser's stated goal in *The Faerie Queene* is to fulfill the *rota Virgilii* by abandoning pastoral life in favor of the martial, imperial, and territorial thematics of epic, as announced in the first lines of his poem, "For trumpets sterne to chaunge mine Oaten reeds," then it is the fluid, dilute, and plastic power of Venus that threatens to turn Spenser's poem away from the war-machine of epic to the erring-desiring machine of romance.

Like the Lucretian seed analyzed in my Introduction, Spenser's "fruitfull seede" are inherently plastic: they give form to life ("Gods . . . Nymphs . . . riuer yet vnred"), but they also expose the dis-unity of life and the pure form of the accident, as announced in Spenser's letter to Sir Walter Ralegh: "*But by occasion hereof, many other aduentures are intermedled, but rather as Accidents, then intendments.*"[2] Spenser's allegorical materialism interrupts "*intention and meaning*" (the *better light in reading*) with an adventure in destructive form. He calls it the accident.[3]

This definition of allegorical materialism sews together both unity and disunity, intention and destructive un-intention, and so registers the premodern sense of "plastic" as both a "principle, virtue, or force in nature," "causing the growth or production of natural forms, esp. of living things"[4] and the more recent definition of "destructive plasticity" theorized by Catherine Malabou as "plastic explosive" ("plastique"). Malabou defines destructive plasticity as the detonation of form and describes it in terms strikingly similar to Spenser's "*continued Allegory, or darke conceit.*"[5] According to Malabou, destructive plasticity is "the dark double of the positive and constructive plasticity that moulds" life.[6] In *Ontology of the Accident*, Malabou echoes Spenser in elevating the "accident," which breaks into life darkly, unforeseen, and without apparent cause, to an a-substantialist philosophy of the "unexpected, unpredictable, dark." "Let's start," Malabou writes,

> with the fact that rarely in the Western imaginary is metamorphosis presented as a real and total deviation from being. Perhaps never once has it been seen in this way. However bizarre the metamorphoses may be—the most striking are found in Ovid—the forms they create, the result of the transmutations of the poor wretches who are its victims, remain, so to speak, very much in the order of things. After all, it is only the external form of the being that changes, never its nature. Within change, being remains itself. The substantialist assumption is thus the travel companion of Western metamorphosis. Form transforms; substance remains.[7]

Destructive plasticity, by contrast, installs something *other* in the order of things. Its sculpture is not the "being" or "substance" of the individual but rather the pure form of the accident, a being "who no longer remembers her self" and who is, thereby, no longer truly a "being" at all but an allegory, a figure of death in life.[8] "Something *shows itself* when there is damage, a cut, something to which normal, creative plasticity gives neither access nor body," Malabou writes. "The deserting of subjectivity, the distancing of the individual who

becomes a stranger to herself. . . . These types of beings impose a new
form on their old form, without mediation or transition or glue or ac-
countability, today versus yesterday, in a state of emergency, without
foundation."[9] Beyond life's metamorphoses and ceaseless transformations lies a dark, unexpected element of destructive plasticity. The
ontology of the accident is, indeed, a "darke conceit." Its artwork, or
summa, is death, a death that *"shows itself"* allegorically as but a detour, hitch, or adventure in form.

Although Malabou credits Freud and Lacan for shedding light on
the "indestructible life"[10] of the unconscious, where plastic sexuality
molds and sculpts the everyday pathologies of the individual and
gives rise to events drawn from the traumas of the past, unendingly,
Malabou draws attention to a different order of events, what she calls
events of material destructivity—"accidents" without hermeneutic
value—where life is "characterized as a metamorphosis unto death or
as a form of death in life."[11] In Spenser's poem, for instance, Venus
seems to have overcome Mars and the drive toward epic, as if precon-
firming Freud's thesis in *Beyond the Pleasure Principle* that, in fact,
and much to the consternation of the literal-minded reader, there is
no *beyond* of the pleasure principle properly speaking. Sexuality, according to Freud, dominates psychic life, and all the many accidents
that seem to contradict this thesis are merely the superficial disguises
that sexuality takes in the theater of the living. Malabou, by contrast,
argues that Freud erred in granting sexuality too much power; for,
in Malabou's view, sexuality may engineer a wide array of disguises
(symptoms, parapraxes, and other unforeseen events), but sexuality
has no sway over the accident:

> This type of transformation unto death, this survival without subla-
> tion, is not only visible in cases of severe brain lesions but is also the
> globalized form of trauma—appearing in the aftermath of wars, ter-
> rorist attacks, sexual abuse, and all types of oppression and slavery.
> Today's violence consists in cutting the subject away from its accumu-
> lated memories.[12]

In Malabou's theory of destructive plasticity, Mars (not Venus)
wins. This standoff between Mars and Venus, which marks a general

impasse not only in Spenser's poetry but also in the wider history of sexuality, should alert us to Spenser's own intervention in the theory of destructive form, a concept that is gaining ground today, for reasons outlined by Malabou above (brain lesions, globalized trauma, terrorist violence, endless war), but that has far deeper roots in the literature and culture of the Renaissance.

Spenserian plasticity is not only life-*giving* but also, in Malabou's sense, life-*destroying*; though "fruitfull seede" give form to Spenser's poetic count (his poem), they also destroy that count, making the art of poetry, for Spenser, "an endlesse worke"—truly, beyond measure. Spenserian plasticity is, in Jacques Derrida's words, "germination, dissemination" in one stroke.[13]

My goal is not to conflate Malabou's theory with Spenser's poem. Instead, this chapter sounds the discord between their respective theories of destructive plasticity. Whereas Malabou cuts the cord between sexuality and destructive plasticity and posits a "new materialism"[14] beyond the indestructible life of sex, Spenserian plasticity is and remains, even after its detonation, stubbornly sexual; in fact, Spenserian plasticity challenges us to rethink—through so many shadowy detours—what exactly we mean by "sex." What is sex, ontologically speaking? Moreover, does the "new materialism" theorized by Malabou constitute an advance beyond sexuality, where the serious matters of realpolitik (wars, violence, trauma) truly begin or does this "advance" merely rob sexuality of its "accidental" structure? For Spenser, destructive materialism is necessarily allegorical materialism, meaning that matter is always "other" to itself (from the Greek *allos*, meaning "other"). In *The Faerie Queene*, this "otherness to self" is the very hallmark of sex. It is not by turning away from sexuality that we arrive at the accidental and traumatic structure of matter. On the contrary, sex, according to Spenser, *is* the battlefield.

Destructive Materialism

Let us look more closely at how destructive plasticity operates in Spenser's poem.

In book 3 of *The Faerie Queene*, Spenser continues his adventure in plastic form, making the Queen's "Chastity" a spur for reflecting on the matter of poetic art. He writes:

It falls me here to write of Chastity,
    The fayrest vertue, far aboue the rest;
    For which what needes me fetch from Faery
    Forreine ensamples, it to haue exprest?
    Sith it is shrined in my Soueraines brest. (3.Proem.1)

In order to represent Chastity, Spenser must represent the inner life of the Queen, the inner temple or sanctum of her heart. However, this task of mimesis is itself impossible. Not only is the matter involved sexual, the Queen's "Chastity" serving here to amplify the speaker's poetic desire; the event of the poem is itself unwilled, unbidden, and underived. Destructive plasticity does not flow from the speaker's life; it *befalls* the speaker. "It falls me here." This "fall" cuts the speaker's life off from the start. Importantly, for Spenser, this life—the life of the poem—is, from the start, a wound. "It," the accident (from the Latin *accidere,* "to fall"), "falls" or happens, and the voice born from that wound is also in a sense borne by it. "My wound existed before me," Gilles Deleuze writes, referring to the incorporeal events that give form to life and, in certain extreme cases, such as Lewis Carroll's wild portmanteaus, also deform it.[15] In Spenser's poem, "It"—the wound—not only preexists the "me" of the poem, but it also preexists the poem itself. The poem's orderly and repetitive structure hinges on the unforeseen and unnameable event. As we will see throughout this chapter, the accident qua traumatic event, though it is held separate from sexuality in Malabou's account of destructive plasticity, cannot be thought apart from sexuality in Spenser's poem. And that is because sexuality, according to Spenser, *is* a matter of parting; it is a germination/dissemination doublet, a dis-unity or trauma inherent to life.

As Spenser continues, he acknowledges that "so liuely in each perfect part" is his sovereign's heart that neither "liuing art . . . / Nor life-resembling pencill it can paynt":

    All were it *Zeuxis* or *Praxiteles*:
    His dædale hand would faile, and greatly faynt,
    And her perfections with his error taynt:
    Ne Poets witt, that passeth Painter farre

In picturing the parts of beauty daynt,
So hard a workemanship aduenture darre,
For fear through want of words her excellence to marre.
(3.Proem.2)

By abandoning the poet's "humble quill" in favor of the refractive powers of the allegorist's oblique "mirrours," Spenser transforms his poem into an allegory of destructive plasticity. Neither the painter's "dædale hand" nor the poet's "witt" can represent the queen's inner "perfections," for the "pourtrait of her hart" exceeds any "liuing art." In the "Letter to Raleigh," Spenser acknowledges that many readers will find "displeasaunt" his "Methode" of using "Allegoricall devices," which are "clowdily enwrapped" at best.[16] The poem, figured as a kind of mirror, makes visible a life that is double: on the one hand, plastic and dynamic; on the other hand, dark and demonic. Spenser cannot represent the queen's inner virtue. However, an apparatus such as allegory provides the optical illusion necessary to create a living poetry, one "clowdily enwrapped"—and therefore one that enacts at the level of form the pleasures as well as the destructions of "clowdily" defined subjective and ontological borders.

Daniel Tiffany describes this conjunction between poetic iconography and scientific apparatus as the very crux of "philosophical materialism," wherein "inquiries into the nature of material substance rely fundamentally on images that do not bear witness to empirical entities, but rather serve as models of unobservable phenomena."[17] For Tiffany, "The foundation of material substance is intelligible to us, and therefore appears to be real, only if we credit the imaginary pictures we have composed of it."[18] Hence "the forms of mediation and imagination proper to . . . poetry begin to resemble the tools and practices of science—especially, as in physics, when it is a question of depicting unobservable phenomena."[19] Both science and poetry proceed by attributing corporeal qualities to events imperceptible to human sight. In this sense, the matter of scientific observation is never quite distinct from the matter of poetic fashioning.

Never distinct and yet, often read apart. This is particularly true of psychoanalytic reading. The history of trauma in both literary and theoretical studies has been for the most part anarchivic (in Derrida's sense of the word): it has necessitated a certain conception of matter as inert and passive with which to record human experience, all the while ignoring the difference that this material substance makes with respect to human life. In considering the medium of the archive, Derrida asks whether the archivic drive can ever *not* be an archive of the remainder. "This drive [the archivic drive] . . . is above all *anarchivic*, one could say, or *archiviolithic*," Derrida writes; "It will always have been archive-destroying, by silent vocation."[20] While psychoanalytic theories of trauma have been adept at illustrating that loss and negativity are intrinsic to human subjectivity, trauma theory foregrounds what I take to be the persistent parochialism of our literary and theoretical understandings of matter insofar as it reads trauma as an event destined *for* and elaborated *by* the human.[21] To echo Malabou, it is not that we do not know that meaning, historicity, and existential indeterminacy pertain to matter—we do; but (and here is the rub) *we do not know what to do with a materialism that is both plastic and, as in Spenser's poetry, life-destroying.*[22]

Cathy Caruth, for one, aligns the impossible experience of living "after the end" with the experience of trauma, stating that traumatic experience is "something that is 'ungrasped' not because it is simply too painful for understanding, but rather because it has remained in the very aftermath of the world—of meaning, experience, historical significance—that it has destroyed."[23] Caruth reads trauma at the level of ontology: trauma, she argues, is not simply a part of history but rather its structure and void. Caruth inquires after what it might mean to "remain after the end," "in a world not suited for human life." "To remain after the end," Caruth writes, "in a world covered in ash—a world after the apocalypse—raises questions for thinking anew the Christian theological framework that itself is left in 'tatters,' covered in ashes, by the unknown yet absolutely catastrophic event."[24] In such a world, "a world covered in ash," survivors are but "remainders of the living," since, in Caruth's argument, "human life" and "living" are identical terms; there is no "life" that is not human life, and so no "remainder," not even "ash," that is not also a witness to a human end.

Caruth's reading runs aground precisely in the conflation of "human life" and "living," "world" and earth ("ash"). Indeed, one could follow Eugene Thacker in distinguishing the "*world-for-us*" from the "*world-without-us*," the former bearing the humanist existential connotations of "worlding" or "being-in-the-world" (recall Heidegger's thesis about the animal, that it is "poor in world"), and the latter the non-anthropocentric connotations of inhuman life-forms.[25] Whatever the case, Caruth's theory of survival repeats a fundamental blind spot of psychoanalytic reading by limiting the experience of trauma to humans alone. My goal in this chapter is to show that psychoanalysis, at times against itself, has not only had recourse to complex figurations of matter but has also made material events central to its articulations of ideation, affect, and ontology, often with explosive results.

The next chapter forms a conceptual diptych with this one. There, I investigate Malabou's claim that the "cerebral unconscious" is the material underside of psychic life and, therefore, the unacknowledged subject of traumatic repetition. Drawing a direct connection between Spenser's wounded bodies in *The Faerie Queene* and psychoanalysis' interest in the unclaimed experience of trauma, I situate Malabou's materialist intervention in the literary history of the Renaissance, from which trauma theory borrows its exemplary image—the figure of a wounded tree. Whereas Malabou seeks to "correct" psychoanalysis by fully naturalizing its claims and limiting its investment in sexuality, Spenser's poem takes the less obvious route. By linking the unclaimed experience of trauma to wooden bodies ("wood" being one translation of the Greek word for "matter," *hyle*), Spenser invites us to read "matter" not only sexually but also allegorically, as "other." Nature, Spenser shows, is riven from the start. Read in connection with Malabou's theory of destructive plasticity, Spenser's *Faerie Queene* foregrounds trauma as a necessary element of his allegorical materialism.

From Sex to Cerebrality

In a short but profound reading of Freud's philosophical "masterpiece," *Beyond the Pleasure Principle*, Deleuze begins with a startling claim. He notes that, contrary to the book's title, Freud's psychoanalytic project fails to deliver on its promise. "There are no exceptions to the [pleasure] principle," Deleuze writes.[26] This is no small matter, for it undermines Freud's whole project. In philosophy, Deleuze explains, "what we call a principle or law is, in the first place, that which governs a particular field." "Pleasure," for Freud, "is a principle insofar as it governs our psychic life. But we must still ask what is the highest authority which subjects our psychic life to the dominance of this principle."[27] What makes pleasure a principle in the philosophical sense? What is its foundation?

The question of the foundation is *the* question on which philosophy typically stumbles, according to Deleuze. As early as *Difference and Repetition*, Deleuze posited that all philosophy begins with a dogmatic "image of thought,"[28] which serves as the implicit foundation for its claims about truth. "Where to begin in philosophy has always—rightly—been regarded as a very delicate problem, for beginning means eliminating all presuppositions. . . . Descartes, for example, in the *Second Meditation*, does not want to define man as a rational animal because such a definition explicitly presupposes the concepts of rationality and animality."[29] A philosophy that knows how to begin has, one presumes, done away with all presumptions. Such a philosophy rests on common sense, in the form of "*Everybody knows, no one can deny.*"[30] Descartes's "no one can deny that to doubt is to think" is one appeal to common sense, which presumes we know what it means to think.[31] "When philosophy rests its beginning upon such implicit or subjective presuppositions, it can claim innocence, since it has kept nothing back—except, of course, the essential—namely, the form of this discourse."[32] Deleuze writes:

> Conceptual philosophical thought has as its implicit presupposition a pre-philosophical and natural Image of thought, borrowed from the pure element of common sense. . . . Thereafter it matters little whether philosophy begins with the object or the subject, with Being or with beings, as long as thought remains subject to this Image which already prejudges everything.[33]

Freud, to his credit, was not content to settle for or to rest his philosophy of mind on common sense. "Freud's problem," Deleuze contends, "is the very opposite of what it is often supposed to be, for he is concerned not with the exceptions to the [pleasure] principle but with its *foundation*."[34] What is it that founds the field of sexuality and the principle of pleasure? Freud's problem, in short, isn't an empirical one but rather "a transcendental one: the discovery of a transcendental principle—a problem, as Freud puts it, for 'speculation.'"[35]

Years later, Malabou will repeat Deleuze's observation by critiquing Freud's failure to set psychoanalysis on a firm foundation. "*There is no beyond of the pleasure principle*," Malabou laments in her book, *The New Wounded*, which posits the notion of "cerebrality" or the "cerebral event," terms denoting the material dynamics of the brain in contrast with the dynamics of the libido as mapped by Freud, as well as the theoretical frontiers of neuroscience, neurophilosophy, and neuropsychoanalysis, as providing the missing foundation that Freud sought and, according to Malabou, failed to uncover.[36] Put simply, Freudian psychoanalysis failed to go beyond the veil of unconscious fantasy, wish fulfillment, disguise, and equivocation, to witness something foundational—that is, *real*—beyond the workings of the pleasure principle. The twin concepts of "cerebrality" (which encompasses "the affective, sensory, and erotic fabric without which neither cognition nor consciousness would exist") and "plasticity" (the reception, donation, and annihilation of material form) are not just the latest attempts at integrating psychoanalysis and science; they are, moreover, Malabou's solution to Freud's greatest problem. They provide psychoanalysis with its missing foundation: "the affective brain."[37] Not only that, these concepts promise to fill the gaps left by the regime of sexuality. What is beyond the pleasure principle? For Malabou, the answer is the suffering brain. "Although Freud was a thinker of the event, could it be," Malabou asks, "that he was not a true thinker of the accident?"[38]

Despite their shared concern for philosophical foundations, Deleuze's reading of Freud draws far different conclusions than Malabou's. We will return to Deleuze and the problem of psychoanalytic foundations later. For now, let us take stock of the difficulty that Freud's theory of sexuality poses to any attempt at going beyond it, according to Deleuze:

> All the apparent exceptions which he considers, such as the unpleasure and the circuitousness which the reality principle imposes on us,

the conflicts which cause what is pleasurable to one part of us to be
felt as unpleasure by another, the games by means of which we try to
reproduce and to master unpleasant experiences, or even those func-
tional disturbances or transference phenomena from which we learn
that wholly and unequivocally unpleasurable events are nevertheless
reproduced with obstinate regularity—all these are treated by Freud
as merely apparent exceptions which could still be reconciled with the
pleasure principle.[39]

To repeat: there is no beyond of the pleasure principle, no event, no
matter how terrible, how violent, that cannot, in principle, be turned
into a source of unconscious pleasure. Not even blunt force trauma—
such as head injuries, amputations, and deadly explosions—escape
the omnipotence of the sexual drive. To put matters crudely, Freud
separates the empirical event (the wound) from the event of sexuality (including unconscious fantasy), not because the former is of no
importance to Freud—it is—but because the former only *becomes*
important to Freud in relation to what people *say* about it. This is
the source of Malabou's contention with psychoanalysis: "Freud posited . . . that shocks or external events constitute only secondary factors
whose damage does nothing in reality but 'trigger' or 'activate' the endogenous causes—the true, sexual causes—of a given disturbance."[40]
There is no denying it. In talk therapy, for example, the analyst listens
not to the content of what we say, our complaints, our miseries, the
whole human comedy of our experience; the analyst's object is not the
empirical event (what happens to us), but what *fails* to happen except
by way of the gaps, elisions, and contradictions in our speech. Slips
of the tongue, jokes, and shattering sexual encounters—these symptoms point to that other subject, the subject of the unconscious, who
speaks at our expense.[41] What is more, these symptoms are, in Freud's
view, the human animal's way of translating events *into* sexuality. A
slip of the tongue is never simply the result of "confused thinking"; it
is, in fact, highly logical since it attests to that other tongue (the subject of the unconscious) that hollows out our discourse.

Whither the wound? Regarding Freud's flight from cerebrality
and the traumas it endures, Malabou pulls no punches: "For Freud, a
wound such as a brain lesion is, unto itself, psychically mute. The lips

of the wound must be closed to allow the 'other mouth' [sexuality] to speak. Victims of brain lesions must be recognized as 'people who are crippled in sexuality.'"[42]

Malabou's argument is twofold: First, Freud abandoned the field of materialist inquiry by leaving his "Project for a Scientific Psychology" unfinished; in other words, he left the science of the brain to the scientists, to the detriment of both psychoanalysis and neuroscience. Second, by giving up on the material foundations of psychic life, Freud missed the opportunity to theorize, once and for all, the beyond of sexuality. Falling short of that, Freud had no choice but to cede ground to sexuality. "Could it be that psychoanalysis hasn't said everything on the subject of psychic suffering?" Malabou asks. "Could it be, precisely, that it ignores the suffering of the brain and, along with it, the emotive and emotional dimension of the brain?"[43] In posing these questions, Malabou proposes to finish the work that Freud left unfinished. Malabou's goal is not to abandon psychoanalysis but to wrench it from the grip of sexuality—to put the mind on material foundations. What is beyond sexuality? According to Malabou, the answer is "destructive plasticity," precisely what Freud ruled out— namely, the brain and what happens to it.

Before turning to the consequences of Malabou's argument, let us look closely at how Malabou distinguishes cerebrality from sexuality. Notably, Malabou describes her intervention as a form of "new materialism," and indeed much of the force and novelty of her writing on neuroplasticity—the brain's agency, malleability, and above all its power to self-destruct—owes to the fact that it refuses both biologism and humanism. Cerebrality is, if anything, a natural history of psychic damage. "I consider it incontestable," Malabou writes, "that the structures and operations of the brain, far from being the glimmerless organic support of our light, are the only *reason* for processes of cognition and thought; and that there is absolutely no justification for separating mind and brain."[44] This separation, we are told, is what Freud fell victim to. Although the theory of the sexual drive is scandalous in the eyes of traditional philosophy because it links mind (ideation) and body (sexual drive)—this, after all, is what remains so shocking about the Freudian theory of sexuality, not that it reduces everything to sex, but that it *elevates* sex to the element of thought;

in Freud's view, the unconscious *thinks*—Malabou maintains that Freud could not help but separate mind and brain. This separation directly informs the theory of the "event" in psychoanalysis and, more broadly, the failure of psychoanalysis to treat psychic suffering. Could psychoanalysis be the result of a missed encounter? For Malabou, the answer is more complicated:

> For Freud, . . . a "psychic event" always has two sides—an "exogenous" side and an "endogenous" side. Every event implies an unexpected occurrence, an element of surprise. This is the exogenous aspect of the event. The endogenous aspect, then, comprises the way in which the psyche elaborates this exteriority in order to integrate it into the history of the subject. Sexuality (in both of its senses, "empirical" and "transcendental," as it were) thus appears to Freud as the privileged site of an encounter between the exogenous and the endogenous, or, more precisely, as the privileged site of the encounter and connection between an *incident* and a *signification*.[45]

Drawing on Paul Ricoeur's reading of Freud, Malabou identifies "sexuality" with hermeneutics, going so far as to say that it—sexuality—is the "privileged site of the encounter" with exogenous events because it results in a *signification* and *translation*. Sexuality is a regime of meaning, which is why, Malabou claims, Freud could not think beyond it. "The course and regime of events governed by cerebrality is completely different." Although "brain damage is itself an event that, insofar as it affects the psychic identity of the subject, reveals a certain connection between the exogenous and the endogenous," no interpretation of the event is possible. "In the case of a brain lesion, for example, the external character of the accident remains external to the psyche itself. It remains exterior to the interior. It is constitutively inassimilable."[46] Malabou adds:

> The accidents of cerebrality are wounds that cut the thread of history, place history outside itself, suspend its course, and remain hermeneutically "irrecoverable" even though the psyche remains alive. *The cerebral accident thus reveals the ability of the subject to survive the senselessness of its own accidents.*[47]

Absolutely cut off from history and biography and external to hermeneutic recovery, "destructive plasticity" ushers in a new regime of
accidents utterly unknown to psychoanalysis. "Contrary to what
Freud affirms," Malabou argues, "sexuality is always exposed to a
more radical regime of events: the shock and the contingency of the
ruptures that sever neuronal connections."[48] Malabou calls "destructive plasticity" an "adventure in form," since, ultimately, cerebrality
refers to accidents that are blind to hermeneutic recovery and beyond
any law or principle.

What is beyond the pleasure principle? Freud was not wrong in
calling this "beyond" the death drive; he erred in denying it any material foundation. For Malabou, "destructive plasticity" is the work of
the death drive; it is the senseless artistry of the brain—a material
negation without reason.

Herein lies the major difference, finally, in how Malabou and
Freud theorize the "event": both start from the evidence of the exogenous event (after all, shit happens), but whereas Freud interprets the
event in and through the discourse on sexuality, Malabou criticizes
Freud for drawing the sexual curtains too tight. Put differently, it is
because the discourse on sexuality is so all-encompassing, as Freud
himself argued, that the cerebral accident and its mannequins of
destruction went unrecognized. The cerebral accident is Malabou's
answer to Freud's question: What is beyond the pleasure principle?
Nothing short of neuronal revolution. The senseless accident and destructive plasticity have been prohibited by the discourse on sexuality
for too long. At a minimum, Malabou contends that her new materialist approach to psychic suffering enables us to fill in the gaps left
by Freudian psychoanalysis. What we read is no longer the subject of
the unconscious, but the "cerebral psyche . . . in the process of claiming its rights."[49]

Malabou, Lacan, and the Allegorical Event

But does Malabou state the problem of the event accurately? While
it is true that Freud has little of use to say about "the brute accident,"
it is not true that he refused to think of material events beyond the
hermeneutic seal of sexuality. The problem comes down to what
we mean by a "material event." On this point, Deleuze was far more

forgiving of Freud, and for a good reason. In Deleuze's estimation, Freud does not retreat from the matter of events. Instead, he wrestles with a very specific problem; that problem emerges as soon as we consider the foundation of any law, including the law of the pleasure principle, as an element of time, which is what Freud does. According to Deleuze, Freud did not retreat from the event; he made it into a foundation, and a terrible one at that:

> We remarked earlier that repetition characterized the binding process inasmuch as it is repetition of the very moment of excitation, the moment of the emergence of life. Repetition is what holds together the instant; it constitutes *simultaneity*. Nevertheless, inseparable from this form of repetition we must conceive of another which in its turn repeats *what was before the instant*—before excitation disturbed the indifference of the inexcitable and life stirred the inanimate from its sleep. How indeed could excitation be bound and thereby discharged except by this double action of repetition, which on the one hand binds the excitation and on the other tends to eliminate it? Beyond Eros we encounter Thanatos; beyond the ground, the abyss of the groundless; beyond the repetition that links, the repetition that erases and destroys.[50]

There are two repetitions at work in Freud's theory of pleasure: there is Eros, repetition that creates "life" and "holds together the instant" by binding excitation (exogenous events) into a sensible and predictable pattern or law—what Malabou calls the hermeneutic side of the event, insofar as repetition makes the event not only pleasurable but also recognizable within the lifestream of the individual—and there is Thanatos, repetition that unbinds the "instant," and, consequently, undoes the "*simultaneity*" of the event and its meaning. This second repetition is Freud's version of "destructive plasticity." It is cut off from the instant and from history and is, therefore, "constitutively inassimilable" to life. It is the form of the unassimilable. Death drive, according to Freud, is truly an "adventure in form." What is absolutely essential in Deleuze's reading is that he refuses to separate Eros and Thanatos as dueling forces. As two forms of repetition—binding and unbinding—they are, Deleuze says, "inseparable." This is the problem that Freud encounters beyond the pleasure principle: there is no exception to the law of pleasure (Eros), but there is, nonetheless, a residue, something unaccountable which gives form to pleasure, and that, Deleuze argues, is the traumatic event itself, "*what was before the instant.*" In other words, Freud does not fail to go beyond the pleasure principle. Neither does he retreat from materialist foundations, contra Malabou. Rather, Freud discovers beyond pleasure the gap qua event that *constitutes* sexuality. The foundation of Freud's materialism is a gap, and there is nothing antimaterialist in saying so. Isn't this gap exactly what Malabou claims to be after—the pure, senseless cut, "the wound without hermeneutic future"?[51]

One can imagine Malabou protesting: *Aha! You have banished the accident once again! Your talk of sexuality knows no limits.* And, in a sense, that would be right. As the theory of what happens to us, cerebrality has no place in a theory of sexual binding; the accident is what, in Malabou's words, cannot be bound to signification. Once again, it would seem that the discourse on sexuality has locked away the new wounded and thrown away the key. Worse still, there is no key. It is because we hold so tightly to metaphors of disclosure and meaning that, according to Malabou, we miss seeing those who have been cut off from meaning entirely. The discourse on sexuality and the psychoanalytic establishment have banished the new wounded from sight.

Cerebrality, therefore, is Malabou's answer to the problem of sex: What is beyond the horizon of sexual meaning? Brain damage; the pure, unassimilable accident. Malabou ends *The New Wounded* by calling for a new psychotherapy that would not try to embed the traumatic event within a world of (sexual) meanings but would instead "[recognize] the existence of destructive plasticity" and furthermore "recognize in cerebrality the other of sexuality—which Freud always sought without ever finding it."[52]

Freud's theory of destructivity is actually more complicated than Malabou lets on, and far less romantic. Whereas Malabou calls on us to "recognize" the "other of sexuality" as both materially present and prohibited by the discourse on sexuality, Freud's point is that the "other of sexuality" is . . . sexuality. For all of Malabou's emphasis on the instant of trauma, Freud maintains that what is traumatizing comes "*before the instant*"; it is "the abyss of the ground-less," in Deleuze's words. This gap, or this abyss of nonmeaning, grounds Freud's theory of sexuality, so that it is only right to say *there is sexuality* insofar as sexuality repeats a nonsignifying, "hermeneutically irrecoverable," gap in ontology. By contrast, Malabou's version of things rests on the sheer presence of the wounded brain, as if the event of wounding could be relegated to a mere accident, something that *befalls* the subject. We must instead say, after Deleuze, "my wound existed before me,""*before the instant.*"

Let us consider what happens when, following Malabou, we separate the wound from sexuality. Malabou's critique of Freud rests on his use of an unfashionable dualism, the separation of mind and body. To Malabou's credit, cerebrality offers a blow to mind-body dualism and constructs a theory of the subject that is fully material. We are the thinking-feeling of what happens to us in Malabou's argument. However, Malabou resorts to a no less problematic dualism when speaking of the "pure accident." To whom does it befall? Not the subject of the unconscious. "If it is necessary to elaborate the concept of cerebrality today, it is because, insidiously but unmistakably, cerebrality has usurped the place of sexuality in psychopathological discourse and practice," Malabou tells us.[53] Instead, the pure accident befalls the "psychic identity of the subject." Malabou gives an example: "What patients with Alzheimer's disease show us . . . is precisely the plasticity of the wound through which the permanent dislocation of one identity forms another identity—an identity that is neither the sublation nor the compensatory replica of the old form, but rather, literally, a form of destruction."[54] In a related example, Malabou waxes poetic about the nature of this sudden "dislocation":

> In the usual order of things, lives run their course like rivers. Sometimes they jump their bed, without geological cause, without any subterranean pathway to explain the spate or flood. The suddenly deviant, deviating form of these lives is explosive plasticity.[55]

Herein lies the problem with separating cerebrality from sexuality: lives are not like rivers. Or, if they are like rivers, we must rethink the foundations of Malabou's metaphor. For what we end up with when we say that "lives run their course" until they are dislocated and that the "dislocation of one identity forms another identity" is a romantic notion of psychic identity that replays all the tired tropes of the metaphysics of presence. It assumes (1) that the psyche is a continuous stream (before it is interrupted), (2) that psychic identity is in place (before it is displaced), and (3) that matter is predictable (before it is made "deviant"). In all cases, the accident so theorized is not only external to sexuality but also external to identity. This makes for a rather simplistic form of politics. What are we to do with our brain? Quite simply, we recognize it. In the absence of Freud's theory of sexuality, the brain becomes the subject of full speech.

Jacqueline Rose has written powerfully on the problems that arise when, in the interest of constructing "a radical Freudianism," we separate the event from the identity it harms:

> Each time the psychoanalytic description of internal conflict and psychic division is referred to its social conditions, the latter absorb the former, and the unconscious shifts—in that same moment—from the site of a division into the vision of an ideal unity to come.... Thus sexual radicalism seems to construct its image of a free sexuality in the image of the ego, without flaw or error, as the pre-condition, or ultimate object, of revolutionary change. Idealization of the unconscious and externalization of the event have gone together in the attempt to construct a political Freud.[56]

Instead of "sexual radicalism," Malabou posits cerebral radicalism. Instead of "unified subjects," cerebrality proposes the identity of the brain-subject "as the pre-condition, or ultimate object, of revolutionary change." The constant, however, is the "externalization of the event." Thus we read of "psychic accidents that cannot be translated into the language of sexual infirmity" and of "traumatized people" who "have all *fallen* ill in the sense that they have been exposed to an accident."[57] Although Malabou displaces one dogmatic image of thought (mind-body dualism), she replaces it with another: inside-outside, or identity-event. The result is an idealization of cerebral identity on the one hand and a no less idealized image of the "accident" on the other. The accident befalls us. The task of cerebral politics, therefore, is to recognize this fallen condition and the "ideal unity" that's been sundered, which may still be "to come." Even the language of the "pure accident" suggests that what is, in fact, being purified here is not "sexual meaning," but the dross of sexual division—a division that, for Freud, does *not* befall us randomly but, in a precise sense, shapes us, molds us, makes us the plastic figures we are, as subjects *of* this division.

For all of its emphasis on inscrutability and untranslatability, "destructive plasticity" remains an idealization of both matter and event: we jump, like a river jumping its bed, from one psychic identity to the next, from the brain-subject unity to the "new wounded," who are *symbols* of the pure event in that they symbolize the "instant," the event of pure destruction. "At every instant," Malabou writes, "we are all susceptible to becoming *new wounded*, prototypes of ourselves without any essential relation to the past of our identities."[58] But the sequence here is actually quite relatable: identity, dislocation, new wounded. There is nothing "hermeneutically irrecoverable" in this. Indeed, because the instant defines "destructive plasticity," the latter takes part in a long aesthetic history of plastic form.

In *The Origin of German Tragic Drama*, Walter Benjamin defines the symbol as the instantaneous unity of matter and meaning, in which the latter, pure form, destroys the former in what we might as well call "destructive plasticity." Here is Benjamin:

> The artistic symbol is plastic. . . . The measure of time for the experience of the symbol is the mystical instant in which the symbol assumes the meaning into its hidden and, if one might say so, wooded interior.[59]

What Freud calls "sexuality," Benjamin calls "allegory." At its etymological root, "allegory," unlike symbol, speaks of something "other" than itself. So too, Freud's discourse on sexuality speaks only and always of the "other of sexuality," its own absence of full speech. And that is because sexuality interlaces the event of nonmeaning (Thanatos) in and with every instant of sense (Eros). In Deleuze's reading of Freud, Eros repeats "*what is before the instant*" of the symbol, which is why, technically speaking, we must say that sexuality is impossible, that it is the very discourse of the impossible. This impossibility of meaning is, oddly enough, the very "thing" Malibou went looking for on the other side of Freud's failed materialism—that is to say, on the other side of sex.

What might an allegorical materialism look like? Famously, Benjamin compares allegory to the events of natural history. Neither plastic form nor the symbolic instant captures the work of the allegorist; his medium is nature—nature as "a death's head."

Whereas in the symbol destruction is idealized and the transfigured face of nature is fleetingly revealed in the light of redemption, in allegory the observer is confronted with the *facies hippocratica* of history as a petrified, primordial landscape.[60]

Notably, while Benjamin's emphasis is on the outlook of the observer, he adds that nature itself is no less allegorical: "If nature has always been subject to the power of death, it is also true that it has always been allegorical."[61] The difference, again, between allegory and symbol is that allegory undoes the "instant." (Think, for example, of Spenser's failed "count," another example of allegorical ruin.) Benjamin cites Schopenhauer on precisely this point: "It is true," Schopenhauer says, "that an allegorical picture can in just this quality produce a vivid impression on the mind and feelings. . . . For instance, if the desire for fame is firmly and permanently rooted in a man's mind . . . and if he now stands before the *Genius of Fame* [by Annibale Carracci] with its laurel crowns, then his whole mind is thus excited, and his powers are called into activity. But the same thing would also happen if he suddenly saw the word 'fame' in large clear letters on the wall."[62] Schopenhauer objects that allegory is too literal. When one looks at an allegorical painting, the letters are all that one can see: "allegory." He characterizes allegory as a form of writing. Unlike the accidental destruction obtained in the symbol, allegorical destruction is far less meaningful. Allegory pertains to the materiality of the letter qua gap, and this gap, or this lack of foundation, makes allegory a difficult object at best. Benjamin, in fact, reverses Schopenhauer's criticism into a form of ironic approval, one that gets us to the heart of allegorical matter, including the matter of sex. Benjamin writes: "It is not possible to conceive of a starker opposite to the artistic symbol, the plastic symbol, the image of organic totality, than this amorphous fragment which is seen in the form of allegorical script. . . . At one stroke the profound vision of allegory transforms things and works into stirring writing."[63]

Now, it may come as a surprise to some readers, but the Lacanian reading of Freud comes quite close to what Benjamin says about allegory. Lacan's claim is not that matter is an effect of language. Rather, it is that language, understood as a system of material letters, is implicated in a gap. Whereas Malabou speaks of a suffering brain, and Benjamin of the suffering of the allegorist, Lacan speaks of the suffering of the letter:

> Our detour is thus validated by the very object which leads us into it: for we are quite simply dealing with a letter which has been *detoured*, one whose trajectory has been *prolonged* (this is literally the English word in the title ["The Purloined Letter"]), or, to resort to the language of the post office, a letter *en souffrance* (awaiting delivery or unclaimed).[64]

This is a far cry from saying that the brain suffers from external accidents. In Lacan's version of things, the material letter (the letter *en souffrance*) *is the accident*. The gap in language, which, for Lacan, is identical to the gap in sexuality, curves the material world around itself. Thus, the psychoanalytic theory of the event is rigorously *nonaccidental*; if I forget a proper name, it is not because an accident has befallen me, dislocating the stream of my thoughts; rather, it is because "my" thoughts have already been shaped by an event that happened long ago, before there was a "me" to forget it. Where Malabou sees a random event of wounding, psychoanalysis sees a highly logical symptom of the wound, which is no less inscrutable for that reason. As we saw with Freud, sexuality repeats an unassimilable remainder. If forgetting is an everyday example of that remainder, it proves sexual not because it hides an illicit content but because it repeats the impossibility lodged in sex.

The problem with allegory, then, is not that it reduces everything to language; it is that readers like Malabou still reserve the instant of the symbol as the true, nonallegorical site of political identity. Destructive plasticity is one thing, so long as it produces recognizable symbols, but an allegorical plasticity that reduces life, meaning, and culture to the *suffering of the letter*, is another thing altogether. I call this allegorical materialism, devoid of symbol, "the environmental unconscious."

Lacan gives his own allegory; in fact, he gives us two. In both cases, Lacan challenges the way we "see" matter. In Lacan's tree diagram, for example, we see "tree," not tree (see Figure 1). Lacan's allegory is a strange natural history of the letter. Nowadays, at least in ecocriticism, it has become common to look to the nonhuman world around us and say, yes, trees speak; forests think.[65] We can and no doubt should extend this observation about the hidden life of trees, taking arboreal language to its etymological root in the Greek word for "matter," *hyle* or "wood," as just one example of the wider world of thinking, speaking matter. As Lucretius showed long ago, all matter is structured like a language, down to the letter. Lacan takes Lucretius's metaphor at face value. In his example of the signifier "tree," the letter has replaced the living symbol (tree). Lacan adapts his tree diagram from Saussure's *Course in General Linguistics*. In Saussure's version, tree (as concept or signified) and "tree" (as signifier) are reversed, maintaining, in Lacan's reading of it, the dominance of the signified over the material letter. "The two elements [concept (tree) and signifier (tree')] are," in Saussure's words, "intimately united, with each calling the other to mind."[66] Saussure's arboreal sign has a circle drawn around it, forming a single, unified symbol. Moreover, the bar separating the two levels indicates that the two levels are two sides of the same coin. Saussure's sign, like Malabou's wounded, forms a unified identity.

Lacan's diagram could not be more different. In his version of things, the signifier dominates the signified. Put differently, "tree" becomes an allegory; it is always *other* than itself. Bruce Fink summarizes Lacan's metaphysical reversal: "According to Lacan, there is no mutuality between signifier and signified, no reciprocal penetration or determination of the one by the other. . . . The signifier dominates the signified without the signified ever having a chance to dominate the signifier."[67] What makes a "tree" a tree is not the intimate unity of matter and meaning; against the *hylomorphic* view of language, which holds that language serves the purpose of representing the idea,

TREE

FIGURE 1. Lacan's "Tree" diagram. Reproduced from Lacan, "The Instance of the Letter in the Unconscious, or Reason since Freud." From *Écrits: The First Complete Edition in English*, by Jacques Lacan, translated by Bruce Fink. Copyright 1996, 1970, 1971, 1999 by Éditions du Seuil. English translation copyright 2006, 2002 by W. W. Norton and Company, Inc. Reprinted by permission of W. W. Norton and Company, Inc.

Lacan anticipates his later theory of sexuality (the famous *Il n'y a pas de rapport sexuel* [There is no such thing as a sexual relationship]) by insisting that there is no relationship between "tree" and tree. To the extent that there is one, the relationship is effectuated by the bar, no longer serving to represent, as in Saussure's model, the two sides of a coin, but rather serving its own function as division or gap.

Decades of deconstruction have taught us to read this bar, yet we have not taken the Lacanian diagram seriously enough. The letter does not stop at the word; it slides along the bar from one language to the next, from linguistics to poetics to the discourse on sexuality and materialism, so that if we now say, rightly, that trees speak and forests think, we must add that they *suffer* the breakup of the letter. Though it was not his intention, Lacan's tree diagram owes more to Lucretius than to Saussure; in it, we find "no reciprocal penetration" of matter and meaning, no intimate unity, identity, or symbolism of the instant. Instead, we find the *lack* of ecological rapport (my update to Lacan's theory of the lack of sexual rapport). We find allegory.

This brings us to Lacan's second diagram, "Gentlemen and Ladies" (see Figure 2). Whereas the tree diagram left open the possibility that a relationship between word and image could be formed eventually,

GENTLEMEN   LADIES

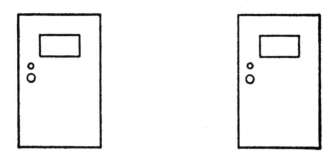

FIGURE 2. Lacan's "Gentlemen and Ladies" diagram. Reprinted from Lacan, "The Instance of the Letter in the Unconscious." From *Écrits: The First Complete Edition in English*, by Jacques Lacan, translated by Bruce Fink. Copyright 1996, 1970, 1971, 1999 by Éditions du Seuil. English translation copyright 2006, 2002 by W. W. Norton and Company, Inc. Reprinted by permission of W. W. Norton and Company, Inc.

Lacan's second diagram cancels that promise. He calls it a "low blow" to functionalist theories of language, but it is equally a low blow to those who put faith in the unity of matter and meaning. Although it appears to have lost the naturalist trappings of the tree diagram, "Gentlemen and Ladies" drives home the message hinted at above: there is no ecological relationship. According to Lacan's second diagram, what defines "ladies" and "gentlemen," men and women is the gap separating two signifiers. Although one could say that the signifier enters the bathroom doors, there is no reassuring destination. Just as there is no relationship bridging the two levels, so there is no relationship between "Ladies" and "Gentlemen." The sexual relationship is barred, or, rather, the relationship is this bar. Fink makes the spurious claim, unsupported by Lacan's text, that the signifiers "Ladies" and "Gentlemen" could be seen (if one were to squint) written on the bathroom doors: "[Lacan] does not provide little stick figures representing men and women," Fink writes. "Instead, he provides pictures of the doors themselves, complete with little plaques on which are undoubtedly found the same signifiers Lacan writes above the bar."[68] Such an unfounded assumption—that if we look closer, the letters will magically appear in place—risks reinstating the intimate unity between levels that Lacan's diagram derails. Moreover, while it is true that a certain notion of sexual difference plays an important role in the psychic itineraries of psychoanalysis, the bathroom doors that Lacan depicts are gender neutral. The plaques *are* blank. And no amount of squinting will fill in that gap, since what we are dealing with here is something pertaining to the very nature of the letter in psychoanalysis: the letter as "impediment, failure, split."[69] Quite literally, Lacan's signifiers are out of order. What the reader confronts in the image of the two identical doors is not a simple arithmetic or count (one plus one) but the impossibility of One. The gap in the diagram, which is identical to the gap in the signifying chain, makes the meaning of sex impossible to locate. As Andrea Long Chu argues, "sex" in psychoanalysis is an "ontological, not biological" affair.[70] It does not pertain to a biological essence but to the very incompletion and impossibility of "matter." Although "psychoanalytically uncontroversial," this point is still widely misunderstood: "Castration," says Chu, "happens *on both sides.*"[71] Although it seems far removed from the arboreal diagram that preceded it, Lacan's second diagram is, in fact, an extension of the former. It tells us that ontology, specifically sexed ontology, is at its foundation split. Material life is plastic, dynamic, and ever changing because of the gap (event) it encircles. This holds true for all speaking beings, trees included.

Disentanglements

Our journey from sex to cerebrality to allegory and back again via the Lacanian diagrams was necessary for two reasons: First, it was necessary in order to pry a theory of events loose from the grip of symbolic reason. Even a materialist thinker such as Malabou holds tight to the image of a materiality *beyond* the letter of sex, and thus ends up reproducing yet another transcendental signified: Malabou calls it "cerebrality." This retention of symbolic form obviates the difficulty of reading matter in relation to *"what was before the instant"* (Deleuze)—namely, the impasse or impossibility of "sex." The second reason for our detour was to theorize the allegorical event as the very substance of this deadlock, as the twisting together of death and sexuality (in Freud) and the (im)materiality of the letter (in Lacan). The psychoanalytic "view" of sexuality is confounding, especially to the ecomaterialist, because it uproots our sense of foundation. The "other of sexuality" is ... sexuality. Sexuality is radically asexual.

To be sure, ecocriticism, new materialism, and posthumanism— these branches of theory have long sought to destabilize our images of matter. Terms such as mesh, entanglement, intra-activity, and natureculture all work to desubstantialize any kind of foundationalist or essentialist understanding of nature; moreover, they subvert *hylomorphism* by theorizing matter as plastic—that is, not only form-*receiving* but also, as in Malabou's theory of material plasticity, form-*giving*. Nevertheless, it is not clear that ecocriticism has a strong account of negativity, precisely that which does *not* enter entanglement. Recall Lacan's two doors: yes, the signifiers "Ladies" and "Gentlemen" enter the picture, but there is no endpoint or destination. The destination was dislocated from the start.[72] We can think of negativity in the psychoanalytic sense as the unassimilable minus or gap that enables the warp and woof (animal pun intended) of our ecological relations, keeping in mind that these "relations" are always contentious since they include something that necessarily falls out. Malabou mistakes this falling for the falling of the accident. In Spenser's *Faerie Queene*, however, it is not just the accident that concerns us; in Spenser's allegorical view, matter is already *felled*.

TWO

TRAUMA IN THE AGE OF WOOD

(Spenser after Malabou)

> In comparing modern thought with ancient records, we
> must remember the difficulties of translation. . . . For
> instance, how differently would Aristotle's metaphys-
> ical reflections read if we persisted in translating one of
> his metaphysical key words by the English term *wood*,
> and also insisted on giving the most literal meaning to
> that word.
>
> —Alfred North Whitehead, *Modes of Thought*

In "The Legend of Holinesse," the first book of Spenser's *Faerie
Queene*, Redcrosse Knight enters the dark deep of the romance
genre's signature wooded labyrinths. There, he encounters a wooden
figure named Fradubio. Trauma mediates the encounter: "He pluckt a
bough; out of whose rifte there came / Smal drops of gory bloud, that
trickled down the same" (1.2.30). Drawing on a long literary archive
of trauma that, time and again, de-centers human subjectivity via the
pain and suffering of nonhuman bodies, Spenser's Fradubio (whose
name means "brother doubt" or "amidst doubt") stands as a plangent
reminder of the romance genre's chimerical and often vexed relationship to allegory. After explaining to Redcrosse how he came to be "in
this rough rynd embard," how he, now a tree, was seduced by Duessa
and thereby became transformed into his current woody state; after
relating his story to Redcrosse, whose own beloved, Fidessa, is we

learn none other than the seductive Duessa in disguise, we are confronted with what Patricia Parker calls the essentially "dilatory" nature of romance: whether Redcrosse Knight will witness his own fate reflected in this bleeding, speaking tree, or whether he will repeat Fradubio's error and wander in the woods of romance without end.[1]

Spenser's tree allegory is not unlike Lacan's arboreal signifier, which we saw in the previous chapter. In both cases, "matter" (wood) is implicated in a gap, or "rifte." Lacan's rift-work therefore repeats and doubles Spenser's allegorical materialism. To better understand Spenser's allegory, let us look more closely, first, at the archive of trauma from which Spenser's tree figure grows and departs.

Spenser borrows his tree allegory from Torquato Tasso's epic, *Gerusalemme liberata,* in which estranged lovers exchange words in the dark as the hero, Tancred, wounds an unknown tree. The tree speaks:

> "Alas! Too much," it cried,
> "have you, O Tancred, wronged me! Now let be!
> … Would you assail (ah cruel and perverse!)
> your dead foes in their very sepulchres?
> "I was Clorinda, not the only soul
> lodged here in rough, hard plants.
> … These branches and these trunks can feel. If you
> hew down their wood, you murder what you hew."
>   (13.42–43)[2]

Clorinda embodies a long literary tradition in which the boundary between human and plant was ceaselessly crossed.[3] Ovid, for example, turns many of his transformations upon this boundary. In the *Metamorphoses,* Daphne's flesh changes into bark as she resists Apollo's amorous pursuit, transforming her body into a branching laurel: "Her soft white bosom was ringed in a layer of bark, her hair was turned into foliage, her arms into branches" (1.545–50).[4] What is more, Tasso's depiction of Clorinda partakes of a rich archive in the history of literary and theoretical interpretations of trauma: from its brief mention in Freud's *Beyond the Pleasure Principle* to its central role in Cathy Caruth's study, *Unclaimed Experience.* In each of these texts, key questions of violence, materiality, and history are at stake.

However, the main question that these texts pose is *where to locate the traumatic event*. Freud turns to Tasso's poem to account for the violent repetitions at the heart of traumatic experience. He writes:

> The most moving poetic picture of a fate such as this is given by Tasso in his romantic epic *Gerusalemme Liberata*. Its hero, Tancred, unwittingly kills his beloved Clorinda in a duel while she is disguised in the armour of an enemy knight. After her burial he makes his way into a strange magic forest which strikes the Crusaders' army with terror. He slashes with his sword at a tall tree; but blood streams from the cut and the voice of Clorinda, whose soul is imprisoned in the tree, is heard complaining that he has wounded his beloved once again.[5]

Following Freud, Caruth explains that, "as Tasso's story dramatizes it, the repetition at the heart of catastrophe—the experience that Freud will call 'traumatic neurosis'—emerges as the unwitting reenactment of an event that one cannot simply leave behind," since, as Caruth argues, it is an event that one never simply *had* in the first place.[6] Trauma, according to Caruth, is an experience (or rather, a nonexperience) of deferred, retrospective action, or "afterwardsness,"[7] in which the present replays the past through an endless series of uncontrolled and uninvited repetitions, eviscerating the present through their unassimilable force. Just as we do "not hear Clorinda's voice until after the second wounding, so trauma is not locatable in the simple violent or original event in an individual's past." Rather, trauma appears in its very absence, in "the way it was precisely *not known* in the first instance" and in the ways it "returns to haunt the survivor later on."[8]

Caruth distinguishes her idea of trauma from Freud's by highlighting the distinctive character of the voice. Caruth argues that "what seems to me particularly striking in the example of Tasso is not just the unconscious act of the infliction of the injury and its inadvertent and unwished-for repetition, but the moving and sorrowful *voice* that cries out, a voice that is paradoxically released *through the wound*."[9] Here what is paradoxical for Caruth is the surprising communicativeness of the wound. Clorinda's vegetable body, needless to say, goes without mention. We read instead that Tasso's story "represents traumatic experience not only as the enigma of a human agent's repeated and unknowing acts but also as the enigma of the otherness of a human voice."[10]

While Caruth's description of trauma rests on the assumption that meaning (or the lack thereof) and experience (albeit unclaimed) inhabit only those regions of the living that obtain for human life, Freud entertains the idea that meaning, consciousness, and historicity are precipitates of traumatic events that have no human referent. Freud anticipates recent challenges to anthropocentrism by speculating on a time before the human, offering the reader another nonhuman figure no less wounded than Clorinda and no less germane to the generic traits of epic romance. Freud writes:

> Let us picture a living organism in its most simplified possible form as an undifferentiated vesicle of a substance that is susceptible to stimulation. . . . This little fragment of living substance is suspended in the middle of an external world charged with the most powerful energies; and it would be killed by the stimulation emanating from these if it were not provided with a protective shield against stimuli. It acquires the shield in this way: its outermost surface ceases to have the structure proper to living matter, becomes to some degree inorganic and thenceforward functions as a special envelope or membrane resistant to stimuli. . . . By its death, the outer layer has saved all the deeper ones from a similar fate.[11]

Freud's passage illustrates the limits of determining what Derrida refers to as the "enigmas of the 'first time' and of originary repetition" in Freud's texts: whether the very movement of the organism "described as the effort of life to protect itself by *deferring* a dangerous cathexis"— that is, an outside force or disturbance—is "not already death at the origin of a life which can defend itself against death only through an *economy* of death, through deferment, repetition, reserve."[12] Recall that, for Freud, life emerges from the attempt to master death (the unassimilable) through repetition. The idea of the "first time"—of a life separated from death—becomes enigmatic precisely because of a deferment of death at the origin of life, a deferment which installs repetition and delay *in the beginning*. "No doubt life protects itself by repetition, trace, *différance*," Derrida writes, "but we must be wary of this formulation: there is no life present *at first* which would *then* come to protect, postpone, or reserve itself in *différance*." On the contrary,

> Life must be thought of as trace before Being may be determined as presence. This is the only condition on which we can say that life *is* death, that repetition and the beyond of the pleasure principle are native and congenital to that which they transgress. . . . It is thus the delay which is in the beginning.[13]

Or, to return to Freud's text, we can say that in the beginning there was delay. Freud's origin story locates the "undifferentiated vesicle" at the beginning of human life; in doing so, he installs a nonhuman "delay" at the origin of human autogenesis, one that works both narratively and ontogenetically to forestall human presence.[14]

Unlike Caruth's analysis, Freud's description of trauma does not *begin* with the human subject. Rather, Freud's speculative account is posthuman avant la lettre. Focusing on a rudimentary organism, "an undifferentiated vesicle" that is at once living and dead ("its outermost surface ceases to have the structure proper to living matter"), Freud enables us to consider the agency of this nonhuman entity as both an antecedent to and a condition of human life. As Freud later writes, "In highly developed organisms the receptive cortical layer of the former vesicle has long been withdrawn into the depths of the interior of the body."[15] Thus, far from hailing any sort of turn *to* the posthuman, Freud points to the always already of the inhuman within humanity, the outer within the inner, and the wound that comes *before* life.

How does this involution of outer and inner abut with Freud's larger narrative? Although Freud has recourse to nonhuman figures (Clorinda, the tiny vesicle) and ultimately undoes the dichotomy human/nonhuman, his narrative frame remains a humanizing one. Writing between wars, Freud turns to Tasso's epic romance and the figure of Clorinda as an example of traumatic neurosis; as a result, he uses Tasso's story to fulfill essentially metaphorical ends: Clorinda's wound symbolizes a loss of self-mastery and misrecognition on the part of the hero, Tancred.

It seems we are at a standoff: although Malabou displaces the traumatic event from mind to brain, her theory of the accident leaves the matter of the brain firmly in place; meanwhile, Freud and Caruth displace the location of the event by calling into question the notion of the "first time." Still, like Malabou, they stop short of reading matter allegorically, as something *other* than a symbol.

Allow me to venture the following allegorical reading: While Freud thought he was working from brain to psyche, and Malabou from the psyche to cerebrality, matter was pulling them in both directions at once. When Freud writes of "the receptive cortical layer of the former vesicle," he states that this cortical layer becomes the material lining of our "inner" world, much like a glove when turned inside out. Turned outside in again, Freud's receptive cortical layer becomes Malabou's suffering brain. In both cases, however, language is not so stable. The destructive plasticity Malabou attributes to the brain becomes most apparent when the materiality of the letter veers off course. For example, in botany, "cortex" refers to the outer layer of tissue in a plant. In Latin, "cortex" means "bark." Not only are these botanical figures eccentric to the authors' stated intentions, they excenter the event of destructive plasticity beyond symbolic recovery. Cerebrality, in both cases, becomes an allegory not unlike Lacan's "tree" allegory; indeed, it is the unintended displacement of human and vegetal life one into the other that makes the matter in question cryptic. Although Freud and Malabou both use material figures (the brain, the tiny vesicle) to speak of events, they operate as if the materiality of these figures made no difference. Is it possible, however, that these figures were using them?

In Benjamin's natural history of allegory, the allegorist is subject to precisely this dialectical reversal: "Allegorical intention is, as natural history, as the earliest history of signifying or intention, dialectical in character," which means that allegory is the "death of the *intentio*."[16] Benjamin explains: "Allegories are, in the realm of thoughts, what ruins are in the realm of things."[17] The very figures used to say one thing (brain), in allegory, say something other (plant). It is this collapse of intention into the errancy of the letter that Benjamin associates with natural history. In this collapse, "history has physically merged into the setting."[18] To echo Lacan's "tree" diagram, there is, for the allegorist, no natural relationship between cortex and "cortex." Just when we think we are speaking of matter, "matter" speaks us.

The Obscure Life of Plants

But perhaps the slippage between cortex and "cortex" is not so strange after all. Or it is the right amount of strange. As Michael Marder argues in *Plant-Thinking*, the powers we associate with the mind may, after all, be inherited from the material plasticity of plants. Marder writes:

> It is questionable . . . whether the sensory and cognitive capacities of the psyche, which in human beings have been superadded to the vegetal soul, are anything but an outgrowth, an excrescence, or a variation of the latter. The sensitivity of the roots seeking moisture in the dark of the soil, the antennae of a snail probing the way ahead, and human ideas or representations we project, casting them in front of ourselves, are not as dissimilar from one another as we tend to think. Assuming then that the "higher" part of the soul is based upon, or better yet emanates from, the "lower," what does it inherit from its progenitor? How, that is, do human beings derive their identity from their inconspicuous vegetal other?[19]

We will have occasion to revisit this construal of the human psyche as an increase out of vegetal growth when considered through the lens of Milton's *Paradise Lost* later (see this book's Conclusion). For now, I wish to highlight Marder's provocation to think of vegetal life not merely as an unfortunate slippage down the signifying chain from humanity to vegetality but rather as synonymous with the allegorical event we have been tracing.

Thus far, we have traveled from sex to cerebrality to the natural history of allegory in Lacan's "tree" diagram and Freud's (unintentional) botanical references above. Might we have come full circle? Could it be possible that the reason why so many poets and theorists have turned to plants as the allegorical representatives of trauma is that plants think allegorically? Might our "inconspicuous vegetal other," whose life is always an afterlife and who grows at the intersection of light and shadow, be the obscure progenitor of allegory? It is suggestive that

Malabou, in a discussion of her grandmother's subjection to Alzheimer's disease, compares destructive plasticity—precisely that which,
in her argument, takes us beyond the hermeneutic circle—to a vegetative state. Malabou writes: "We are supposed to be satisfied with
the implicit diagnosis of vegetative state. Everyone thinks it without
daring to say it aloud: my grandmother, along with all her companions
in misfortune, had simply become 'vegetables.'"[20] In *Ontology of the Accident*, Malabou repeats the Ovidian transformation of Daphne into
a branching laurel; again, she compares destructive plasticity and its
sculptural work to the formation of plants:

> Plasticity is the form of alterity when no transcendence, flight or es-
> cape is left. The only other that exists in this circumstance is being
> other to the self. It is all too true that Daphne can only escape Phoe-
> bus by transforming herself. In a sense, flight is impossible for her too.
> For her too, the moment of transformation is the moment of destruc-
> tion: the granting and suppression of form are contemporaneous:
> "Her prayer was scarcely finished, when a heavy numbness seized on
> her limbs. Her soft breast was enveloped in a thin bark, her hair grew
> into foliage and her arms into branches; her foot that was just now so
> quick was stuck in sluggish roots, a tree top covered her face; only her
> radiance remained in her." Nothing left of the former body other than
> a heart that for a time beats under the bark, a few tears.[21]

Underwriting both these explosions of form—Alzheimer's disease
and Ovidian metamorphosis—is a conception of vegetal life that,
while "other" to the self that it replaces, remains oddly self-identical.
In other words, while vegetable life serves as an example of alterity,
vegetality is not, according to Malabou, existentially self-distancing.
Hence Malabou's frustration with the diagnosis of "vegetative state."
It seems to ignore the existential condition of her grandmother. Nevertheless, the speed at which we dismiss such comparisons to vegetal
life may say more about our own lingering commitments to human
identity, as if humans were the only beings capable of going outside
ourselves and becoming "other." Malabou relegates vegetal life to the
shadows by rescuing destructive plasticity for the brain. She makes
cortex and "cortex" symbols of human identity.

This is the point at which Marder's intervention into vegetal life proves essential to our argument. Although the identity of plants seems fixed due to their apparent rootedness in the soil, the modern word "vegetable" contains "two opposed, if not mutually exclusive, senses."

> While the predominant usage of the verb "to vegetate" is negative, . . . its subterranean history relates it to the exact opposite of this privileged meaning: the fullness and exuberance of life, vigor, and brimming energy, the *ergon* of plant-soul. Vegetal activity encrypts itself in its modes of appearance by presenting itself in the guise of passivity, which is to say, by never presenting itself as such. The life of plants, therefore, poses a special challenge before hermeneutical phenomenology, incapable of elucidating that which does not appear in the open, that which emphatically does not give itself.[22]

Thinking allegorically is not coincidentally but deeply connected with plant-thinking. We might say that plants are allegorical creatures, for their very way of being is a form of encryption. If Malabou was after the "other of sexuality," understood as the other of hermeneutic recovery, she could have found it in plants. In plants, life and death, sex and otherness, matter and *phusis*, are already encrypted in the soil. Allegorically speaking, plant plasticity is irreducibly "other," which is why Marder calls plants "non-objects": their excessive growth, fecund sexuality, and obscurity pose a "special challenge" to hermeneutics.

Spenser's Trees

Like Freud after him, Spenser followed Tasso in making the pain of traumatic repetition sound out through trees. Unlike Freud, Spenser, in anticipation of Marder, grafts his vision of trauma to the obscure life of plants and his "darke conceit," his allegory, to a version of the environmental unconscious that (in Marder's words) "emphatically does not give itself." In the following lines, Spenser's wounded tree speaks:

> Therewith a piteous yelling voice was heard,
>   Crying, O spare with guilty hands to teare
> My tender sides in this rough rynd embard,

But fly, ah fly hence away, for feare
Least to you hap, that happened to me heare,
And to this wretched Lady, my deare loue,
O too deare loue, loue bought with death too deare.
Astond he stood, and up his heare did houe,
And with that suddein horror could no member moue.
　(1.2.31)

The encounter with Fradubio is just one in a series of traumatic misrecognitions in which Redcrosse's subjectivity is threatened by strange figures (Error, Orgoglio, Duessa, the dragon) whose physicality overwhelms his ability to fashion symbolic meaning. The pertinent word for this failure to fashion is "frame."

And thinking of those braunches greene to frame
A girlond for her dainty forehead fit,
He pluckt a bough; out of whose rifte there came
Smal drops of gory bloud, that trickled down the same.
　(1.2.30)

Seeking not only psychic but also stylistic compensation for the battle against Error, Redcrosse frames "A girlond," an image of allegorical closure, to crown his beloved (and false) Fidessa, for whose "Faire seemely pleasaunce" and "falsed fancy," Redcrosse, "to expresse, . . . bends," that is, perverts, "his gentle wit" (1.2.30). However, this attempt to frame (fashion) allegorical closure immediately results in failure (failed "fit"). Redcrosse, the play on words suggests, is not yet ready to frame (too "greene to frame"), and so not being consummate in his ability to fashion Holinesse, instead exposes a "rifte," or wound, within allegory itself. This wound surfaces, in Lacanian terms, as the traumatic "Thing" that both inaugurates subjectivity through processes of misrecognition and haunts subjectivity as its material-psychotic surplus. The result is a framing mise en abyme. What horrifies Redcrosse is not so much this thing, be it man or tree, but the recognition that he *is* this Thing. Spenser breaks the frame of human recognition, the frame that distances and represents the material world as a reserve for human utility.

Already at the outset of "The Legend of Holinesse," this potential to misrecognize and to frame nonhuman matter as always already human appears written on trees, carved into the archetypal Wandering Wood, whose "couert," "shadie groue" shades Redcrosse and Una as they wander out of epic and into the dark deep, the *selva oscura*, of romance (1.1.7). The transition from epic to romance, like the transition from pastoral, is "compeld," constrained ("constrain"), and indeed, "enforst": "with pleasure forward led" (1.1.5, 6, 7, 8). Redcrosse and Una are passively "led" to the Wandering Wood, a type of *hortus conclusus* "shrouded from . . . dred" (1.1.8). There they encounter a catalog of trees whose names are framed according to human use:

> Much can they praise the trees so straight and hy,
> The sayling Pine, the Cedar proud and tall,
> The vine-propp Elme, the Poplar never dry,
> The builder Oake, sole king of forrests all,
> The Aspine good for staues, the Cypresse funerall. (1.1.8)

Marder notes that in the history of Western thought, plants have mostly been viewed not in terms of their emergence as forms of life (*phusis*) but in terms of their actuality, as fetishized objects, or, in Martin Heidegger's words, "standing reserve" for human use.[23] "On Heidegger's reading, the emergence of nature, or nature *as* emergence, as a surge into being, is at the same time its retreat, a giving withdrawal and an inexhaustible generosity."[24] For this reason, Heidegger defines the work of art, especially poetry, as a dis-closure of *phusis*: the artwork lets nature appear as a *work*. Moreover, Heidegger calls the ontic/ontological divide between nature as appearance and nature as *phusis* the "rift-design."[25] What makes the artwork different from a thing of utility ("standing reserve") is that the former does not exhaust itself in its usefulness; instead, it sets to work the "rift" between concealedness and unconcealedness that allegory, or the work of art, is.

Marder, for his part, follows Heidegger in critiquing the "philosophical denegation of vegetal existence" as standing reserve.[26] This denigration, Marder writes, "has had palpable effects on the human approach to natural environment, so that, for example, the woods are treated as nothing more than wood, a mass of lumber 'produced' in a gigantic and infinitely stocked factory of planetary proportions."[27] The example of wood is not accidental, "given that the concept of *matter* arose in Aristotle's thought by way of adopting the everyday word for timber, *hulē*, for rigorously philosophical purposes."[28] What is more, because of the "indispensability of wood as the primary energy source underpinning subsistence and manufacture in the preindustrial era," Vin Nardizzi reminds us that the age of humanism was also, in many ways, the "age of wood."[29] "*The age of wood* is, I trust, an epochal designation unfamiliar to literary scholars," Nardizzi writes; "it names a swath of time that stretches from prehistory to the second half of the eighteenth century, when coal generally replaced charcoal (an energy source plucked from the ashes of cone-shaped piles of lumber that had been charred) in industrial iron making and fuel-wood homes, where it heated food and consumer alike."[30] By the time Shakespeare's Globe was in full swing, the age of wood had already entered an age of ecological crisis, as shortages of wood and timber resulting from deforestation threatened to bring the ligneous era to a state of economic and ecosystemic collapse.[31] The rapid deforestation of England proves Marder's philosophical point: that "all that is required is to project the impoverished notion of matter back onto its pre-philosophical source (*hulē* or timber) and so to confirm, in a vicious circle, that the woods are wood awaiting its elevation . . . or the sublation of its immediate existence into the form of a house, a page in a book, or logs in the fireplace."[32]

Listed according to their use value, the trees in Spenser's catalog of the Wandering Wood are an emblem of human consumption and a marker of poetic accomplishment. The "Laurell, meed of mightie Conquerours" is also the crown of "Poets sage," linking Spenser's epic to Virgil's *Aenied* (1.1.9). The "Firre that weepeth still" and the "Willow worne of forlorne Paramours" recall Ovid's *Metamorphoses*, in which Orpheus has the power to arouse the passions of trees and gather a forest to his lyre (1.1.9). And unlike Redcrosse, who "bends his gentle wit" to frame reluctant matter, here the "Eugh" is "obedient to the benders will," the "Birch" gives itself "for shaftes," and "the Sallow for the mill" (1.1.9).

Such an image of nature in harmony with human desire would seem to re-seal the "rifte" opened by Redcrosse, were it not for the melancholy hexameter line that closes, or rather breaks open, the eighth stanza. "Cypresse funerall" speaks to the negative dimension of desire, in which the desired object ("matter") is already absent, thus provoking an endless series of metonymic displacements: pine, cedar, elm, poplar, oaks, and so forth (1.1.8). Against the inviting appearance of the Wandering Wood, which is described as a "shadie groue" and "Faire harbour," a maternal house and dwelling (*oikos*), what we find is the quintessential lost object. Instead of trees, we find "trees." While the allegorical frame that lured ("led") Redcrosse and Una is the type that promises "pleasure," the kind of pleasure that comes from voy-euristically distancing nature so as to possess it, "Cypresse funerall" implicates Redcrosse and Una in a dying world. The Wandering Wood offers pleasure, but an ek-static, destructive pleasure (*jouis-sance*). It preserves the melancholy quality of life in the form of a dead emblem. The Wandering Wood has a baroque form.

When we reach the end of the catalog of trees, we do so silently, mournfully: the last line reads, "the Maple seeldom inward sound" (1.1.9). Literally, the maple is un-sound: corrupted, and therefore si-lent, enigmatic. Benjamin writes that because nature is fallen, nature is mute: "fallen nature mourns."[33] The presentiment of mourning in the silence of the maple tree foreshadows a death. The death it fore-shadows (the monster lurking inside the allegorical Wood, Error) is already announced from the very beginning of book 1, starting with the first stanza:

> A Gentle Knight was pricking on the plaine,
>> Ycladd in mightie armes and siluer shielde,
>> Wherein old dints of deepe woundes did remaine,
>> The cruell markes of many a bloody fielde. (1.1.1)

And "Yet":

> Yet armes till that time did he never wield. (1.1.1)

Spenser's "Yet" disjoins the living present; it points to "dints," "markes," and "deepe woundes," forms of violence but also forms of writing, which Redcrosse wears and inherits without having been present to the event of their reception: "deepe woundes did remaine," and *yet*, "armes till that time" (what time?) "did he never wield." Redcrosse's physical description doubles as a description of the traumatic event in that the symptomology of his "woundes" comes as much from the future as from the past: we do not (yet) know from whence these "woundes" came; only a future event, a traumatic repetition, can bring "old" wounds to the surface.[34]

Hence, it is not until after the battle with Error, in which Redcrosse receives fresh injuries, that "His Lady," Una, says to him, "Well worthie be you of that Armory" (1.1.27). Spenser's "Yet" delays the moment of recognition when Redcrosse becomes identical to, and not just a simulacrum of, "A Gentle Knight." Or so it seems. For it is not until after we read Spenser's "Letter to Raleigh," which comes at the end of book 3 in the 1590 *Faerie Queene*, that we learn that the "Armory" belongs to Una. Una gives "the Armes of a knight" to Redcrosse (another instance of the gift, of inheritance), who, before that time, was described as "a tall clownishe younge man . . . unfitte through his rusticity for a better place."[35] The gifting of Redcrosse takes us back to the problematic of the proem—that is, to the "unfitter taske" of turning pastoral into epic. Or better still, it takes us back to the "Januarye" eclogue of *The Shepheardes Calender*, in which the mirroring of "gifts," from Hobbinol to Colin Cloute and from Colin to Rosalind, ends in the humiliation of refused return: "Ah foolish *Hobbinol*, thy gyfts bene vayne: *Colin* them gives to *Rosalind* againe" ("Januarye," 59–60).[36] As Jonathan Goldberg notes, "The same 'vayne' effect is achieved in each case—[the gift] passes through several hands and is yet refused. Although it is the same, it is no one's and never proper, a text circulating from hand to hand, always out of hand, never arriving."[37] Never arriving and yet, never let go: while the circulation of gifts proceeds ineffectually on either side of the colon, the "rurall musick" which Colin "broke" off in his failed courtship of Rosalind[38] persists in Spenser's *Faerie Queene* as the failed "fit" of pastoral into epic and epic into romance. The "rusticity" of Colin Cloute clings to Spenser's epic hero Redcrosse like a clot of dirt clings to one's shoe. The name Cloute, though rightly attributed by E.K. in the "Januarye" gloss to the writings of John Skelton and Clément Marot, refers to a "lump of earth."[39] Thus the progression from pastoral to epic begins, as E.K. explains in the "Dedicatory Epistle," in "the base-ness of the name," Colin Cloute.[40] Rather than unfold pastoral into epic, Spenser "chose . . . to vnfold great matter of argument couertly" ("Dedicatory Epistle," 139–40); he fashions a knight from georgic, who repeats Colin's failure to fashion base matter into greatness.[41] Just as Colin "broke his oaten pype" in a fit of melancholy, so Redcrosse breaks the frame of allegory.

Although much Spenser criticism focuses on the boundedness of Spenserian subjects, I follow James Kuzner in asserting that experiences of unboundedness, of trauma and vulnerability, are just as important to Spenser's sense of ecological subjectivity.[42] The iteration of the wound is not locatable, is not fixable to a discrete temporal or characterological identity. Much less a human identity. Moreover, this is because subjectivity in Spenser's poem is profoundly, traumatically, relational. Perhaps this explains why, without cause or referent, Spenser's "iolly knight" appears so melancholy: "But of his cheere did seeme too solemne sad; / Yet nothing did he dread" (1.1.1, 2).

Environing Nothing

The "nothing" that Redcrosse encounters in the Wandering Wood is Error. Error is the manifestation of this empty signifier, "nothing"; she is the dark and occluded object of Redcrosse's aimless "dread." Yet despite her apparent monstrosity, she is also gendered (as my switching between "she" and "it" will indicate), adding another layer of significance to Redcrosse's paradoxical "dread." Error is the traumatic "nothing" of female castration.[43] "She" is the "it" (id) that Lacan calls *objet petit a*, the "nothing" that distances the unconscious "Real" from its symbolization, creating a surplus, or remainder, that desire tries to fill.[44] Whereas conventional knowledge has it that "the return of the repressed" (the symptomatic no-thing that haunts subjectivity) signals a return from the past, Žižek argues that the traumatic "thing," insofar as it drives a wedge between conscious and unconscious subjectivity, comes not from the past but the future. "The past exists as it is included, as it enters (into) the synchronous net of the signifier. . . . [T]hat is why we are all the time 'rewriting history' . . . because the symptom as a 'return of the repressed' is precisely such an effect which precedes its cause (its hidden kernel, its meaning), and in working through the symptom we are precisely 'bringing about the past'—we are producing the symbolic reality of the past, long-forgotten traumatic events."[45] Hence, the process of working through trauma (the interminable process that Freud calls "melancholy") does not entail deciphering hidden meanings but rather letting oneself be overcome by the "nothing" that a future misreading can only temporarily occupy and conceal. This is what Lacan calls "misrecognition": it installs a "nothing" (what Žižek calls the "rock" of the Real, an expression I find apt in the case of Redcrosse, whose semblance is Saint George: George derives from the Greek *geos,* meaning "earth") in subjectivity itself. In a felicitous phrase, Žižek describes the "time structure" of misrecognition as a passage through "error." Although he models it on psychoanalysis, it is in truth the structure of romance:[46]

> The time structure with which we are concerned here is such that it is mediated through subjectivity: the subjective "mistake," "fault," "error," misrecognition, arrives paradoxically *before* the truth in relation to which we are designating it as "error," because this "truth" itself becomes true only through—or, to use a Hegelian term, by mediation of—the error. . . . We overlook the way our act is already part of the state of things we are looking at, the way our error is part of the Truth itself.[47]

Is this not the time structure of "The Legend of Holinesse"? When Redcrosse and Una enter the Wandering Wood, Una knows the truth of their error. She implores Redcrosse:

> Be well aware . . .
>> Least suddaine mischiefe ye too rash prouoke:
>> The danger hid, the place vnknowne and wild,
>> Breedes dreadfull doubts: Oft fire is without smoke,
>> And perill without show: therefore your stroke
>> Sir knight with-hold, till further tryall made.

> . . . the perill of this place
>> I better wot then you, though nowe too late,
>> . . . .

This is the wandring wood, this *Errours den,*
A monster vile, whome God and man does hate.
(1.1.12–13)

As the symbol of feminine humility (she is first seen riding "Vpon a lowly Asse") and truth (her name means "the One, the True"), Una knows ("I better wot then you") that "the return of the repressed"— their journey's "danger hid, the place vnknowne"—lies ahead. She knows that for every image of feminine unity—herself, the Wandering Wood—there are abjects: Duessa, the Whore of Babylon, and Error. What is more, she describes their task as an interminable task of reading and deciphering the "nothing" that lurks within the Wood's "hidden shade" (1.1.12). In an effort to prevail upon Redcrosse, she says: "Therefore I read beware" (1.1.13), where thinking is a matter not of uncovering hidden meanings, but, as Žižek puts it, of going darker and deeper into "the paradoxical structure in which the Truth arises from misrecognition."[48]

Una's motto is this: Truth comes from misrecognition; therefore, beware of wandering into the dark. Her double warning ("Be well aware," "I read beware") doubly insists not to give way to desire, not to be premature in one's dark desires, for this can only lead to error. Hence her admonition: "therefore your stroke / Sir knight with-hold, till further tryall made" (1.1.12). And again: "Yet wisdome warnes, whilest foot is in the gate, / To stay the steppe, ere forced to retrate" (1.1.13). Una advises against entering the Wood too early, prematurely, before Redcrosse has ripened—"further tryall made." Yet her admonition indicates already the paradoxical time structure, the revisionary "re-trate" that she seeks to keep at bay. Error, err, *errare*: the meanings of "to wander" are already internal to the "before" ("ere") of "ere forced," and so the errant step, too, is already in motion in the "steppe" not taken. To "stay the steppe" is already double, of a piece with the logic of the *pas/ne pas* (step/no step) that Derrida articulates, whereby action and nonaction cancel and overlap (the active/passive "retrate" of the trace).[49]

Redcrosse's motto is more exorbitant: not that we should not give way *to* desire, but that we should not give way *on* desire. Having entered the Wandering Wood, Redcrosse is drawn ("Led with delight") to the promise of "nothing," which guarantees both the "pleasure" of substitution and the ecstasy of annihilation. By mapping the fear of female castration, as well as the scopic pleasure of fetishistic substitution, onto the Wandering Wood, Spenser proffers this "nothing" in the form of a "darksom hole," into which we the readers, along with Redcrosse, enter and look:

> But full of fire and greedy hardiment,
>> The youthfull knight could not for ought be staide,
> But forth vnto the darksom hole he went,
> And looked in. (1.1.14)

From the very first line of Spenser's epic romance, Spenser describes Redcrosse's "greedy" desire as a form of "pricking" (spurring, wounding)—that is, urging one's horse, but with the added connotation of phallic penetration. "Pricking" is desiring, but it also makes holes. Combining chivalry and violence, the *equus eroticus* (or, in Karen Raber's queer construction, "equeer" romance)[50] imagined in the first line joyfully envisions the pleasure and pain associated with bestial coupling. Redcrosse feels the spur of desire. (Later on, it is the horse who suffers in this desiring assemblage: "He prickte with pride / And hope to winne . . . / Forth spurred fast: adowne his coursers side / The red bloud trickling staind the way, as he did ride" [1.2.14].) Entering "*Errours den*," that "darksom hole," Redcrosse becomes hard ("full of . . . greedy hardiment") with anticipation:

> his glistering armor made
> A litle glooming light, much like a shade,
> By which he saw the vgly monster plaine,
> Halfe like a serpent horribly displaide,
> But th'other halfe did womans shape retaine,
> Most lothsom, filthie, foule and full of vile disdaine.
>> (1.1.14)

Loss saturates the whole scene. Redcrosse's "glistering armor" provides "A litle glooming light," but this "light" only produces more "shade." The adjective "glooming" derives from the verb "gloom": to gloom means to glow; but its primary sense is to make dark, solemn, or melancholy. Redcrosse's armor fills the "darksom hole" with more dark; he merges with the dark "like a shade." Himself a shadow, he experiences what Hegel calls "the night of the world," the uncanny "nothing" glimpsed in the gaze of the Other—the night of the eye, the empty dimension of subjectivity, "a Night which turns terrifying," Hegel writes.[51] Environed by this "nothing," Redcrosse experiences a radical ontological negativity, the uncanny darkness of the *oikos*.[52] The Wandering Wood, rather than being a safe haven or respite, forces Redcrosse darker and deeper into the uncanny materiality of allegory. Exit nature. Enter Error.

Error embodies in her monstrous flesh the disavowed objects of Protestant masculine identity, abjected but strangely familiar. Her stomach is "full of great lumps of flesh and gobbets raw," material leftovers, Linda Gregerson argues, of the Catholic doctrine of transubstantiation.[53] "Her vomit" is "full of bookes and papers," an image that conjures not only the outpouring of Catholic textuality, as Lawrence Rhu argues,[54] but also the excessive generic outpouring of romance, a genre that resists the classical Aristotelian unities of space and time by overpouring their boundaries.[55] Shifting from a materialist to a hermeneutic register, Gregerson and Maureen Quilligan both stress the textuality of Error's body, claiming that, in the Protestant poetics championed by Spenser, Error's monstrous body serves as an allegory warning Redcrosse and the reader not to be seduced by surfaces, not to be "Led by delight" and "thus beguile the way," but rather to read beyond the letter of the text and so, as Una warns, "read beware."[56]

While such readings find their warrant in Spenser's writings, I concur with Joseph Campana that there is more to Error than the medium or mechanism of textuality.[57] Also interesting is the ecological dimension of Error's monstrous body, which limns the borders of Redcrosse's physical and psychic geography as the abjected, yet still intimate, waste product of Protestant masculine identity. She is half-human, half-beast, an unraveling, perpetually moving, self-generating assemblage of inchoate matter. She is also a mother. In the following lines, we witness this unholy "dam" giving suck to her creaturely "brood":

And as she lay vpon the durtie ground,
… Of her there bred,
A thousand yong ones, which she dayly fed,
Sucking vpon her poisonous dugs, each one
Of sundrie shapes, yet all ill fauored. (1.1.15)

Error's vomiting, excreting body returns the abjects of post-
Reformation England to the surface of textual visibility. Not only
that, her unbounded flesh, a collocation of material entities—animal,
serpent, frog, and so forth—confronts Redcrosse with his own chimerical identity: not only is he compared to a "Lyon" in a scene
of animal mimicry ("he lept / As Lyon fierce" [1.1.17]), but also the
poem's insistence on Error's snake-like body, which slithers on the
"durtie ground," doubles as a reminder of Redcrosse's own lowly beginnings, his "rusticity," not to mention his name, Saint George (or
Saint Earth).

Shame in the Allegorical Fold

Although the Wandering Wood had first been a source of pleasure,
the confrontation with Error marks the symptomatic return of the
repressed last line of the catalogue of trees, making the uncanny materiality of the allegorical Wood akin to the irreducible strangeness
of sex.

When we first see Error, deep within the depths of a "darksome
hole," much like the "keyhole" scene Jean-Paul Sartre describes in
Being and Nothingness,[58] what we see, though darkly, is the most chimerical body that "The Legend of Holinesse" has to offer us in its
vast vegetal-zoo-ontology. Indeed, Error's "beastly bodie" becomes
a prototype of monstrosity in "The Legend of Holinesse," already
containing in her serpentine coils and "poisnous dugs" the dragon's
"hundred foldes," Orgoglio's "monstrous mas," and Duessa's "mis-
shaped parts" (1.1.15; 1.11.11; 1.8.24; 1.8.46). Later allegorists, such as
Milton, repeat Spenser's depiction of Error. In *Paradise Lost*, Sin is
represented as a category error, "The one seemed woman to the waist,
and fair, / But ended foul in many a scaly fold" (2.650–51), while the
very act of creation—natal, cosmological, poetic—is compared to a
primordial chaos or "abyss":

thou [Spirit] from the first
Wast present, and with mighty wings outspread
Dove-like sat'st brooding on the vast abyss
And mad'st it pregnant. (1.19–22)

Milton's universe begins from original chaos, a birth suggestively metaphorized as a form of "brooding" done by an animal who, in this case, "Dove-like," hatches a cosmos. We, humans, are, presumably, along with the rest of creation, the animal's chaotic "brood" (the first entry for "brood" in the OED pertains to an animal's young, "esp. of animals that lay eggs, as birds, serpents, and insects, etc.");[59] what is more, in a stunning speech act that sublates "brooding" into a form of mental incubation while losing none of its peculiarity, the speaker asks that the Holy Spirit make him pregnant too: "what in me is dark / Illumine" (1.22–23). Though it is easy to pass over these lines as a clear-cut statement of poetic intent, what is notable is the *non-intentional* and therefore *unconscious* folding together of spiritual and bestial intercourse, mental and physical parturition, masculine and feminine genders, form and matter, active and passive, and high (epic) and low (beast fable) modes of poetic invention. Milton's speaker is not only "Dove-like" but also Sin-like: impregnated by his "brooding" creator (Satan gives birth to Sin just by thinking of her) and transfigured by the act so that even he "seemed woman," the speaker and all of creation, we learn, are a brood of animals. This chaos ever "brooding" continues apace in the garden, where error appears in the "wanton ringlets" (4.306) of Eve's vine-like hair ("As the vine curls her tendrils" [4.307]), and even extends well beyond the early modern period to the postmodern "body horror" of cinema auteur David Cronenberg, whose film *The Brood* (1979) replicates to the letter Spenser's plastic materiality in the technoscientific biohorror of a transhuman (animal-plant) mother who communicates telepathically with her monstrous young.

That both senses of "brooding" (i.e., moody meditation, and chaotic generation) intertwine in the above examples, such that nursing an idea and hatching an egg are metaphorically interchangeable, if not identical, actions, is not all that surprising when one considers the etiology of mental contemplation. In the *Three Essays on the Theory of Sexuality*, Freud devotes a chapter to "The Sexual Researches of Childhood," stating that "the instinct for knowledge in children is attracted unexpectedly early and intensively to sexual problems and is in fact possibly first aroused by them." Freud adds:

> At about the same time as the sexual life of children reaches its first peak, between the ages of three and five, they also begin to show signs of the activity which may be ascribed to the instinct for knowledge or research. This instinct cannot be counted among the elementary instinctual components, nor can it be classed as exclusively belonging to sexuality. Its activity corresponds on the one hand to a sublimated manner of obtaining mastery, while on the other hand it makes use of the energy of scopophilia. Its relations to sexual life, however, are of particular importance.[60]

A master of self-contradiction, Freud posits a nascent will to knowledge that emerges from sexuality but that cannot "be classed as exclusively belonging to sexuality"; it is the case, however, that "its relations to sexual life . . . are of particular importance" to the child's sexual researches, so much so that a stifled sexual curiosity in childhood can result, Freud says later on in the chapter, "in a renunciation which not infrequently leaves behind it a permanent injury to the instinct for knowledge." Despite Freud's characteristic wavering on the consequences of his theory, the thesis regarding the sexual researches of children makes clear that avidity toward research (whatever the subject: history, biology, Renaissance literature . . .) not only originates from but also remains identical to the earliest experiences of sexual arousal. When it comes to the sexual researches of children, the instinct for knowledge is rooted in a unique kind of problem, what Freud calls "sexual problems"—"sexual" because they have no solution.

Among the bevy of sexual problems that psychoanalysis uncovers, the biggest problem that the child confronts, according to Freud, is the question of where babies come from. "The threat to the bases of a child's existence offered by the discovery or the suspicion of the arrival of a new baby and the fear that he may, as a result of it, cease to be cared for and loved, make him [the child researcher] thoughtful and clear-sighted."[61] No wonder, then, that even in the most abstract realms of continental philosophy, philosophers treat the question of the *event* not only as a trauma (Malabou) but also as "natality" (Arendt), "birth to presence" (Nancy), and "incarnation" (Badiou).[62] As we have seen, error is built into the very fabric of the event insofar as the event (birth) is part and parcel of a thinking that is, from its earliest beginnings, sexual. Confronted with the riddle, Where do babies come from? the child researcher offers up an endless array of "sexual theories" that, "in spite of their grotesque errors," "show more understanding of sexual processes than one would have given their creators credit for."[63] We noted earlier Malabou's suspicion of the imperiousness of the hermeneutic fold of sexuality. Witness, however, what happens when Freud's infantile researchers begin to read "sex."

> The anatomical answers to the question [of childbirth] were at the time very various: babies come out of the breast, or are cut out of the body, or the naval opens to let them through. . . . [Also,] people get babies by eating some particular thing (as they do in fairy tales) and babies are born through the bowel like a discharge of faeces. These infantile theories remind us of conditions that exist in the animal kingdom—and especially of the cloaca in types of animals lower than mammals.[64]

When it comes to sexual brooding, Freud's offhand remarks about "animals" and "fairy tales" are more accurate than he thinks. For, it is not any one empirical observation that matters in these inquiries, but the event or gap that suspends a final answer. Sexuality, according to Freud, is the absence of a *wherefore*. Consequently, the shame so often associated with sexuality is, contrary to the cultural or repressive argument, not due to the inordinate nature of sex, its "dirtiness"; rather, in psychoanalysis, shame is the affective correlate of an interruption or gap—precisely the interruption or gap that the ontological negativity of sex (a problem *without* solution) brings about.

While critics have mostly focused on the monstrosity of Error's body, the category of monster does not sufficiently capture the physical ontology of Error, who is both woman and beast in the first instance. Error is not only monstrous; that is putting the matter too simply. Error is monstrous *because* she represents a snag or tear in the visual field. She is a chimera. In the following lines, we witness another chimerical scene, one in which Duessa, having been stripped of her disguise, stands naked as an animal. As in Freud's description of the sexual theories of children, in Spenser's brooding description below, "nudity" and "animality" become allegorical—that is to say, not just empirical but *problematic*—figures. Here is Duessa:

> Her neather parts, the shame of all her kind,
>   My chaster Muse for shame doth blush to write;
>   But at her rompe she growing had behind
>   A foxes taile, with dong all fowly dight;
>   And eke her feete most monstrous were in sight;
>   For one of them was like an Eagles claw,
>   With griping talaunts armed to greedy fight,
>   The other like a beares vneuen paw:
> More vgly shape yet neuer liuing creature saw. (1.8.48)

The "shame" registered in the first two lines, doubled and repeated between Duessa and Spenser's blushing Muse, prefigures the mirror-play of shame that Derrida recounts in the opening pages of *The Animal That Therefore I Am*. There, Derrida narrates a scene in which he is looked at, naked, by his cat (a cat that, as Derrida insists, is also female), and describes it as an experience of "impropriety": "The single, incomparable and original experience of the impropriety that would come from appearing in truth naked."[65] The name that Derrida gives to this "naked truth" is *animot*. It is a portmanteau, a chimerical word denoting "neither a species nor a gender nor an individual" but rather "an irreducible living multiplicity of mortals," "a chimera waiting to be put to death by its Bellerophon."[66] *L'animot* is an allegory, a word that means "word" (*mot*) and which points to something other than itself—namely, to the heterogeneous assemblage of animals "whose plurality cannot be assembled within the single figure of an animality." "There is no Animal in the general singular," Derrida writes, "separated from man by a single, indivisible limit."[67]

The same holds true in the encounter between Redcrosse and Duessa. From the outset of "The Legend of Holinesse," Spenser describes the Redcrosse Knight as a hunter: he journeys "To proue his puissance in battell braue / Vpon his foe, ... / ... a Dragon horrible and stearne" (1.1.3); he journeys to kill "that balefull Beast" (1.12.2). When he reaches the Wandering Wood, shame compels him forward: "Ah Ladie (sayd he) shame were to reuoke, / The forward footing for an hidden shade" (1.1.12). And when he is nearly overcome in battle with Error, it is shame that he considers: "Thus ill bestedd, and fearefull more of shame" (1.1.24). Redcrosse, like Bellerophon, is put to the test of overcoming shame. The Legend of Holinesse allegorizes that test. However, when Redcrosse sees Duessa, after she has been stripped naked ("Ne spared they to strip her naked all" [1.8.46]), the shame that Spenser records before blazoning Duessa's chimerical body does not so much lead to improved modesty but rather interrupts, in a moment of self-reflexivity, the poetic allegory, turning the poem's allegory into a scene of writing, materiality, and what is more, into a reflection (in words) on Duessa's animality; the poem becomes an *animot*, an utterly chimerical allegory, and hence, a source of shame for Spenser's muse: "My chaster Muse for shame doth blush to write" (1.8.48). Redcrosse's encounter with Duessa breaks the frame of human recognition, so much so that Spenser's allegory becomes more akin to a beast fable, a genre, Spenser acknowledges, not fit for his "chaster Muse ... to write."

This is not the first time that we encounter Duessa's beastly body in the flesh. Already in canto 2, Fradubio recalls seeing Duessa standing waist-deep in a pool of water, "Bathing her selfe in origane and thyme" (1.2.40). Then, as though witnessing a trauma too much for human sight, he "chaunst to see her in her proper hew," not a "Faire Lady," but "A filthy foule old woman I did vew":

> Her neather partes misshapen, monstrous,
>> Were hidd in water, that I could not see,
>> But they did seeme more foule and hideous,
>> Then womans shape man would beleeue to bee. (1.2.41)

Fradubio misrecognizes Duessa's "misshapen" body, including her "skin as rough, as maple rind," and so becomes her victim, a prisoner in "rough rynd embard" (1.8.47). Because he "could not see" Duessa's false disguise, he has to live out his days as a thing to be misrecognized: "a tree I seme, yet cold and heat me paines" (1.2.33).

The pain of misrecognition that Fradubio suffers returns in Duessa's full exposure in canto 8. There, the shame that interrupts Spenser's muse also immobilizes Redcrosse, leaving him "amazd" at Duessa's monstrous form (1.8.49). Duessa's wooden-animal-body would all but overwhelm the Knight of Holinesse were it not for Una's timely reconstruction of the allegorical frame. Whereas Redcrosse stands in dumb amazement (the Old English root of "amazd," *masse*, means "to stupefy, to make dumb") at the spectacle of Duessa's chimerical body, Una mobilizes the most potent power of allegorical expression—namely, the violent and instrumental imposition of abstract form. Here is Una:

> Which when the knights beheld, amazd they were,
>   And wondred at so fowle deformed wight.
>   Such then (said *Una*) as she seemeth here,
>   Such is the face of falsehood, such the sight
>   Of fowle Duessa, when her borrowed light
>   Is laid away, and counterfesaunce knowne.
>   Thus when they had the witch disrobed quight,
>   And all her filthy feature open showne,
> They let her goe at will, and wander waies vnknowne.
>   (1.8.49)

In *Allegory and Violence*, Gordon Teskey argues that allegorical meaning is not, as it is commonly understood, "a simple object or goal," nor is it a mere "representation of any kind."[68] Rather, allegorical meaning, for Teskey, "is an instrument used to exert force on the world as we find it, imposing on the intolerable, chaotic otherness of nature a hierarchical order in which objects will appear to have inherent 'meanings.'" In the stanza quoted above, Una, whose name denotes the One, the True, summons the instrumental force of allegory to give form or meaning to the "deformed" body of Duessa, whose very image as a chaotic assemblage of plant and animal parts threatens to tear a rift in the poem's allegorical frame. Duessa's naked body lacks the "wholeness" (Holinesse) of human form. As such, it exposes a rift or wound, a trauma that Una deftly repairs (remember Una's motto: "read beware") by suturing the reader's gaze away from "deformed" matter, the bestiary that is Duessa's body. Duessa represents "falsehood"; she bears its "face" or figure. Thus the reader can rest assured that her "falsehood" has been exposed, her "counterfesaunce knowne." The instrumental force that Una applies to Duessa's body, turning matter into (human) meaning, is all the more strange given the gendered dimension of allegory. For, as Teskey writes, all allegory is gendered: "As a father stands to his sons, so form stands to its instances, which are begotten in and propagated through an alien subject, matter-as-woman."[69] By these lights, to fashion allegory is not just to instrumentalize inchoate matter into sensible form, but to violently erase the feminine in the production of human meaning. Phallogocentrism and humanism go together.

Still, having just mobilized the instrumental force of allegory in the interest of securing the poem's masculinist and humanist framework, Redcrosse and Una nonetheless return Duessa back to the wild, like an animal released from captivity:

> Shee flying fast from heauens hated face,
>   And from the world that her discouered wide,
>   Fled to the wastfull wildernesse apace,
>   From liuing eies her open shame to hide. (1.8.50)

More than any other book in Spenser's *Faerie Queene*, scholars tend to agree that "The Legend of Holinesse" reaches the greatest level of allegorical and narratological closure. Harry Berger Jr., for example, summarily contrasts "The Legend of Holinesse" to book 6, "The Legend of Courtesie," writing that whereas the latter reflects the problems and lacunas faced by "the Renaissance poet trying to make sense of the world around him," such that "almost every episode is left unresolved" (see this book's Interlude), the former is "self-contained. . . . The allegorical dimension . . . has its main purpose in illuminating the character and quest of the fictional hero—the holiness (wholeness) of Redcross."[70] Similarly, Campana, while alert to the "textures of suffering and sympathy" that disrupt the smooth surface of Spenser's text, maintains that by its conclusion, "The Legend of Holinesse" "witnesses the correction of Redcrosse by Protestant ideology and the defeat of the problems of pain and sympathy (in the form of Duessa, Orgoglio, and the dragon)," the same problems that, as Campana poignantly observes throughout his study, are the source of the legend's antinomy.[71]

While such readings ground their understanding of the legend's final resolution in the wedding scene between Redcrosse and Una, this so-called resolution raises more questions than answers about the hero's final "correction." For example, how does the legend's conclusion, the marriage of Holinesse and Truth, square with the freedom granted to Duessa? Although Duessa is cast off into the wild, the inhuman configuration of pain and materiality that she, along with Error, represented does not simply vanish but rather returns under different guises, leaving exposed the "rifte," or wound, that has haunted Redcrosse from the beginning.

Take, for instance, the opening lines of canto 12, in which the materiality of the poem surfaces once again in the figure of a "feeble barke":

> Behold I see the hauen nigh at hand,
>> To which I meane my wearie course to bend;
>> Vere the maine shete, and beare vp with the land,
>> The which afore is fairely to be kend,
>> And seemeth safe from stormes, that may offend;
>> There this faire virgin wearie of her way
>> Must landed be, now at her iourneyes end:
>> There eke my feeble barke a while may stay,
> Till merry wind and weather call her thence away. (1.12.1)

Recalling the "blustring storme" that first drove Redcrosse and Una into the Wandering Wood, Spenser elaborates his elemental conceit by imagining a fragile vessel, "my feeble barke," exiting the tempest and returning to safe harbor. The "barke" of the poem, "wearie" and "feeble," doubles as a portrait of the poet as navigator, a nautical persona who emerges in the last instance to bring the legend's "wearie course to bend." More than an author function, or an attempt on the part of Spenser to bring his "wearie" ship to harbor by securing narrative closure, the figure of the poem as a sailing "barke" harkens to the figure of the dragon, whose

> … flaggy wings when forth he did display,
> Were like two sayles, in which the hollow wynd
> Is gathered full, and worketh speedy way. (1.11.10)

No idle metaphor, the image of the wooden vessel, here used as a simile for the dragon's monstrous bulk, points to exorbitant mirrorings: the dragon's body as double of the poem, the poem's body as double of the dragon, Error, and Duessa. And then there is Christ's body, the image of suffering materiality, Catholic idolatry, masculine vulnerability, and so forth, which has as one of its most common metaphoric figures the image of the wooden vessel, as in John Donne's divine poem, "A Hymn to Christ": "In what torn ship soever I embark, / That ship shall be my emblem of thy ark" (1–2).[72] Finally, there is Fradubio, "a man … now a tree," whose "piteous yelling voice" vitiates Redcrosse in excruciating, abjecting "horror."

When we reach the final episode of the wedding between Redcrosse and Una, Spenser's deployment of poetic conventions at cross-purpose with their familiar significations persists as the trauma of the bleeding tree disruptively resurfaces. Whereas Redcrosse failed to fashion a "girlond," symbol of allegorical unity, out of Fradubio's wooden body, Una, we are told, assumes a "girlond greene" and at last becomes the rightful image of a "Queene":

> Then on her head they sett a girlond greene,
> And crowned her twixt earnest and twixt game;
> Who in her self-resemblance well beseene,
> Did seeme such, as she was, a goodly maiden Queene.
> (1.12.8)

By virtue of her own "self-resemblance," Una brings art and nature into mirroring accord and thus becomes what she always was, "a goodly maiden Queene." Redcrosse's error of framing a "girlond" for false Duessa comes full circle in the once erring, now obedient body of nature: "braunches" too "greene to frame" transform into a "girlond greene" as Redcrosse ripens into maturity and completes his allegorical journey.

Were this the end of the story we could agree with C. S. Lewis's influential argument that *The Faerie Queene* completes the history of the love allegory by synthesizing the material and the immaterial in a dialectical union of married pairs. For Lewis, courtly love speaks to the erotic and often abject nature of human experience; in it, "the lover is always abject."[73] By contrast, allegory takes place in "married pairs of sensibles and insensibles";[74] it speaks to the abstract union of concrete substance and ideal form. In his book-length study, Lewis argues that the intertwining history of love and allegory culminates in *The Faerie Queene*, representing "the last phase of that [history]— the final defeat of courtly love by the romantic conception of marriage."[75] Allegory, for Lewis, achieves a discordia concors whereby the material substance of love and romance culminates in the ideal of heterosexual union, of matter married to essence. He focuses his argument on book 3 of *The Faerie Queene*, "The Legend of Chastity," specifically on the freeing of Amoret from Busyrane and her subsequent reunion with the grief-stricken Scudamour, which he describes as "the triumphant union of romantic passion with Christian monogamy"—Amoret and Scudamour represent romantic passion, which Chastity must reunite.[76] However, in book 1, the triumph of allegory over romance appears less certain. Indeed, whereas Lewis claims that the heterosexual union represents the positive triumph of allegory over passionate materiality, in the marriage between Redcrosse and Una, Spenser proceeds to shadow the conclusion of his legend with material events inassimilable to narrative closure.

No sooner has Una been crowned with the "girlond" and the wedding ceremony been set underway when that obedient and pliant symbol of unity—a crown made of leaf and bark—is undone by its opposite. In the very next stanza, the dragon's dead body stubbornly clings to the scene of the wedding like a stain too dark to rub out:

> But when they came, where that dead Dragon lay,
> Stretcht on the ground in monstrous large extent,

The sight with ydle feare did them dismay,
Ne durst approch him night, to touch, or once assay.
    (1.12.9)

Continuing with the wedding ceremony despite the looming presence
of the dragon's monstrous corpse, the allegorical motif introduced
by the circular "girlond," now complete, repeats in the tying together
of hands. Nevertheless, just as art and nature, love and holiness, are
brought together in the binding of hands, the poem yields to an exorbitant repetition that undoes the work of binding and brings the
poem's allegory and Redcrosse's re-formation to an open-ended and,
what is more, disastrous close. Beginning with the following lines:

> Thus when that Princes wrath was pacifide,
> He gan renew the late forbidden bains,
> And to the knight his daughter deare he tyde,
> With sacred rites and vows for euer to abyde.

> His owne two hands the holy knotts did knitt,
>   That none but death for ever can diuide;
> His owne two hands, for such a turne most fitt,
>   the housling fire did kindle and prouide,
> And holy water thereon sprinckled wide. (1.12.36–37)

Moving from the immaterial register of Protestant theology to the
material register, Una's father, Adam, patriarch and "Lord of all that
land," Eden, calls upon the ancient Roman marriage rites of fire and
water to supplement "sacred rites and vows." The initial invocation
of binding ("bains") ties Redcrosse and Una in a spiritual union.
However, as if to supplement that spiritual bond, the second stanza
repeats the act of binding by tying "holy knotts" in material bands.
Una's father, acting as a priest, mediates the relation to the divine
by administering the sacraments of fire and water. "His owne two
hands," a line repeated twice, registers the material dimension of the
ceremony while also taking part in a passive syntactical structure in
which divine agency circulates: "holy knotts did knitt." In this way,

Una's father embodies a pre-Reformation spirituality that accords the power of the sacraments to the mediating body of the priest. Including the elements of fire and water, physical mediators in the transfer of power over Una, the land, and its resources to Redcrosse, the wedding ceremony's continued reliance on material signs as supplements to "sacred rites" attests to the ongoing attachment to material forms of spirituality even in the aftermath of a post-Reformation English society. Along with fire and water, the dragon's beastly body, and the "barke" of Spenser's wooden ship, one final ecological force threatens to disrupt the allegorical unity of the poem: Duessa's letter.

Last seen secreted in shame, Duessa returns from the wild via a messenger, Archimago in disguise. The messenger interrupts the wedding vows and proceeds to read a letter addressed to the "most mighty king of *Eden* fayre" (1.12.26). The letter reads:

> . . . be advized for the best,
> Ere thou thy daughter linck in holy band
> Of wedlocke to that new vnknowen guest:
> For he already plighted his right hand
> Vnto another loue, and to another land. (1.12.26)

Duessa echoes the language of the wedding: she refers to a "holy band," "sacred pledges," and warns of "hasty . . . / . . . knitting" (1.12.27, 28). More important, she reveals that she and Redcrosse have already been married: "To me sad mayd, or rather widow sad, / He was affyaunced long time before" (1.12.27). Duessa, who declares herself "neither friend, nor foe," makes of Redcrosse an "vnknowen guest," a stranger at his own wedding (1.12.28, 26). Redcrosse echoes this estrangement: "It was in my mishaps, as hitherward / I lately traueild, that vnawares I strayed / Out of my way, through perils straunge and hard" (1.12.31). Acknowledging his "breach of loue, and loialty betrayed," Una interrupts Redcrosse and again endeavors to reseal the rift that Duessa has rent open (1.12.31). She exposes Duessa as a "false sorceresse," and proves the latter's messenger to be the false Archimago, "The falsest man aliue" (1.12.33, 34). Having done so, the king her father "with suddein indignation fraight, / Bad on that Messenger rude hands to reach" and "bound him strait":

Who seeming sorely chauffed at his band,
As chained beare, whom cruell dogs doe bait,
With ydle force did faine them to withstand,
And often semblaunce made to scape of their hand.
(1.12.35)

The emphasis on binding, along with the repetition of "band," "hand," and "bound," is not coincidental. Duessa returns to disrupt the ending by unbinding the vows made between Redcrosse and Una. Although he means it literally, Spenser's emphasis on forms of binding approximates Freud's notion of *Bindung* (binding), which plays a key role in the discussion of trauma as the effort on the part of the psychic apparatus to cathect—that is, to bind—an excessive and unwanted force. With *Beyond the Pleasure Principle,* the problem of binding moves to the forefront of Freud's thought as he considers how "a failure to effect this binding would provoke a disturbance analogous to a traumatic neurosis."[77] Apropos of the repetition of unpleasurable experiences in trauma, Freud insists "only after the binding has been accomplished would it be possible for the dominance of the pleasure principle . . . to proceed unhindered. Till then," Freud writes, "the other task of the mental apparatus, the task of mastering or binding excitations, would have precedence."[78] This task, the task that Freud gives "precedence" in the psychic apparatus, is that of the death drive. It is the site of the demonic, the masochistic, and the melancholic in Freud's psychic economy, and it surfaces in Spenser's text in the return of Duessa's letter.

What beastly images are conjured by this return? With Duessa's pretense of "breaking . . . the band" between Redcrosse and Una exposed, and with Archimago in chains, the ceremonial "knitting of loues band" and the triumph of allegory can go on unhindered. Those critics who attribute allegorical closure to the legend undoubtedly find their warrant in this ending. Yet the logic that tries to do so is quite perverse. Clearly, bestiality is at issue in this ending. Just as Redcrosse broke his vows to Duessa, so he breached the divide between human and animal by falling for this chimerical figure. Paradoxically, the language of bearbaiting that surfaces here not only evidences this breach but also displaces the shame of Redcrosse's

crime onto Archimago. In other words, Redcrosse's beastly sexuality gets transformed into violence against animals. Archimago,
"chained" and dehumanized, becomes a "beare, whom cruell dogs
doe bait." Duessa's crime against nature—her disruption of the allegorical ideal, the heterosexual union—is met with a moralizing and
dehumanizing response as Archimago, her messenger, is "bound" and
"bait[ed]," "As [a] chained beare."

Erica Fudge has written extensively about the particular (il)logic
that grounds violence against animals in the early modern period.
In the case of bearbaiting, Fudge explains that this violence was (at
least) twofold: On the one hand, "the entertainment is a representation of wild nature controlled and choreographed (in the main)
by humans."[79] At the same time, humans who "watch a cruel entertainment such as baiting . . . sink below the level of the beasts." "In
proving their humanity," Fudge writes, "humans achieve the opposite.
The Bear Garden makes humans into animals."[80] Quite similarly,
the binding of Archimago is a choreographed representation of wild
nature controlled by knights and ladies. Holinesse (wholeness) has
been achieved—but only on the surface. The binding of Archimago
also binds Redcrosse to this animal "other." The wildness of this animal figure to whom Redcrosse is bound evokes all the strange figures
whom the hero has encountered on his journey to slay the dragon,
such that Eden, his final home and destination, more and more
resembles the Wandering Wood that was the site of his earliest di-
vagations. Archimago, far from being the only one in chains, binds
Redcrosse to melancholy:

> And all the while sweete Musicke did apply,
> Her curious skill, the warbling notes to play,
> To driue away the dull Melancholy;
> The whiles one sung a song of loue and iollity. (1.12.38)

The materialism I have highlighted in this chapter evinces many av-
atars, some animal, some tree, but in all cases wooden with respect
to its etymological root, *hyle*. In a certain sense, no ending is more
wooden in its mundane conventionality than a wedding. And yet, in
Spenser's hands, the "song of loue and iollity" proper to a romance

ending is not the dominant strain here. What hangs largely are the "dull" and heavy tones of "Melancholy." Rather than appeal to epic expectations, Spenser downplays a triumphant conclusion. His legend does not subsume the pains of materiality; instead, it ends on a "wearie" note, racked by the traumas of its making, a "feeble barke."

Materialist Melancholy

I began this journey by looking at the sea's destructive plasticity, particularly as it informed my reading of Spenser's "*darke*" allegory and the allegorical materialism therein. I conclude now by looking at another image of allegorical materialism, oriented not just to the ordeals of the accident (its surprises, its repetitions, its clouds of unknowing), but also to the communities of the wounded that such accidents, events, and traumas unfold.

In book 3 of *The Faerie Queene*, we join the knight Britomart gazing upon a mirror fashioned by the "Magitien *Merlin*," whose "deepe science" produced a "looking glasse" capable of "shew[ing] in perfect sight / What euer thing was in the world contained" (3.2.18–19). Britomart sees in this "world of glas" the "semblant of a knight, / Whose shape or person yet [she] never saw," but whose image, she remarks, "Hath me subjected to loues cruell law" (3.2.19, 38). No sooner is Britomart "subjected to loues cruell law," than she is changed irreversibly:

> The Damzell well did vew his Personage,
>   And liked well, ne further fastned not,
>   But went her way; ne her vnguilty age
>   Did weene, vnwares, that her vnlucky lot
>   Lay hidden in the bottome of the pot;
>   Of hurt vnwist most daunger doth redound:
>   But the false Archer, which that arrow shot
>   So slyly, that she did not feele the wound,
> Did smyle full smoothly at her weetlesse wofull stound.
>   (3.2.26)

> And if that any drop of slombring rest
>   Did chaunce to still into her weary spright,
>   When feeble nature felt her self opprest,

> Streight way with dreames, and with fantastick sight
> Of dreadful things the same was put to flight,
> That oft out of her bed she did astart,
> As one with vew of ghastly feends affright:
> Tho gan she to renew her former smart,
> And thinke of that fayre visage, written in her hart.
>
> (3.2.29)

At once an object of human "shape" and a figure of love's inscrutability, the "Personage" whom Britomart encounters in the "looking glas," far from being a mere representation of a knight, is best understood as a figure of conjunction. This figure is akin to the "melancholy assemblage" theorized by Drew Daniel, which "joins together its sufferers and its witnesses into tenuous perceptual communities."[81] Britomart, "weetlesse" of Cupid's arrow, "thought it was not loue" she suffered, "but some melancholy" (3.2.27). The "semblant" that enables her to see "her Loue . . . magnifyde" also subjects her to love's "tyranny."

The joining of sufferer and witness that melancholy enables begins when "fayre *Britomart*" looks into the "mirrhour playne." From this "did grow her first engraffed payne, / Whose root and stalke so bitter yet did taste" (3.2.17). The image itself entangles seer and seen, just as the language of vegetable love engrafts foreign bodies. Later the image of "engraffed payne" transforms into an image of writing, as Britomart turns her gaze inward "to renew her former smart, / And thinke of that fayre visage, written in her hart" (3.2.29). From the initial graft of "root and stalke" to its engraved repetition in Britomart's "hart," the image takes on the phantasmatic or dreamlike quality that again confounds the objective perception of external objects with internal, subjective experience. Shrouded by this image-world, this "Night," in which the "beautie of the shyning skye" is "Defaste," and "reft" is the "worldes desired vew," Britomart suffers "dreames" and "fantastick sight / Of dreadfull things . . . As one with vew of ghastly feends affright" (3.2.28–29). Under "loues cruel law," Britomart's "liuely cheare" turns more "dead" than "liuing"; the negative obverse of Spenser's herbal metaphor, it loses "Both leafe and fruite, both too vntimely shed" (3.2.31).

This assemblage of image-plant-heart that joins Britomart's melancholy to the wider ecological surround includes forms of relationality that go beyond the bounded subjectivity that would seem to ground Spenser's purported aim of fashioning persons of "vertuous and gentle discipline." Britomart's nurse, Glauce, for example, would seem the exemplary voice of such disciplinary measures. Reasoning with Britomart, Glauce urges Britomart not to be carried away by "despeire," since no love, no matter how "sore," is beyond the "salue" of reason (3.2.35). However, Glauce, too, suffers melancholy's web of entangled relationality. Having just "auow[ed]" to "ease [Britomart's] griefe, And win [her] will" from the "knowen signes and passions" of love (3.2.33), Glauce undergoes the same melancholy transformation: "So hauing sayd, her twixt her armes twaine / Shee streightly straynd, and colled tenderly, / And euery trembling ioynt, and euery vaine / Shee softly felt, and rubbed busily" (3.2.34). This compassion—or fellow-feeling—has the effect of taking Britomart out of herself. Seeing her nurse thus tormented, Britomart exclaims: "Ah Nurse, what needeth thee to eke my paine? / Is not enough, that I alone doe dye, / But it must doubled bee with death of twaine?" (3.2.35). The reciprocal grief shared by Britomart and Glauce makes visible the joining of sufferer and witness that scholars such as Daniel and Gail Kern Paster attribute to melancholy's involuntary processes of ecological assembly.[82] Britomart's melancholy resists anthro-determinacy.

Journeying to find her "semblant" knight and "Following the guydaunce of her blinded guest," Cupid, Britomart arrives at the "seacoast" (3.4.6). There she reactivates the memory of her inner scar—"her wound she fed"—and "to the seacoast at length she her addrest" (3.4.6):

> Huge sea of sorrow, and tempestuous griefe,
>   Wherein my feeble barke is tossed long,
>   Far from the hoped hauen of reliefe,
>   Why doe thy cruel billowes beat so strong,
>   And thy moyst mountaines each on others throng,
>   Threatening to swallow vp my fearefull lyfe?
>   O doe thy cruell wrath and spightfull wrong

At length allay, and stint thy stormy stryfe,
Which in thy troubled bowels raignes, and rageth ryfe.

For els my feeble vessell crazd, and crackt
    Through thy strong buffets and outrageous blowes,
    Cannot undure, but needes it must be wrackt
    On the rough rocks, or on the sandy shallowes,
    The whiles that loue it steres, and fortune rowes;
    Loue my lewd Pilott hath a restless minde
    And fortune Boteswaine no assuraunce knowes,
    But saile withouten starres, gainst tyde and winde:
How can they other doe, sith both are bold and blinde?
    (3.4.8–9)

More than just a metaphor for Britomart's inner grief, Spenser uses
the Petrarchan image of a "feeble vessell crazd, and crackt" to illustrate the material linkage between Britomart's love ("my lewd
Pilott") and the environment. Britomart loses her fixed identity by
dissolving into the sea. The sea's "deuouring" currents not only mirror
Britomart's "deep engord . . . hart" but also magnify and deterritorial-
ize her physical body, remapping the topography of her "hart" away
from the fixed body and the land's "craggy clifts" to the disassembling
movements of the sea (3.4.7, 6, 7). In Britomart's benthic imaginary,
"deepe" (inner "sorrow") echoes "deepe" ("tempestuous griefe") (3.4.6).
Although temporary, this moment of dissolution showcases a fundamental lesson in Spenserian ontology: the lover does not impose
her "sorrow" on the world. The lover is proof that the world is already
broken. Both the lover and the environment are "crazd, and crackt."

The Animal Complaint

Book 6, canto 10 of Spenser's *The Faerie Queene* begins with a question: "Who now does follow the foule *Blatant Beast*" (6.10.1)? For all of its apparent urgency and its insistence on "now," the question masks what I would dare call an unreadable inscription or, better yet, a thousand-tongued complaint. "Blatant," in modern parlance a synonym for what is obvious, conspicuous, and "obtrusive to the eye," means primarily that which is noisy, offensive, and clamorous.[1] The *Oxford English Dictionary* credits Spenser with coining the word "blatant." The word, we read in the dictionary's etymological account, was "invented by Spenser, and used by him as an epithet of the thousand-tongued monster begotten of Cerberus and Chimaera, the 'blatant' or 'blattant beast,' by which he symbolized calumny."[2] Allegorically speaking, the Blatant Beast symbolizes the court's falsity, misrepresentation, and slander. The book's hero, Calidore, knight errant, has vowed to the Faery Queene to capture the Blatant Beast, thus undertaking a task that, according to Derrida, humans have been undertaking since time immemorial: that of tracking, hunting, and domesticating the animal that, Derrida says, we are (following).[3]

What interests me is the next sentence in the OED's definition of "blatant," and, in it, something that sets Spenser's idea of following apart from the *bêtise*, the foolishness of the philosophers whom Derrida upbraids. Let us follow the OED's etymology carefully: "It has been suggested that he [Spenser] intended it ['blatant'] as an archaic form of bleating (of which the 16th cent. Scots was *blaitand*), but this seems rather remote from the sense in which he used it."[4]

When I first read this sentence, I confess that I stopped in my tracks, unable to follow its logic. Why remote? After all, "bleat" means "to cry, as a sheep, goat, or calf."[5] Something that is "blatant" is, likewise, noisy, clamorous, even offensive to the ears. We can follow this train further. In addition to being loud, something that is "clamorous" is also "the excited outcry of vehement appeal, complaint, or opposition: commonly, but not always, implying a mingling of voices."[6] A clamor, then, isn't just a sound, however monstrous; it is also a "mingling" or a swarm, of the kind that Milton's fallen angels transform into at the end of book 1 of *Paradise Lost*, "As bees / In springtime . . . / . . . So thick the airy crowd / Swarmed" (1.768–69, 775–76).[7] It seems in fact that one never clamors alone. But then, this would imply that one never complains alone, either.

Spenser's complaint, "Who now does follow the foule *Blatant Beast*," mingles with the thousand-tongued complaint it is after. Or rather, Spenser's outcry shares in the same complaining, bleating, and vociferating cry that the animal in question symbolizes. Both complain. Both are bleating. The outcry of one redoubles the other. This comingling of complaints gives a different meaning to Spenser's question, for it is now a matter of following both *after* and *before*, in both senses of the verb "to follow": Spenser's question follows, that is to say, comes after, the animal that we are—hunting. Spenser's question evolves *out of* and, in an important sense, *derives from* the animal that we are.[8]

I repeat, why remote? If anything, I would say that Spenser's question plunges us into the semiotic realm of the nonhuman, where Milton's bees, Spenser's animal, and the many posthuman figures that populate the theoretical landscape today all clamor (mingle, swarm, complain).

In defining "blatant" as that which is loud, offensive, and perhaps untrue, the OED gives voice to human language while silencing the querulous cry of the animal, the "bleating" from which Spenser's language derives. It makes the animal complaint inaudible, unreadable, or, in any case, "remote." Moreover, as a metalanguage whose sole purpose is to make legible the proper meaning and use of the English tongue, the OED, in this case, conceals that which it opens. It conceals itself, as though it were covering its tracks.

At once given and taken away, the animal complaint is banished before making itself heard in Spenser's question. Still, certain questions persist. For starters, what is the meaning of this question that complains about the very nature of complaint and that summons an entire bestiary to its call? Moreover, what are we being asked to hear in following this nonhuman call? Two observations follow from the OED's definition: (1) The silencing that takes place in the OED's definition works to conceal Spenser's entanglement with the very thing he is after. It conceals the animal complaint and thereby disentangles human language from nonhuman language. (2) Although this silencing contradicts the very definition of the word "blatant," it is a contradiction that matters for how we read Spenser's poem and early modern poetry more generally. For it is not just that the OED fails to offer a satisfying reading of the Blatant Beast. More precisely, my claim is that such failure *is* the condition of reading. Were we to give the animal complaint its due—which, to be clear, is my goal here—it would still contain silences. Such is the nature of desire for every speaking being, human and nonhuman: language conceals as it opens. What the OED makes clear by its very silence, its animal silence, is that in complaint, as in reading, the thing that matters most is not the shout but the silence of the outcry.

Beyond the manifest content of Spenser's poem, I am interested in what the OED labels remote and improbable and so writes off as exorbitant in Spenser's text. What I am after, in short, is the exegesis of the exergue.

The improbable interpretation is this: Spenser's question is *about* reading. Not only that, it is a *complaint* about reading, specifically, about a certain failure to read matter *to the letter*—and not just Calidore's failure; Spenser's open interrogative "who" enfolds the reader as well. This failure pertains to what *cannot* be read in the text of complaint, no matter how loud. It pertains to what in language, and in poetry especially, falls out: namely, the remote, the untranslatable—hence the poem's emphasis on foreign tongues. Just as the OED would have us forget what seems remote in Spenser's text, namely, the mingling of human desire with the bleating of an animal, so too readers today, among them animal studies scholars, ecocritics, and new materialists, take the complaint in its most blatant form, as literal or given: they hasten the reader to recognize the immediacy and vitality of nonhuman figures.

In the widely influential book *Vibrant Matter*, Jane Bennett foregrounds the act of following as critical to her book's materialist methodology. In the preface, Bennett cites Derrida and aligns her methodology with his: "Derrida points to the intimacy between being and following," Bennett writes. "To be (anything, anyone) is always to be following (something, someone), always to be in response to call from something, however nonhuman it may be."[9] Bennett's book represents what has come to be called the "new materialist" turn in contemporary theory. As Bennett's book makes plain, making space for more-than-human worlds requires both response and responsibility to matter's call, "however nonhuman it may be." My book shares the new materialisms' interest in answering matter's "call." However, the difference in my book is that I remain equally committed to the enigmatic voice that crackles beneath matter's message, disrupting its telos and tele-phono-centrism.[10] What if there is a bad connection?

In fact, the bad connection is what most concerns me in the new materialisms' insistence on relationships of call and response. The new materialisms ignore, or disavow, the impasse—or failure of full speech—in relationality's web. I am referring to what Lacan calls the language of the unconscious. It is what in language, above all the language of complaint, refuses to be read, even as it makes its refusal noisily heard. What is the "literal," Lacan asks? It is not the matter (or content) of the statement, such that by turning to matter, we overcome the lack that a literal reading would seek to fill. According to Lacan's etymological interpretation, the literal meaning of "literal" is the letter—which certifies materialism as an abyssal form.[11] As Lacan writes in the "Seminar on 'The Purloined Letter,'" "The signifier [or letter] is a unique unit of being which, by its very nature, is the symbol of but an absence. This is why we cannot say of the purloined letter that, like other objects, it must be *or* not be somewhere but rather that, unlike them, it will be *and* will not be where it is wherever it goes."[12] In contrast with Bennett's new materialist approach, this book makes a fervent call to read matter to the letter—where every complaint, human and nonhuman, encounters an inherent minus, something that is intractably *without*. To read matter to the letter—to read early modern poetry to the letter—we must not assume the complainer knows what they are after, for the letter of the law in psychoanalytic discourse is this: the unconscious thinks, but it thinks in a foreign tongue. It is a thousand-tongued complaint.

In light of Freud's discovery of the unconscious, psychoanalysis revolutionizes how we read language, particularly the language of complaint, which, from the Old Testament to now, is vast. As Aaron Schuster argues in *The Trouble with Pleasure*, the goal of the psychoanalytic talking cure is not to get at the root of complaint by finding the missing cause of the subject's dissatisfaction, since this would imply two things: first, that a preexisting coherence of the subject can be remade, and second, that a preexisting cause was there to begin with. Both of these are things that the theory of the unconscious rejects. Instead of a coherent subject of desire, psychoanalysis gives us the split subject. Furthermore, instead of a coherent object of desire, psychoanalysis posits strange nonobjects, or partial objects of desire—little nontotalizable fragments that, because they never cohered as objects, set the subject on her impossible journey of rediscovering what is by definition undiscoverable. Lacan calls these partial objects *objet a*. Unlike the myriad bodies, objects, and things proposed by the new materialisms, these partial objects do not exist but rather *insist* in the world as a wound, rupturing the material world from within. To be clear: the object-world proposed by the new materialisms is, from the vantage of psychoanalysis, always already a fantasy world, or a screen made up of bodies-objects-things; the *real* they seek is elsewhere, in the cracks of the unconscious. Instead of finding the fully satisfying object-relation, the goal of psychoanalysis becomes that of an interminable reading. And in contrast with those who would seek to fill the negativity of our desires with "lively matters," this book never stops reading desire as constitutively dis-contented. Schuster writes:

> One should not overlook the greatness of the neurotic complaint, which bears witness, through its fidelity to dissatisfaction and endless ironic challenges to the Other, to the glorious maladaptedness of the

human being in spite of its insertion into the social world, structures of authority, kinship ties, sexual norms, metaphysical programs, etc. Neurosis is the name for the crack in these frameworks, the protest that stems from their internal fissures and inconsistencies.[13]

According to Schuster's Lacanian reading of Freud, the complaint represents the subject's "fidelity to dissatisfaction" and the lack that inheres in language rather than to any specific content of the mind. It is the lack of the thing, in other words—the lack of the fully satisfying object—that truly drives the subject and enables her to voice the thousand-tongued complaint that Spenser registers so provocatively. When I complain, it is not because I crave "x," but because my complaining enables me to repeat a fundamental absence. The complaint, in other words, disarticulates its object, showing that failure was there from the beginning, from the very first object-relation.

We recall that Calidore, the knight tasked with capturing the Blatant Beast, was diverted—pleasurably so. The speaker complains:

> Vnmyndfull of his vow and high beheast,
> Which by the Faery Queene was on him layd,
> That he should neuer leaue, nor be delayd
> . . . .
> He [Calidore] mindeth more, how he may be relieued
> With grace from her, whose loue his heart hath sore
>   engrieued. (6.10.1)

Turned away by love for "that faire Mayd," Pastorella, Calidore has become "Vnmyndfull of his vow." Indeed, "Vnmyndfull" is an understatement. For he has become perforce un-minded by love. He is, to use Lacan's pet phrase, a "headless subject," driven by desire alone. Henceforth, Calidore "meanes no more to sew / His former quest, so full of toile and paine." He no longer wishes to be left "sayling . . . on the port," porting dangerous "blaste[s]" in exchange for the empty words of the court. Instead, as the verb "sew" suggests, Calidore pursues "Another quest, another game," and begins weaving not just another fantasy but, as the homonym "sow" suggests, another genre. Like Odysseus trading places with Penelope, or Theseus with

Ariadne, Calidore weaves the threads of fantasy by planting the seeds of pastoral. He dreams of the *oikos*. And sure enough, he finds it:

> One day as he did raunge the fields abroad,
>> Whilest his faire *Pastorella* was elsewhere,
>> He chaunst to come, far from all peoples troad,
>> Vnto a place, whose pleasaunce did appere
>> To passe all others, on the earth which were:
>> For all that euer was by natures skill
>> Deuized to worke delight, was gathered there,
>> And there by her were poured forth at fill,
> As if this to adorne, she all the rest did pill. (6.10.5)

By turning away from the "toile and paine" of epic, Calidore "sew[s]" a new life, but a life that reads alarmingly like the insubstantial "shadowes" and empty tropes of the court. Nature, here, is a matter of artifice ("skill"), and so does not hesitate to pillage ("pill") other natures in order "to worke delight." Nature so imagined promises mastery and control, the very same mastery and control that Calidore so sorely lacks.

Calidore embodies the mindset of the environmental humanities today: like the proverbial "good enough" mother who reflects to the child his (desired) unity, Calidore's "mynde" is reflected in the gestalt of this "place," imagined as female. Most troublesome of all is that Calidore's new "game" repeats his former "hunt," the hunt for the Blatant Beast, by making Pastorella the object of his game—the "game" itself, an animal hunted. No longer "fed" on "courtly fauour," Calidore now feeds on the fantasy of "woman," the object par excellence in heteronormativity's narrative of completion. The hunt for Pastorella merely displaces the hunt for the Blatant Beast. This environmentality, however, "remaine[s]" a wish.

Haunted by the desire to "remaine" in this place without remainder (the other sense of "remaine"), Calidore ends up "sew[ing]" an impossible fantasy. Not coincidentally, "sew" is one of the possible translations of the German *Bindung*, Freud's word for the "binding" operation that weaves, ever so tenuously, the network of signifiers around the body. *Bindung*, or binding, gives meaning to the tumult of the organism. More accurately, this text or textile *makes* the organism what it is: parts (organs) connected to a great whole (the body and its environment). Binding, sewing, and making: this primal poetic activity is the prehuman condition of sense in that it gives narrative direction (*sens*) to the body. Freud calls this binding operation the pleasure principle, or Eros. From the very beginnings of the organism, Eros casts a line into chaos (sensory bombardment) and pulls back a life raft: the small flotilla that we call human meaning or sense.

Nevertheless, beyond Eros, Freud discovers something else entirely—he discovers sexuality. The same binding operation that captures sense captures us; we become captives of the image. Except for the fact that this binding operation inevitably fails. The Blatant Beast evades capture:

> Thus was this Monster by the maystring might
>   Of doughty *Calidore*, supprest and tamed,
>   The neuer more he mote endammadge wight
>   With his vile tongue, which many had defamed,
>   And many causelesse caused to be blamed:
>   So did he eeke long after this remaine,
>   Vntill that, whether wicked fate so framed,
>   Or fault of men, he broke his yron chaine,
> And got into the world at liberty again. (6.12.38)

As a symbol of complaint, the Blatant Beast defies easy capture, slipping the bonds that Calidore seeks to impose.[14] Moreover, as an image of nature's discord, the Blatant Beast suffers no false unity, easily escaping the muzzle that a final reading would impose. Calidore, however, is a different kind of headless subject. Un-minded by the fantasy of a final reading, he knows nothing of the pleasures of loss.

PART II

What Does Nature Want?

THREE

THE OCEANIC FEELING

(*Ralegh*)

> Certainely, as all the Riuers in the world, though they
> haue diuers risings, and diuers runnings; though they
> some times hide them-selves for a while under ground,
> and seeme to be lost in Sea-like Lakes; doe at last finde,
> and fall into the great Ocean: so after all the searches that
> humaine capacitie hath; and after all Philosophical con-
> templation and curiositie; in the necessitie of this infinite
> power, all the reason of man ends and dissolves it selfe.
>
> —Walter Ralegh, *The History of the World*

In the preface to Walter Ralegh's six-volume magnum opus, *The History of the World* (1614), Ralegh imagines his life as a tempest of misfortune, physical ruination, and inexorable time. A life and death meditation at the bleeding edge of contemporary biopolitics, including such concepts as Achille Mbembe's necropolitics, "the living dead," and Giorgio Agamben's "bare life,"[1] Ralegh's *History* begins, in derelict fashion, as a confession of his life's "dissability":

> I confess that it had better sorted with my dissability, the better part
> of whose times are runne out in other trauailes; to have set together
> (as I could) the unioynted and scattered frame of our English affaires,
> than of the Uniuersall: in whome had there beene no other defect,

(who am all defect) then the time of the day, it were enough; the day
of a tempestuous life, drawne on to the very euening ere I began.[2]

Ralegh's *History* is a history in ruins. From the beginning, Ralegh
cancels the very prospect of his *History*, a history so massive as to ex-
tinguish the author's life long before its writing began. In part, this
chapter argues, the problems arise from what Laurie Shannon and a
host of other ecologically minded critics refer to as the "human excep-
tionality" of the term.[3]

History, Shannon argues, tends to be a narrative for and about
personhood. Absent persons, there is no subject of history. Thus
the efficacy or continuity of the term always seems to depend on the
marginality of nonhuman agents. Nevertheless, as Ralegh proceeds
from the altered states of his "dissability," in which the boundary
between life and death seems little more than the dilation between
day and evening, to the "frame" of "our English affaires," he imagines
human history as itself "unioynted," as a "scattered" and disabling confrontation with the Earth's troubling liquidity: "How unfit, and how
unworthy a choice I haue made of my self, to undertake a worke of
this mixture; mine own reason, though exceeding weake, hath sufficiently resolved me. For had it been begotten then with my first
dawne of day," Ralegh muses, "I might yet well haue doubted, that
the darkenesse of Age and Death would haue couered ouer both It
and Mee, long before the performance."[4] This vision of life and death
testifies not only to Ralegh's own waning health but also to the disabling force of "a worke of this mixture," a work in which human
history—the history "of our English affaires"—dissolves into the
deterritorializing flows of "Uniuersall" time, "beginning with the Creation."[5] History undergoes a radical transvaluation, becoming a study
not just of persons, but of the whole *world*.[6] In Ralegh's "Uniuersall"
history, human activity collapses time and again into the sea, becoming a plane of immanence for life's forces to reconfigure.[7] As the
human civilizations that Ralegh details over nearly three thousand
pages move steadily toward destruction, Ralegh reminds the reader
that just as all the rivers of the Earth must end in the "great ocean," so
"after all the searches that humaine capacitie hath," including Ralegh's
own ill-fated searches, "in the necessitie of this infinite power, all the

reason of man ends and dissolves it selfe." History becomes ocean, and only the ruins are left to attest to man's ending.

Biopolitics at Sea

I begin with Ralegh's *The History of the World* to reframe such biopolitical factors as Ralegh's "dissability"—a term that animates paradoxically life and death ontologies of matter, including the fragile boundaries between animacy and inanimacy, as Mel Y. Chen theorizes with respect to so-called "inanimate" materialities[8]—around a concept that has less to do with human world-making and more to do with the "states of exception" under which inhuman agencies come to matter for world history (often by disabling human epistemologies).

Among contemporary theorists of biopolitics, Giorgio Agamben has been the most successful at calling our attention to a series of "states of exception" in which human freedoms grounded in the law of sovereign nations are suspended, and all for the purpose of reconstituting the law by furthering its forms of calculation, management, and instrumental reason. For Agamben, the defining feature of biopolitics is that of "bare life" (*zoē*), which he opposes (in ways we will want to question) to the political life (*bios*) of man. In Agamben's formulation, it is only in the modern era, when the exception "everywhere becomes the rule," that "bare life—which is originally situated at the margins of the political order—gradually begins to coincide with the political realm."[9] When the exception becomes the rule, *bios* (human life, us) and *zoē* (nonhuman life, them) "enter into a zone of irreducible indistinction," and politics becomes biopolitics, a system of managing life and death ontologies through elaborate forms of calculation and instrumental reason.[10]

And yet, as Claire Colebrook points out, although Agamben is critical of the power of sovereign nations to suspend the rights of man, he nevertheless sees the law's suspension as ushering in a real potential for human redemption:[11] for "only within a biopolitical horizon will it be possible to decide," Agamben writes, "whether the categories whose opposition founded modern politics [*bios* and *zoē*] . . . will have to be abandoned. And only a reflection that . . . interrogates the link between bare life and politics . . . will be able to bring the political out of its concealment and, at the same time, return thought to its practical calling."[12] For Agamben, the project of return-ing "thought to its practical calling"—of going beyond the politics of bare life and death to regain a sense of life's quality or freedom—requires that man once again think of life's proper "calling" as an act of *creation*, in other words, that he think of politics as something *made* and just not given. Badiou voices a similar "call" in his reading of Saint Paul. In opposition to the calculations of bare life and death wrought by "false universality"—the church in Paul's case, or world capitalism in Badiou's—Badiou endeavors to "refound a theory of the Subject" based on Paul's own evental state of suspension: "Let us say that, for Paul, it is a matter of investigating which law is capable of structur-ing a subject devoid of all identity and suspended to an event whose only 'proof' lies precisely in its having been declared by a subject."[13] As with Agamben, life's proper calling, according to Badiou, requires a suspension of law and normativity precisely to return human life to its practical calling: that of "subtracting truth from . . . any objective aggregate."[14] For both thinkers, the return to "life" proper can only be founded on the exclusion of bare life (*zoē*) from the human polis and the suspension of calculation and techno-reason. Only then can man (for it is always a question of man with these thinkers) become an opening to future horizons and return politics to its proper calling.

But one can think here, *with* Ralegh, of a state of exception that does not return politics to its so-called "human" grounding. What if, for example, we recognized the Earth's liquefaction as an agent of sus-pension? Would the "Ocean," "Riuers," and "Sea-like Lakes" of which Ralegh writes count as an opening to future political horizons, such that we would then have to speak not of man's "practical calling," but of the sea's? For the Ralegh of the *History*, as well as *The Discoverie of Guiana* (1596) and *Ocean to Cynthia* (1592), the Earth's waters do just that: they suspend life and death's proper boundaries by redefining problematic notions of "liveliness," "bodily integrity," and "disability" in the light of inhuman exigencies and anarchic temporalities—life and death (de)compositions of matter in contretemps with human world-making. In short, there is no pure realm outside of *bio*-politics, no way to wash clean of our inhuman condition, since the matter of the Earth is already politically active in "our" designs.[15] Rather than try to return man to his "proper" calling, Ralegh puts forth the very real possibility of a state of suspension that returns man to the sea. This is not a posthumanist rapture, much less a return to an organic vitalism, but rather an attempt to live life among the ruins, at the "infinite" speed at which Ralegh imagines human thought destroys itself by becoming ocean.

Ralegh's aquacentric discourse thus represents a sustained philosophical and poetic meditation on the suspension of sovereignty, bodily integrity, and world. However, it does not represent a return to "life" understood in Agamben's and Badiou's sense as the practical life of man. Ralegh's "tempestuous life" does not represent a praxis that could be used to re-found the human polis or to awaken politics to its proper calling. Whereas Michel Foucault, at the end of his archaeology of man, famously imagines a future time, a *post*human time when "man would be erased, like a face drawn in sand at the edge of the sea," Ralegh attests to man's erasure from and in the beginning.[16] And this is so because man has always existed as a being who attempts to survive himself through an "autoimmunitary process" of endings.[17] Man as *Homo faber*, as the being who exists by exiting himself through endless self-fashioning, has always been this self-erased being, this posthuman being who survives his own ending. The end of man, then, is perhaps the only history of man that "we" have ever known.

What we need instead, and what Ralegh's texts offer us, is an image of life not based on human survival. Against a redemptive future, a posthuman future in which man, having been erased by the tides of the sea, surpasses himself by returning to life and ecology, against this image of reproductive futurity, Ralegh figures the "tide of man's life" as nothing other than a state of suspension without end.[18] I call this state of suspense, after Freud, the oceanic feeling.

Becoming Ocean

Writing on the concept of the "oceanic feeling" in the opening pages of *Civilization and Its Discontents*, Freud disparages the notion of oceanic selves, of selves bleeding into their surroundings, and of bodies melting into other bodies, on the basis that such an affective transverberation of bodies entails a regression to an earlier state of narcissistic indifference.[19] Recent psychoanalytic theorists writing to the side of Freud, among them Leo Bersani and Kaja Silverman, have asked whether there might be a way of retooling narcissistic indifference to allow for an experience of the world's flesh.[20] Whereas Freud dismisses the oceanic feeling of being extended in space and time beyond the envelope of one's skin, Ralegh bids welcome to the hospitality of a difference within the self, of a self that overflows itself, indifferent to its own difference.

This sense of (in)difference that Ralegh—nicknamed "Ocean"— absently represents appears in Spenser's address to Queen Elizabeth. There, Ralegh's pseudonym "Ocean" provides the material and semantic substrate of Spenser's liquefacient verse:

> But if in liuing colours, and right hew,
>   Thy selfe thou couet to see pictured,
>   Who can it doe more liuely, or more trew,
>   Then that sweete verse, with *Nectar* sprinckeled,
>   In which a gracious seruaunt pictured
>   His *Cynthia*, his heauens fayrest light?
>   That with his melting sweetnes rauished,
>   And with the wonder of her beames bright,
> My sences lulled are in slomber of delight. (3.Proem.4)

In Spenser's poem, the liquid dynamics of male–male friendship detailed by Jeffrey Masten[21] ebb and flow in relation to the paradox of Elizabeth's "chaste" pleasure, a pleasure portrayed by Ralegh not as singular, chaste, or inviolable virginity but as "melting sweetnes." "Sweete" conjures a highly motile sense of desire and affection between bodies.[22] A significant signifier in the rhetoric of early modern friendship, "*sweet* indicates," according to Masten, "the fungibility of male friends—not merely the exchangeability and indistinguishability of identities or selves but also the way in which what we have regarded as an identity trope is imagined in this culture as literally embodied."[23] This "sweetnes" collates, first, the taste of colonial power abroad with the importation of sugar at home, linking Ralegh's seagoing and colonial ventures in the Americas to the erotics of domestic and poetic consumption;[24] and second, the disaggregation of sovereign bodies—human, national, and territorial—which, by over-flowing the opposition between inside and outside, makes way for a different kind of bodily becoming, one that dissolves human subjects in watery undertows and combines them with ecological forces.

By mirroring Elizabeth's narcissism, Ralegh not only welcomes the oceanic feeling of bodies melting into other bodies, he turns the speculum of narcissistic indifference against itself, revealing, in Iriga-ray's words, "the other of the other"—not just the specularized Other of the masculine subject but the irreducible otherness internal to all subject positions. This "other of the other" surfaces in Irigaray's eco-materialist reading of Friedrich Nietzsche as an elemental "marine lover"; in Ralegh's hands, the marine love that threatened to undo Spenser's poetic count in chapter 1 returns in the image of Elizabeth qua Cynthia.[25]

Whereas critics such as Stephen Greenblatt, Mary Fuller, and Richard Helgerson have each wanted to see Ralegh's writings as evidence of an imperial ideology in service of the English nation,[26] I suggest that to fully appreciate Ralegh's involvements in the Ca-ribbean and American tropics, we need to be less *geo* and more *aqua*-centric in our accountings.[27] Only then can we begin to under-stand "forms of nationhood" (Helgerson) in their proper relational context, *not* as reflections of discrete national bodies exerting unilat-eral control over colonial environments, but as imbroglios of material (human and nonhuman) agents.[28] To echo Steve Mentz, "Too often [in literary studies] the sea quickly becomes a metaphor for the artis-tic process . . . or mutability itself. The real taste of the ocean gets lost in the flux. It shouldn't. It's there."[29]

In what follows, I trace the uncanny "thereness" of the ocean in three parts: from the amorous disaggregation of bodies in *Ocean to Cynthia* to the abyssal encounters of *The Discoverie of Guiana* to the techno-oceans of the *History*. More than just a cipher or thing to be crossed, the ocean in Ralegh's writings represents an agency of bio-political suspension, an archive or *mal d'archive* of the Earth's shifting transformations of matter. Oceans *world* in Ralegh's archive. To fig-ure that inhuman worlding is the task of this chapter.

Cinders

Beginning in the alluvial sands of once-flowing tides, rivers, and streams, Ralegh's *Ocean to Cynthia* does nothing but lament a barren existence bereft of the fructifying powers of the sea:

> Lost in the mudd of thos hygh flowinge streames
> which through more fayrer feilds ther courses bend,
> . . . .
> from frutfull trees I gather withred leves
> and glean the broken eares with misers hands,
> who sumetyme did injoy the waighty sheves
> I seeke faire floures amidd the brinish sand. (*The 21th: and last booke of the Ocean to Scinthia*, 17–24)[30]

The speaker's identity materializes as the mineralized effect of fluidities become solidities, and vibrant materialities become dead beaches. From "withred leves" to "broken eares," the landscape of Ralegh's poem is one of drought and desiccation: "I seeke faire floures amidd the brinish sand." "[A] boddy violently slayne" by once "pleasinge streames"—"the messengers sumetymes of my great woe"—the speaker addresses his wounds to the dead, "as to the dead, the dead did thes unfold," asking: "what heat in Cynders of extinguished fiers?" A necropolitical question of extreme duress, the speaker invites the reader to pay "wittnes" to "joyes interred . . . under dust," to a life more dead than living, and more spectral than human. It would be wrong to say that Ralegh's allegory of the ocean merely allegorizes the human, for at every turn the allegory in question refigures the speaker as less than human, as utterly inhuman, as "Cynder" and "dust." Ralegh's *Ocean to Cynthia* does not give face to the figure of the ocean; it does not try to re-create the abyss in man's best image. Instead, it elaborates seasons of drought and flood so severe as to render the human face beyond recognition. In the following lines, the speaker (here known as "Ocean") writes "as onn . . . / whom love, and tyme, and fortune had defaced"; he writes his face in the "dust":

> Alone, forsaken, frindless onn the shore
> with many wounds, with deaths cold pangs inebrased

writes in the dust as onn that could no more
whom love, and tyme, and fortune had defaced. (89–92)

Ralegh's poem is about defacement, yet it is not tragic because it
offers not loss but change. From drought and desiccation to flood and
flowing waters, the speaker's essential question, "what heat in Cynders of extinguished fiers?" returns with surprising force as "dust" and
"cinder" give way to energies of liquefaction within the environment
itself, disintegrating (or indeed melting) the desert ocean into "suddayn streames":

so did my joyes mealt into secreat teares
so did my hart desolve in wastinge dropps
and as the season of the year outweares
and heapes of snow from of the mountayn topps
with suddayn streames the valle[y]s overflow
so did the tyme draw on my more dispaire
then fludds of sorrow and whole seas of wo
the bancks of all my hope did overbeare. (134–41)

In Ralegh's *Cynthia* poem, "fludds of sorrow" and emotions of "joye"
and "dispaire" are not projected onto the outside environment; they
have their source in it. From "seasons" to "mountayn topps," "valle[y]s"
and finally river "bancks," Ralegh welcomes the oceanic feeling of
bodies melting into other bodies as affects of despair, disquietude,
torment, and love channel through him, from him, and without him,
making it true what the speaker says: "All is desolvde" (235). This shift
from a poetics of defacement to a poetics of ecological assemblage
allows us to abandon the elegiac orientation that Ralegh so often
adopted and that many of his critics, most notably Greenblatt, have
taken for granted. According to Greenblatt, Ralegh's work consists
of an "unending dialectic . . . between optimism and despair, between
the vision of a world made over in the image of man's desires and the
vision of a world of lies, disappointment, and death."[31] For Agnes
Latham, "Everything [Ralegh] did seems to have been tainted by a
curious impermanence."[32] To be sure, Ralegh saw his life as an epi-
taph upon ruins, as a tempest of misfortune, stagnation, and death.

However, beyond this elegiac terrain of bare life and death, Ralegh describes transformations of the human body that are at once literal and allegorical and that render the possibility that lovers' wounds are not simply human because they move with the ocean and partake of its watery stirrings.

To read Ralegh's poetry in this way, as a force of ecological assemblage, is to insist on the advantages of thinking the land-nation-body of Renaissance writing in relation to the water-flow-abyss of the sea. Édouard Glissant's theory of relation unfolds some of those advantages. Writing nearly four centuries after Ralegh, Glissant identifies what he calls a "cross-cultural poetics" distinct from (but not unrelated to) the literary traditions of the West.[33] This "cross-cultural poetics" consists of "the memories of cultural contact," Glissant argues, "which are put together collectively by a people before being dispersed by colonization."[34] In the example of the African epic, Glissant observes: "I am aware of a certain 'suspension' of the narrative: as if, while composing the discourse, the poet seems *to be waiting for something* that he knows he cannot stop. The succession of kings does not give rise to [nor is it based on] a theory of legitimacy. The epic is disruptive."[35] Shifting focus from the "disruptive" past of cross-cultural contact to the afterlives of colonization in the Caribbean, Glissant makes of the "suspension" of epical time in the West (which he identifies with the time and telos of the imperial nation) an opportunity to reimagine history as itself errant, as an "estuary" of overlapping desires, cultures, temporalities, and locations. "Caribbeanness, an intellectual dream," represents this errant possibility of shared history while suspending the "need for nationalism" on the one hand and anthropocentrism on the other:

> Lived at the same time in an unconscious way by our peoples, [Caribbeanness] tears us free from the intolerable alternative of the need for nationalism and introduces us to the cross-cultural process that modifies but does not undermine the latter. What is the Caribbean in fact? A multiple series of relationships. We all feel it, we express it in all kinds of hidden or twisted ways, or we fiercely deny it. But we sense that this sea exists within us with its weight of now revealed

islands. The Caribbean Sea is not an American lake. It is the estuary of the Americas.[36]

Displacing the mass of the Americas into the Caribbean Sea, Glissant emphasizes the way that the sea forges relations and transcorporealizations that, in addition to impacting bodies and things ("this sea exists within us"), also catalyze sedimentations that express not the feeling of isolation endemic to the British island but instead the openness of the land-sea.[37] "In the Caribbean each island embodies openness. The dialectic between inside and outside is reflected in the relationship of land and sea."[38]

Like Glissant, Ralegh imagines the Caribbean Sea and the Guiana coastline as a type of estuary, a rhizomatic body of terraqueous connection linking the maritime environments of the Atlantic Ocean with the intercontinental flows of rivers and sediment. As we shall see in the following section, this vision of Guiana as a land-sea zone—as a tissue of watery transport and connection—is far from utopic, for it describes liquid bodies that repeatedly threaten to engulf Ralegh's voyage. Continuing my analysis of the personification of material entities (of the giving and taking away of face), I argue that Ralegh's attempt at personifying the Guiana territory as a virgin landscape already enthralled by the English nation meets with, and ultimately comes undone by, apocalyptic undertows of rivers and lakes extending from the lower Orinoco to the Guiana Basin to the Atlantic Ocean. Starting with Ralegh's aquacentric account of relation in *The Discoverie of Guiana*, I show that far from vanishing human agency, Ralegh's fascination with the Earth's liquefaction holds open the possibility for a different kind of material agency, something akin to what Jonathan Goldberg, in *Tempest in the Caribbean*, identifies as the "different kind of creature" made possible by inhuman genealogies.[39]

Transatlantic Ecologies

Writing to Sir Philip Sidney in the "Dedicatorie Epistle" to his *Divers Voyages Touching the Discouerie of America, and the Ilands Adiacent vnto the fame, made first of all by our Englishmen, and afterward by the*

Frenchmen and Britons (1582), Richard Hakluyt—student of geography and later proponent of England's colonizing efforts in Virginia and South America—enjoins his readers to consider England's precarious economic, political, and cultural position after the "so great conquests and plantings of the Spaniardes and Portingales" in the West, stating: "I Maruaile not a little (right worshipfull) that since the first discouerie of America (which is nowe full fourescore and tenne yeeres) . . . that wee of Englande could neuer haue the grace to set fast footing in such fertill and temperate places, as are left as yet vnpossessed of them."[40] Chafed not only by the desire to annex New World territories from England's geopolitical rivals, Spain and Portugal, but also by England's seeming reluctance to contend for maritime supremacy in a newly globalized environment, Hakluyt, an inveterate propagandist of England's imperial expansion, nonetheless states that "I conceiue great hope, that the time approcheth and nowe is, that we of England may share and part stakes (if wee will our selues) both with the Spaniarde and the Portingale in part of America, and other regions as yet vndiscouered." So hopeful is Hakluyt about the prospect of England partaking in the project of "discovery" in America that he turns to the language of natural history and, in particular, that of bees, to illustrate the biopolitical *necessity* of colonial conquest in the West:

> Yea if wee woulde beholde with the eye of pitie how al our Prisons are pestered and filled with able men to serue their Countrie, which for small roberies are dayly hanged vp in great numbers euen twentie at a clappe out of one iayle . . . wee woulde hasten and further euery man to his power the deducting of some Colonies of our superfluous people into those temperate and fertile partes of America, which being within sixe weekes sayling of England are yet vnpossessed by any Christians and seeme to offer themselues vnto vs, stretching neerer vnto her Maiesties Dominions, then to any other part of Europe. Wee reade that the Bees, when they grow to be too many in their own hiues at home, are wont to bee led out by their Captaines to swarme abroad, and seeke themselves a new dwelling place. If the examples of the Grecians and Carthaginians of olde time, and the practise of our

age may not mooue vs, yet let vs learne wisdome of these final weake and vnreasonable creatures.[41]

The reference to bees in Hakluyt's passage is not atypical. As Jonathan Woolfson argues, "Both the ancient Judeo-Christian and the Greek and Roman heritage emphasized the special nature of bees, suggesting in different ways that they were comparable to humans."[42] For Renaissance authors drawing on these traditions, the ancients' ideas about the specialness of bees exerted a major influence. Aristotle calls them a "peculiar and extraordinary kind of animal" due to their social and gregarious nature.[43] Meanwhile Pliny the Elder regards them as superior to humans because of their commitment to the common interest of the hive.[44] Other ancient writers, notably Virgil in his *Georgics*, celebrate bees for their industry, organization, and division of labor.[45] "These writers, and Virgil especially, exercised a huge influence," Woolfson argues, such that "medieval and Renaissance authors often continue to consider bees the most outstanding of all animals, or . . . at least the most noble of the insects."[46]

For Hakluyt, moreover, the analogy between "her Maiesties Dominions" and the dominion of bees carries an overtly sexual connotation in that it alludes to one of the most hotly contested problems in Renaissance natural history: the autogenesis of bees. As historian of natural science David Freedberg writes, "If there was a central natural historical problem—let us not yet call it biological— . . . it was precisely the problem of generation and reproduction." Because "the ancients maintained [that] bees were autogenetic," early modern naturalists, including Galileo, believed that bees "reproduced without any kind of sexual congress, and were therefore particularly pleasing to Diana," goddess of both the hunt and chastity.[47] Here again Virgil is instructive. In the *Georgics*, he writes "that bees refrain from intercourse, their bodies never weaken into the ways of love, nor suffer pangs of labour."[48] That the autogenesis of bees would have seemed an apt metaphor for "her Maiesties Dominions," her majesty the virgin queen—Hakluyt's text leaves little doubt.

And yet, what is most fascinating about Hakluyt's analogy to bee society, hierarchy, and asexual generation is its vitalist rationale, a

rationale that highlights issues of security, territory, and population—
the trivium of concerns punctuating Foucault's late writings on
biopolitical organization—as key to the stability and furtherance of
the English nation.[49] Targeting the overpopulation of England's pris-
ons as a reason for undertaking colonizing expeditions to America,
Hakluyt's bee analogy layers the spatial coordinates of the "iayle" cell
with that of the hive in order to demonstrate the necessity of imperial expansion. In vitalist terms, Hakluyt's call to "swarme abroad" is
consubstantial with the desire to maximize and preserve life through
colonial occupation. Hakluyt's image of the "swarme," an image of
life's profusion and circulation, is thus correlative to the image of the
cell, an architectural model emblematic not only of life's absorption
by, and contribution to, a larger republic but also of life's division and
appropriation in the colonies, and of the grids of knowing that Anglo-
Europeans used in the classification of New World environments.

For literary scholars, the genre typically associated with this process of division and classification is that of the blazon. Drawing
on Nancy Vicker's influential analysis[50] of blazon writing's central motif—the fragmentation and metonymization of the female
body—Patricia Parker and Louis Montrose detail the relation between blazon as a form of *writing* and nature as a *material surface* in
the ideology of colonial conquest. For Parker, the blazon's rhetorical techniques of amplification or dilation by division in which a
whole body—here, the body of a woman—is distributed into parts
finds its New World expression in the gendering of America as female, as in John Donne's erotic line, "O my America, my new found
land" (27).[51] Similarly, for Montrose, the "gendered body of America calls attention to the affinity between *discovery* and the *blazon*,
two Renaissance rhetorical forms that organize and control their
subjects—respectively, the body of the land and the body of the lady—by means of display, inventory, and anatomy."[52] Following
Michel de Certeau, Montrose argues that the affinity between the
discourse of discovery and that of the blazon is "emblematic of the
inception of a distinctively modern discursive practice of historical
and cultural knowledge," one that ruptures the relation, in de Certeau's words, "between a *will to write* and a *written body* (or a body to
be written)."[53] The blazon enacts "the writing subject's textualization

of the body of the Other, neither as mere description nor as genuine encounter but," as Montrose observes, "as an act of symbolic violence, mastery, and self-empowerment."[54]

If we return to the image of the beehive, we note that the same logic of partition—of parts taken for wholes, and of subjects *who write* and objects *written*—informs Hakluyt's wish to "part stakes . . . both with the Spaniarde and the Portingale in part of America," and to bring order to "regions as yet vndiscouered" in the image of an atomized and highly regulated honeycomb. Rather than follow Parker and Montrose, however, I want to put forth an alternative understanding of the relation between part and whole in the discourse of discovery.

According to French historian and philosopher of science Georges Canguilhem, even in the limited context of seventeenth-century discussions of "cell theory," which Hakluyt's cell image anticipates, there were competing understandings of the relation between part and whole. Whereas Robert Hooke, in 1665, coined the term "cell" after looking at a magnified piece of cork and noting its compartmentalized structure, Nehemiah Grew, by contrast, writing just a few years after Hooke's discovery, theorized that "cells are preceded by and grow out of a so-called vital fluid."[55] The difference, Canguilhem notes, is that of "continuity versus discontinuity": "Some thinkers imagine living things growing out of a primary substance that is continuous and plastic; others think of organisms as composites of discrete parts, of 'organic atoms' or 'seeds of life.'"[56] Pointing to the persistence of this difference in modern scientific concepts such as particle and wave, Canguilhem suggests that the dissensus between theories of continuity and discontinuity dates as far back as classical mythology and the earliest representations of life's emergence from the sea. Canguilhem asks:

> For what, in the end, is this continuous initial plasma, this plasma that biologists have used in one form or another ever since the problem of identifying a structure common to all living things was first posed in order to deal with the perceived inadequacies of the corpuscular explanation? Was it anything other than a logical avatar of the mythological fluid from which all life is supposed to arise, of the frothy wave that bore Venus on its foam?[57]

Canguilhem's question returns us to the mythical waters of chapter 1, to the "seas abundant progeny" and the "fruitfull seede" of Spenser's *The Faerie Queene*. There I argued that Venus's fructifying waters both disturbed *and made possible* Spenser's poetic "count," bringing into view a biopolitics in which the life represented is not simply opposed to calculation, systemization, and measure but rather produces forms of organization and metastability from its liquid excess. Spenser's poetic "count" can be read as an emergent structure rising from and collapsing back into Venus's "frothy wave." The same can be said of Hakluyt's bees. Recall that for Virgil and much of the natural historical tradition, bees were thought to generate without sex. As Freedberg explains, "The process of generation started with the honey itself. This was the basic formative material out of which the bee emerged."[58] From this vital honey, "boundaries are firmly established, parts are formed. . . . The parts and figures of the body are thus formed by a process in which the basic particles both move and are moved, dissolve and are dissolved, until the necessary connections for the formation of the animal are coordinated, ordered, and established."[59] Parts of bodies flow together and dissolve, assemble and reassemble, just as the seminal substance of bees, the honey fluid, overflows the walls of each partitioned cell, forcing the bees to flow elsewhere.

I have been arguing that what makes Ralegh's poetry so "sweete" (to quote Spenser) is precisely this conceptualization of bodies as parts not confined to any given form but rather open to the movements of honey-like, or sealike, flows. Whereas Vickers, Parker, and Montrose each critique the body in parts as emblematic of the kinds of colonial violence that Hakluyt's image promotes, they, like Hakluyt, remain committed to the idea of the body as a potential whole, whether in the Lacanian inflected criticism of Vickers or in the anticolonialist criticism of her followers. The body remains *ideally* what it was in Hakluyt's image of the beehive: a whole-body containing many individuated parts. And yet, it is precisely the idea of the body as a potential whole that grounds the humanist subject as *bios politikos*, as the kind of being capable of detaching *from* and holding dominion *over* the material world. For critics of the blazon's rhetoric of division and fragmentation, the environment is an elemental condition of our being in the world, yet the world remains structurally *for us*: it environs *us*, sustains *us*, and thus *we* are called to protect *it* from the destructive illogics of the Enlightenment subject. For all of its seeming radicalism, then, the critique of the body in parts—which for many scholars is synonymous with the critique of the human- ist subject as such—merely repeats rather than ruptures the idea of the "human" insofar as it regards the human body as single and self- identical over time despite the diverse materials that flow through it.

Ralegh's aqueous bodies demand a different materialism of the body. In *The Discoverie of the Large, Rich, and Bewtifvl Empyre of Gviana* (1596), Ralegh's aquacentric account of his travels to the Ca- ribbean and the Guiana river basin, the blazon's rhetoric of division and fragmentation is set in sharp relief, only the bodies we "discover" there are neither singular nor self-identical; Ralegh does not relate their parts to a greater (if fragmented) whole. Rather, he makes of the human body's dissolution and disaggregation into parts a vehicle for reframing the materialism of the body in accord with the active intru- sions and cavitations of the environment.

Consider the following passage taken from the final pages of the *Discoverie*, in which Ralegh inventories the New World territory for the reader's probing eye:

> To conclude, *Guiana* is a Countrey that hath yet her Maydenhead, neuer sackt, turned, nor wrought, the face of the earth hath not beene torne, nor the vertue and salt of the soyle spent by manurance, the graues haue not been opened for gold, the mines not broken with sledges, nor their Images puld down out of their temples. It hath neuer been entred by any armie of strenght, and neuer conquered or possessed by any Christian Prince.[60]

Ralegh uses the similitude of the land and a woman's body to provoke Elizabethan subjects toward New World colonization. Earlier in the narrative he makes a similar analogy, but to different effect. Recalling his conversation with the native peoples of Trinidad, he states:

> I made them vnderstand that I was the seruant of a Queene, who was the great *Casique* of the north, and a virgin, and had more *Casiqui* vnder her then there were trees in their Iland: that she was an enemy

to the *Castellani* in respect of their tyrannie and oppression, and that
she deliuered all such nations about her, as were by them oppressed,
and hauing freed all the coast of the northern world from their serui-
tude had sent me to free them also, and with al to defend the countrey
of *Guiana* from their inuasion and conquest. I shewed them her maiesties picture which they so admired and honored, as it had beene
easie to haue brought them Idolatrous thereof.[61]

Ralegh stages the discourse of discovery in terms of the competing
connotations of the virgin body, whose exemplary figure is that of the
virgin queen. On the one hand, Ralegh blazons the Guiana territory
as a naked virgin awaiting Old World occupation; on the other hand,
he projects the inviolable female body of the monarch onto the islands
of the Caribbean, offering protection from a common "enemy," the *Castellani* of Spain. Queen Elizabeth's presentation of chastity thus had
the paradoxical effect of intensifying the sexual field of politics, not
delimiting it. We see one instance of this in the passage above, wherein
a servant's praise for his queen's inviolability transitions smoothly to a
scene of "Idolatrous" gazing at "her maiesties picture." We see another
instance in the "Armada Portrait" of Queen Elizabeth (see Figure 3).
As many critics, among them Montrose, have pointed out, this paint-
erly representation of the defeat of the Spanish Armada has at its
pictorial and ideological center the queen's virginal body. However,
we do not so much *see* the queen's body but rather intuit its existence beneath the surface of her garments. The queen's clothes are as
impenetrable as they are ornate, at once luring the viewer's eye and de-
feating ocular penetration. In Montrose's reading, the presentation of
chastity is signaled by a white bow resting at the bottom of Elizabeth's
stomacher, which figuratively represents the queen's "virgin-knot."
"This demure iconography of Elizabeth's virgin-knot suggests a
causal relationship," Montrose argues, "between her sanctified chastity
and the providential destruction of the Spanish Catholic invaders."[62]
For Montrose and others, Elizabeth's power depends on the containment of her—and by extension the English nation's—erotic body as
a knotted, bounded whole. The containment of the queen's body thus
yields an emerging discourse of nationalism and imperialism, figured
most dramatically by the queen's hand resting atop the globe.

FIGURE 3. The Armada Portrait of Queen Elizabeth I, circa 1588. Oil on oak panel, 105 x 133 cm. Woburn Abbey. Formerly attributed to George Gower.

By contrast, Valerie Traub identifies in the Armada portrait an erotic assemblage of human and animal parts that breaks mens' bodies and scatters them at sea. Noting the uncanny semblance of the queen's body in the figure of a mermaid, Traub observes:

> Elizabeth is turned slightly away from the only other figure in the frame: a small statue of an exquisitely carved "mere-maid," whose genitals are effaced by the smooth and continuous impenetrability of her aquatic appendage. In Renaissance typologies of the monstrous, the hybrid bodies of mermaids, like those of sirens and nereides, defy what Ambroise Paré calls the "confusion and conjunction of seeds," that is, the reproductive potential that is every woman's lot. The mermaid's vagina is precisely a point of non-entry, overwritten by the fantasized space of a mythical marine topos. No line separates her torso from tail; surfaces overlap, in an eerie reminder of Elizabeth's dress. Representing genital impossibility, the mermaid is endlessly desirable: like the sirens, she lures men into the boundless sea of desire;

but because her body is devoid of a genital opening, the psychic threat of "erotic drowning" is displaced away from her body and onto the sea that is her element.[63]

A figure of "non-entry," the mermaid displaces the body's interior onto a "smooth and continuous" surface of pleasure points and folds coextensive with the surface and folds of the sea. A bridge between the engulfing power of the ocean ("mere") and the bounded body of Elizabeth ("maid"), this aquatic assemblage of human and animal parts splits the optic of the painting as it disperses the queen's body across the surface of the canvas. Like the blazon, the Armada painting invites fragmentation; only this fragmentation does not relate the body in parts to a greater whole. If the mermaid's "genital impossibility" evokes ruin, this is not because of a lack in the body but because of a fullness that drowns mens' bodies and combines them with the elements.

If we return now to the previous "picture," in which Ralegh personifies the Guiana territory as a naked virgin awaiting Old World fabric, what we encounter is another figure of "non-entry" akin to the mermaid. Continuing the quotation, Ralegh writes: "There is therefore great difference between the easiness of the conquest of *Guiana*, & the defence of it being conquered." And this is true, Ralegh asserts, because "*Guiana* hath but one entraunce by the sea (if it haue that) for any vessels of burden, so as whoeuer shall first possesse it, it shall bee founde vnaccessable for anie Enimie, except he come in Wherries, Barges, or Canoas, or els in flatte bottom boats."[64] Of course, as many critics are quick to point out, the (mythical) Empire of Guiana, sometimes called *El Dorado*, was never discovered; what is more, the "entraunce by the sea," which Ralegh immediately calls into question ("if it haue that"), was never entered. All of this supports the logic of difference and deferral that, according to Mary Fuller, structures the movement of nonentry or non-discovery that Ralegh's text paradoxically elaborates.[65]

Nevertheless, granting these deferrals, Ralegh does more than just personify a virgin landscape in honor of a virgin queen; he details in excruciating prose the disruptions to his journey brought about by the rivers and floods that mark the Guiana territory and that connect it to the sea. Whereas Montrose and others read the virgin body as a container for the English nation, one that extends across the Atlantic Ocean to encompass the whole globe, such a work of containment, I argue, is itself impossible, and for the simple reason that it presumes the separation of the human body from the natural world. In fact, in page after page of the *Discoverie*, what we "discover" is not a prima facie landscape, naked and serene; what we discover is that "the face of the earth" has a history, and that this history is written in the relation of the land-sea.

Developing the idea of the nonseparation of human bodies from colonial environments, Monique Allewaert asserts that "in the American tropics, bodies were often experienced as disorganized and disorganizing, and, what is more, it seemed possible that parts once organized into bodies might well evince autonomy outside of this organization. This transformation of human and other bodies was a key anxiety," Allewaert observes, "of Anglo-Europeans writing in and about the American colonies," for whom individual "identity depend[ed] on the organization of matter into individual bodies."[66] From debilitating heat to impassable waters, poisonous snakes to penetrating insects, the American tropics foregrounded not just the vulnerability of the body to environmental influence but far more radically the deformation, penetration, and disaggregation of the human body and its potential for disorganization into parts by climatological and other material forces. For the Ralegh of the *Discoverie*, the body's nonseparation from and consequent disorganization by colonial ecologies made the work of personifying the American tropics for the economic, objective, and aesthetic use of the English nation physically impossible. In the opening pages of the *Discoverie*, he describes his journey to America and the island of Trinidad as one of unilateral progress and unimpeded entrance, a kind of coasting carried out on the horizontal surface of the ocean: "I my selfe coasted in my barge close abord the shore and landed in euery Coue, the better to know the Iland, while the ships kept the chanell."[67] While Ralegh's fixation with the island and its inhabitants seems predicated on a belief in the ultimate horizontality and navigability of the water's surface, his description of Guiana belies a greater concern with fluid depths. There, amid river-crossings and vertiginous channels, instead of coasting on the water's smooth surface, Ralegh gets pulled into a quickening environment of liquid and sedimentary flows, of liquefactions inimical to the body's sensory-motor-schema, and of histories and cultures in contretemps with the hegemonic time of English expansionism. If, as Allewaert asserts, Anglo-Europeans understood the body to be essentially what it was for Hakluyt—a whole body containing many individuated parts—then what we find in Ralegh's description is the body in extremis, that is, pulled into parts so that it becomes a body without organization. Already in his "Dedicatorie Epistle" to Charles Howard and Sir Robert Cecil, Ralegh attests to the body's potential for disorganization, writing:

> I did therefore euen in the winter of my life, undertake these trauels, fitter for bodies lesse blasted with misfortunes, for men of greater abilitie, and for mindes of better incouragement.[68]

To which Ralegh adds:

> Of that little remaine I had, I haue wasted in effect all herein, I haue undergone many constructions, I haue been accompanied with many sorrows, with labor, hunger, heat sicknes, & perill. . . . I doe not then knowe whether I should bewaile my selfe either for my too much trauel and expence, or condemne my selfe for doing lesse then that, which can deserue nothing. From my selfe I haue deserued no thankes, for I am returned a begger, and withered, but that I might haue bettred my poore estate, it shall appeare by the following discourse.[69]

Ralegh's conditional "might" signifies a rhetoric of elegy and loss consistent throughout his writerly corpus, from the wasted life of the speaker in Ocean to Cynthia to the "wasted" and "withered" body of the explorer turned "begger" in the lines above. However, what interests me is not this mournful rhetoric but the ecology it yields.

Ralegh capacitates a sense of becoming in which the breakdown of the body into parts does not signify death but rather opens the body up to an alternative form of assembly. Starting with the preface "To the Reader," Ralegh describes this material assembly as a kind of tempest or temporization (from the Latin tempus, meaning "time"); time grows abyssal as land becomes sea, and as the tempestuous life that Ralegh "discovers" in Guiana drives his body further into the deep:

> There were on this discouerie, no lesse than 100 personnes, who can all witnesse, that when we past any braunch of the riuer to vewe the land within, and staid from our boats but six houres, wee were driuen to wade to the eyes, at our returne: and if we attempted the same the day following, it was impossible either to forde it, or to swim it, both by reason of the swiftnesse, and also for the borders were so pestered with fast woods, as neither bote nor man could finde place, either to land, or to imbarque: for in Iune, Iuly, August, and September, it is impossible to nauigate any of those riuers, for such is the furie of the Current, and there are so many trees and woods overflowne, as if anie boate but touch vppon anie tree or stake, it is impossible to saue any one person therein: and ere we departed the land, it ran with that swiftnesse, as we draue downe most commonly against the winde, little lesse then one hundred miles a day.[70]

Suspending time, space, and forward action, the tempest that Ralegh encounters in the Caribbean draws bodies into the abyss of multitudinous rivers, unnavigable currents, shifting sediments, and labyrinthian islands connecting the lower Orinoco that Ralegh "draue downe," unsuccessfully, to the greater Atlantic Ocean (see Figure 4). In this transatlantic ecology, survival is put into question, as "it is impossible to saue any one person therein."

Rather than construct a virgin body, a whole body, an image of land and discovery, Ralegh gives rise to a liquid ontology, a language of inhuman depths, and of depths in which it is right to say, as Derrida says of his encounter with his cat, that "what is here called the '. . . abyss' is not a hole, a gulf, but too much being."[71] Ralegh imagines the Guiana territory as a body in parts, a body so divided by river-crossings as to become an image of archipelagic and rhizomatic affiliation between land and sea: "For I know," Ralegh writes, "all the earth doth not yeeld the like confluence of streames and branches, the one crossing the other so many times, and all so faire and large, and so like one to another, as no man can tell which to take."[72] Here Ralegh encounters a figure of nonentry, for the body of America

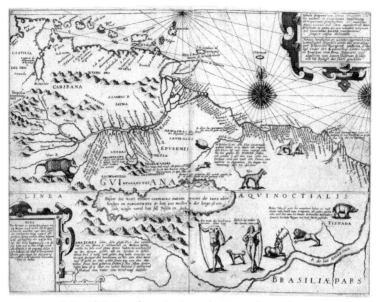

FIGURE 4. Map of Guiana from the Lago de Maracaibo to the Amazon River. Cartographic elements include the Orinoco River and its branches. From Theodor de Bry's *Americae pars VIII*. Frankfurt am Main, 1599. Courtesy of the John Carter Brown Library.

is already multiple, already transgressed by its vertiginous abyss. Where critics have seen only the projection of "text" onto a New World landscape, Ralegh sees his relation to the environment as one of "breach[ing]," "border"-crossing, and translation across "multitudes," a *scene of writing* enacted in and by the materials of the earth. I argue that such a scene of writing constitutes an assemblage or a *worlding* practice in which parts not confined to a greater whole *have world* insofar as they relate to their "outsides" through a palimpsestic eco-nomy of breaching, crossing, ontological spacing, and temporization.[73] This is a writing *of the earth* rather than a writing that *writes the earth*. More than anything, it is what constitutes the major "discovery" of Ralegh's text, namely, that there is something rather than nothing in the abyss, and that this something resists—is a force against—the history and artifacts of colonialism.

If it has been convenient to assume, as most critics do, that Ralegh treats the Guiana territory as an abyss, a tabula rasa devoid of history, this is because the abyss itself—the vertical, intertidal, and oceanic zone—has largely been overlooked by critics who see it simply as a surface, empty and void. And yet, Ralegh devotes most of his time in the *Discoverie* to describing precisely these waters and to recognizing that there is, indeed, "being rather than nothing" in the deep.[74] In the following section, I return to Ralegh's *The History of the World* in order to draw out the consequences of this oceanic perspective for a reading of what is often called, all too stubbornly, "life" or "life itself." For Greenblatt, Ralegh's sense of the "'tide of man's life' lies at the heart of his entire *History*," and yet "its particular expressions are often highly conventional, . . . reaching back through centuries of histories, sermons, and orations to the Bible and to classical moralists," even if "the effect of the whole is profoundly personal."[75] Against this reading (itself highly conventional), I show that the "personal" in Ralegh's *History* is, from the beginning, as much techno-logical as it is bio-logical, as much a matter of convention, ornamentation, and framing as it is a matter of creation, poeticization, and life. Whereas Greenblatt, among others, treats Ralegh's "tempestuous life" as merely figural, I ask: What is "life" such that it necessitates figures of "tide," "tempest," and "deep"? What does "highly conventional" here mean? Rather than return to life's practical calling, to a life that would be just life, Ralegh ushers in the sense of life's difference and multiplicity and of worlding powers beyond the human.

Writing in the Deep

The History of the World was never completed, a fact that compounds Ralegh's anxious accounting of his so-called "dissability" with a "defect" identical to and seemingly exacerbated by the scene of writing. Written late in life, Ralegh stages his *History* as a competition between incommensurable speeds, between the speed of human life, of writing, and the spectacular speed of the earth's shifting transformations of matter. From the outset of the first book, "Intreating of the Beginning, and First Ages of the Same, from the Creation vnto Abraham," Ralegh's engagement with these differential speeds devolves upon the question of beginnings, from the meaning of the word "beginning" to the "meaning of the words Heaven and Earth" in Genesis: "This word *beginning* (in which the *Hebrewes* seeke some hidden mysterie, and which in the *Iewes Targum* is conuerted by the word *Sapientia*) cannot be referred to succession of time, nor to order, as some men haue conceived, both which are subsequent."[76] Time for Ralegh is not now, not movement, not before and after (which are more spatial than temporal). Dealing with Genesis and the problem of the creation of Heaven and Earth, Ralegh posits an initial mixture of cotemporal and interstitial states, of chaos turning into solid and solid into chaos. He writes:

> It is more probable and allowed, that by the wordes *Heaven and Earth*, was meant the solid matter and substance, as well of all the Heavens, and Orbes supernall, as of the Globe of the Earth and Waters, which couered it ouer, (to wit) that very matter of all things, *materia, Chaos, possibilitas, siue posse fieri*. Which matter (saith *Calvin*) was so called, *quod totius mundi semen fuerit; Because it was the seede of the Vniuersall*, and opinion of ancient Philosophers long before.[77]

Invoking a Lucretian universe of vital and recomposeable matter, of atoms or "*seede*," Ralegh goes on to explain how differences emerge within this "*Vniuersall*" matter. Whereas for Lucretius all things emerge from the chance meeting of atoms, in Ralegh's universal history, the clinamen in question is less that of atoms and more that of oceans and waters—aqueous bodies that separate and connect at the same time the earth's terrestrial masses. In the beginning, Ralegh posits, there was neither speech nor act nor atom but "*Deepe*":

> *The Earth was couered with the Deepe* (meaning with waters) *as with a garment,* saith *David*. And if by naturall arguments it may been proued, that water by condensation may become earth, the same reason teacheth vs also, that earth rarified may become water: water, aire: aire, fire; and so on. . . . For the Heauens and the Earth remained in the same state, though there was afterwards added multiplicitie of perfection, in respect of beauty and ornament.[78]

From the beginning of the world, or of what we might call *globalization,* there will have already been "multiplicitie," "ornament," and instrumentation. Ralegh compares his "*Deepe*" to a text or textile, "*a garment,* saith *David*," playing on both meanings of the word creation:

creation as the invention ex nihilo of something new, and creation as a form of technology or reproduction—poiesis and techne, then. Whereas the one speaks prima facie of a primordial, untouched and unpolluted emergence, the other speaks of creation as a form of technology or prosthesis. This latter, essentially *parergonal* (to use Derrida's phrase, borrowed from Kant) conceptualization of the world simultaneously "constitutes . . . and ruins" the world of pure creation by supplementing, "*as with a garment*," that which is already complete.[79] The garment "would have the function of a *parergon* and an ornament," Derrida writes, meaning "that which is not internal or intrinsic . . . to the total representation of the object but which belongs to it only in an extrinsic way as a surplus, an addition, an adjunct, a supplement."[80] The garment separates the inside from the outside, the intrinsic from the extrinsic, and yet: "One wonders, too, where to have clothing commence. Where does a *parergon* begin and end."[81]

Derrida's analysis of the *parergon* bridges the intrinsic and the extrinsic, showing them to be interdependent. Ralegh goes one further: for it is not just the human body that is contaminated by its outside, but the whole world. Ralegh's ocean is, to quote Patricia Yaeger, a "techno-ocean": it *begins* with "the recognition that our relation to the sea is always already technological."[82] In his *Upon the first Invention of Shipping* (1650), subtitled *A Discourse of the Invention of Ships, Anchors, Compasse &c*, Ralegh furthers this eco-techno-poetic vision of the sea by stating

that the Ark of *Noah*, was the first Ship, because of the Invention of God himself, although some men have believed, yet it is certaine, That the world, being planted before the Flood, the same could not be performed without some transporting vessels; It is true, & the successe proves it, That there was not any so capacious nor so strong to defend itself against so violent, as so continued a powring down of raine, as the Arke *Noah*, the Invention of God himself, or of what fashion or fabrick soever, the reft withall mankind perished, according to the Ordinance of God. And probable it is that the Anchors, whereof *Ovid* made mention of, found on high Mountains: *Et inventa est in montibus Anchora Summis*, were remaining of ships wrackt at the generall flood.[83]

Ralegh's world history cannot be known outside a techno-ocean, for even God is an inventor, or better still, a builder of ships. Even "before the Flood," the world had already been "planted," seeded, and artificially yoked by "some transporting vessels." In this way, Ralegh does to Genesis what Derrida does to Plato's pharmacy: he shows that the world's creation is already a de-creation, and yet the *pharmakon* in question does not diminish the world "in respect of [its] beauty and ornament." Taking a page from George Puttenham's *The Art of English Poesy,* which admonishes against *too much* "ornament" but necessitates it nonetheless,[84] Ralegh entertains the (rather Ovidian) idea that well before humans began making the world over in their image, before the invention of ships, anchors, and compass, the Earth had already begun to write itself, to create and de-create its own globalizing tapestry or blazon: its own *technopoiesis.* For Ralegh (as for poet Derek Walcott)[85] the sea is this history: a "garment" as long as Penelope's in Homer's *Odyssey,* and as bottomless as the darkest "*Deepe.*"

In recent decades, scholars of world history, imagined community, and globalization have begun to turn their sights to the Renaissance to track the emergence of the "globe" as a transnational and techno-national phenomenon in the advancements of early modern print and other related technologies (most notably mapmaking). In literary scholarship, the study of print technology has fueled expanded forms of book history, which treat the invention of the printing press as the key to understanding early modern transformations of knowledge of and around the globe.[86] For world-systems theorists Pascale Casanova and Franco Moretti, the global spread of print in and outside of Europe and its colonies in the Renaissance and beyond constitutes what Casanova conceives of as a "World Republic of Letters," in which writers of different nations from different periods—from Dante Alighieri to Samuel Beckett—compete to have their works (and the nations they represent) become part of an abstract network of literary and cultural influence and global dominance.[87] In *Graphs, Maps, Trees,* Moretti promotes "distant reading"—"a process of deliberate reduction and abstraction"—as a way of contending with the enormous bibliographic troves that comprise the "World Republic of Letters."[88]

Similarly, for New Historicist critics Mary Fuller and Richard Helgerson, the notion of a globalized world of information exchange is tied to the imperial ambitions of the English nation, which relied on the global dissemination of print to level cultural and geographic differences and to reflect back—from Virginia to South America to the Elizabethan court—its own "forms of nationhood." In Helgerson's study, the England represented in Richard Hakluyt's *The Principal Navigations of the English Nation* (1589) as well as other overseas narratives, including Ralegh's *Upon the first Invention of Shipping*, is "an England defined by its relations to those other more or less similar entities, an England reconstituted in response to a new global system of differences."[89] For Helgerson, Hakluyt's *Principal Navigations* is the first among voyage narratives to insist on "the nation as ultimate actor" in world affairs and "to promote English expansion abroad."[90] It is thus exemplary for Helgerson not as a nautical text but rather as a representation of nationhood and territorial expansion. In Helgerson's reading, it is not the voyages themselves that constituted the "age of discovery," but rather the books printed about them.

Likewise, in Fuller's *Voyages in Print,* she begins with an epigraph from Francis Bacon's *Novum Organum* (1620) reminding the reader of "the force, effect, and consequences of inventions which," according to Bacon, "are nowhere more conspicuous than in those three which were unknown to the ancients, namely printing, gunpowder, and the compass."[91] Whereas Bacon opines that the inventions of print, gunpowder, and the compass "have changed the appearance and state of the whole world," Fuller isolates the first invention in Bacon's series, printed texts, arguing that printed voyages "were both generated by and helped to generate England's entry into American discovery and colonization."[92] Focusing on "the importance of the Elizabethan and Jacobean voyage texts as central to forming the idea of the English nation," Fuller writes that "Ralegh's expedition [in *The Discoverie of Guiana*] is literally a search for the referent, a place to which can be attached the proper names 'Manoa' and 'El Dorado.'"[93] For Fuller, as for Helgerson, the printed text animates and precedes the voyage; it invents the voyage as it invents the globe, making it the true agent of discovery. Between land, nation, and text, the sea is merely a cipher: *terra mundi,* not *aqua mundi.*

By contrast, Shannon is the rare scholar who reads Ralegh's writings about oceans and ships as above all *about* the lives that inhabited oceans and ships. Reacting against "the beast-machine doctrine" forged in the seventeenth century by René Descartes, who "grant[ed] the free agency of thought to all humans" while "classifying the entire balance of creatures, from the oyster to the ape, as uniformly hardwired," Shannon looks to natural-historical accountings of species-being and cross-species relating (what Shannon calls "cosmopolitics") in order to chart an alternate, "zoographic" history that runs counter to "the modern constitution" theorized by Bruno Latour, which places humans on the side of politics and culture and nonhumans on the side of mechanized and homogenous nature.[94] In the last chapter of *The Accommodated Animal,* Shannon turns from the landed cosmopolitics of Shakespeare's plays to the ocean ecologies of Ralegh's *History.* There, in contradistinction to the nation-based focus of Fuller and Helgerson, Shannon locates (and at the same time de-locates, that is, unmoors) the biopolitical and technological center of Ralegh's *History* in the hull of Noah's ark: "The story of Noah's ark taxed the early modern imagination," Shannon writes, triggering "doubt about how Noah could have built a craft sufficient to hold all the earthly kinds" while driving "early modern commentators into the cold waters of mathematical calculation."[95] Among these commentators, Shannon singles out Ralegh for "weeding out such creatures as could easily be reconstructed rationally," thus conserving space on Noah's ship: "For those beasts which are of mixt natures," Ralegh writes, "either they were not in that age, or else it was not needfull to praeserve them: seeing they might be generated againe by others."[96] From the hull of Noah's ark to the shores of the "Black Atlantic," Shannon shows how Ralegh's speculative calculations about animal life and death on Noah's ark prefigure the transatlantic traffic in "human chattel," making the sea voyage itself and not just the text written about it key to understanding the biopolitics of race and early modern globalization.[97] In this way, Shannon not only critiques Foucault's biopolitics and Agamben's "bare life," which "remain essentially human in reach," but also critically supplements New Historicist accounts of nationhood by torquing our attention toward the multivectored zones between land, nation, and print.

Even so, while Shannon is critical of the human-exceptionalism of Agamben's biopolitical formulation, she nevertheless shares with Agamben an interest in returning thought to its practical foundation—that is, to a conception of life that is not that which has already been shaped by efficiency and techno-reason. Cosmopolitics, in her argument, thus stands for the inclusion of species difference within the human polis and for the specifically pre-Cartesian ability to think the world-making capacities of nonhumans. Nevertheless, we should ask whether "life," as both Agamben and Shannon conceive of it, can simply be added back to the polis, or whether a more radical suspension of life and the political is needed in order to think life beyond the human.

Returning to the world-making power of oceans, I want to foreground Ralegh's relation to the earth as one of infinite speed. Rather than add more, respect more, Ralegh's relation to "life" is purposefully abstract: that is, beyond animal and human, what it requires is not greater inclusivity but, in the words of Deleuze and Guattari, greater *intensity*.[98] Deleuze and Guattari write that the problem with theoretical models "is not that they are too abstract but, on the contrary, that they are not abstract enough."[99] The opposite of "life" for Deleuze and Guattari is not techne, not even death, since life "itself" is already a machinic assemblage of recomposable dead matter. Instead, what stands in opposition to life for Deleuze and Guattari is the organism or organ: the body, the nation, the printed book. Against these, the "body without organs" is at the same time real and abstract: real because it is *of* life, and abstract because it takes life beyond its human, national, and organic confines. As Brian Massumi explains, "The charge of indeterminacy carried by a body is inseparable from it. . . . Far from regaining a concreteness, to think the body in movement thus means accepting the paradox that there is an incorporeal dimension *of the body*. Of it, but not it. Real, material, but incorporeal."[100] Real but abstract. Among the elements that carry out this deterritorializing or abstracting movement, Deleuze and Guattari single out the earth's liquefaction as a primary agent in the creation and de-creation of human knowledge: "Concepts are like multiple waves," they write, "rising and falling, but the plane of immanence is the single wave that rolls them up and unrolls them."[101] The "plane of immanence" describes the earth's processes of abstraction, its own speeds of deterritorialization, which are incommensurable to human reason. "The plane envelops infinite movements that pass back and forth through it," like waves crashing on the shore. Folding and unfolding, the plane *produces* the potential for "infinite speed," or the thought of life as the potential for infinite relations: "From Epicurus to Spinoza the problem of thought is infinite speed. But this speed requires a milieu that moves infinitely in itself—the plane, the void, the horizon. Both elasticity of the concept and fluidity of the milieu are needed. Both are needed to make up 'the slow beings' that we are."[102]

Along with Epicurus and Spinoza, we can add Ralegh to the list of thinkers who problematize the relation of the earth's "infinite speed" to human reason. "True philosophy," Ralegh writes, "is an ascending from the things which flow, and rise, and fall, to the things that are for euer the same."[103] Not "life itself," then, not some pure organic sameness that then falls into alienation, technologization, and difference, but rather differences *within* the same: this is what characterizes the life that Ralegh calls "tempestuous," and what constitutes the sea as a potential plane of immanence. Whereas Shannon, Helgerson, and Fuller each consider Ralegh's writings to be emblematic of a biopolitical dispensation in the service of the English nation, together with Deleuze and Guattari, we might begin to see Ralegh's writings, especially his writings on Creation, on the essential *technopoesy* of Creation, not as an escape from difference but rather as a proliferation of differences carried out at the absolute speed of deterritorialization. Speed of writing, speed of deterritorialization: from the outset, Ralegh's writings are about this movement, a movement that makes the writer more, not less, heterogeneous. "A writer," Deleuze and Guattari argue, "is not a writer-man; he is a machine-man, and an experimental man ... who thereby ceases to be a man in order to become ... inhuman."[104] To become inhuman, Deleuze and Guattari aver, "is to participate in movement."[105] Such a movement Ralegh attributes to the earth's waters:

> This Masse, or indigested matter, or Chaos created in the beginning was without forme, that is, without the proper forme, which it

afterwards acquired, when the Spirit of God had separated the Earth, and digested it from the waters: *And the earth was voide*: that is, not producing any creatures, or adorned with any plants, fruits, or flowers. But after *the Spirit of God had moued upon the waters*, and wrought this indigested matter into that forme, which it now retayneth, then did *the earth budde forth the hearbe, which seedeth seede, & the fruitfull tree according to his kinde, and God saw that it was good*; which attribute was not giuen to the Earth, while it was confused, nor to the Heauens, before they had motion, and adornment.[106]

Both meanings of creation are active in this passage: creation as poetic production ex nihilo, and creation as separation, digestion, supplementation, and "adornment." God supplements the world of pure creation by adding, "*as with a garment*," the earth's fructifying waters. These waters re-create the world by adding "motion, and adornment." Neither "*budde*" nor "*hearbe*," "*seede*" nor "*fruitfull tree*" appears without the *paregonal* supplement of the earth's techno-waters, which "had not only motion," Ralegh writes, "but also power to procreate or bring forth liuing creatures."[107]

In book 1, chapter 6 of the *History*, Ralegh considers "*how it is to be understood that the Spirit of God moued upon the waters*," how, in the words of Psalm 147, "*the winde from the face of God did blow under, driue, or remoue, or did blow upon . . . stirring upon the face of this double liquor*."[108] Resolved that God's ways "cannot bee conceiued by any minde, or spirit, compassed with a mortall body," Ralegh nevertheless maintains, so as to "eschew curiosity," that this much at least "is true": "that the English word (moued) is most proper and significant: for of motion proceedeth all production, and all whatsoeuer is effected."[109] Movement, production, and water: how compelling that, for Ralegh, it is the inhuman face, the face of an anonymous materiality or faciality (as Deleuze and Guattari would say) that constitutes the very possibility of our being and becoming human; how compelling that it is the inhuman face, "*the face of this double liquour*," that constitutes our very forms of worlding.

The Ends of Man

Flying over the land between Baghdad, Beirut, Haifa, and Tripoli, Gayatri Chakravorty Spivak notes: "I am making a clandestine entry into 'Europe.' Yet the land looks the same." "I know the cartographic markers," Spivak observes, writing from the airplane above, "but, in search of a springboard for planetarity, I am looking at the figure of land that seems to undergird it. The view of the Earth from the window brings this home to me."[110] The figure of planetarity, in contrast to that of the national or international, makes our home *unheimlich* or uncanny, Spivak argues, in that it introduces the idea of "land" as continuous with the earth. "Land" is the element that makes possible the displacement of the national into planetarity, a term that, for Spivak, goes beyond cosmopolitanism in that it reminds us of the inhumanness of the place that we call "home" or "mother earth": "The planet is in the species of alterity," Spivak argues, "belonging to another system; and yet we inhabit it, on loan. . . . When I invoke the planet, I think of the effort required to figure the (im)possibility of this underived intuition."[111]

For Spivak, the alterity of the land signals the limit, or rather the impossible possibility, of thinking the planet in a human-centered frame. Nevertheless, for those travelers living in the era of exploration and discovery, it was not the figure of land but rather that of water—vast expanses of water, sea, and oceanic abyss—that both made the territorializing ambitions of the English nation possible and, in the case of Ralegh, set them catastrophically off course. As Peter Sloterdijk argues succinctly, "The fundamental thought of modernity was articulated *not* by Copernicus, but rather by Magellan."[112] By displacing land into ocean, nation into sea, Ralegh (dis)figures the face of planetarity by rendering the matter of the Earth as "depe": "And the earth was without forme & voyde, and darkeness was vpon the depe."[113]

Ralegh's "tempestuous life" is not *for us*; it is an image of inhuman durations, of speeds of life that leave "our" time, the time of persons and nations, "unioynted and scattered." To say (à la Shakespeare's *Hamlet*) that time is out of joint is one thing; the real question that "we" should ask is: Whose time? As Foucault makes clear, "Man is neither the oldest nor the most constant problem that has been

posed for human knowledge."[114] Rather than think of life in terms of
man's ending, we might begin to think of the inhuman abyss *within*
man himself. Perhaps only then, "after all Philosophical contemplation and curiositie," after "all the reason of man ends and dissolves
it selfe," might the (im)possible and underived intuition of a world
without us start to take hold.

FOUR

ARCHITECTURAL ANTHROPOLOGIES
(*Marvell*)

There are two quite distinct phases in a sunset. At first, the sun acts as an architect. Only later (when its rays are reflected and not direct) does it become a painter. As soon as it disappears behind the horizon, the light weakens, thus creating places of vision which increase in complexity with every second. Broad daylight is inimical to perspective, but between day and night there is room for an architecture which is as fantastic as it is provisional.

—Claude Lévi-Strauss, *Tristes Tropiques*

In the preface to his *De re aedificatoria* (*On the Art of Building*, 1452), Leon Battista Alberti writes: "Our Ancestors have left us many and various Arts tending to the Pleasure and Conveniency of Life, acquired with the greatest industry and diligence."[1] These "Arts," "tho' they all pretend, with a kind of emulation, to have in view the great end of being serviceable to Mankind; yet we know that each of them in particular has something in it that seems to promise a distinct and separate Fruit."[2] Ascribing to the "Arts" a "serviceable" and delectable "end" in the species of "Mankind," Alberti delineates the various kinds of "Fruit" that men, either for industry or for pleasure, tend to follow: "Some Arts we follow for necessity, some we approve for their usefulness, and some we esteem because they lead us to the knowledge of things that are delightful."[3] "Architecture," Alberti writes, "is not to be excluded from that number. For it is certain, if you examine the matter carefully, it is inexpressibly delightful, and of the greatest convenience to Mankind in all respects, both public and private; and in Dignity not inferior to the most excellent."[4] A delight and "convenience to Mankind," the art of architecture is nonetheless a fruit distinct from its labor: "For it is not," Alberti argues, "a Carpenter or a Joyner that I thus rank with the greatest Masters in other Sciences; the manual Operator being no more than an instrument to the Architect." Rather, drawing on the Platonic distinction between true model and false copy, Alberti classifies the architect as a cogitator of forms:

> Him I call an Architect, who, by a sure and wonderful Art and Method, is able, both with thought and invention, to devise, and, with execution, to compleat all those Works, which, by means of the movement of great Weights, and the conjunction and amassment of Bodies, can, with the greatest Beauty, be adapted to the uses of Mankind: and to be able to do this, he must have a thorough insight into the noblest and most curious Sciences. Such must be the Architect.[5]

Returning to the mathematical principles first established in his *De pictura* (*On Painting*, 1435), Alberti attributes to the architect the geometer's "insight" into "the basic principles of nature."[6] Just as "mathematicians measure the shapes and forms of things in the mind alone and divorced entirely from matter," so "the whole Art of Building consists in the Design," which, according to Alberti, is the *archē*, the archetype or order, internal to every structure. "We can in our Thought and Imagination contrive perfect Forms of Buildings entirely separate from Matter," Alberti argues, "by settling and regulating in a certain Order the Disposition and Conjunction of the Lines and Angles. Which being granted, we shall call the Designs a firm and graceful pre-ordering of the Lines and Angles, conceived in the Mind, and contrived by an ingenious Artist."[7]

The true Architect, writes Alberti, invents "Designs" ex nihilo, or better still, *ex geometrico*. The *Oxford English Dictionary* notes that in the period in which Alberti was writing, the word "design" (used by Alberti's translator, James Leoni) underwent a formal and semantic differentiation: between "a plan or scheme conceived in the mind and intended for subsequent execution" on the one hand, and "the completed product or result" of said plan on the other.[8] Although the history of this semantic shift would not be complete until the end of the eighteenth century, we can see in the architectural writings of Alberti that this process of mutation was already well underway in the fifteenth century and that the hierarchizing of "Number" as consubstantial with "Mind" entailed—for Alberti and his followers—the subtraction of "Matter" as supplemental and thus derived. For Alberti, there are pure forms given to the human knower, gifted by geometry and yet separate from any geo-logical or geo-graphical determination. Architectural figures communicate across time and space, regardless of their material coordinates. The true architect thus has unique access to a universal, immaterial, and true knowledge, at once gifted by the earth and yet separate from any earthly inscription. From this perspective, although he is a figure *of* the earth, the architect stands radically outside nature, elevated above the earth as its measurer or surveyor.

While this (temporal) differentiation of form/matter underscores Derrida's assertion that "linearism," the temporal priority given to certain entities or events (in this case, the "Mind"), "is . . . inseparable from phonologism," or speech/writing—a point made all the more salient here by the Euclidean linearism of "Lines and Angles"—it is more precisely the problematic of *figure* that I wish to address in this chapter, beginning with Lucretius.[9]

A Dance of Figures

Writing several centuries after Alberti in an essay titled "Figura," German philologist Erich Auerbach asks the following architecturally related question: "How is it possible," Auerbach wonders, "that both words [*forma* and *figura*], but particularly *figura*, the form of which was a clear reminder of its origin, should so quickly have taken on a purely abstract meaning?"[10] From the narrower concept of "plastic form" (what it was originally for the Greeks) to the concept of abstract schema (what it became after the Hellenization of Roman education), *figura*, according to Auerbach, underwent both a dramatic drawing away from plastic matter and a global reduction in the concept of form:

Greek, with its incomparably richer scientific and rhetorical vocabulary, had a great many words for the concept of form: *morphē, eidos,
schēma, typos, plasis,* to mention only the most important. . . . It was
only natural that *forma* should come to be used in Latin for *morphē*
and *eidos,* since it originally conveyed the notion of model; sometimes
we also find *exemplar;* for *schēma* on the other hand *figura* was usually
employed. But since in the learned Greek terminology—in grammar,
rhetoric, logic, mathematics, astronomy—*schēma* was widely used in
the sense of outward shape, *figura* was always used for this purpose
in Latin. Thus side by side with the original plastic signification and
overshadowing it, there appeared a far more general concept of grammatical, rhetorical, logical, mathematical—and later even of musical
and choreographic—form.[11]

What distinguishes Auerbach's philology of "origins" from the work
of his near contemporary, a no less gifted philologist and thinker—
Martin Heidegger, who famously connects building, dwelling, and
thinking as sister arts—is that unlike the latter, Auerbach's focus on
the Hellenization of Greek grammar does not dwell on the "concealment" of Being *(ousia)* by mathematical abstraction but rather on the
multiplicity of beginnings (without origin) opened up by the concept
of "form." Pointing to what Louis Althusser would later call "the underground current of philosophy,"[12] Auerbach charts an alternative
historiography of *figura* in the Epicurean philosophy of Lucretius.
There, Auerbach states, "Lucretius uses *figura* in the Greek philosophical sense, but in an extremely individual, free, and significant
way."[13] Lucretius does not reduce *plasis* to *schēma,* plastic form to
abstract model; instead, "he starts with the general concept of 'figure,'
which occurs in every possible shading from the plastic figure shaped
by man . . . to the purely geometric outline."[14] The result, Auerbach
argues, is a veritable reversal of the Platonic division between sensible
copy and abstract form:

A special variant of the meaning "copy" occurs in Lucretius' doctrine of
the structures that peel off things like membranes and float round in
the air, his Democritean doctrine of the "film images," or *eidola,* which
he takes in a materialistic sense. These he calls *simulacra, imagines,*

effigies, and sometimes *figurae;* and consequently it is in Lucretius that we first find the word employed in the sense of "dream image," "figment of fancy," "ghost." . . . All these meanings clung to *figura.*[15]

Lucretius turns to the subject of figures in book 4 of *De rerum natura* to describe an image-world in which images or ideas *(eidola)* are themselves material entities, what he elsewhere refers to as "atoms" or "seeds." These images move, they assemble and reassemble, and from these shifting assemblages derive the physical world:

> These images are like a skin, or film,
> Peeled from the body's surface, and they fly
> This way and that across the air.

> So there are, all around us, shapes and forms
> Of definite outline, always on the move,
> Delicate, small, woven of thread so rare
> Our sight cannot detect them. (4.33–35, 85–88)[16]

If, according to Deleuze, the project of modern philosophy has been to "reverse Platonism," then there is perhaps no philosophical precedent better fitted to that task than the inverted world of Lucretius, for whom ideas in the Platonic sense take on a strange bodily existence.[17] In his first and most important philosophical axiom, Lucretius states that "nothing comes from nothing," meaning that all things derive from the same stuff, the same matter, and that behind every event is a series of other events, each constituting a swerve in the world's becoming. "Whatever has been done may be called an accident *[eventum]* either of the whole earth or of the region in which it occurred," Lucretius briefly states.[18] Whatever the case, the principle guiding these events is the same throughout *De rerum natura:* that all things emerge from the chance meeting of atoms and that from these meetings, multiple/incommensurable scales of space-time, matter, and causality are put in play. "So it comes about," Auerbach remarks, "that [Lucretius] often calls 'forms,' *figurae.* . . . The numerous atoms are in constant motion; they move about in the void, combine and repel one another: a dance of figures."[19]

Here the point to be emphasized concerning Lucretius is that the "*structures* that peel off things" are without center or model; they compose what is. Atomic figures are both immaterial (they cannot be seen) *and* corporeal (they compose the sense-event of animal perception).[20] Consequently, atemporal figures like the circle and the triangle become plastic, not static, defined by affects and collisions. In turn, the surface of the earth becomes a radical differential calculus or ahuman geometry. Instead of man surveying the earth from above, in Lucretius's philosophy, man is one of nature's figures—a thinking being not because he stands above extended substance, but because extended substance is already thinking. Lucretius's universal architecture is without "Design" in Alberti's sense, but it nonetheless affirms the status of figures as both real and abstract, making the dance of figures the universal condition of what is.

"This use of the word [*figura*] does not seem to have gone beyond Lucretius," Auerbach observes, thus bringing to an abrupt conclusion his genealogy of plastic form.[21] Later Renaissance writers, including the Italian humanist and biographer Giorgio Vasari, who devotes an entire chapter to Alberti in *The Lives of the Artists* (1550), repeat Alberti's architectural Platonism, making mathematical form the structure of all things. In his preface to the *Lives*, Vasari says of the architect's "design" that it "existed in absolute perfection at the origin of all other things."[22] A form later incarnated in matter, it reveals to man his own "first image," perfected by God algorithmically before "Time and Nature" existed.[23]

According to Renaissance art historian Rudolf Wittkower, this new scientific approach to human nature advanced by Alberti's architectural theory "had a notable share in consolidating and popularizing the mathematical interpretation of all matter," since "architecture was regarded . . . as a mathematical science which worked with spatial units: parts of that universal space for the scientific interpretation of which they had discovered the key in the laws of perspective."[24] Artists and scientists both, from Leonardo da Vinci to Isaac Newton, "were made to believe that they could re-create the universally valid ratios and expose them pure and absolute, as close to abstract geometry as possible." The geometrical definition of God made incarnate in architectural structure had its roots, for Alberti and his followers, in ancient cosmology, and above all in Plato. In the *Timaeus*, Plato defines the physical universe as fundamentally mathematical: the universe, he writes, is "a circle, a single solitary universe," which is then divided into polygonal shapes, since "everything that has bodily form also has depth," and "depth, moreover, is of necessity comprehended within surface, and any surface bounded by straight lines is composed of triangles."[25] Euclidean geometry appealed to Plato as a model for his Ideas because it defined static, unchanging, and self-identical forms. Following this Pythagorean tradition, Alberti's theory of architectural "Design" not only helped formalize the Renaissance interest in perspective but also helped radicalize the geometrical definition of God and Man as manifest in the universal laws of nature, as can be seen in the following passage from Alberti, wherein nature "herself" is imagined as an enumerating machine, a calculator of shapes and units:

> It is obvious from all that is fashioned, produced, or created under her influence, that Nature delights primarily in the circle. Need I mention the earth, the stars, the animals, their nests, and so on, all of which she has made circular? We notice that nature also delights in the hexagon. For bees, hornets, and insects of every kind have learned to build the cells of their hives entirely out of hexagons.[26]

After Galileo published his mathematical interpretation of the material world in *The Assayer* in 1623, nature came to be understood as the orderly manifestation of a set of internal laws whose precise architectural consequences could be deciphered and read using the geometer's figurative language. "Philosophy is written in this all-encompassing book," Galileo observes, "that is constantly open before our eyes, that is the universe."

> It is written in mathematical language, and its characters are triangles, circles, and other geometrical figures; without these it is humanly impossible to understand a word of it, and one wanders around pointlessly in a dark labyrinth.[27]

The most important and far-reaching consequence of Galileo's insight is the idea that universal constants like "triangles, circles, and other geometrical figures" could be mathematically described, thus eliminating time and change from science's image of nature. The universe described by Galileo was essentially static; the idea of an evolving nature was as unreasonable as the idea of an evolving God, whose image this "all-encompassing book" reflects. Within this architectural description of nature, progress was, as Ernst Cassirer explains, human progress.[28] Hegel's march of the human Spirit only makes sense in a world where physical differences mask an underlying unity. By learning to recognize mathematical figures beneath the surface of sense, the human subject becomes, as in Cartesianism, both a cogitator of architectural forms and, paradoxically, a mind removed from matter.

The Vaulted Brain

Alberti's mathematization of matter prefigures Galileo's universal "book" while also redoubling its humanist puzzle: the *mathesis universalis* described by nature's laws both does and does not include man as one of its many figures. In reading this universal book of nature, humanity stands strangely outside it, both inside and outside nature's figurative work.[29]

Turning to Andrew Marvell's seventeenth-century country-house poem, *Upon Appleton House*, a poem written in honor of his lord and patron, Lord General Thomas Fairfax, we witness a curious involution of the relation between Being and dwelling that, in the case of Alberti, signified "man's" essence as the identity between "Mind" and "Number." While this relation of Being and dwelling, spirit and number, remains operative throughout the history of architectural theory in the West—from Lévi-Strauss's structural anthropology to Badiou's claim that "mathematics *is* ontology"[30]—there is, nonetheless, a curious complicity in Marvell's poem between inner and outer form, between the design on the one hand and matter on the other, such that the exteriority of matter in Marvell's poem, rather than being secondary or derived as in the case of Alberti, constitutes an inside that is nothing other than the figure or fold of an outside. Here is Marvell:

Within this sober frame expect
Work of no foreign architect;
That unto cave the quarries drew,
And forests did to pastures hew;
Who of his great design in pain
Did for a model vault his brain,
Whose columns should so high be raised
To arch the brows that on them gazed.

Why should of all things man unruled
Such unproportioned dwellings build?
The beasts are by their dens expressed:
And birds contrive an equal nest;
The low-roofed tortoises do dwell
In cases fit of tortoise-shell:
No creature loves an empty space;
Their bodies measure out their place. (1.1–8, 2.9–16)[31]

Written in eight-line stanzas of octosyllabic iambic couplets, Marvell's poem is a model of architectural sobriety, appearing uniformly on the page as a sequence of identical figures or squares. In *The Art of English Poesy*, subtitled, "Of the Square or Quadrangle Equilateral," George Puttenham describes the figure adopted by Marvell's poem as a steadfast and solid figure most "likened to the earth," reasoning that "the square is of all other accounted the figure of most solidity and steadfastness, and for his own stay and firmity requireth none other base than himself."

> Therefore as the roundel or sphere is appropriate to the heavens, the spire to the element of the fire, the triangle to the air, and the lozenge to the water, so is the square for his inconcussable steadiness liked to the earth, which perchance might be the reason that the Prince of Philosophers, in his first book of the *Ethics*, termeth a constant-minded man, even equal and direct on all sides, and not easily overthrown by every little adversity, *hominem quadratum*, a "square man."[32]

Though future philosophers will denounce the repressiveness of one-dimensional man,[33] and others will trace the diamond or lozenge (*poinçon*) separating man from his desires (Lacan's $a formula), Marvell's "square man" presents no such obstacle to enjoyment. The two-dimensional *hominem quadratum* combines, in Puttenham's terms, both the simplicity of geometric proportion and the steadfastness of nature's living art, giving to both poet and reader not less art, but more—the "better for [its] briefnesse and subtiltie of deuice."

Still, although Puttenham and Marvell highlight the quadrature's metrical unity and praise such unity for "keep[ing] him [the reader] within his bounds," the surface regularity of Marvell's earth-poem masks the volatility of its unplumbed depths. By wandering the edges of the "sober frame," we bend in the direction of nonhuman metrics: "The beasts are by their dens expressed," the square man muses, "And birds contrive an equal nest." If the sober frame is indeed a figure of the earth, it is perhaps the genius of Marvell's poem to literalize that figure, moving from one creaturely architect to the next. Rather than restricting matter's movement, the sober frame provides a site of poetic disequilibrium, allowing for endless material, architectural drift. "Within this sober frame," thought—or what amounts to the same, measurement—becomes a part of nature's endless work, with bodies serving as the framework for homes that do not separate inside from outside but rather fold inner and outer space—fitting tortoise-body within "tortoise-shell," earth-matter within earth-dwelling.[34]

This, we could say, is an architecture *of* the outside, to use Elizabeth Grosz's Deleuzian-inspired terminology. For Grosz, bodies, minds, cultures, and passions all take shape in relation to territory and frame, making architecture—or the act of framing—first among the arts. "The first artistic impulse," Grosz writes, "is thus not body-art but architecture-art. . . . This roots art not in the creativity of mankind but rather in a superfluousness of nature, in the capacity of the earth to render the sensory superabundant."[35] Before there is a self who makes, before there is a body to shelter, there is the art of framing, there is the constitution of the empty frame, which bodies and cultures later come to inhabit. The earth provides thought with sensory materials, and the frame organizes those materials into sensible compounds, always leaving open the possibility for future framings, future deterritorializations of the earth. The thinking thus inspired by Marvell's "sober frame" is altogether unlike Alberti's architect, who surveys and measures land from above. And whereas the "foreign architect" in the first stanza "vault[s] his brain" above the surface of the earth, leaving emptied "quarries" and felled "forests" in his wake, Marvell's poem foregrounds a creaturely geometry in which "bodies"—all bodies—"measure out their place."

A poem is also a type of house, and philosophers have variously celebrated and bemoaned the house that language provides. In Marvell's hands, the house in question is not a prison house, much less a place in which man truly dwells, but is more akin to a bird's "nest" or "tortoise-shell," in that it attests to a writing that happens from below, in the measurements, bisections, and arrangements of the earth. As we shall see, such earth-writing (or geo-metry) is made possible by the "sober frame," which, being emptied, allows for a structural poetics in which framing, rather than operating from above in either Alberti's or Plato's sense, emerges dynamically, materially, from the ground up.

In *What Is Philosophy?*, Deleuze and Guattari offer their own definition of the vaulted brain. In their definition, the relation between thought and earth takes center stage. They write:

> Vitalism has always had two possible interpretations: that of an Idea that acts, but is not—that acts therefore only from the point of view of an external cerebral knowledge . . . ; or that of a force that is but does not act—that is therefore a pure internal Awareness. . . . If the second interpretation seems to us imperative it is because the contraction that preserves is always in a state of detachment in relation to action or even to movement and appears as a pure contemplation without knowledge. . . . Even when one is a rat, it is through contemplation that one "contracts" a habit. It is still necessary to discover, beneath the noise of actions, those internal creative sensations or those silent contemplations that bear witness to a brain.[36]

Just as Marvell literalizes the subject of his poem, taking the "square man" or square poem as a figure of the earth, so too Deleuze and Guattari take the subject of "contemplation" literally: for them, contemplation is not separate from brain and body but is, rather, a form of physical contraction. The body contracts a stimulus. It folds that stimulus into perception. Contemplation, thus defined, is radically decentralized. "Even when one is a rat," Deleuze and Guattari wager, "it is through contemplation that one 'contracts' a habit." We become what we are—human, nonhuman (these distinctions start to break down)—by contracting the outside, like an inverted glove. The question is not, for Deleuze and Guattari: What is thought? The is-ness of the question masks its grounding in a field of material forces. Thought, conceived as sensation, pertains directly to the thought-brain and what is given to thought by earth, sky, water, and cosmos. "It is the brain that thinks," Deleuze and Guattari argue, "and not man." This holds true "even if one is a rat," or bird, or tortoise.

Although we typically look for thought housed in the human head, Deleuze and Guattari ask us to consider a thought without subject, without head. They write: "If the mental objects of philosophy, art, and science (that is to say, vital ideas) have a place, it will be in the deepest of the synaptic fissures, in the hiatuses, intervals, and meantimes of a nonobjectifiable brain, in a place where to go in search of them will be to create."[37] The higher functions of cognition only serve to habituate active–reactive circuits (the stuff of recognition), whereas the synaptic fissures, hiatuses, intervals, and so on of the thought-brain preserve thought in "a state of detachment," holding thought in creative suspense in relation to any end. The intervals of the thought-brain—we could say, too, the thought-poem, since poetry is language stretched across intervals, hiatuses, and gaps— militate against mastery and narrative ends, allowing, in Marvell's words, for an "easy" philosophy of material conversion. "I was but an inverted tree," Marvell's speaker relates (71.568).

Contemplation contracts the outside and folds it into the very stuff of thought. Unlike the vaulted brain of Marvell's "foreign architect," Deleuze and Guattari's thought-brain accords with the "easy philosopher" of *Upon Appleton House*, who, like the animal architects of the second stanza, forsakes activity to become a part of the material surround: sensing, folding, creating. A passionate passivity.

This is what it means to become a "square man" in Marvell's poem. In any case, Puttenham was right about the following: the "square man" or the contemplative man is low to the earth, his house more akin to the "low-roofed" tortoise dwellings than the vaulted house (or head) of man. But whereas Puttenham praises the "sober frame" for its straight lines and metrical unity, this proves only a passing figure, or a phase state in flux. Increasingly, the dance of figures takes over, and the poem's architecture becomes plastic, desultory, unbound. In the speaker's prosopopoeia of Nature, he welcomes this unbounded state and adopts a passive attitude toward nature's art, stating:

> Nature here hath been so free
> As if she said, "Leave this to me."
> Art would more neatly have defaced
> What she had laid so sweetly waste. (10.75–78)

It is this unique form of "leave"-taking that sees the speaker take leave of himself, ecstatically, among nature's inhuman art, that I foreground in this chapter. We see it foregrounded in the following:

> In ev'ry figure equal man. (6.48)

On the one hand, this line represents a conservative social order intent on reinscribing the human figure at every turn, making, as the saying goes, "man" the measure of all things. Within this inscriptive space, poetry stops short of altering man's image of himself: man's figure remains "ev'ry"-where the same, eternal, like Plato's triangle. On the other hand, as much as "In ev'ry figure equal man" inscribes "man" at every turn, it also works to de-scribe man from the space of inscription by effacing or de-facing man's sovereignty. In other words, Marvell's architectural anthropology reveals man to be continuous with, and everywhere the same as, the figures of the earth, utterly unexceptional. In the geometric language of Marvell's poem, the figure "man" is homeomorphic to all the rest; "man" is a deformed circle or a deformed square. Marvell: "I was but an inverted tree." From a topological viewpoint, these figures, while metrically distinct, are the *same* at a nonmetric level. The legible becomes illegible in this nonmetric space. Vision blurs.

Lee Edelman has a word for this nonmetric space: he calls it "homographesis." Always keen to bend rhetorical figures into untoward

shapes, Edelman's homographic writing resonates with the homeo-
morphisms at play in Marvell's architectonics. Both result in a certain
fading of the human subject. Edelman explains:

> "Writing," especially when taken as a gerund that approximates
> the meaning of "graphesis," functions to articulate identity only in
> relation to signs that are structured, as Derrida puts it, by their "non-
> self-identity." Writing, therefore, though it marks or describes those
> differences upon which the specification of identity depends, works
> simultaneously . . . to "de-scribe," efface, or undo identity by framing
> difference as the misrecognition of a "différance" whose negativity,
> whose purely relational articulation, calls into question the possibility
> of any positive presence or discrete identity. . . . In this sense homo-
> graphesis . . . de-scribes itself in the very moment of its inscription.[38]

"Nature," read homographically, takes on the status of a "writing"
in Marvell's poem, "writing" conceived as a differential articulation
or *différance* without fixed borders. Notable for my purposes, Derrida describes the figure "a" in *différance*, which is neither a word nor
a concept, as a kind of "tomb," a silent geometric marker that resists
metaphor and the interpretation of fixed meaning.[39] The letter "a,"
like all letters or figures in the alphabet, houses nothing, neither spirit
nor essence. Instead, the letter "a," written architecturally by Derrida
in the figure of a triangle, △, entombs every signified—including
the signified of "man"—in a play of untimely forces, materials,
and events.[40]

Passive Vitalism

Numerous critics have pointed to *Upon Appleton House*'s unique
place in the country-house tradition, to its untimely politics in a time
of civil war, and to its reactionary response to the rebels who were
challenging the very system of property and patronage that made
the country-house genre ideologically viable in the first place.[41] John
Rogers synthesizes these scholarly commentaries—the generic and
the political—by reading Marvell's poem alongside the writings of vitalist philosopher and puritan revolutionary Gerrard Winstanley. As
Rogers remarks:

In the country-house poem's idealist representation of his retreat
to his patron's [Lord Fairfax's] wood, Marvell . . . seems to validate
that mode of passive political aspiration, embraced most famously
by Winstanley, that concedes political change to the forces of natural development and growth. Entering the "yet green, yet growing
Ark" of Fairfax's wood (an ark superior to Noah's, fashioned without
the squaring and hewing of trees), the speaker, retreating from the
flooded fields, identifies his submergence in natural process with Noah's redemptive mission, hoping to purify a world corrupted by war.[42]

For Rogers, the "strangenesse of the action" in Marvell's poem denotes a negative, regressive action or inaction; it is because Marvell
retreats to the pastoral genre and its corresponding system of patronage that Rogers characterizes *Upon Appleton House* as an "evasion of
historical agency," a "green" dream in which nature (emblematized by
Fairfax's trees) supplants human action by restoring the earth to a
truly "leveled" plane—paradise regained.[43] Rogers exposes the failure
of Marvell's "green idealism" by turning to the latter's Mower poems,
where the green revolution envisioned in *Upon Appleton House* falls
into self-mutilating contradiction, self-resignation, and poetic irony.
Rogers writes:

> If in *Upon Appleton House* the retreat into Fairfax's wood constitutes
> Marvell's attempt, however transitory, to embrace the green idealism
> of a passive revolutionary such as Winstanley, then the Mower lyrics
> surely represent the poet's more distanced, ironic reflection on the vi-
> ability of a vitalist politics. Marvell lingers in the country-house poem
> over the exciting possibility of the participation of mankind and na-
> ture in a vitalist revolution; the Mower lyrics, however, persistently
> stage a troubled recognition that such a revolution is unachievable.[44]

From "vitalist politics" to "troubled recognition," the immanent conception of agency that Rogers detects in *Upon Appleton House* gives
way to a reading of the speaker's struggle for recognition against an
impassive nature.

This reading of *Upon Appleton House* points in the direction of
two different political horizons, both of which were legible in the

time Marvell was writing. They can be summarized as follows: Hegel or Spinoza—the first the philosopher of dialectics and universal Spirit, and the second the philosopher whose political naturalism reinserted God and man into the universal laws of nature. Rogers does not reference either philosopher, but he captures the problem of their aporia as it appeared to Marvell in the incipient struggles of seventeenth-century English radicalism. According to Rogers, "Marvell's pastoral poems struggle with one of the most troubling questions his century posed: what is the point of political action in the face of a revolution overseen and perhaps even controlled by a higher, inhuman power?"[45] Rogers answers this question in the same manner that Hegel answers Spinoza. In his lectures on the history of philosophy, Hegel remarks that "thought must begin by placing itself at the standpoint of Spinozism, to be a follower of Spinoza is the essential commencement of all Philosophy."[46] For Hegel, Spinozism is *only* the beginning, however, and a dangerous one at that. Spinoza's single substance, according to Hegel, is lifeless:

> The moment of negativity is what is lacking to this rigid motionlessness, whose single form of activity is this, to divest itself of their determination and particularity and cast them back into the one absolute substance, wherein they are simply swallowed up and all life in itself is utterly destroyed.[47]

For Hegel, the grandeur of Spinoza's single substance is what guarantees its ruin. Without the self-determination of individual agents, "whose single form of activity" is the outward projection of thought, Spinoza's single substance becomes passive and self-consuming, a motionless activity awaiting its own destruction.

Whereas Hegel saw Spinoza's naturalism as presaging the end of history, we might better understand Spinoza's naturalism as opening up history to an infinite play of figures—an architectural anthropology free of every teleological design. In the *Ethics* (1677), Spinoza famously remarks that he will "consider human actions and appetites just as if it were an investigation into lines, planes, or bodies."[48] With this geometric redefinition of human actions and appetites, the architectural language of lines, planes, and bodies serves as the theoretical foundation for what Hasana Sharp describes as Spinoza's "politics of renaturalization," whereby an impersonal politics of nature supplants the idea of man as self-determining, self-moving agent.[49] According to Spinoza, "Most of those who have written about the emotions [*affectibus*] and human conduct seem to be dealing not with natural phenomena that follow the common laws of Nature but with phenomena outside Nature. They appear to go so far as to conceive man in Nature as a kingdom within a kingdom."[50] Those who imagine man as "a kingdom within a kingdom" misunderstand human action as "phenomena outside Nature." Spinoza, by contrast, "mobilizes mathematics to reinsert human action into nature."[51] Nature, according to Spinoza, does not stand in opposition to the free activity of thought (Hegel), since all beings that exist are explications—Deleuze calls them "folds," alighting on the Latinate *pli* in the word explication—of the same universal substance: nature's book. Early on in the *Ethics*, Spinoza suggests that a narcissistic understanding of nature might have imprisoned us forever "had not Mathematics, which is concerned not with ends but only with the essences and properties of figures, revealed to men a different standard of truth."[52] Because mathematics provides us with an alternative lens in which to see ourselves and our place in nature, mathematics denies human exceptionalism in any form. In Sharp's words, "The lens of geometry exposes humanity as continuous with nature, operating according to the same norms and regularities."[53] Spinoza uses architectural figures "to make possible a new measure of ourselves, a new measure of 'man.'"[54]

In the following stanza, Marvell, too, introduces "a new measure of man" by conceiving of human form as one in a myriad of nature's "designs." He writes:

Humility alone designs
Those short but admirable lines,
By which, ungirt and unconstrained,
Things greater are in less contained.
Let others vainly strive t'immure
The circle in the quadrature!
These holy mathematics can
In ev'ry figure equal man. (6.41–48)

Unlike Alberti's architectural anthropology, in which the "design" alone figures humanity's elevation above the earth, as figure is to ground, Marvell's poem raises the ground to meet the figure. In the above lines, the *humus* (ground, earth) that is the etymological origin of "humility" becomes complicit in Marvell's "holy mathematics,"[55] such that, instead of "Humility alone designs," we may read: "Earth alone designs." The geo- in geometry has become strangely articulate.

SQUARING THE CIRCLE

As a figure of "Humility," man no longer builds eternal essences out of temporal clay. The ancient problem of squaring the circle, which had burdened mathematicians for ages and which Marvell humorously attributes to those who, beginning with the area of a circle, "vainly strive t'immure / The circle in the quadrature," amounted to imprisoning infinity (∞) within four corners. The problem, according to Zeno, was achingly simple: infinity is nonmetric. Just as one cannot fit infinity within the duration of time's arrow nor outrace a tortoise in the quicksand of infinite regress, so too one cannot fit a perfect circle in a perfect square. The reason why this is so disconcerting if you are a Euclidean geometer, or worse, if you are Thomas Hobbes, is that not being able to square the circle means that geometry is an imperfect system. As Amir Alexander explains, "If geometry is fully known, as [the followers of Euclid] declared it must be, then it should have no unsolved, not to mention insoluble, problems. The fact that it does suggests that it possesses dark corners where the light of reason does not shine."[56] Because followers of Euclid equated "holy mathematics" with timeless and knowable laws, they could not be satisfied with shapes that were irregular and imperfect. Postulate 5 of Euclid's *Elements*, known as Euclid's "parallel postulate," states, for example, that two straight lines, being parallel, will not touch if their interior angles are 90 degrees.[57] In other words, Euclid's geometry rules out of court the possibility that a line may curve and that two parallel lines may meet.

Fast-forward to the seventeenth century: Gottfried Wilhelm Leibniz was among the first to lay the foundations for the mathematical study of topology, the branch of geometry concerned with the properties of figures preserved under continuous deformation, such as bending, twisting, crumpling, and stretching. His post-Euclidean claim that the straight line is a curve and that parallel lines do meet made him the subject of Deleuze's late study *The Fold*, which saw in Leibniz's metaphysics a materialism that is "ceaselessly dividing," ceaselessly fractal: "The parts of matter form little swirls within a swirl, and in them there are other, smaller ones, and still more in the concave intervals of the swirls which touch one another. Matter thus offers a texture that is infinitely porous, that is spongy or cavernous without empty parts, since there is always a cavern in the cavern."[58] Whereas active perception detects only discrete shapes—triangles and squares—Leibniz's sub-representational materialism registers shapes that are perpetually folding, twisting, and connecting. Such an ontology poses serious problems for Euclidean rigor, both then and now. As historian of mathematics Carl B. Boyer explains, beginning in the seventeenth century with "the introduction of analytic geometry and the systematic representation of variable quantities,"[59] a chasm opened up between sensory experience and mathematical knowledge, roughly akin to the "dissociation of sensibility" described by T. S. Eliot in his essay on metaphysical poetry.[60] The problem, according to Boyer, is that while "mathematics knows no minimum interval of continuous magnitudes," the senses surely do.

> Inasmuch as the laws of science are formulated by induction on the basis of the evidence of the senses, on the face of it there can be no such thing in science as an instantaneous velocity, that is, one in which the distance and time intervals are zero. . . . The power of every sense organ is limited by a minimum of possible perception. We cannot, therefore, speak of motion or velocity, in the sense of a scientific observation, when either the distance or the corresponding time interval becomes so small that the minimum of sensation involved in its measurement is not excited—much less when the interval is assumed to be zero.[61]

We cannot speak of vanishing intervals. Science, however, was doing just that: by looking beyond the threshold of the possible into intervals infinitesimally close to zero, science was pushing the very boundaries of the sensible, tracing incipiencies and potentialities of matter at nonlocal, nonrepresentational intervals—that is to say, at speeds beyond capture. Brian Massumi writes of a similar problem in *Parables of the Virtual*. There, he refers to a study of the "missing half-second," in which sensory stimuli applied to the body of patients went undetected by cognition. The reason? The duration of the stimulus was less than half a second, "the minimum perceivable lapse."[62] The study thus raised an important, if underexplored, question: What is missed during the missing half second? The answer: everything. "The half second is missed not because it is empty, but because it is overfull, in excess of the actually-performed action and of its ascribed meaning."[63] What the study, in fact, showed was that conscious perception only makes up for a small fraction of the superfluity of bodily sensation. Or to put this in the language of Boyer above, there is an ocean of potentiality going unnoticed between zero and one. The conclusion that Massumi draws from this subcognitive superabundance is that the old philosophical hobbyhorses, "will and consciousness," are, in fact, "*subtractive*. They are *limitative, derived functions* that reduce a complexity too rich to be functionally expressed."[64] Whereas philosophy tends to think of the mind as something added to matter, as in the case of Marvell's mind-vaulting architect, the missing half-second shows that mind is actually subtractive. "This requires a reworking of how we think about the body," Massumi writes. Marvell's architect is a bit like an inverted tortoise, surveying from above when he should be surveying from below, in the middle of things, where everything happens.

Leibniz was not the only one to craft a geometry at imperceptible speed (close to zero, but not quite). Marvell's country-house poem performs a similar feat by subjecting architectural figures, including the figure "man," to a continuous process of deformation. A topological survey of Fairfax's estate, *Upon Appleton House* deforms both its "place" and its visual perspective, resulting in the poem's notorious "misshapen" images, the blurriness of which T. S. Eliot denounced.[65] Although Eliot singles out stanza 7 for special opprobrium, criticizing "the attitude of the house toward its master" as "absurd" and accusing Marvell of falling "into the even commoner error of images which are over-developed or distracting," and "which support nothing but their own misshapen bodies,"[66] he misses the fundamental aspect of the poem's composition: its movement, its speed. In the following stanza, we are given architecture at a blur:

> Yet thus the laden house does sweat,
> And scarce endures the Master great:
> But where he comes the swelling hall
> Stirs, and the square grows spherical;
> More by his magnitude distressed,
> Than he is by its straitness pressed:
> And too officiously it slights
> That in itself which him delights. (7.49–56)

Where philosophers and mathematicians failed, *Upon Appleton House* succeeds: the square house becomes circular. Everything here begins with movement: "the laden house does sweat"; "the Master great . . . comes"; "the swelling hall / Stirs"; "the square grows spherical." "Ungirt and unconstrained," Marvell's humble geometry lacks in Euclidean rigor, but it more than makes up for it in non-Euclidean elasticity. By raising illegitimate figures up to the earth's surface, his poem brings infinity down to earth, not by immuring the "circle in the quadrature," but by beginning elsewhere, on "unconstrained" soil. He begins, that is, in the excluded middle, with shapes that are similar but inexact: not circular but "spherical," not square but "straitness pressed." In short, Marvell's poem thinks figuration in Massumi's sense as virtual.

The "sober frame" is, therefore, "sober" not because it restricts material excess. This interpretation has led to confusion among critics who see a contradiction between the ecstatic transformations of the previous stanza (stanza 7) and the conservative semantics of the next:

> So Honour better lowness bears,
> Than that unwonted Greatness wears.
> Height with a certain grace does bend,
> But low things clownishly ascend.
> And yet what needs there here excuse,

Where ev'ry thing does answer use?
Where neatness nothing can condemn,
Nor pride invent what to contemn? (8.57–64)

How to square this stanza's emphasis on "neatness" and "use" with the
round peg of stanza 7, where nothing seems to "answer use," but answers only to the excitement, the sub-representational nonmetrics, of
rounding, of queering the line? Again, Eliot is a useful foil. For, despite Eliot's criticisms of Marvell, the answer is already to be found in
Eliot's interpretation of the structure of metaphysical poetry. Before
Raymond Williams, before Brian Massumi, Eliot pinpoints what
he calls a "*structure* of . . . feeling" operating beneath the language of
the poem:

> It is to be observed that the language of these poets is, as a rule, sim-
> ple and pure; in the verse of George Herbert, this simplicity is carried
> as far as it can go—a simplicity emulated without success by numer-
> ous modern poets. The *structure* of the sentences, on the other hand,
> is sometimes far from simple, but this is not a vice; it is a fidelity to
> thought and feeling.[67]

In addition to George Herbert, Eliot singles out Marvell for "producing an effect of great speed" in his poetry, an effect not opposed to
simplicity but in resonance with it. Eliot's theory of structure is already poststructuralist because it theorizes structure in tension with
an affective base that is indifferent to cognitive aims. Indifferent, but
not opposed. Whereas language produces regular, metric units (the
"square man" celebrated by Puttenham, for example), it also mixes
with nonmetric depths, plumbing areas of thought-feeling that are
detached from anticipation—generative, but not reproductive.

The same holds true for geometry. As Carla Mazzio points out,
"Although 'mathematics' [in the early modern period] is idealized as
the vehicle of cognitive orientation and cultural organization, basic
geometric form poses problems of being and knowing."[68] This is
because "the former [mathematics] was aligned with rational abstraction and the latter [geometric form] with sensory and affective
subjection."[69] Quoting John Dee's "Mathematicall Preface" to the

first English translation of Euclid's *Elements* (1570), Mazzio writes, "God of course created the world in number, weight, and measure, but when we separate these categories, we . . . see that geometric 'formalities,' while potentially 'rauishing,' prove uncomfortable allurements at best." "Geometric figures inhabit an ideal realm, but come to life only when that realm fractures and turns against itself. Affect is produced within an increasingly disoriented geometric realm."[70] Mazzio differentiates physical form from abstract number in order to put "the three-dimensional" body back in our accounts of early modern calculation. In doing so, she underscores the emotional drama of mathematical shapes. While I share Mazzio's interest in a *more geometrico* form of physical ravishment, my goal is not to *add* the body back to geometrical figures, just as it is not my attempt, qua Badiou, to *subtract* mental figures from material substance; both of these arguments rest on the linearism that they seek to subvert. That is, they connect body and number in a linear sequence of addition and subtraction (body plus number, in the case of Mazzio; number minus body, in the case of Badiou). However, neither the addition of the body nor its subtraction addresses the *supplementary* nature of figures. To read the mutual implications of form-matter rather than their sequence (form and *then* matter) would be to reinvent geometric figures not as supports for humanity's mental abstractions but rather as proofs of the earth's incredible geometry. Nature in this sense is not the object of human measurement but instead the *event* of matter's masturbatory self-involvement—its writing, measuring, and framing of itself: a strange geo-poesy.

Against the law of noncontradiction, Marvell shows that the "sober frame" can and does exist in an ecstatic, drunken state. (Eliot says as much, though he forgets.) Whereas Ben Jonson's "To Penshurst" (1616) lays out the importance of algorithmic proportion, contrasting "Those proud, ambitious heaps" of foreign form to the modest yet harmonious proportions of Penshurst, where, it is said, the human body not only lives but "dwell[s]" within the architectural frame (101, 102),[71] Marvell's poem sees dwelling as something other than the containment or expression of human form. Whether he is referring to birds' nests, or tortoise shells, or nature's art, architecture, for Marvell, emerges from outside, from the thinking earth-brain itself. Moreover, because poetry, like thought, already comes prefilled by poetic convention (the entire image repertoire of what has been said before), Marvell turns to the "sober frame" to empty it of its human contents and return thought to the writing of the earth. Deleuze and Guattari explain why: "The painter does not paint on an empty canvas, and neither does the writer write on a blank page; but the page or canvas is already so covered with preexisting, preestablished clichés that it is first necessary to erase, to clean, to flatten," to sober, as Marvell would say, "even to shred, so as to let in a breath of air."[72]

The "sober frame" performs this act of erasure by turning the subtractive ontology of Alberti and company on its head.[73] As critics have long noted, the speaker of *Upon Appleton House* fades from the frame, as if caught up in the very same "matter" surveyed. The speaker, in other words, is less an active "I"/eye surveying the poem from above than he is a figure among figures, emerging only to collapse back into the groundwork of the poem. Marvell's poem subtracts the human subject. The result: not emptiness at all, but rather material multiplicity, erotic potentiality, figural excess, and folds within folds. Marvell's "slow eyes" contain multitudes:

> While with slow eyes we these survey,
> And on each pleasant footstep stay,
> We opportunely may relate
> The progress of this house's fate. (ll.81–84)

The "slow eyes" of Marvell's poem, though blurry, slow down the action–reaction circuits of human perception so that the missing half-second or zero-degree of change can enter the frame of our attention—if only fleetingly.

Architecture of Perversion: A Deleuzian Digression

In the middle, load-bearing chapter of *Difference and Repetition*, Deleuze takes aim at what he calls the dogmatic "Image of thought": the figure of the rational mind that synthesizes the chaos of sensory experience to produce stable, recognizable objects.[74] By contrast, one can imagine, Deleuze argues, a geometry of pure mutation, so that figures are defined not by their discreteness but by their potential for transformation.[75]

Such a geometry was initially proposed by the ancient geometer Archimedes in "On the Method," who tried to show that a square could achieve the same area as a circle if and only if we relax Euclidean rigor. By decomposing geometric figures into their infinitesimal parts, Archimedes pointed the way toward a practical geometry, one that better reflects the experience of living in a world of movement and change, where a straight line is not the closest distance between two points and where parallel lines do bend and meet. Deleuze's mutational image of thought adheres to the practical geometry of Archimedes and others and is therefore inclusive of discordant figures—figures that are not merely sensible but *insensible*, that produce a shock to thought. As Claire Colebrook explains in her gloss of Deleuze, if we do without the dogmatic image of thought, the one that, in the Euclidean language of Alberti and others, makes a circle a circle, and a square a square, "and consider the syntheses of images in themselves then we may have to consider a discordant subject. There would not be a self *who thinks,* but a thinking that occurs as an unwilled event and that cannot be reduced to a single locus or genesis."[76]

Although Deleuze turns to Freud and Antonin Artaud to imagine this discordant subject, for whom thought is no longer active or willed but rather passive and *forced* (Deleuze uses the language of the "intruder" to imagine this forcing of thought), it is primarily art—or the free connection of images—that provides Deleuze's philosophy with images freed from Euclidean reason. According to Deleuze, one always begins to paint, to write, or to think in confrontation with the images handed down by tradition, by reason, and by the man of good sense; these images are always clichés of thought because they relate the diversity of sense experience to the demands of recognition. For Deleuze, by contrast, true thinking, or true art, begins in the absence of the image, after one has, after great struggle, emptied the frame. Unlike the architectural anthropology of Alberti, which figures man's elevation above the earth, as figure is to ground, Deleuze's "thought without image" raises the ground to meet the figure, thus sending the human along virtual paths.[77]

"Everything culminates," Deleuze writes, "in the great principle: that there is—before all else, and despite everything—an affinity or a filiation—or perhaps it should be called a philiation—of thought with the truth; in short, a good nature and a good desire, grounded in the last instance upon the *form of analogy in the Good*."[78] What is the Good, exactly? In the mind of reason, it is the resemblance between the object of thought and the thought of the object. Between these two poles, there is both a "filiation," in the form of analogy—the object of thought only becomes an "object" when thought is imagined as a unifying machine—and a "philiation," in the form of amorous accord. Philosophy is not only a resemblance machine but also, Deleuze claims, an Oedipal machine because it structures thought in accordance with a desire for the unit, the whole, the metrical—that is to say, the phallus. Thus it is no surprise that Deleuze characterizes the whole of Plato's philosophy as an Oedipal operation. In the *Logic of Sense*, Deleuze writes: "The theory of Ideas must be sought in a will to select." "The purpose of division is not at all to divide a genus into species, but, more profoundly, to select lineages: to distinguish pretenders; to distinguish the pure from the impure, the authentic from the inauthentic."[79] Plato traces transcendental Truth from the empirical given, selecting only those traits that accord with the principle of Identity; in short, he traces lineages. Like Charles Darwin in *The Descent of Man*, philosophy begins with the empirical object ("Man") and traces its emergence back to the very conditions of thought. In Kant's *Critique of Pure Reason*, for instance, Kant defines the man of reason as a being endowed with the faculties of apperception, comprehension, and recognition. In this way, Kant weds the object-form ("object = x") to the emergence of thought; he folds the empirical into the transcendental, making thought itself, the foundation of thought, one of pure recognition. If the empirical resembles the transcendental, and if the world of appearance resembles itself in the image of the true, that is because, Deleuze argues, the image of thought comes from outside. Like the image of wholeness reflected in the mirror, the image of thought has been conceived as a container of the identical, a house of pure forms, or a memorandum of objects to be encountered. The measure of space and time, the synthesis of parts, and the recognition of the "object = x" are the building blocks of universal "man," who by these means becomes, indeed, the measure of all things. The house of Being presumes *philia* as its foundation and the man of good reason as its architect and custodian.

Nevertheless, given that the image of thought has, since Plato, been conceived of in Euclidean terms as the joining of parts under one self-same roof, and has thus domesticated thought by marrying it to function or recognition, can we, instead, think of thought as an intruder—as what is not contained but rather deforms both the container and the contained?

In the first image, "thought is thereby filled with no more than an image of itself, one in which it recognizes itself the more it recognizes things: this is a finger, this is a table, Good morning Theaetetus."[80] The unity of form and function in this image gives rise to both the man of good reason, who recognizes stable objects and the man who is "master of his own house," who recognizes himself in the image of one who cognizes recognizable objects. Like the "I function" in Lacan's analysis of the "mirror stage," the child who perceives the outer image (prototypically the mother) is "filled with no more than an image of itself."[81] What is outside is therefore folded inward, becoming the "future perfect" foundation of the child's progressive mastery of time and space: in the image, I become what I will have been. Man is an essentially retroactive animal: although the thought of our world emerges in non-Euclidean space (chaos), we imagine conceptual lineages, or the always already of "good sense." Deleuze suggests an alternative image of thought, which is that of a primordial discord. Instead of preformed concepts, which dictate in advance what is possible for me to say or think and only relate thought to the sensible objective world, Deleuze proposes perverse folds—that is to say, encounters with objects that do not unfold meaning or identity (the "I" of recognition), but rather peel away that identity, revealing a groundless ground beneath the architecture of sense, "a thought without image." Its exemplary figure is not the man of reason, for whom even the absence of the image is, like the missing phallus, an image to be recalled; its figure is the problematic figure of the "body without organs," created, with no shortage of cruelty or "misosophy," by Artaud:

Artaud pursues ... the terrible revelation of a thought without image, and the conquest of a new principle which does not allow itself to be represented. He knows that difficulty as such, along with its cortège of problems and questions, is not a *de facto* state of affairs but a *de jure* structure of thought; that there is an acephalism in thought just as there is an amnesia in memory, an aphasia in language and an agnosia in sensibility. He knows that thinking is not innate, but must be engendered in thought. He knows that the problem is not to direct or methodically apply a thought which pre-exists in principle and in nature, but to bring into being that which does not yet exist.[82]

How does one create "an acephalism in thought," as Artaud proposes?

Although Kant and the phenomenological tradition after him theorize the proprioceptive powers of the body as a primary unit of measure, or a matrix of good sense, achieving ever-greater forms of coordination and mastery over itself and the world outside it, the alignment of motor function, thought, and aesthetics has a much longer history. The history of the aesthetic organism can be traced back to Plato, but it finds a striking articulation in the ancient Roman architect Marcus Vitruvius's *Ten Books on Architecture*. There, Vitruvius writes how "Nature has planned the human body so that the members correspond in their proportions to its complete configuration," and how "if a man lies on his back with hands and feet outspread, and the center of a circle is placed on his navel, his fingers and toes will be touched by the circumference."[83] If, for Kant, "x" marks the spot of transcendental apperception, for Vitruvius, that spot or that "x" is the navel. The body from navel to circumference provides the architect schooled in geometry with the measurements needed to master the world of sensation. Although the body of phenomenology and likewise the Vitruvian body both give form to the world of matter and so find their forms everywhere reflected, as in Marvell's poem, "in ev'ry figure equal man," this body like any architectural body is, according to Deleuze, built on quicksand. In fact, the definition of ideal figures proves a sleight of hand within the history of scientific thought because it selects from problematic figures those that fall in line with an axiomatic order, which is always a paternal order of resemblance.

Platonism is, in this sense, a paternal model. It begins with the figure of the father and distinguishes legitimate from illegitimate copies. However, like other paternal narratives, such as Freud's *Totem and Taboo*, the omnipotent father is always already a dead father. The primal father is a myth. For example, in *Totem and Taboo*, the murderous sons obey the father only after the father is dead. The name of the father only works retroactively, in the father's absence. Likewise, in Darwin's *On the Origin of Species*, the primal ancestor is an asymptotic figure. As Darwin explains, any attempt to find a genetic blueprint that would explain the evolution of man must contend with the infinite variety of species. From this perspective, humanity is no longer a blueprint unfolding through time but rather a deviation among deviations. Like the phallic father in Freud's narrative, humanity only appears against the backdrop of its own absence.

On the one hand, Plato presents the myth of the ideal model: he "constructs the immanent model or the foundation-test according to which the pretenders should be judged and their pretensions measured."[84] On the other hand, this same model can only be defined in relation to simulacra. The image of the body as a totalized whole fills thought with an image of itself, but this image is radically discordant. Before thought falls in love with its own image, thought first contends with perverse doubles, images that fly away from the body in illegitimate figures—figures that are *against* the father—a misosophy of thought. Thus when Lacan speaks of the phallus as symbol of the father, he speaks of it as hopelessly detachable, as coming and going, forever missing from its place, and does so in architectural terms: the phallus is not the penis, Lacan says; it is the body's imaginary keystone, the "tip" of the image, its imaginary steeple.[85] This is why the phallus is always at risk of falling off. Indeed, this falling off has always already happened; that is its future perfect threat: not that it may someday go missing, but that, from the vantage of the child's anxiety over its own image, the phallus is always already lost. The virtual body is a body in pieces. There is always one part too few. Read as an Oedipal structure, then, the image of thought that subtends our apprenticeship to ideal figures—including the figure of the phallus—submits thought to the promise of future completion, to the dream of being in a well-ordered house, where everything belongs.

Deleuze's architecture of perversion follows psychoanalysis in turning thought against the image of a well-ordered house. No doubt, psychoanalysis has been rightly attacked for limiting sexuality to an image of resemblance, to an image modeled, moreover, on the vital order of need. Nevertheless, elsewhere in the *Three Essays on the Theory of Sexuality*, Freud overturns this very model. Freud is the first to reverse Freudianism. By freeing sexuality from the body's sensory apparatus, Freud unhinges sexuality from its object. Sexuality, Freud suggests, is an architectural abnormality—a thought without image. Freud writes:

> It has been brought to our notice that we have been in the habit of regarding the connection between the sexual instinct and the sexual object as more intimate than it in fact is. Experience of the cases that are considered abnormal has shown us that in them the sexual instinct and the sexual object are merely soldered together—a fact which we have been in danger of overlooking in consequence of the uniformity of the normal picture, where the object appears to form part and parcel of the instinct. We are thus warned to loosen the bond that exists in our thoughts between instinct and object. It seems probable that the sexual instinct is in the first instance independent of its object; nor is its origin likely to be due to its object's attractions.[86]

"Soldered together": it is as if Freud, the same Freud who later submits sexuality to resemblance, forgets his prior argument about the discordance of the sexual subject—which is to say, a subject *subjected* to the disorder of sex.

Consider a mythical image: the child coupled to his mother's breast, in full harmony with the image of this omnipotent, adult figure who not only caters to his every need but also mirrors the self-sufficiency that the child imagines to be his own. Now, from the vantage of the "soldered together" object, this image can only appear in retrospect as myth. For what Freud says, before forgetting his own argument, is that the sexual instinct has no object. "At its origin," Freud writes, "[sexuality] attaches itself to one of the vital somatic functions; it has as yet no sexual object, and is thus auto-erotic."[87] Like Lucretius's simulacra, which peel away from bodies in unforeseeable directions, sexuality, according to Freud, peels or folds away from the "vital somatic functions" in unforeseeable ways, causing them to become airy, detached, and free-floating. Sexuality distills the vital order in a dance of figures. In the case of the sexualized mouth, Freud writes, "if that significance persists, these same children when they are grown up will become epicures in kissing, will be inclined to perverse kissing."[88] The reason why this statement is so striking is that it reverses Freud's previous claim about resemblance; here, the finding of an object is, in fact, a refinding—not of the mother, not of original wholeness, but of a morcellated, "soldered together" object. Resemblance begins to appear more like a machinic assemblage of parts. With the onset of sexuality, mouth and breast no longer join metaphorically; the parts of the body have become free-floating and only meet by way of perversion. Jean Laplanche uses the figure of the Lucretian "clinamen" (the swerve) to describe sexuality's deviant course: "Sexuality in its entirety is in the slight deviation, the *clinamen* from the function. It is in the *clinamen* insofar as the latter results in an autoerotic internalization."[89]

Sexuality is a problematic figure because it links parts without telos or model. Sexuality deviates from life's course. Although Freud vacillates on this point, it is clear from the *Three Essays* that the perversions detected in later life, such as "perverse kissing," are the foundations or unfoundations of "normal" object choice. Sexuality as ontology is problematic from the start. What it aspires to is not the complete object but rather parts soldered together by chance. Instead of the subject conceived as the architect of the body's aims and desires, sexuality happens *to* the subject, passively, and continues to incline toward parts that are always incomplete and roughly sketched: mouth, breast, voice, gaze, and so on. Sexuality begins with the desiderata of parts, a picture that is never complete.

To incline this discussion back in the direction of Marvell, let us consider one of Freud's earliest case studies. In his 1910 essay, "Leonardo da Vinci and a Memory of His Childhood," Freud investigates the Renaissance artist's reputation for problematic figures, including many unfinished pieces and grotesque anatomical drawings. Freud speculates that da Vinci's tendency to leave work either unfinished or monstrously disproportioned owes to the indefatigability of his *"infantile sexual researches"*—that is, his search for sexual knowledge:

> If we reflect on the concurrence in Leonardo of his over-powerful instinct for research and the atrophy of his sexual life . . . the core of his nature, and the secret of it, would appear to be that after his curiosity had been activated in infancy in the service of sexual interest he succeeded in sublimating the greater part of his libido into an urge for research.[90]

The result, Freud says, of da Vinci's sublimated sexuality is an exhaustive series of figures—faces, torsos, viscera, fragments—with no recognizable outlines. Outside his best-known works of art, "he was no longer able to limit his demands, to see the work of art in isolation and to tear it from the wide context to which he knew it belonged. After the most exhausting efforts to bring to expression in it everything which was connected with it in his thoughts, he was forced to abandon it in an unfinished state or to declare that it was incomplete."[91] Freud claims that da Vinci's *"infantile sexual researches"* were triggered early in life by a traumatic encounter with his mother, whose exorbitant affections overwhelmed his childish understanding. What is noteworthy about Freud's conclusion is not that it reduces artistic and intellectual struggle to sex; what is noteworthy is that it defines sexuality as impossible, such that no effort at exhausting its combinatorics can succeed. Da Vinci's failures, if we can call them failures, testify to a sexual drive that has no object (no recognizable object) other than the unfinished work.

Green Thought

What does it mean to think green with Marvell? This question turns on what Marvell himself, in his 1668 pastoral poem, "The Garden," calls "green thought," which critics such as William Empson have rightly interpreted as Marvell's most "analytic" statement on the relationship between being and dwelling, earth and world. Analytic, but also highly perplexing. Marvell sets several poetic traps before the reader, and it is part and parcel of the "green thought" imagined by Marvell that we, the readers, become tangled in his verbal nets. "The chief point of [Marvell's 'The Garden']," Empson argues in *Some Versions of Pastoral*, "is to contrast and reconcile conscious and unconscious states, intuitive and intellectual modes of apprehension."[92] In other words, the point of the poem is to reconcile thought and world. "And yet," Empson adds, "that distinction," between mind and world, "is never made, perhaps could not have been made; [Marvell's] thought is implied by his metaphors."[93] Though it goes unremarked, Empson's use of "implied" here is crucial, for it derives from the root word *pli* (fold). Marvell's "implied" way of thinking connotes perplication, complication, implication, explication, and replication—the many senses of "folding" that we have thus far attributed to Marvell's architectural figures.

The first poetic snare (the lesser of the two) that we encounter in "The Garden" resembles the figure of the vaulted "brain" that we saw in the first stanza of *Upon Appleton House*. Just as the "architect" in that poem "did for a model"—"in pain"—"vault his brain" by seeming to transcend the materials of the earth, so the poet, in Marvell's "The Garden," tries "vainly," through "uncessant labours," "To win the palm, the oak, or bays"—figures of military, civic, and poetic achievement, respectively (1.1, 3, 2).[94] Whereas the architect extracts materials by emptying quarries and leveling forests, the poet, similarly, extracts glory in the form of a crown made of laurel. The propinquity of the two stanzas is further buttressed by the architectural structure of "The Garden," which repeats *Upon Appleton House*'s eight-line stanza of tetrameters, giving it the same "square" structure that Puttenham "likened to the earth." The structure of "The Garden" mimics once again the vain striving of those "foreign architect[s]" and poets who, by thought alone, "vainly strive t'immure / The circle in the quadrature"—this time not in Palladian villas, but rather in crowns of palm, oak, and laurel. Poetry becomes mere "toil," mere building, when it imposes form from above (1.6). In "The Garden," nature not only "upbraid[s]" such "toils" (1.6), but also loosens (un-braids) the grip humans have on artistic creation, giving us a poetry that is, as in *Upon Appleton House*, "ungirt and unconstrained." One need not enclose nature, tame and domesticate it, the speaker of Marvell's "The Garden" suggests, for "all flow'rs and all trees" here "do" already "close /

To weave the garlands of repose" (1.7–8). Nature *creates*. Better still, nature "weave[s]" (1.8) materiality by abstracting it from mere use and re-posing it as art. Nature is an art of framing. And like the "sober frame" of *Upon Appleton House*, which we said grounds architecture in the figures of the earth, so "the garlands of repose" woven by Marvell's earth-poem *pose* the problem of thinking green—*with* and not against the materials of the earth.

This is the poem's first snare—thinking as a form of tangling removed from productive "toil." In the seventeenth century, it was common to call a hunting net used for catching game a "toil," after the Middle French *toile*, meaning a spider's web.[95] The word later lost its animal derivation and with it the spider's architectural prowess, becoming a form of reverse capture instead: a snare for wild animals. Marvell's use of "toil" is, therefore, all the more peculiar. In Marvell's hands, to "toil," in the sense of laboring to enclose nature, ultimately leaves one toiled—that is, tangled in a net not of one's choosing, but nonetheless of one's making. Marvell's active subject is hopelessly self-thwarting. Such overdetermined meanings come to a point in the figure of the "garland." This figure lays bare the vexed relation between symbol and allegory that we saw in chapters 1 and 2, highlighting the poet's symbolic mastery over nature on the one hand while braiding multiple temporal and material forces on the other, forces that do not testify to a higher, sublimated meaning, but rather peel away in the direction of multicausal relations—referential nets.

The closest allegorical references are to Spenser and Milton. Marvell's "garland" closely replicates that of Spenser's Redcrosse Knight, who, in book 1 of *The Faerie Queene*, before "two goodly trees," tries "to frame / A girlond" to symbolize his love for Fidessa (the false Duessa in disguise). Likewise, in book 9 of *Paradise Lost*, Adam frames a "garland wreathed for Eve"—"a garland, to adorn / Her tresses, and her rural labors crown." At the news of Eve's trespass, Adam "Down dropt" the garland, "and all the faded roses shed." Layered within these allegorical references is a thicket of material forces that resist human toil. The tree that Redcrosse wounds exposes a "rift" or trauma that, try as he might, no garland can suture or heal (see chapter 1 of this book).

Similarly, when Eve "Forth reaching to the [forbidden] fruit," "plucked," and "ate," triggering a planetary phase shift of epic proportions, the earth registers this trauma in the form of a scar: "Earth felt the wound" (I explore this wounded figure in chapter 5). As with Redcrosse, Adam's "garland" points to a "rift" in the geologic record; his allegorical symbol becomes a record of extinction: "and all the faded roses shed." Artistic toil, read through this net or network of allegorical references, reveals a chaos of material forces that problematize and ensnare human attempts at mastery. This is why in his writing on the German *Trauerspiel*, Walter Benjamin defines allegory as a fundamentally natural historical mode of dramatization because it intensifies and "upbraid[s]" our relation to the earth. In allegory, nature and art are woven together. They are mutually intensifying.[96]

This brings us to the second snare set by Marvell's poem: How should we read the mind's "withdrawal" in the following stanza?

> Meanwhile the mind, from pleasures less,
> Withdraws into its happiness:
> The mind, that ocean where each kind
> Does straight its own resemblance find;
> Yet it creates, transcending these,
> Far other worlds, and other seas;
> Annihilating all that's made
> To a green thought in a green shade. (6.41–48)

Critics have tarried over the competition of forces seemingly in opposition in the above lines. Rogers, we saw before, reads Marvell's vitalism as a "green dream" in which nature does all, obviating the need for human action or struggle. For Empson, by contrast, "the point is not that these two," nature and thought, "are essentially different but that they must cease to be different so far as either is to be known."[97] I want to pose a different reading that takes the mind's "withdrawal" neither as a separation from nor fusion with nature but rather as an *intensification* of the earth's chaos. Thinking here derives from "pleasures less," which could mean a lessening of pleasure, or a lessening of the self from too much excitement, as in, I become less myself due to the ego-shattering intensity of too much pleasure. Or, as Marvell puts in the lines that follow, "pleasures less" could have to do with the experience of passing out of existence, as when the speaker says, "I pass," or I expire (note, too, the language of falling and the "fall," of "Stumbling," below). The more the pleasure–unpleasure tension of "pleasures less" increases, the "less" the speaker becomes:

> What wondrous life is this I lead!
> Ripe apples drop about my head;
> The luscious clusters of the vine
> Upon my mouth do crush their wine;
> The nectarene, and curious peach,
> Into my hands themselves do reach;
> Stumbling on melons, as I pass,
> Insnared with flow'rs, I fall on grass. (5.33–40)

Here again we are "Insnared" by nature's web, only this time not because of excessive "toils," but because the speaker, having relinquished toil, is free to "pass" out of existence, to "fall," wander, and become less human and more plantlike by absorbing "pleasures less." The final line, "I fall on grass," closely replicates Isaiah 40:6, "All flesh is grass," but with a playful twist, as if to fall were the opposite of man's fallen condition. Here, falling, going outside oneself, is a homecoming—a return to grass.

A return, but also a displacement. Although Marvell's poem is surely interested in place, in this case, the place of the garden, its topographic measures stress far more the active displacements— both sexual and creative—of a writing that has no fixed location. Marvell's topographic descriptions *de*-scribe the place of the speaker. The result is less that of a topographic survey, written from above, than a writing generated from below.

In *The Interpretation of Dreams*, Freud uses a topographic language to describe the landscape of the mind and its division into three houses: conscious, preconscious, and unconscious. As in Marvell's "The Garden," Freud uses the topographic model in order to map the distribution of "pleasures less"—what he calls "psychical locality."[98] Freud's psychic topography takes place at the very frontier of the mind-body, where libidinal energy folds and unfolds to generate psychic interiors. Freudian psychology is quite literally a land survey, taking his metaphoric language of topography seriously as a mapping of physical space. Still, Freud was never content with this spatial analogy. Despite the spatial unity of his architectural drawings, the unconscious, as Freud theorizes it, isn't a "place" at all but rather a series of seismic shocks, testifying to the indeterminacy of the land qua psychic locality. "Strictly speaking," Freud writes, "there is no need for the hypothesis that the psychical systems are actually arranged in a *spatial* order. It would be sufficient if a fixed order were established by the fact that in a given psychical process the excitation passes through the systems in a particular temporal sequence."[99] Although Freud borrows the language of topography from the physical sciences, his topographic survey is never fully presentable in a "spatial order," despite what his architectural figures would have us think; they are, rather, the effects of a "temporal sequence," and are thus the aftereffects of an energetic process passing from one system—unconscious, preconscious, conscious—to the next. Freudian figures are therefore only knowable in *transit*; as soon as Freud maps the interior spaces of the mind onto Euclidean figures, he demolishes those figures as the frozen forms of an otherwise unruly process of figuration or earth-writing. In this way, Freudian psychology repeats and unearths the plastic *figura* described by Auerbach. Like Marvell, he renders the self the mere aftereffect of underground displacements, figural transformations, and unchecked libidinal energy—excitations that never remain in place but expire from one figure to the next; they "pass."

In other words, Freud's metaphors are no less "implied" (to use Empson's word) than Marvell's. Nor is Marvell any less concerned with the problem of reconciling the dynamic transformations of "pleasures less" (a pairing that is itself highly unstable) with the "*spatial* order" of the poem—itself a highly regular object. We see this tension increase with each passing line, as pleasure turns to more pleasure, and as these intensifying transitions lead to a diminution of the self—a "mind, from pleasures" *made* "less." By the end of stanza 5, the "I" that first "lead" a life of pleasure retires (fittingly, in that "The Garden" is a retirement poem) into the tangled intensities of the earth's prodigious excess.

Marvell's poem is not alone in this regard. "The Garden" owes its flare for erotic self-dismissal to the pleasure-seeking man of Milton's "L'Allegro," whom, Gordon Tesky notes, all but disappears from the poetic frame for lack of a grammatical subject. "The speaker's object presence is so vague," Tesky writes, "that he at first lacks any clear grammatical subject, being introduced into the landscape by the participial phrases, 'Oft list'ning how the hounds and horn' (line 53) and 'Sometime walking not unseen' (line 57)."[100] "Not unseen" is a circumspect form of visibility, to be sure, but Milton's peripatetic subject fades in and from the landscape like a form of verbal parapraxis or a slip of the tongue: the poem's dreamwork lets *slip*—"pass," "fall," or "stumble"—an absent subject, driving the poem toward grammatical incompletion. Like a column without its capital (from the Latin *caput*, meaning "head"), the lines of "L'Allegro" wander headless. Milton's pleasure-seeking man is a headless subject.

Now, it is this headless condition that, strangely enough, leads to what Marvell calls "green thought." For it is not simply thought *about* the environment that greens Marvell's speaker, as if mind and matter met from opposite locales. More radically, Marvell imagines thought as topographically "implied": thought derives, it enfolds and unfolds from the material outside. This is not to say that thought turns *away* from matter toward airy abstraction; rather, the more interesting point is that matter is already a process of abstraction. Matter thinks in Marvell's poem. Readers have taken "the mind" in line 41 of Marvell's poem as evidence of a vaulted figure—*the* vaulted figure, that of human cognition—whereas the poem gives no such proof. If the tendency has been to read "the mind" as housed within the human head, we have already seen that Marvell (like Milton) pays no mind to such vaulted figures, preferring the agrammatical and ahuman wandering of the poem's empty frame instead. Again, "the mind" has no given location, and the errant topography of Marvell's poem should alert us to thought's wandering displacements: from sexual objects like "Ripe apples" and "curious peach" to their sublimated form as "green thought." Thought is nowhere present, yet it is everywhere renewed, refreshed, repeated. This is what it means to green in the intransitive sense of the verb. By "Annihilating all that's made," all that is sedentary in the world of thought, thought throws open its windows to a little chaos, to the winds of "nihil" coming from outside. This repetition of annihilation/creation, like the increase and decrease of "pleasures less," and the stanza's final rhyming couplet, "made" and "shade," suggests that thought—the architecture of thought— emerges ever so precariously against the background of nature's superabundance, its force. In the lines, "The mind, that ocean where each kind / Does straight its own resemblance find," we encounter again the logic of Marvell's "In ev'ry figure equal man." Just as the human body measures out perfect forms, the human mind also measures and encompasses all things. The human figure is everywhere *implied*. And yet, the same deterritorializing force of Marvell's figures applies here as well. "Green thought" is not the same as "resemblance." Whereas "resemblance" suggests that we are at home in our thoughts, "green thought" is perforce *unheimlich*; it comes from outside. "Green thought" frames matter's superfluous energy, its "pleasures less," by creating structure, form, resonance (the architecture of "resemblance") and by casting a shadow on whatever falls from that frame ("green shade"). The repetition of "green" in "a green thought in a green shade" implies that the difference between thought and shadow is not subsumable to the difference between human and nonhuman, since the former is internal to the latter, and vice versa. "Green thought" emerges from a background of material forces, but the connection between thought and matter remains. Even bees cogitate.

In the poem's final stanza, Marvell slips once more into the groundwork of his poem. He unearths an unexpected figure, "th'industrious bee":

> How well the skillful gard'ner drew
> Of flow'rs and herbs this dial new;
> Where from above the milder sun
> Does through a fragrant zodiac run;
> And, as it works, th'industrious bee
> Computes its time as well as we.
> How could such sweet and wholesome hours
> Be reckoned but with herbs and flow'rs! (9.65–72)

Marvell's poem ends with the image of a clockwork garden—a clockwork green—one in which the tangle of implied metaphors and subject-"less" snares have all but resolved in the metric order of a skillfully drawn world, knowable down to its tiniest of architects, the bee, who here "Computes its time as well as we." Although the line is certainly a check to human exceptionalism, the image of a tiny computer serves to exalt the mathematical uniformity of all things over the chaos of "pleasures less." The bee cogitates, but it does so only for industry; Marvell's bee is the exemplary figure of the protestant masculine work ethic, reimagined as the animal work ethic. However, does the bee wander, do its figures err?

This question becomes all the more pressing as we turn to Marvell's writing in honor of Lord Fairfax, not only *Upon Appleton House* but also Marvell's minor poems written during his stay at Nun Appleton. In "Upon the Hill and Grove at Bilbrough, To the Lord Fairfax," Marvell imagines the hill of Fairfax's estate much like the bee of "The Garden," as a mathematical figure commendable for its architectural regularity. In the following lines, the earth draws itself:

> See how the archèd earth does here
> Rise in a perfect hemisphere!
> The stiffest compass could not strike
> A line more circular and like;
> Nor softest pencil draw a brow
> So equal as this hill does bow.
> It seems as for a model laid,
> And that the world by it was made. (1.1–8)[101]

Like M. C. Escher's *Drawing Hands* (1948), which depicts two hands rising from the groundwork of the image to draw each other into existence, Marvell's image of Bilbrough hill travels the paradoxical loop of art in nature and nature in art, as the hill serves as both "model" and artist, drawing and being drawn at the same time. This landscape qua Möbius strip again registers the plasticity of Marvell's figures. The human face, for one, is implied by the hill's hemispheric "brow," suggesting that whatever the human face is, it derives from inhuman nature, from the lines and planes of this "archèd earth." Deleuze and Guattari further Marvell's poetic observation, claiming that "there is even something absolutely inhuman about the face."[102] "Architecture," they write, "positions its ensembles—houses, towns or cities, monuments or factories—to function like faces in the landscape they transform. Painting takes up the same movement but also reverses it, positioning a landscape as a face, treating one like the other."[103] Thus Deleuze and Guattari make the somewhat romantic assertion that "all faces envelop an unknown, unexplored landscape," just as "all landscapes are populated by a loved or dreamed-of face."[104] Facialization, Deleuze and Guattari's word for Marvell's anthropomorphic landscape, was indeed a reoccurring element of Renaissance art, including such iconic examples as Wenceslaus Hollar's *Landscape Shaped Like a Face* and Giuseppe Arcimboldo's fantastical, elemental portraits.

But as much as Marvell's implied figures deterrorialize the human face by seeing it en-"compass"-ed in hill and earth, they also reterritorialize in the same movement, giving us a figure related to what Kathryn Yusoff calls "geologic life," referring to the material practices of racialization and extraction that divide matter (corporeal and mineralogical) into active and inert.[105] Yusoff's concern is for the many lives inscribed in the earth that do not have "face" in the sense of Marvell's anthropomorphic model. One of those lives without "face" is the body of the disabled. In the following stanza, ideal geometry collides with tectonic movement to create a scene of interpolation in which the earth's craggy surface is hailed as unequal, "unjust":

> Here learn, ye mountains more unjust,
> Which to abrupter greatness thrust,
> That do with your hook-shouldered height
> The earth deform and heaven fright,
> For whose excrescence ill-designed,
> Nature must a new centre find. (2.9–14)

While the body may serve as a topographic model in Marvell's poetry, as we saw in "The Garden," here, at least, the disabled body stands in for the wild abruptions ("abrupter greatness"), tectonic folds ("hook-shouldered heights"), and variations of the earth's surface ("ill-designed"). No longer read via the architectonics of the (ideal) face, with its smooth lines and "equal" measures, Marvell

188 ARCHITECTURAL ANTHROPOLOGIES

interpolates the earth as monstrous "excrescence," that is to say, as abnormal, excessive, delinquent, and off-"centre."[106] The speaker hails
the landscape as cripped.[107]

Nevertheless, green thought does not result solely in ableist
figures. The bee's clockwork measurements, the garden's sundial
proportions, and the hill's brow-like visage, though consistent with
the architectural theory of Vitruvius, for whom the entire universe,
down to the human face, is like a "compass" ("For there the power of
nature like an architect, has contrived and placed the poles like cen-
tres"),[108] spin off-center in Marvell's post-Ptolemaic universe, such
that "Nature must a new centre find." Green thought shows that nature is off-kilter. It is "excrescence" all the way down. So that if nature
does "draw" perfect figures, we are compelled to read those figures as a
form of writing, precisely the kind of deconstructive writing signaled
by Marvell's "In ev'ry figure equal man," in which there is no "brow,"
"hill," or "hook-shouldered height" to limit the errancy, the disabled
geo-metry, underwriting nature's art.

In *Upon Appleton House*, trees build as well, they write. Marvell's
word for this strange geo-metry is "wood," which, in addition to referring to woodland, refers to a state of madness.[109] "And here am I,
and wood within this wood" (2.1.192), says Shakespeare's mad lover,
Demetrius, in *A Midsummer Night's Dream*.[110] Marvell's dreamer
and "easy philosopher" is no less mad; he converses with birds and
trees, treating them as "equal."

> Thus I, easy philosopher,
> Among the birds and trees confer.
> . . . .
>
> Already I begin to call
> In their most learned original:
> And where I language want, my signs
> The bird upon the bough divines. (71.561–62, 72.569–72)

Here again, "In ev'ry figure equal man" is less the multiplication of
man's unique architectural ability than an exercise in earthly humility

(*humus*), a lack ("I language want") in exchange for vital "signs." As we will see, all the earth's figures—flora and fauna—are mad, are wood. Marvell invites us to get tangled in their verdant arches.

Wooden Oedipus

"When first the eye this forest sees," the speaker of *Upon Appleton House* says, having wandered from the poem's ostensive center, the Fairfax home, to the outer forest, "It seems," he remarks, emphasizing the difficulty of blurred vision, "indeed as wood not trees,"

> As if their neighborhood so old
> To one great trunk them all did mould. (63.497–500)

"Mould" suggests both the plasticity of architectural design, lending credence to Auerbach's definition of *figura* as a malleable shape, and something rotten, decayed. Both plastic art and plastic death, "mould" conveys the impermanence of all things while also highlighting the forest's art, which is to resist devouring time in the shape of a green— ever-greening—monument. Let us not forget that "mould" also pertains to the earth's dirt, loam, and humus. "Mould" is thus an extraordinarily plastic as well as humble material and word; moreover, it echoes the poem's language from before, "Humility alone designs," this time referring to the design of trees. Marvell's square poem has become the literal embodiment of Puttenham's earthly metaphor: like Fairfax's elastic estate, and like the contradictorily static yet growing (and decaying) forest art before him, Marvell's poem takes these figures as models for his poetry. The poem is an earthen "mould."

What is more, this "mould" takes on a classical architectural shape. The forest wood molds itself, just as a sculptor molds clay—by separating inside from outside, "Dark all without" from "fires" within—into a "temple green." We could say that the wood *woods* in Marvell's poem. It matters; it builds. In the following lines, the topography of Marvell's poem is reversed, mutated, or turned inside out, like a topological knot. Having left the site of human design, we are right back in it, only the "we" has been crossed out. The "sober frame" proves highly mobile, its figure disfiguring to man's architectural ambition. If "In ev'ry figure equal man" seemed like a paean to human universalism, here the universal equivalent—"man"—disappears in nature's geometry, revealing an ecology in which "home" and *oikos* exist without us:

> Dark all without it [the wood] knits; within
> It opens passable and thin;
> And in as loose an order grows,
> As the Corinthean porticoes.
> The arching boughs unite between
> The columns of the temple green;
> And underneath the wingèd choirs
> Echo about their tunèd fires. (64.505–12)

When Marvell thinks of trees, he thinks of Corinthian columns.

He is not alone. In *De architectura*, Vitruvius provides the origin story for the three classical columns—Doric, Ionic, and Corinthian— and suggests they derive from human form. The Doric was designed for the Temple of Apollo in ancient Greece and took inspiration from the human body: "They measured a man's footstep and applied it to his height. Finding that the foot was the sixth part of the height in a man, they applied this proportion to the column. . . . So the Doric column began to furnish the proportion of a man's body, its strength and grace."[111] The Ionic was designed for the Temple of Diana and featured "a new kind of style." According to Vitruvius, "they ornamented the front, and, over all the trunk (i.e., the shaft), they let flutting fall, like the folds of matronly robes; thus they proceeded to the invention of columns in two manners; one, manlike in appearance, bare, unadorned; the other feminine."[112] Marvell's version of things echoes Vitruvius. In his poem, Vitruvian columns appear as "ancient stocks" as Fairfax and his wife, Vere (Anne Fairfax), stand in for deeply rooted genealogies. Marvell writes:

> The double wood of ancient stocks
> Linked in so thick, an union locks,
> It like two pedigrees appears,
> On one hand Fairfax, th'other Vere's. (62.489–92)

However, neither Vitruvius nor Marvell stop at the number two. As comforting as this heterosexual division of matter into male and female may appear to Vitruvius, two proves an odd number. Although the number two can easily reproduce the one (as Simone de Beauvoir argues in *The Second Sex*), it also creates strange bedfellows, Oedipal thirds.

We know the story of the man from Corinth, Sophocles's Oedipus, whose feet were pierced and bound as a child, leaving him exposed to the elements and, in some versions of the story, bound to a tree, plantlike and disabled, with "swollen foot."[113] But Vitruvius offers a different version of human–plant hybridity. In the following passage, we learn not of Oedipus and his tragic ending, but of the girl from Corinth and her posthumous life:

> A girl, a native of Corinth, already of age to be married, was attacked by disease and died. After her funeral, the goblets which delighted her when living, were put together in a basket by her nurse, carried to the monument, and placed on the top. That they might remain longer, exposed as they were to the weather, she covered the basket with a tile. As it happened the basket was placed upon the root of an acanthus. Meanwhile about spring time, the root of the acanthus, being pressed down in the middle by the weight, put forth leaves and shoots. The shoots grew up the sides of the basket, and, being pressed down at the angles by the force of the weight of the tile, were compelled to form the curves of volutes at the extreme parts.[114]

To this day, the Corinthian column bears the imprint of this human–plant, living–nonliving assemblage; "It imitates the slight figure of a maiden."[115] Unlike Oedipus, who lived to repress his former life as an unwilling plant, the girl from Corinth lives on after death in the image of a Corinthian column, part "maiden," part acanthus plant. Marvell reimagines her spectral presence in the image of the "young Maria," Fairfax's daughter.

Only in Marvell's version of things, the "curves" and "volutes" of the acanthus plant appear straightened, not curved: "She *straightness* on the woods bestows" (emphasis added), with all that this entails for the "green thought" that, at least in other moments of Marvell's poem,

queered nature's art along nonlinear paths.[116] The "young Maria,"
it would seem, oedipalizes the girl from Corinth, representing, in
Lee Edelman's terms, the reproductive futurism of the symbolic
order or law, which is what the speaker of Marvell's poem says: "She
that already is the law / Of all her sex, her age's awe." Such is the
"young Maria."

> 'Tis she that to these gardens gave
> That wonderous beauty which they have;
> She straightness on the woods bestows;
> To her the meadow sweetness owes;
> Nothing could make the river be
> So crystal-pure but only she;
> She yet more pure, sweet, straight, and fair,
> Than gardens, woods, meads, rivers are. (87.689–95)

The "law" in this case, as in every case of Oedipal straightness, is
properly Euclidean. If at first the "temple green," Marvell's dream
house, was seen "loose" in geometric composure ("in as loose an order
grows, / As the Corinthean porticoes"), it soon recalls itself, which
is to say, it retroactively rewrites itself in the image of law and order,
the order that Mary Fairfax represents: "See how loose Nature, in
respect / To her, itself doth recollect; / . . . The sun himself, of her
aware, / Seems to descend with greater care" (83.657–62). If, before,
all nature, including the speaker, could "pass" from one "loose" figure
to the next, "Annihilating all that's made" in a geometry of pure deformation, here, all nature appears frozen ("vitrified") by the image
("So crystal-pure") of the "young Maria": "by her flames . . . / Nature
is wholly vitrified," that is, turned into glass—a static figure.

But even this figure betrays a strange topography. For example,
the above stanza ends by rhyming "fair" and "are," and each rhymed
couplet suggests the same synthesis of two becoming one that the
symbolic order propagates. However, ghosting this synthesis is the
word "err," which doubles as a queer homophone of the final key
word, the ontological word, "are" (to be). If, on the one hand, being
is aligned here with "straightness," on the other hand, being is also
curved, crooked, and inclined, like the Lucretian *clinamen*, toward

errant figures. In other words, the being of straight lines and Euclidean figures is not only homophonic with error ("are" echoing "err") but also homographic: the place of the garden, its symbolic positioning within a topographic survey, is structurally no-place. Marvell's architectural figures are structured by *involution*, like the volutes of the acanthus plant: inside becoming outside, one becoming many, and the "young Maria" becoming a ghostly offshoot of the girl from Corinth. This wildness of being persists surreptitiously up to the final stanza, where the madness of the wood resurfaces, against all correction, in the image of a "shod" off head.

> But now the salmon-fishers moist
> Their leathern boats begin to hoist;
> And, like Antipodes in shoes,
> Have shod their heads in their canoes.
> How tortoise-like, but not so slow,
> These rational amphibii go! (97.769–74)

Once again, Marvell's poem does the impossible: it squares the circle, circling back to one of its earliest images of animal architecture, "The low-roofed tortoises." If the first image was meant to decenter architectural man, the second image goes a step further: as if capitalizing on the Medusa head that the Corinthian capital represents with its snaking tendrils, distributed morphology, and female description, the image of "salmon-fishers" with shorn-off heads (literally: their heads are housed within the boat's carapace) likewise points to the decapitation and castration of the figure "man." Whereas Freud famously reads the Medusa head as an image of castration, the snake-like hair of Medusa serving as figurative compensation for the absence of the phallus,[117] Lacan reads castration in strictly architectural terms. What matters, Lacan says, is not the penis but the idea of the body as one. The phallus is the keystone, the "tip" of the body image. And because this keystone is precariously placed, it is always at risk of falling off. (Indeed, it has always already fallen off, as Marvell's "The Garden" showed us.) Marvell's "In ev'ry figure equal man" registers this sense of castration anxiety by claiming that no figure is ever self-identical.

Still, Marvell is not Freud. Unlike the latter, Marvell delights in the figural possibilities of castration and even exclaims with fascination the joys of the headless subject, here writ in the image of "rational amphibii," the flip side of "In ev'ry figure equal man." This image repeats and therefore takes pleasure in reading "man" as "tortoise-like," as laterally (dis)assembled—mad.

But the joy of madness has been a part of Marvell's wood all along. Marvell gives the poem's penultimate image of pleasurable castration in the image of the human body as an "inverted tree": "turn me but, and you shall see, / I was but an inverted tree," the speaker says (71.567–68). Like the volute turns of the Corinthian arbor, Marvell turns the "I" upside down, once again removing the head of the speaker by burying it underground, revealing limbs like tree branches. In the following stanza, we read of the pleasures of this posthuman inversion:

> Bind me ye woodbines in your twines,
> Curl me about ye gladding vines,
> And oh so close your circles lace,
> That I may never leave this place:
> But, lest your fetters prove too weak,
> Ere I your silken bondage break,
> Do you, O brambles, chain me too,
> And courteous briars nail me through. (77.609–16)

Marvell's is perhaps the earliest example of tree-sitting, a form of environmental activism in which activists sit in trees, often chaining themselves to the trunks in order to protect forests from logging. These activists occupy the wood. Oddly enough, the logger in Marvell's poem is the "young Maria," Fairfax's daughter and symbol of the Edelmanian Child. Insofar as the Edelmanian Child is supposed to represent the future, while clandestinely laying waste to that future, Marvell's child represents a similar paradox: by straightening Fairfax's "ancient stock," she bestows on the wood the ideal geometric shape for cutting. The opposite is true for Marvell's "rational amphibii" and headless speaker. Although both are lopped figures, they embrace their lack of future so that other figures, human and nonhuman, can enter the poem's frame. What is more, by rejecting the future that reproductive futurism bestows on the wood, and by embracing the nonreproductivity, not to mention queer Christianity, of that image of a pseudo-Christ nailed, in ecstatic reverie,[118] to his bed of "brambles," Marvell repeats, and thus gives life to, the repressed topology of the poem, its archeology of prohibited passion, erotic conversion, whispered lesbianism, and religious ardor, which, true or not, is the fantasied underside of all that is raised (both elevated and erased, in both senses of the verb "to raise") on the Fairfax estate.

I am referring to the Catholic nunnery on which the Fairfax home was originally built and the scenes of female sexuality that the poem imagines therein. By erasing this queer history as the underlying groundwork of the poem, *Upon Appleton House* seeks to straighten and so "recollect" itself. But it does so only by repeating this queerness in other forms, a queerness that it contains only by imagining it as "other," as the fantasy of a specifically female, unreligious, and unmanly threat to life and futurity. Despite its erasure, Marvell's speaker reawakens this archive of imagined pleasure and becomes the "other" that the future rejects. Chained and nailed through, the speaker repeats in his "silken bondage" the "billeted" flesh of the personas non grata of the poem's not too distant (and, for Fairfax, not distant enough) past, the childless paramours of Christ's broken body, the nuns of Nun Appleton Priory. In the following stanzas, the speaker ventriloquizes their seductive invitation:

> What need is here of man?
> . . . .
>
> 'Each night among us to your side
> Appoint a fresh and virgin bride;
> Whom if Our Lord at midnight find,
> Yet neither should be left behind.
> Where you may lie as chaste in bed,
> As pearls together billeted,
> All night embracing arm in arm
> Like crystal pure with cotton warm. (23.183, 24.185–92)

The invitation is addressed to Isabel Thwaites, ancestor to Thomas Fairfax and wife of William Fairfax. Like "the young Maria," her descendant, the poem imagines "the blooming virgin Thwaites, / Fair beyond measure," as "an heir / Which," like her future offshoot, "might deformity make fair"—that is, straight. But in the poem's recollection, this straightening ancestry gets diverted by "the subtle nuns" of Nun Appleton Priory, whose question, "What need is here of man?," not only ensnares the "virgin Thwaites," but also poses the very problem that Marvell's poem and this chapter have been interrogating: the ontological question—What need of man?

As the archeology of this question unfolds, "man," we find, is thrown into doubt as the nuns' "subtle" speech gives voice to a libidinal unconscious that is anything but "human." Sexuality, more likely, is the site of the inhuman. It is as if, in an anticipatory nod to Freud's *Three Essays*, Marvell's poem looked back at the ontogeny of "man" and found something wanting and inexplicable, an ontosexuality that neither resembles nor guarantees the emergence of the human. Well before Freud and Lacan named "woman" the site of this ontological impossibility, Marvell saw the risk and the pleasures of a world with no "need . . . of man." Inside the imagined interiors of Nun Appleton, the future imagined as "fair" "straightness" reconfigures into polymorphous contact zones, where bodies, instead of connecting to sustain the future, connect "As pearls together billeted." Valerie Traub has shown that the ornamental "pearl" could be used as a metonymy of female pleasure in Renaissance representations of chastity.[119] In Marvell's use, "chaste" bodies multiply rather than subdue female pleasure as bodies, like pearls, move in and out of spatial relation—"[be]side," "behind," "together"—a string of contiguous pleasures. Even Christ, the original figure of pleasures "billeted," partakes of their spatial erotics. To be "billeted" means to be assigned a place or position, like pearls on a string, but a "billet" also refers to a piece of wood (from the medieval Latin *billa* and *billus*, "branch, trunk of a tree").[120] "As pearls together billeted," Marvell's pearls not only metonymize female pleasure but also link ecstatic joys to the place of Christ's passion. The vehicle of Christ's suffering, a tree, is made a sexual plaything, with the added implication that those who link "arm in arm" are "billeted" (penetrated) by this tree. "Embracing arm in arm," each is nailed in imitation of and out of love for Christ's penetrated body.

Marvell's "nail me through" thus finds its Cistercian echo in the architectural interior of Nun Appleton Priory. Although the destruction of this space and rescue of Isabel Thwaites serves a triumphalist and teleological version of Protestant, masculinist history, which the poem later repeats with the appearance of "young Maria," who forces the poem and the wood to recollect its former "straightness," Marvell's "easy philosopher," like the "blooming . . . Thwaites," is so easily ensnared by the enervating chains of "briars" and "brambles" that it is impossible not to see Marvell's speaker as a kind of S&M Christ "billeted" by the wood. The poem's archeology of silence, though covered over by Appleton House and its mythology of undeviating (straight, patriarchal) family lines, reappears in the poem due to the wood's "loose" (I would say, queer) order, not only in the scene just mentioned, the speaker's ecstatic bondage, but up to the very last lines, in the image of a headless canoer.

Marvell's Spinozist affinity for getting tangled in the lines, planes, and bodies of the wood amounts to a similar form of occupation by dispossession. "Here," Marvell's speaker says, "in the morning tie my chain, / Where the two woods have made a lane" (78.617–18). Marvell ties his fate to the fate of the wood. Read queerly (that is, against history's grain), Marvell's poem also ties its "chain" to the anonymous individuals, environmental activists, and tree-sitters the world over, who occupy the wood today, from the Northern California redwoods to the great tropical rainforests that gird the earth.[121] The first lines of *Upon Appleton House* showcase futurity's destructive gambit against the earth in the image of emptied "quarries" and leveled "forests." Against this image of architectural extraction, Marvell extracts the human from futurity's figural frame. Call it mad love. Call it joyful castration. The image is one of wild connection. It refuses to lie straight.

The Undergrowth

I began this chapter by reflecting on the critical dissensus surrounding Marvell's passive vitalism. While critics such as John Rogers and others label Marvell's pastoral poetry a "green dream," in part because it retires from the space of politics proper (deemed human) to greener pastures (deemed apolitical), and because the nature it depicts seems, at least to a point, to straighten all that's odd about the wood, my reading follows a different path. Specifically, it shows that the space of politics, so framed by Rogers, works only to fix, not unfurl, the topographic connections, movements, and lines of flight that Marvell's poem generates. Fred Moten and Stefano Harney call this generative space "the undercommons" and contrast it with the enclosures of "self-possession": "It is recourse to self-possession in the face of dispossession (recourse, in other words, to politics) that represents the real danger," Moten and Harney write.[122] The undercommons is what self-possessive politics tries to enclose by giving it a fixed identity, a location. Nevertheless, they argue, "We cannot represent ourselves. We can't be represented."[123] By assuming the place of opacity and non-localization, Moten and Harney enact a diagrammatic politics of escape that closely resembles Marvell's desire to "retire" and to be (in Milton's words) "not unseen." Indeed, the very language of "enclosure," still no less pressing today, cuts through Marvell's *Upon Appleton House* and the geopolitics it frames. Instead of faulting Marvell's poetry for taking flight in more-than-human directions—that is, outside the enclosures of humanity—we can read *Upon Appleton House* in Moten and Harney sense as an escape from representation. Moten and Harney call this space of escape "the undercommons." I call it, after Marvell's wood, the undergrowth.

The undergrowth, like the undercommons, is a space in which being is forever beside itself, un-enclosed, tangling in the roots and brush. To pass into imperceptibility is, for Moten and Harney, what is required today to think outside of ecological enclosure (which, as Guattari points out in *The Three Ecologies*, is also the mind's enclosure). Whereas the house and all its related figures—the fort, the settlement, the Heideggerian fourfold, even the poetic stanza—represses the undergrowth, we have seen that Marvell's square poetry is built on "loose" foundations. The undergrowth is constantly escaping itself. By wandering farther and farther outdoors and into the open, away from its human center, Marvell empties the frame of his poem much like the painter, in Deleuze's description of modern painting, empties all the clichéd figures that occupy the canvas:

Modern painting is invaded and besieged by photographs and clichés that are already lodged on the canvas before the painter even begins work. In fact, it would be a mistake to think that the painter works on a white or virgin canvas. The entire surface is already invested virtually with all kinds of clichés, which the painter will have to break with. This is exactly what [Francis] Bacon says when he speaks of the photograph: it is not a figuration of what one sees, it is what modern man sees. It is not dangerous simply because it is figurative, but because it claims to *reign over vision*.[124]

One never begins to paint on an empty canvas, Deleuze tells us. To begin to paint or to create, one must, with great struggle, clear the frame of all the images that still cling too close to the lived. Deleuze's aestheticism is, in this sense, strictly avital. Art never derives from the lived. It only derives from what is unlivable and therefore unrepresentable in life. That is why the great artists are, according to Deleuze, all martyrs in their own way. In order to create the new, they had to retire from life.

Marvell's ecological martyrdom takes up this strange sense of retirement. "Annihilating all that's made" to become "a green thought in a green shade," Marvell's poetry takes place not by way of a politics of self-possession; it takes place by *giving up place*.

> But I, retiring from the flood,
> Take sanctuary in the wood,
> And, while it lasts, myself embark
> In this yet green, yet growing ark,
> Where the first carpenter might best
> Fit timber for his keel have pressed.
> And where all creatures might have shares,
> Although in armies, not in pairs. (61.481–88)

Here, both senses of creation, *creating* and *creature*, intermingle in Marvell's poetic frame. The "I" that tops the stanza is the strangest creature of them all in that it flickers in and out of existence. "Retiring," trading flesh for bark ("myself embark"), the "I" fades so that

"armies" of other "creatures" (and no longer just the heterosexual cou-
ple, "The double wood" of Fairfax and Vere) can have their "shares." At
the same time, however, some residue of this "I" remains: "But I." "But
I" is no longer exceptional, but it does mark an exception, an opening
through which to peer. Hovering between life and death, the "I" is an
implicit point of view in the poem. It does not stand apart from nature's work. "But I" is the minimum of anthropogenesis that Marvell's
architectural poem gives us to see: a speaker who all but passes out of
existence, except for the barely human eye it presents.

FIVE

QUEER LIFE, UNEARTHED

(Milton)

Time hath endless rarities, and shows of all varieties;
which reveals old things in heaven, makes new discoveries
in earth, and even earth it self a discovery. . . . a large part
of the earth is still in the Urne unto us.

—Sir Thomas Browne, *Hydriotaphia, or Urne-Buriall*

The being of Spirit is a bone.

—G. W. F. Hegel, *Phenomenology of Spirit*

Midway through the first book of Margaret Atwood's *MaddAddam*
trilogy, so named for its postapocalyptic retelling of Genesis, the
book's title character, Crake, says to the novel's protagonist, Jimmy:

"Want to play Extinctathon?"
"Extinctathon?" said Jimmy. It took him a moment, but then he re-
membered it: the boring Web interactive with all those defunct animals
and plants. "When was it we used to play that? It can't still be going."
"It's never stopped," said Crake. . . .
He went onto the Web, found the site, pulled it up. There was the
familiar gateway: EXTINCTATHON, *Monitored by MaddAddam.*
Adam named the living animals, MaddAddam names the dead ones. Do
you want to play?[1]

In the post-Edenic, postapocalyptic world imagined by Atwood, it is not the Tree of Knowledge that figures man's disobedience, but rather multinational corporations set on biological manipulation ("RejoovenEsence" is the name of one such corporation), postgenomic experimentation, and life management. The invitation to play "Extinctathon" surprises Jimmy ("It can't still be going," he exclaims), but that is nothing compared to the shock of what follows:

> A new sentence popped up: *Adam named the animals. MaddAddam customizes them.*
>
> Then there was a string of e-bulletins, with places and dates—CorpsSeCorps issue, by the look of them, marked For Secure Address Only.
>
> A tiny parasitic wasp had invaded several ChickieNobs installations, carrying a modified form of chicken pox, specific to the ChickieNob and fatal to it. The installations had had to be incinerated before the epidemic could be brought under control.
>
> A new form of the common house mouse addicted to the insulation on electric wiring had overrun Cleveland, causing an unprecedented number of house fires. Control measures were still being tested.
>
> Happicuppa coffee bean crops were menaced by a new bean weevil found to be resistant to all known pesticides.
>
> A miniature rodent containing elements of both porcupine and beaver had appeared in the northwest, creeping under the hoods of parked vehicles and devastating their fan belts and transmission systems.
>
> A microbe that ate the tar in asphalt had turned several interstate highways to sand. All interstates were on alert, and a quarantine belt was now in place.
>
> "What's going on?" said Jimmy. "Who's putting this stuff out there?"[2]

What started as a simple game of life and death (*"Adam named the living animals, MaddAddam names the dead ones"*) became an all-too-real network of posthuman actors or actants—terrorist figures without easy ontological definition—playing under the quasi-Adamic title of "MaddAddam." Their goal? To rename life and thereby bring about a new Eden. These posthuman figures turn life into nonlife and the undead into the living (the chickenpox virus and its parasitic host; the chemical monoculture and its pesticidal-kin; the interstate highway and its rapacious commuter, the tar microbe). As numerous scholars have pointed out, if the Adamic art of naming was an operation of making *sense* of the world's primordial entanglements, then MaddAddam's monstrous assemblages foreground those entanglements with mad abandon.[3] As products of the biopolitical naturecultures that Atwood describes in her novel, they defy traditional categories of life, identity, time, and space; neither the (post) modern categories of nature versus culture nor the Aristotelian categories of substance and change capture their distributed forms of agency.[4] More recent ideas drawn from the new materialisms approximate their shifting coordinates: "the parasite" (Serres); "the rhizome" (Deleuze and Guattari); "terrorist assemblage" (Puar); "hyperobject" (Morton).[5] None of these are names per se, at least not in the Adamic sense of fixing an identity or essence; instead, they are mobile concepts used for grappling with matters and events on the move. Puar, for one, emphasizes the *queerness* of such assemblages: "There is no entity, no identity, no queer subject or subject to queer, rather queerness coming forth at us from all directions, screaming its defiance. . . . The assemblage, as a series of dispersed but mutually implicated and messy networks, draws together enunciation and dissolution, causality and effect, organic and nonorganic forces."[6]

One thing, however, that does bear a name, and so with it, the knowledge that *it too will die,* is humanity—Adam's offspring.[7] As Jimmy watches the real-life *Extinctathon* unfold, he knows that one day, in the not-too-distance future, humanity too will be one of the many "defunct" species on MaddAddam's list. Looking out at a futureless horizon scarred by ruins, he imagines humanity's total disappearance from the earth, leaving only the exoskeletal remains of past monuments for future life-forms to reconfigure:

The buildings that didn't burn or explode are still standing, though the botany is thrusting itself through every crack. Given time it will

fissure the asphalt, topple the walls, push aside the roofs. Some kind
of vine is growing everywhere, draping the windowsills, climbing in
through the broken windows and up the bars and grillwork. Soon this
district will be a thick tangle of vegetation. If he'd postponed the trip
much longer the way back would have become impassable. It won't be
long before all visible traces of human habitation will be gone.[8]

Life, as envisioned by Jimmy, is not the future-flowing life of Adam
and his children, for whom death—always the singular death of this
or that living being—still makes *sense,* so long as it is redeemable, either in this life or in the next; instead, Jimmy's image of life is *mad*
and mad in the unique sense theorized by Michel Foucault in his
queer-archaeology of the present: "My intention was not to write the
history of that language [the language of madness]," Foucault writes,
"but rather draw up the archaeology of that silence."[9] To write the
history of madness, to "draw up" or exhaust its meaning, one ought
to interpret the history of the present not as a continuous line of development, from birth to maturation, but as a jagged line crossed by
geological strata: "Where might this [archaeological] interrogation
lead," Foucault asks, "following not reason in its horizontal becoming,
but seeking to retrace in time this constant verticality," the geological
layers, "which, the length of Western culture, confronts it with what it
is not, measuring it with its own extravagance?"[10]

If Foucault's archaeological and genealogical methods have been
aegis defining for queer theory, his emphasis on the madness of the
geological archive, on silences encased in stone, should alert us to the
queerness of geology itself. Like the history of madness, which extrudes itself into discourse as reason's chthonic double, the geological
archive—now more so than ever—extrudes itself into the present as
an archive of past and future extinction. To exhaust this "silence," to
"draw up" the silent ground of lives fossilized by time's arrow, is to interrupt the ongoingness of life, to confront life with "what . . . is not"
life, life's own forgotten record of "extravagance": the monstrousness
of the earth.[11]

In *The Order of Things,* Foucault registers the earth's mad "silence"
as a "catastrophe" or "monstrosity" discontinuous with life's becoming.
He writes:

If it is necessary for time, which is limited, to run through—or perhaps to have already run through—the whole continuity of nature,
one is forced to admit that a considerable number of possible variations have been encountered and then erased; just as the geological
catastrophe was necessary to enable us to work back from the tax-
onomic table to the continuum, through a blurred, chaotic, and
fragmented experience, so the proliferation of monsters without a
future is necessary to enable us to work down again from the continuum, through a temporal series, to the table.[12]

From the vantage of reason, the fossil makes sense only as a deviation
from the "continuum" of life, making it akin to Foucault's better-
known "abnormals": the masturbating child, the hysterical woman,
the sodomite.[13] But if we read the earth's monsters, as both Foucault
and Atwood suggest, not as deviations *from* life's "continuum," but as
the fundament-al deviance *of* life itself, its bottomless nonidentity,
nonbecoming, and nonthriving, we would have to conceive of the
earth as inexhaustibly mad—as queer *sub*-stance all the way down.[14]

Life, then, would no longer be so reasonable, its "horizontal becoming" so assured by geological time. As Jimmy envisions it, life
would be an archive of extinction. Under the assemblage of plant life
and mutant biota, a geology of exhausted life waits to be read.

Queer Remains

Of course, MaddAddam is not the only post-Adamic figure to raise
questions about the monuments of the dead. Long before Atwood's
novel, a young John Milton had already begun to name, in poetic
fashion, the mysteries of the earth:

> What needs my Shakespeare for his honoured bones,
> The labour of an age in pilèd stones,
> Or that his hallowed relics should be hid
> Under a star-ypointing pyramid?
> Dear son of memory, great heir of fame,
> What need'st thou such weak witness of thy name?
> Thou in our wonder and astonishment
> Hast built thyself a live-long monument.

For whilst to th' shame of slow-endeavoring art,
Thy easy numbers flow, and that each heart
Hath from the leaves of thy unvalued book,
Those Delphic lines with deep impression took,
Then thou our fancy of itself bereaving,
Dost make us marble with too much conceiving;
And so sepulchred in such pomp dost lie,
That kings for such a tomb would wish to die. (Milton, "On
     Shakespeare")[15]

Although Milton's first published poem, "On Shakespeare," written
for the Second Folio, seems to dismiss stone's animating power ("weak
witness of thy name"), the rhetorical chiasmus that follows, "Thou in
our wonder and astonishment," interrupts life's vital continuum by fig-
uring life as a kind of sepulcher. "Thou in . . . astonishment" doubles
in Milton's poem not only as "a live-long monument," uncorrupted by
stone's "slow-endeavoring art," but also as a figure of life's extinction
(to *astonish* means "to deprive of sensation, as by a blow," i.e., to make
stony). If, in the lines above, Shakespeare's "honoured bones" speak
from beyond the grave—with "Delphic" foresight—the converse must
also be true: life itself must be "a tomb." (No wonder, then, that the
poem ends with a "wish to die.") Shakespeare's "hallowed relics" petrify
the living: "our fancy of itself bereaving, / Dost make us marble with
too much conceiving." In rhetorical terms, this is the trope of *prosopopoeia*, which Paul de Man has defined as "the fiction of an apostrophe
to an absent, deceased, or voiceless entity"—in this case, Shakespeare's
bones—"which posits the possibility of the latter's reply and confers
upon it the power of speech. Voice assumes mouth, eye, and finally
face, a chain that is manifest in the etymology of the trope's name,
prosopon poien, to confer a mask or a face (*prosopon*)."[16]

De Man famously focuses his attention on the anxiety produced
by this trope in Wordsworth's *Essays upon Epitaphs* and traces its rhetorical effects to the lines of Milton's early poem. A similar anxiety
can be found in many early modern encounters with relics, including
John Ray's encounter in *Three* Physico-Theological *Discourses* (1693).
In that text, Ray strains to provide a speculative account of the "deep
time" of the earth in accordance with scripture, writing:

Concerning the *Chaos* and Creation of the World, if it were not an-cienter than the scripture, it is likely it had its Original from the first Chapter of *Genesis*, and the *Chaos* from the second Verse, *And the earth was without form and void, and darkness was upon the face of the deep.* But if it were more ancient, it must still in all likelihood be Di-vinely revealed, because Man being created last, [was] brought into a World already filled and furnished.[17]

Historian of science Martin J. S. Rudwick notes that in "the age of scientific giants such as Galileo and Newton, most people in the Western world, whether religious or not, took it for granted . . . that not just the Earth, but the whole universe or cosmos, and even time itself, are scarcely any older than human life."[18] Not only did Gen-esis "set out a brief narrative in which Adam ('The Man') had been formed on the sixth day of creative action," but also "it seemed obvi-ous *common sense* to them that the world must always have been a *human* world, apart from a brief prelude in which the props necessary for human life had been put on stage: Sun and Moon, day and night, land and sea, plants and animals."[19] Deep history, or the history of the earth's formation, consisted of the five days before God created Adam. In Ray's account, although "there is no particular mention made of the Creation of Metals, Minerals and other Fossils [in Gene-sis], they must be comprehended in the word Earth."[20] And this is so, Ray argues,

[because] it would hence follow, That many Species of Shell-fish are lost out of the World, which Philosophers hitherto have been unwilling to admit, esteeming the destruction of any one Species a dismembering of the Universe, and rendering it imperfect: whereas they think the Divine Providence is especially concerned to secure and preserve the Works of Creation: and that it is so, appears, in that it was so careful to lodge all Land-Animals in the Ark at the time of the general Deluge.[21]

Although Ray confronts the evidence of species extinction, of lives "lost out of the World" in the form of fossil remains (see Figure 5), he relegates these figures—nature's archive of extinction—to the history of humanity and the story of the Flood. Denuded of their "dismembering" power, which is the power to *rend* the "Universe" by "rendering it imperfect," instead they reveal life's seamlessness. Unlike Foucault's fossils, which interrupt life's "continuum" with a jagged silence, or Shakespeare's bones, which ossify the living, Ray's fossils speak *not* of extinction, but of "that innate *Prolepsis* we have of the Prudence of Nature, (that is, the Author of Nature)."[22] Figured therefore as the prudent figure of "Prolepsis," nature so figured guarantees life's continuum; it guarantees that, against all evidence to the contrary, life cannot rend its own fabric. Life, in other words, delays or puts off the catastrophe of (non)identity, which the fossil represents, as something to be avoided or overcome. Consequently, we never encounter the catastrophe of the present, life's intolerability to our images of sustainability, because we put life in the service of metaphor, life's futural form.[23]

Today, however, there is a name for this catastrophe. The environmental epoch known as the "Anthropocene," the period of geological time in which human impact on the planet has reached geologic and meteoric scale, marks the collapse not only of the (post)modern distinction between nature and culture, but also the more fundamental distinction between life and nonlife. We are witnessing, we are told, the emergence of humanity as a "geological agent."[24] Consequently, the distinction between life and nonlife, which has taken a backseat in recent years to various animist, new materialist, and biopolitical theories of matter focused on "life itself," reasserts itself today in the form of mass extinction of species, mutated carbon cycles, and military and national defense budgets aimed at laying hold to the earth's remaining stores of precious minerals, gas, and oil.[25] All of this spells a general shift in the political paradigm from a theory of *bio*-power, which Foucault defined and others have since popularized as the governance of life through "life itself,"[26] to what Elizabeth Povinelli terms "geontopower": the maintenance of the distinction between life *(bios)* and nonlife *(geos)*. "This distinction," Povinelli argues, "revolves not only around that which had life but is now deprived of it but also that which never was alive in the first place, the undead, the geological."[27] Povinelli defines geontology, or (riffing on Foucault) geontopower, in relation to biopower, *not* as the power to make live and

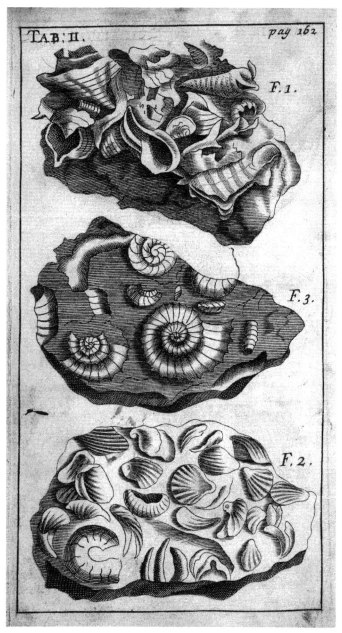

FIGURE 5. Depiction of fossils in John Ray's *Three* Physico-Theological *Discourses*. Courtesy of the Lownes History of Science Collection, John Hay Library, Brown University.

let die (i.e., biopolitics) but as the power to manage and regulate the affective and discursive relations separating life and nonlife. We have been too focused on the biopolitical, Povinelli argues, to the exclusion of the geontological; but the threat of climate change, resource scarcity, and endless war enables us to see that nonlife (by which Povinelli means the geological and meteorological) undergirds and even makes possible our fascination with "life itself."

As early as *Society Must Be Defended,"* Foucault was already experimenting with metaphors of geological depth in order to confront histories of the present with a "bottom-up" approach attuned to "subjugated knowledges."[28] Instead of "totalitarian theories" (Marxism, psychoanalysis), Foucault was interested in unearthing "knowledges from below."[29] The sexual connotations of Foucault's "bottom-up" approach would be made explicit elsewhere. In his essay on Deleuze, for example, Foucault outrageously professes that "a dead God," the famous reversal of Platonism, "and sodomy are the thresholds of the new metaphysical ellipse."[30]

Foucault's "bottom-up" approach, along with his sodomitic language of geologic depths, points to a related shift within queer theory, which today spills more and more in the direction of the inhuman. Elizabeth Grosz, for one, mines the evolutionary philosophies of Darwin, Bergson, and Deleuze to theorize a "nonorganic life" in which nonlife bequeaths life, and life, in turn, restores art and agency to nonliving matter.[31] As these figures of nonlife leak into and interpenetrate with the figure of the human, and as the figure of the "homo" (the gay and lesbian adult) becomes an integral part of "homonationalism," new figures of the queer are beginning to take shape.[32]

This chapter posits Milton's earth as one such figure. Turning to what Cleanth Brooks once described as "the absurdity of a battle in which the contestants cannot be killed," this chapter explores the exhaustion of epic tropes in the battle of book 6 of *Paradise Lost*.[33] Here, the exhaustion of both bodies and images in Milton's poem is linked to the exhaustion of the earth—what Milton calls the "originals of nature in their crude / Conception; sulphurous and nitrous foam," and "mineral and stone" (6.511–12, 517).[34] These fossils (the word originally meant "things dug up") power the fallen angels' "devilish enginery," which is in turn used to mine the earth further (6.553). As the earth itself is exhausted, so too are the angels. Traditionally read as an allegory of the English Civil War, in which diggers and levelers laid claim to a common ground, *Paradise Lost* foregrounds the earth's deep history, which seventeenth-century naturalists such as Robert Hooke, John Woodward, and John Ray were just beginning to uncover.[35] Read as an archive of nature's prehuman past, Milton's poem confronts the reader with the truth of extinction or the "slow violence" of geological time.[36] It enables us to see what Quentin Meillassoux refers to as the "arche-fossil": "Not just materials indicating the traces of past life," but, far more radically, "fossils of creatures living prior to the emergence of the first hominids, the date of the accretion of the earth, the date of the formation of stars."[37]

While several scholars have commented on the rise of coal mining practices in the sixteenth century and have attributed capitalism's current fossil-fuel dependency to the rise of "cheap energy" in the form of English coal, the real shock of *Paradise Lost* is not its supposed break with Mother Earth but rather its break with human duration.[38] Read from the vantage of the earth's deep history, Milton's poem foregrounds what Ray and others feared and found monstrous about the earth: inhuman durations out of sync with human history and disjunct temporalities with the power to rend the universe. For this reason, Milton's poem not only challenges the idea that the Anthropocene one day arrived—earlier accounts suggest that we have always already been geological agents, that is, queer mixtures of life and nonlife—it also opens the archive of queer theory to new figures of the geologic past.

Queer theory *needs* Milton: in fact, queer theory's recent embrace of "life" and "ecology" as obvious "goods" in themselves appears increasingly symptomatic of a pastoral turn in queer theory, driven by our unrelenting commitment to living on, to seeing ourselves as part of the web of life, and to birthing our own, more sustainable future.[39] Rosi Braidotti's statement on prophecy typifies the new materialist turn to life in queer theory: "A prophetic or visionary dimension is necessary in order to secure an affirmative hold over the present, as the launching pad for sustainable becoming or qualitative transformations. The future is the virtual unfolding of the affirmative aspect of the present, which honors our obligations to the generations to come."[40] Braidotti emphasizes connection, life as a collaborative network, mutual redefinition, resignification, becoming: that is, the future. But what if this plays too much into a fantasy of human world-making, survival, and meaning?[41] Geontology, according to Povinelli, defines the political project of separating out life and nonlife, *bios* and *geos*. This project is all the more relevant today to discussions of the Anthropocene, humanity's geological force on earth. The emphasis in much Anthropocene writing is on survival, on redefining life as an open network of mutuality. Consequently, extinction—humanity's end—gets endlessly deferred, resignified, repurposed. If, for Lee Edelman, the image of the Child is the figure representing our violent devotion to the future, it is I think time to revise that figure to represent what it was always already about: life itself. Equally suspicious of the biontologization of life as purposive, self-organizing, intentional life, queer theorists such as Edelman and Leo Bersani posit a "real" that is neither life nor its opposite, biological death, but nonlife. Edelman calls it the "rock of the Real" and argues that it is the undead, never-to-be-alive remainder of the intentional subject.[42] The neovitalists who eschew the psychoanalytic "real" by way of Deleuze tend to forget that Deleuze, too, always insisted on figures of the inorganic: the machine, the desert, the exhausted. These figures are a part of life, according to Deleuze, because life expresses itself not only as vitality but also as inert, as nonlife. Indeed, according to Deleuze, thought entails an encounter with what is intolerable to thought: the oft-discussed "plane of immanence" he describes is a desert; we must rediscover the desert—the rock of the real—to become otherwise than what we are.[43]

Milton can help here. When so many posthumanisms—however queer—speak of life as a flowing, unending force of affirmation and creativity, Milton includes rupture, negativity, and violent encounter as necessary conditions for making and unmaking the earth. That is, far from determining how life *works*, Milton confronts the reader with the "absence of a work"—nature's archive of extinction.[44] So rendered, queerness registers not only the absence of place, as I will show in the next section, but also the absence of any lived in relation to affect.

Milton's Ungrounded Earth

If there is a commonplace of ecocriticism, it is that a poet's place is rooted to *place*. Ken Hiltner's important book, *Milton and Ecology*, makes this point axiomatic with respect to Milton. In the book's opening pages, Hiltner asks:

> When we, like Eve (tempted by the thought of what we might become) forget, even for a moment, that we still need our roots to run deep into our place on Earth, what happens to the place? Milton's answer is that the place will surely suffer as Earth feels the wound of our uprooting.[45]

To which Hiltner adds:

> In many respects the epic *Paradise Lost* is an answer to a simple, though rarely asked, question: how does one consider the allegory of the Fall, which introduces the Judeo-Christian *ethos*, without pondering our own place on the Earth?[46]

I will return to Hiltner's first answer (let us not say yet that it is Milton's), that "Earth feels the wound of our uprooting," toward the end of this section. For now, however, I would like to focus on the last question concerning our place on Earth. Is it true that *Paradise Lost* affirms *our* place above all else? Is Mother Earth really so homely, so "rooted" to here and now, as to play nursemaid to our wants, our feelings? Lastly, a question that is truly "rarely asked": as the place of place, the presumed anchoring point for time and meaning, for narration, the human subject can consider a future in which she is absent and nonetheless maintain that this will be a future for us. The world environs *us*. Is it easier, then, to imagine the end of the world than it is to imagine a world *without* us, since the world seems to hinge on our being there to witness it?

For Hiltner, "*Paradise Lost* is a call to regain our lost place on Earth" from the ravages of abstract space: "What should trouble us all is that the notion of the Earth covered with particular *places* has almost completely given way to an understanding of the Earth as *space*."[47] He notes that "the dominant Western view is to see such 'undeveloped' places as 'wide open space' onto which a grid of streets, wires, and pipes can be imposed—entirely irrespective of the character of the place already situated in this 'space.'"[48] Whereas Newton's *Philosophiae naturalis principia mathematica* (1687) announces "the manifest triumph of absolute space" as its philosophical masterwork, Hiltner claims that in *Paradise Lost*, "Milton's poetry speaks—or more accurately, rebuffs," "featureless space" as an ecological dead end.[49] I quote Hiltner's argument at length:

> The space Satan must cross from Hell to Earth is clearly featureless space: "a dark / Illimitable Ocean without bound, / Without dimension, where length, breadth, & highth, / And time and place are lost" (2.891–94). Perhaps the only way to characterize this timeless, featureless *space* in *Paradise Lost* may well be to say that it simply lacks *places* of any sort. Shortly after the Fall the devils in the epic approach this space in the same way that England was approaching "unused space" in Milton's time: they set about to develop the "dark / Illimitable Ocean without bound" (2.891–92). Beginning with a massive ocean-dredging operation, the devils toss up "what they met / Solid or slime" (10.285–86) to form the base for a bridge, "a passage broad, / Smooth, easie, inoffensive down to Hell" (10.304–05), "a Monument / Of merit high to all th' infernal Host" (10.258–59). What the devils dredge up is viewed as merely "material" for the making of the bridge, and just in case this soil is living, "The aggregated Soyle / Death with his Mace petrific, cold and dry, / As with a Trident smote, and fix't as firm / As Delos floating once" (10.293–96). It is difficult to imagine how the development of "space" could be described in more horrific terms than to have petrific Death touch everything in the place where the expansion is to occur.[50]

Alighting on the first instance of deepwater drilling in *Paradise Lost*, Hiltner reveals that the view toward developing "space" instead of "place" creates dead zones where once-living matter now serves as standing-reserve ("petrific Death") for the fallen angels' terraforming ambitions. This, of course, is how the fallen angels have proceeded from the start of Milton's epic. In book 1, Satan speaks of "one who brings / A mind not to be changed by place or time. / . . . [Which] in itself / Can make a heaven of hell, a hell of heaven" (1.252–55). The mind being "fixed," changeless, apprehends not its rootedness to place but rather its power to see every place as a unit of *space*. No sooner do the fallen angels apprehend their new home, "A dungeon horrible," volcanic, "With ever-burning sulphur," than they begin to remake it in their own image: "There stood a hill not far whose grisly top / Belched fire and rolling smoke; the rest entire / Shone with a glossy scurf, un-doubted sign / That in his womb was hid metallic ore, / The work of sulphur" (1.61, 69, 670–74). Setting upon this hill "with spade and pickaxe armed / . . . to trench a field, / Or cast a rampart," they, like "Men also," "Ransacked the centre, and with impious hands / Rifled the bowels of their mother earth / For treasures better hid" (1.676–78, 685, 686–88). Careless of place, Satan's "crew / Opened into the hill a spacious wound / And digged out ribs of gold" (1.688–90). The result is a spatial marvel exhumed from the materials of the earth:

> Let none admire
> That riches grow in hell; that soil may best
> Deserve the precious bane. And here let those
> Who boast in mortal things, and wondering tell
> Of Babel, and the works of Memphian kings
> Learn how their greatest monuments of fame,
> And strength and art are easily outdone
> By spirits reprobate, and in an hour
> What in an age they with incessant toil
> And hands innumerable scarce perform. (1.690–99)

Ungrounded, acculturated, the "riches" of the earth are with "strange conveyance" transformed by Satan's army into a "temple" of "stately height," "brazen folds," "ample spaces," and "smooth / And level pavement" (1.707, 713, 723, 724, 725, 725–26). It is, architecturally speaking, both a figure of algorithmic "magnificence" (1.718) and, as Hiltner observes, a symbol of "modern efficiency": "Whether the open *space* of chaos, or the distinct *place* of a hill, the devils saw noth-ing but space to attack, kill, or enslave."[51]

But is "space" really the nightmare that Hiltner says it is? If it is true what Satan says, that "Space may produce new worlds," it is also true that *Paradise Lost* is replete with worlds beyond the here and now, where "place" is folded, abstracted, doubled, and *queered* by worlds that are not ours, and definitely not human. In book 5, Eve dreams of a world not "of day past, or morrow's next design," but of "offence and trouble" and "irksome night," a liminal world governed by the "Full-orbed . . . moon," which "Shadowy sets off the face of things" in "more pleasing light" than day (5.33, 34, 35, 42, 43, 42). Eve's dream uproots her from the ground ("Forthwith up to the clouds / . . . I flew" [5.86–87]), giving her a new perspective on place: "and underneath beheld / The earth outstretched immense, a prospect wide" (5.87–88). Eve's dreamwork, like Freud's definition in *The Interpretation of Dreams,* occurs outside time and place, in a nonplace of unconscious desire; the result mirrors Milton's Satan (the latter's fall is doubled, ironized by Eve's ascent), who perceives the earth not as a dwelling place, an *oikos* or ecology, but rather as a "prospect" to be mined. (Indeed, the etymology of "prospect," from the Latin *prospectus,* "the action of looking out," also registers as an "anxiety" for the future ["prospect, n.," OED]; Eve's spatial "prospect" not only speculates on material ends, the literal riches of the earth, it also looks ahead [L. *pro-specere*] to tragic consequences.) All of this would, of course, support the idea that "space" is the enemy of "place" in *Paradise Lost,* were it not, however, for Adam, ever the glossator to Eve's dream life, who says to Eve:

> But know that in the soul
> Are many lesser faculties that serve
> Reason as chief; among these fancy next
> Her office holds; of all external things,
> Which the five watchful senses represent,
> She forms imaginations, airy shapes,
> Which reason joining or disjoining, frames
> All what we affirm or what deny, and call
> Our knowledge or opinion; then retires
> Into her private cell when nature rests.
> Oft in her absence mimic fancy wakes
> To imitate her; but misjoining shapes,
> Wild work produces oft, and most in dreams,

Ill matching words and deeds long past or late.
Some such resemblances methinks I find
Of our last evening's talk, in this thy dream,
But with addition strange. (5.100–16)

So "strange" in fact is "mimic fancy," whose "addition[s]" "misjoin"
higher reason's architectural "frames" (her "joints"), creating a surreal-
istic dreamwork of "knowledge or opinion," that she extends her "Wild
work" (or so says the speaker only a short time after) to all of nature:

for nature here
Wantoned as in her prime, and played at will
Her virgin fancies, pouring forth more sweet,
Wild above rule or art; enormous bliss. (5.294–97)

Where does Eve's dreamwork—her other world—end and begin?
From the echo of book 4 of Eve's "wanton ringlets" and vine-like "tendrils" (4.306–7), where she is first figured as plantlike, to "Wantoned"
nature above, the description of "fancy," which Adam frames as a tres-
passer in the night, soon frames the entirety of nature, which is "Wild
above rule or art."[52] Even the description of "reason," who retires to
"her private cell," conjures the image of wild nature, of a nonhuman
"cell" such as a honeycomb or beehive, whose female sovereign figuratively echoes Milton's borrowings from *A Midsummer Night's Dream*,
wherein, when the Fairy Queen sleeps, chaos reigns. Put differently:
nature is figured as already architectural in Milton's poem, as a wild
frenzy of lines, planes, and geometrical bodies—without any human
supplement. Nature is both spatial and spatializing, both corporeal
(concrete) and incorporeal (abstract) at once: "And corporeal to incorporeal *turn*" (5.413, emphasis added). It is for this reason that
Deleuze, oft-cited for his materialism, claims that "the true opposite
of the concrete is not the abstract"—the language of abstract "space"
does not a bad materialist make—"it is the discrete."[53] Parsing the
concrete from the abstract, or place from space, renders "discrete"
what would otherwise be, for Milton and Deleuze, a perpetual
"turn[ing]" motion of one thing into the other. Not only that, Adam
and Eve praise the "sovereign architect" for "this thine universal frame"

(5.256, 154); Galileo is credited for "Imagin[ing] lands and regions in the moon" (5.263); and, echoing the science fiction of Margaret Cavendish, speed and space combine to emblazon new worlds: "Down thither prone in flight / He [Raphael] speeds, and through the vast ethereal sky / Sails between worlds and worlds" (5.266–68).

Space is not the problem in *Paradise Lost*; if anything, place is.

Not coincidentally, the image of "place" that Hiltner gravitates toward in *Milton and Ecology* is Adam and Eve's "bower" (4.690): "The Bower is a living 'planted house' rooted in place. . . . It is a prelapsarian image not of a house built of the place's 'resources' (as *resurgere*, 'to rise again'), but as a living house still in its act of rising out of its place, it is still a source of life."[54] And what kind of life does this "living house" sustain? To answer that, Hiltner suggests, "it might be more than idle speculation to consider just how Adam's and Eve's future generations would have inhabited their place if there had been no Fall."[55] Translated slightly (but only slightly), the bower becomes the "place" of heteronormative "speculation"—Hiltner's, not Milton's. "Life," according to Hiltner, is not the afutural life of queer dame "fancy," whose strange "misjoinings" produce differences within the garden without concern for self-maintenance or reproduction. "Life" for Hiltner means living *for* the children: "So we can imagine the first young child . . . being led by Adam and Eve to a *particular place* in the Garden which he would be told would be his *domicile*, where he would have *dominion*."[56] Notice the curious doubling here between generational "speculation," in which the future is written in the image of the child and the place-based language of humanity's unchecked "*dominion*," and the poem's previous speculations: the fallen angels' "Ransacked" earth and Eve's "prospect wide." What each of these examples has in common is a view toward being *rooted* to place, toward *taking* place now and in the future, no matter the cost.

Putting aside the obvious threat that (in hindsight) Adam and Eve's "future generations" pose to other species, including those "defunct species" that we read about in Atwood, the cost of taking "place" in the garden is apparently this: queer desire. Hiltner is at pains to put *space* between Adam and Eve's "blissful bower" (4.690) and its literary antecedent, Spenser's "Bowre of Blisse": "Though the outward similarities between these two bowers are many, their role in their

respective works is fundamentally different. Vividly contrasted with
the Garden of Adonis, Spenser's Bowre of Blisse is first and foremost
an enchanting temptation. . . . Milton's blissful bower, though pleas-
ant, is in no sense a temptation—though it is conspicuous."[57] Note
again what can only be thought of as a symptom in the logic of "place,"
as the object of opprobrium, "featureless space"—the term itself is
spaced from its neighbor, "place"—rears its ugly head in the word "conspicuous," which is rooted in the act of speculation (con-*specere*, "to
view or observe mentally," "to theorize upon").[58] If the "blissful bower"
is conspicuous, it is because it forces us to look awry at the language
of place, which is haunted, doubled by the empty, superficial, and for
that reason potentially pleasurable, a futural "misjoinings" of Spenser's
bower. After all, speculation does not guarantee "future generations"
(it is not clear, in any case, that Adam and Eve *know* where future
generations come from . . .). If we take the bower's "conspicuous" delights as just that, pleasures afforded by the garden, then speculation
has less to do with *taking place* (now and in the future) and more to
do with cruising material differences—without a view toward shor-
ing up our "dominion."

This last point is all the more important with respect to Milton's
earth, which Hiltner interprets as a womb:

> Forth reaching to the fruit, she [Eve] plucked, she ate:
> Earth felt the wound, and nature from her seat
> Sighing through all her works gave signs of woe,
> That all was lost. (9.781–84)

Given the cosmic nature of this event—Earth's trauma—it would
be strange, at least, to theorize "the wound" anthropomorphically.
"Earth felt the wound" figures the event of wounding as utterly *inhuman*, beyond or other than the merely "felt" or lived body. "Earth
felt the wound" extinguishes at once any image of place ("and nature
from her seat / Sighing *through all her works*") and any lived being
(the event happens at a geologic scale impossible for any living being
to comprehend); so told, "Earth felt the wound" epitomizes the autonomy of the event, which, though "felt," stands outside human
experience (the event *cuts* the enjambed line with an imperceptible

caesura). Before the wound becomes *this* wounded body, or *this* wounded self, it subsists in matter as the potential *to cut*. Milton's wounded earth is thus radically *unlivable*: it severs not only "our" felt relation to place but also affect from affection and earth from home. Read as *unheimlich* or "unhomely," as the "seat" of inhuman affects, which only become human through a reduction to human sense, Milton's earth appears less as the material support for "our" affections. Rather, like the rectum in Bersani's "Is the Rectum a Grave?," Milton's queer earth figures the earth's "seat," its bottom, as inhuman fundament, one that shatters individual identities along the cutting edge of affect-laden events (affect understood here not as the private affections of the lived body but as relations of inhuman force).[59]

The illusion of affect is to think that because we are thinking–feeling beings, that the mind-body is, therefore, the "seat" of affect. In fact, the mind-body is already a synthesis of myriad inhuman events. To the extent that language and art reach the virtuality of affect, they become vital. At the same time, however, this vital life has nothing to do with the lived. That is why Deleuze characterizes the "event" as a kind of nonsense—to think the event of *wounding*, in the infinitive, is to think outside our relations of sense, of being and knowing. Similarly, Milton's geo-affective-event barely makes sense when read through the humanizing lens of personification; in Milton's hands, it is the earth itself that trembles:

> Earth trembled from her entrails, as again
> In pangs, and nature gave a second groan,
> Sky loured and muttering thunder, some sad drops
> Wept at completing of the mortal sin
> Original. (9.1000–1004)

Richard DuRocher notes that "for all its originality and importance, the significance of this figure has virtually escaped critics' attention."[60] I would suggest that the reason for this oversight is personification itself, or the tendency to read anonymous materiality through the sieve of human signification, such that "Earth trembled" or "Sky loured" become projections or screens for "our" emotion. Hiltner, for one, reads the earth's affect through a humanizing lens; he personifies the earth's wound through the language of birth and separation, writing: "Milton's use of 'pangs' to describe what the Earth felt is telling, since from the sixteenth century through Milton's time 'pangs' was limited to either 'death pangs' or 'pangs of childbirth.'" Hiltner continues: "On the other hand, if we do not think in terms of a literal childbirth, but rather a child's own foolish act that causes a separation from the Mother Earth, then the wound becomes the site (the place of 'root-edness') where human beings and the Earth became separated."[61] Here the affect "pangs" is rooted to "place," but this place is not the chthonic place of earthly "entrails." Hiltner interprets "entrails" as a womb rather than a rectum, despite the predominant early modern usage of "entrails" to denote the bowels or intestines.[62] (The displacement of the rectum for the womb: Is this not precisely the point at which queerness and geontopower intersect? If, as Bersani has taught us, the rectum figures that which is intolerable to our images of sex, sex being the pillar of biopower's investment in life, a life that is undone by queer desire, then a geology of life would need to confront this rectum, or this grave, as the abjected region of "life itself" under geontopower. To return to my earlier assertion: the "rock" of the real—the drive, the negative—takes on a queerly literal significance when geology and ontology become entangled. This is the crisis we are experiencing today. Milton would have us embrace this crisis as our inmost inhuman nature.) What the earth *feels*, therefore, according to Hiltner, is our lived affections, the Mother-Child couplet, and the pains of parturition projected onto an emotionally recognizable (because *humanized*) landscape.

Milton, I argue, offers a far more nuanced understanding of affect. For if personification is the word (the only available word) to describe "Earth trembled," it is a peculiar, queer personification in which the figure of the "face" (Greek *prosopon*) derives from inhuman forces: the Mother-Child is *thinkable* because forces beyond us first actualize it. Milton envisions "pangs" that have nothing whatsoever to do with the lived body—neither *from us* (personification) nor *for us* (hermeneutics), the affects "pangs," "Sky loured," and "muttering thunder," depict affects in their inorganic and incorporeal materiality. To the extent that we too feel the wound, it is because we are seized by forces beyond us—earth, sky, and thunder; we exhaust their inhuman potential. But why take this highly formal approach to the affective, which, in its recent scholarly iterations, has inspired a return to the body and the titillations of the flesh?

The reason why I claim it is necessary to read Milton's inhuman figures as just that, as figures outside our lived experience, is because only such a reading will enable us to encounter what is not us. "Affects," Deleuze and Guattari write, "are no longer feelings or affections; they go beyond the strength of those who undergo them." Instead, "Sensations, percepts, and affects are *beings* whose validity lies in themselves and exceeds any lived. They could be said to exist in the absence of man because man . . . is himself a compound of percepts and affects. The work of art is a being of sensation and nothing else: it exists in itself."[63] To read affect *without us* is to encounter "the absence of man," which is precisely what the geological record makes possible. "Earth felt the wound" figures a trauma of deep historical time. By separating this "wound" from the place of the human sensorium, Milton points to a different economy of affect, one in which matter-energy is no longer a "resource" *for us.* In book 6 of *Paradise Lost,* Milton reimagines the "re" of resource as both repetition and undoing, as what is exhausted from the earth as fossil energy redounds upon the angels themselves, exhausting their power to do or act according to their own interest. In what is the most epical of books in Milton's epic, bodies divest their own bounded energy, becoming subject to the earth's inhuman affect. In this sense, Milton embraces the *amor fati* of Stoic ethics: "My wound existed before me; I was born to embody it."[64] As the figure of this wound, an earthly trauma in-itself, with neither a *from* (personified intentionality) nor a *to* (referent or recipient), the fossil signifies both the autonomy of affect and "the absence of man" in Deleuze's sense: the wound that Satan suffers will, through the repetitive force of the poem, prove to be nothing more and nothing less than the same wound that preexists us—that is, the rending of the earth—which proposes powers and potentials beyond us.

The Seraphic Body in Pain

In *Civilization and Its Discontents*, Freud offers a description of geo-historical events as his metaphor for the unconscious; I begin with Freud's metaphor here as it points the way toward my reading of Milton's earth. Freud writes:

> Let us, by a flight of imagination, suppose that Rome is not a human habitation but a psychical entity with a similarly long and copious past—an entity, that is to say, in which nothing that has once come into existence will have passed away and all the earlier phases of development continue to exist alongside the latest one. This would mean that in Rome the palaces of the Caesars and the Septizonium of Septimius Severus would still be rising to their old height on the Palatine and that the castle of S. Angelo would still be carrying on its battlements the beautiful statues which graced it until the siege by the Goths, and so on. But more than this. . . . Where the Coliseum now stands we could at the same time admire Nero's vanished Golden House. On the Piazza of the Pantheon we should find not only the Pantheon of to-day, as it was bequeathed to us by Hadrian, but, on the same site, the original edifice erected by Agrippa; indeed, the same piece of ground would be supporting the church of Santa Maria sopra Minerva and the ancient temple over which it was built. And the observer would perhaps only have to change the direction of his glance or his position in order to call up the one view or the other.[65]

Unlike the observer in Margaret Atwood's novel, Jimmy, who looks out on a ruined landscape, Freud's observer witnesses the (impossible) intertwining of structure and history, in which everything remains intact. From a certain perspective, the unconscious seems to know no time, as all the buildings of Rome's past constantly remain present. From another perspective, however, the comparison of the unconscious with Rome is radically weighted by time, as the entirety of the city's past pushes upon the present. Freud was the first to recognize the limitations of his metaphor: "There is clearly no point in spinning our phantasy any further, for it leads to things that are unimaginable and even absurd. If we want to represent historical sequence in spatial terms we can only do it by juxtaposition in space:

the same space cannot have two different contents."[66] Freud's logical protestations aside, it is precisely the heterological (im)possibility of *other spaces* contained in the archaeological metaphor that serves as the ungrounded ground of his theory of the unconscious.

Crucial here is Freud's claim that unlike conscious space with its objective contents and relations, unconscious space is subject to the rhythmic formations and deformations of the drives, which mutate, displace, and transform the contents of the past while nonetheless insisting those contents *in* the present. In the unconscious, it is the nonrelations between things, the cuts that separate *and* bind contents of the mind temporarily, that both yield objective relations (such as the familiar relations between an organism and its environment, which allow us to curve a situation around our interests and actions) and *dissolve* those relations as well, as when an affect or event of too much power exhausts our ability to act according to our own interests. Freud's archaeological metaphor not only shows how the present is limned and made possible by the hauntological record; it also undoes that present, the space of our future action. What Freud's observer perceives, then, is not our space but "a" space of potential actions opened by the geological record, a time beneath and beyond the habits of this lived present.

The unconscious in Freud's metaphor is, therefore, an *environmental unconscious*—though with this important caveat: just as everyday life becomes interesting to Freud precisely when systems of speech, memory, and psychic functioning *do not work*, as in the case of the well-known parapraxes or errors in speech (i.e., the Freudian slip), so too, the environmental unconscious becomes meaningful only when living systems do not work—that is, when life is no longer *for us* but involves the suspension or dissolution of the actual as such. Freud's Rome can be grasped only by escaping the perspective of any actual living individual. In the passage quoted above, it is *we* who have been exhausted, whereas the structures themselves appear untimely or atemporal—they reference a time in which we are not.

What might the ethics of this perspective be? It is the claim of this chapter that we need a different ecological ethics, one that can tolerate the nonrelation, or the bottomless nonidentity, of earthly life, if we are to grasp the catastrophe of the Anthropocene on its own terms: both as a queering of human agency via geology, and as an event written in the earth itself. This is an event for all time; therefore, it references a time without us. As Claire Colebrook and Jami Weinstein write: "Something entirely new has occurred with the posing of the Anthropocene, and this is the possibility of human life and *human history after humans*: Humans will be readable in the scar they left upon the earth."[67] Instead of the same old ecological mantras of care, sustainability, interconnectivity, and place, words we *repeat* but do not *feel* outside our own lived experience, it may be time to think about the violence of the nonrelation—such as Foucault's fossils, Ray's rent universe, Freud's environmental unconscious, or Milton's inhuman affect—as a way of opening thought to events beyond us.

Take one of Milton's most illuminating examples, the event of Satan's wound. Near the beginning of book 6 of *Paradise Lost*, pain enters the world for the first time in the form of a cut:

> Together [Michael and Satan] both with next to
>   almighty arm,
> Uplifted imminent one stroke they aimed
> That might determine, and not need repeat,
> As not of power, at once; nor odds appeared
> In might or swift prevention; but the sword
> Of Michael from the armoury of God
> Was given him tempered so, that neither keen
> Nor solid might resist that edge: it met
> The sword of Satan with steep force to smite
> Descending, and in half cut sheer, nor stayed,
> But with swift wheel reverse, deep entering sheared
> All his right side; then Satan first knew pain,
> And writhed him to and fro convolved. (6.316–28)

Notice the delay between the affect or event of cutting, "deep entering sheared," on the one hand, and its affection on the other, "then Satan first knew pain." The entirety of book 6 aims at returning thought exhaustively to that delay—what Milton elsewhere calls that "dreadful interval," the empty, disinterested space of nonaction—by repeating it over and over again (hence the importance of "convolved," to roll, fold, or coil together) in the form of a wound. In other words, the event's structure is double: there is the wound that Satan feels, sword cutting flesh; and there is the power *to wound*, which cuts time in the form of a delay or break in action.

What Milton enables us to see with this structure is the autonomy of the affect free from any lived—not this or that particular wound but "a" power to wound, not this or that body affected in time but "a" power to affect bodies for all of time. The same structure emerges at key intervals of the battle between the angels: before Abdiel "his own undaunted heart explores" in the form of a felt apostrophe, "O heaven!," he is seized by a power of "sight" that is itself unlivable; he "endured [it] not" (6.113–14, 111). The unbearable "sight" is a power of expression that precedes any expressed. Likewise, we read that "Amazement" in its autonomy "seized / The rebel thrones," and that an anonymous "clamour" hovered over the surface of bodies, linking the battle among the angels to the very center of the earth: "And had earth been then, all earth / Had to her centre shook" (6.198–99, 208, 218–19). Whereas the disjunct between affect and affection is *implied* by these earlier moments, the structure of the event, the nonrelation (or cut) between things is most fully realized in the figure of Satan's wound, a wound that is multiply wounding in that it tears affect from affection, time from our time, and sign from referent. Within the space of that tear, epical time—the time of our actions and affairs— comes to a standstill; time is exhausted.

If there is an ethics to be gained from this exhaustive method, it is this: to be *equal* to the event.[68] In one of his rare statements on ethics, Deleuze writes: "Either ethics makes no sense at all, or this is what it means and has nothing else to say: not to be unworthy of what happens to us."[69] Elsewhere he implies that ethics *is* a form of exhaustion: "Only an exhausted person can exhaust the possible," Deleuze writes, "because he has renounced all need, preference, goal, or signification. Only the exhausted person is sufficiently disinterested."[70] Only the exhausted person is certain never to "get up."[71] To be equal to the event to the point of exhaustion: this, no doubt, is a strange definition of ethical practice, one that flies in the face of commonsense notions of human freedom.[72] Nevertheless, it is this definition of ethics, I argue, that we find implicated, folded, convolved, and implied in the exhaustive repetitions of Milton's poem.

Take the word "equal," for example: when God says to the angel Michael that he and his army are "Equal in number to that godless crew," he measures their power to act in accordance with mathematical figures (1+1=2, and so on to infinity). By the end of the battle, however, when both sides have exhausted their powers, God says again: "Equal in their creation they were formed," therefore "in perpetual fight they needs must last / Endless, and no solution will be found" (6.49, 690, 693–94). "Equal" denotes a freedom to act that is represented on both sides of the battle as freedom *from* natural constraint. When outmatched by Michael and his army, the fallen angels bemoan "the too unequal work [they] find / Against unequal arms to fight in pain," and turn to the "Deep underground, materials dark and crude," to power their "devilish enginery" (6.453–54, 478, 553):

> Forthwith from council to the work they flew,
> None arguing stood, innumerable hands
> Were ready, in a moment up they turned
> Wide the celestial soil, and saw beneath
> The originals of nature in their crude
> Conception; sulphurous and nitrous foam
> They found, they mingled, and with subtle art,
> Concocted and adjusted they reduced
> To blackest grain, and into store conveyed:
> Part hidden veins digged up (nor hath this earth
> Entrails unlike) of mineral and stone,
> Whereof to found their engines and their balls
> Of missive ruin. (6.507–19)

If poetry begins with verse (from the Latin *versus*) meaning "to turn"—the ancient metaphor is of turning soil, plowing—Milton exaggerates that metaphor by re-turning poetically to the first upturning of the earth's "celestial soil." This is, in other words, the first instance of what Jason W. Moore, in *Capitalism in the Web of Life*, calls "accumulation by appropriation" of "Cheap Natures," a cyclical process of ecological vampirism by which capitalism "overcomes" its tendency to exhaust energy surpluses. "The normal course of capital accumulation tends to exhaust the establishing relations of re/production that inaugurate a great wave of accumulation," Moore writes.[73] "From the sixteenth century, the appropriation of biophysically rich frontiers, combined with uncapitalized labor-power and sufficiently mobile capital, has periodically resolved the underlying contradiction" of energy exhaustion.[74] From this vantage, capital is a form of vitalism (or vital-vampirism) in that it seeks to resolve its contradictions through a fantasy of endless adaptability—of life *without* negativity, exhaustion, or limits.[75] This is the vitalist fantasy we see not once but repeatedly in book 6, notably after Satan's wound, which "soon he healed; for spirits that live throughout / Vital in every part . . . / Cannot but by annihilating die"; and again after the fallen angels' first defeat in battle, when they turn to the earth's "hidden veins" to power their "engines" and defer further exhaustion (6.44–47). Nor is this tendency to capitalize on the earth's energy—on fossil remains bequeathed by deep time—exceptional to the fallen angels' spatializing practices (pace Hiltner), for Michael and his army, too, repeat the image of earth's wound by cutting the mountains from their seat:

> Their arms away they threw, and to the hills
> (For earth hath this variety from heaven
> Of pleasure situate in hill and dale)
> Light as the lightning glimpse they ran, they flew,
> From their foundations loosening to and fro
> They plucked the seated hills with all their load,
> Rocks, waters, woods, and by the shaggy tops
> Up lifting bore them in their hands:
> . . . .
> The bottom of the mountains upward turned. (6.639–49)

Freedom so imagined rests on the geontological distinction of human and nonhuman timescales, on the interval, that is, separating life ("vital in every part") from nonlife, which is figured as expendable. As Dipesh Chakrabarty writes: "The mansion of modern freedoms stands on an ever-expanding base of fossil-fuel use. Most of our freedoms so far have been energy-intensive."[76]

Milton proposes an alternative to this energy economy. Writing at the advent of the Anthropocene, Milton not only recognizes the energy-intensive nature of epic; he draws on epic "resources"—such as Chaucer's "The Knight's Tale" and the battle between Cambell and Triamond in book 4 of Spenser's *The Faerie Queene*—to illustrate the very "absurdity" that Cleanth Brooks saw as a failing in his poem, namely, "the absurdity of a battle in which the contestants," being equal, "cannot be killed." Against this form of freedom, which reduces the angels' power to an exhausting reductio ad absurdum of epic tropes, Milton envisions an ecological ethics in which the angels themselves, having exhausted their powers to act independently of nature, become equal to the event itself. Nature, in other words, is figured by Milton as self-acting or self-cutting, an inexhaustible agency that is neither redemptive nor nihilistic but multiplicative and creative: when, at the end of the battle, "wonted vigour left them drained, / Exhausted, spiritless, afflicted, fallen," the only thing that remains vital is the *form* of the affect itself (6.851–52). Repetition, in other words, *as form* exhausts the angels' bodies so that all that remains standing is the affect: exhaustion. As a stand-alone form (and here I note parenthetically the significance Milton attributes to the action of standing—as in "Sufficient to have stood, though free to fall" [3.99]) exhaustion reads as a power *to exhaust* not just here and now but for all of time; not just these particular bodies—not even the body of the reader—but also past and future bodies, including Ray's lifeless fossils and Atwood's defunct species.

The queerness of Milton's earth lies in precisely this fact, that only bodies exhausted of any future communicate across the intervals of stratigraphic time, and so too the intervals of life and nonlife, making it possible therefore to think a future difference in which we do more than re-live ourselves. To return to Foucault's dilemma, how to exhaust the earth's record of "extravagance," its "silences" encased in stone, we might begin to reflect on the autonomy of affective forms in Milton's poem (*to exhaust, to wound*) as expressions of an impersonal power. These forms would pose the possibility of thinking the interval or delay between our world (with its habitual relations) and the world without us. Milton's geology of exhausted life does just that: it allows us to witness what Michael Marder, in *Energy Dreams*, describes as *another* "will to energy" antithetical to the war over resources. "By force of habit," he writes,

> we think of energy as a resource—a thought not so outlandish considering that, as a word, it is a substantive. A noun, an object, a cause for wars and diplomatic alliances, something to divide, extract, lay claim to, possess. . . . The effects of energy, however, surpass a strife-ridden or consensual division of resources. Far from a mere object to be appropriated, it energizes us—our bodies, psyches, economies, technologies, political systems. . . . Its sense, then, is evenly split between substantive and verbal significations. The will to energy is none other than the will to willing, where the object, the objective, is not some inert material but an active, activating event—that of the subject. The crisis of energy is that, though treated as a finite resource to be seized in a mad race with others who also desire it, *it* seizes both "us" and "them," taking, first and foremost, our fantasies and our dreams hostage.[77]

Seen as a "finite resource," an object "to be seized in a mad race with others," energy entombs life within a vivophilic quest of vitalistic-vampirism, an exhausting will-to-power that is both deadly and disastrous. A thinking that is *queer* desists from this exhausting repetition—not by returning to life, place, or *oikos* (the home), but by insisting on the already dead force of the drive, a will to exhaust "our" will-to-power by pushing beyond the here and now, the lived, toward an ethics of the unlivable, where life and nonlife con-*volve*. While Milton's "activating event" is not that "of the subject," the implicitly *human* subject—as I have shown, *Paradise Lost* is replete with material events far removed from any human agent—it shares Marder's sense of the "split between substantive and verbal signification," such that *to wound* differs radically from any wounded. Satan's *ressentiment*, his will to be equal, to repeat, no matter the cost, belongs to the substantive pole—he repeats therefore he is; but from the queer perspective afforded by Milton's verbal signification, *to cut, to sheer, to cleave, to rend*, we witness an action without time, a dead time of pure form in which "we" are no longer acting. Such an event can only be *read*—slowly, recursively, to the point of exhaustion. The blade that cuts Satan also cuts—briefly, imperceptibly—the action of the poem, allowing us to read Satan's inner "pain" alongside the many other events of cutting that form and deform Milton's earth. "Earth felt the wound" is not simply "our" lived emotion project outward; rather, as the earth's archive of extinction suggests, our pain is a fold of the earth. To be "convolved" with the earth is to imagine freedom otherwise than as the power to lay hold of the earth as "resource"; to be convolved means to act in concert with the earth, in-*formed* by its very madness, contingency, dehiscence, and queer extravagance.

CONCLUSION
Toward Wild Psychoanalysis

In the environmental humanities, we have become used to saying that
we are not subjects outside of nature; rather, we are (in) nature. We
are intra-active, enmeshed, networked, emergent parts of a greater
whole; the thinking-feeling of what happens; *bios* and *geos* at once.
Nevertheless, what happens when questions of violence, runaway
carbon emissions, and other destructive forces enter the conversation? We reintroduce the notion of a human/nature split. Or we
finesse the split by introducing the "Capitalocene," said to interrupt
our previous balance.[1] According to this argument, humanity really
was enmeshed with nature until, starting in around the sixteenth
century (the dates are fuzzy), humanity went astray. Enter Descartes. Enter mind–body dualism. Enter the Enlightenment and
deleterious capitalism. Descartes's "error" was *only* an error, however.
Now, the task is to correct our errant path and get back to nature,
our home. But if we are indeed parts of nature, and if we take the environmental credo seriously, that *there is no outside of nature*,[2] then
nature cannot be so wholesome, and destruction cannot simply enter
from without.[3] None of the tropes mentioned above (mesh, entanglement, intra-active network) adequately captures the problem of
environmental destruction because they treat loss as external. Time
and again, entanglement serves as a new and improved version of ecological holism. But even this holism has an aggressive slant: we are all
parts of an interactive web, the ecocritic tells us, *don't you forget*.

On the one hand, a concept derived from psychoanalysis, misrecognition, has proven indispensable to ecocriticism, whereby we see ourselves not as separate beings severed from the Earth-system, but rather as the *effect* of that system and as the *realization* of vital networks of living and nonliving agencies. Ecocriticism (be it deconstructed, biopoliticized, or queered) could not operate and would be strictly speaking impossible without the psychoanalytic notion of misrecognition at its disposal.[4] To be sure, what we recognize in ecocriticism is varied. What the new materialist and the posthumanist reveal is not the truth of nature; they point instead to differences upon differences and interacting networks of vital, toxic, and destabilizing bodies. On the other hand, there is a crucial difference between this version of misrecognition and the psychoanalytic one. The former cuts out the latter.

Although Jacques Lacan had theorized misrecognition in the mirror-stage essay, it was not until *Seminar XI* that he theorized it in relation to the gaze. In the later work, "gaze" interrupts vision.[5] Whereas the child before the mirror misrecognizes the image as his own, the gaze further complicates matters by introducing desire, specifically desire for what is *not* visible and therefore *in*explicable to vision itself. What defines misrecognition, according to Lacan, is not that we forget to see ourselves as reflects *of* the Other (the image that promises wholeness); it is that there is no Other. Misrecognition, for Lacan, means that we avoid seeing the unseeable—what he calls little object a—and that vital networks do not simply produce that unseeable "something"; the latter view would amount to yet another version of ecological monism, in which every last thing is accounted for. Instead of the monism of all things, Lacan argues that the gaze is a veritable hole in being. What is more, this hole comes from the Other, which is why the Other cannot explain the subject of desire. It is also why the Other cannot be the totality of our ecological relations. Far from explaining desire, the Other makes desire inexplicable. When we encounter the gaze, we encounter the fact that the network of our vision curves around an absence, and that absence induces us as desiring subjects.

The consequences of this rather technical point about misrecognition are twofold: first, although ecocriticism borrows from psychoanalysis the idea that we are opaque to ourselves and that our images of self come from the Other, be it the personal other of intimate relations or the impersonal Other of ecological interconnectedness, it defangs the idea of misrecognition entirely; second, what distinguishes misrecognition in the psychoanalytic sense and sets it apart from ecotheory is that desire never stops *failing* to realize itself. In other words, while it is true that psychoanalysis and ecotheory both posit subjects who are the *effects* of their environments, psychoanalysis does not argue that subjects *realize* their environments.[6] On the contrary, desiring subjects are those who fail to recognize themselves in the Other, and for whom desire—the object of desire—remains unrealized. Being a desiring subject does not mean that we are produced by the Other and that we must therefore recognize ourselves in the image of the Other; it means that the Other, including the ecological Other of networked beings, is radically incomplete—and not only in the sense of endlessly differing and deferring relations, but incomplete in the sense that the Other houses lack. That hole in the Other triggers our desire, which makes the field of vision something more than the network of our relations.

My claim is that ecotheory misrecognizes and is also hostile to the something more that escapes the panoptivision of our relations. My reference to Foucault's theory of the panopticon is not beside the point, since Foucault's theory of panoptic vision runs parallel to Lacan's theory of the mirror and, like the big Other of ecocriticism, leaves nowhere for desire. This elision is not by accident. Foucault's project, as we know, takes from Lacan's theory of misrecognition the idea that we are first subjects outside ourselves; we furnish our inner world with the images that power bestows on us. We are, in this sense, the image of the Other. Where things go awry is in Foucault's theory of this Other. As Joan Copjec argues, Foucault's Other (biopower) is an upright Lacanian because it has no basis in desire.[7] By aligning the Other with production—this is how Foucault defines power, not as the power to repress but as the power to *produce* and make live—Foucault assumes this Other to be all-encompassing, perfect in its power to produce the social field.

In ecocriticism, which repeats Foucault's emphasis on relations of production, we find a similar semblance of the Other as all: there is no outside, Karen Barad and Timothy Morton both proclaim.[8] There is no outside because relations and their productions are all there is. This proposition, to be sure, can lead to toxifying encounters. Let us imagine the ecocritical rejoinder: saying there is no outside is to claim that we are deeply, inextricably, and transcorporeally entangled with all we abject. This much is true. Nevertheless, my claim is that this autoimmunitary status is, despite its war-torn rhetoric, oddly resistant to the very possibility of resisting the big Other's toxifying embrace. By accepting as true the idea that the Other qua biopower qua biosphere is and says all, we leave ourselves no choice but to recognize our place in the image of the Other and to take pleasure in the relations afforded therein. I say pleasure, not desire. When we speak of pleasure in psychoanalysis, we speak of *habituation*, not deviation. Pleasure, not desire, has become the master signifier of post-Foucauldian readings of the "repressive hypothesis."[9] Queer pleasures, posthuman pleasures, and surface pleasures now interlace with a certain version of bio-deconstruction to stamp out desire and its relation to the unconscious—to everything that is *not* of the environment because it is first of all repressed.

Because psychoanalysis sees the Other as desiring, rather than panoptic, the Other is no less incomplete. As I have been arguing, misrecognition has two potentials, the one Foucauldian, the other psychoanalytic: in the former, misrecognition means that we fail to recognize ourselves in the image of the Other; in psychoanalysis, it means that we fail to recognize that there is no Other. Failure, a prestigious term in psychoanalysis, thus refers not to a failure of perception but to the failure that is perception. Consequently, the social field is not the realization of the Other but the realization of the Other as failure. Contra bio-deconstruction and the smooth interweaving of all things, psychoanalysis holds that there is, in fact, an outside and that this obtrusive outside is the only means of conceiving of a radical politics that can break from the immanence of bodies and their relations. Together, biopower, bioethics, and biopleasures produce the social field by producing subjects who misrecognize their desire and take pleasure in being the Other's mirror. "I'll be your mirror," Nico says, "Reflect what you are, in case you don't know."[10] This is the language of bioethics today.

By contrast, Spenser, Ralegh, Marvell, and Milton show that there is no big Other to guide nature's discourse because environmentalism's big Other does not exist. Far from recognizing their place in environmentalism's big Other (the network that houses our material–symbolic identities), Spenser, Ralegh, Marvell, and Milton make failure the object of their poetics. This is a slow process, to be sure. As late as book 9 of Milton's *Paradise Lost*, we see Adam and Eve protesting their daily labors. Although they work assiduously to tend and cultivate the garden, this work does not offer an end to desire. The opposite is true: the more they work, the less they have to show for it. Eve says to Adam:

> well may we labour still to dress
> This garden, still to tend plant, herb and flower,
> Our pleasant task enjoined, but till more hands
> Aid us, the work under our labour grows,
> Luxurious by restraint; what we by day
> Lop overgrown, or prune, or prop, or bind,
> One night or two with wanton growth derides,
> Tending to wild. (9.205–12)

For Eve, a garden that is forever "Tending to wild" is beyond human measure and, so, beyond human enjoyment. It is a wasted effort. Luxury is, in this sense, the obverse of personal gain. Eve tends to the garden. She enjoys all that it has to offer. However, she claims she has nothing to show for it. Her work is unworkable. The garden, she claims, "grows / Luxurious by restraint." This is as much a poetic problem as it is an ecological one. The more nature outstrips Adam and Eve's efforts, the more it becomes apparent that nature in the garden is not one: nature, like poetry, is skewed from the start. Although Milton's poem tells the story of humanity before the fall, we can read Adam and Eve from the vantage of Milton's own time as capitalist subjects in the making. The garden is their training ground in the logic of accumulation.[11] Although it would seem that they have everything, a veritable paradise, "something" is missing.[12]

Milton's paradise is a paradox. Indeed, Eve's statement suggests that paradise and paradise lost are structurally identical. Although she has a wealth of things, the paradise around her only generates more loss. Meanwhile, Eve's desire to restrain the garden's "wanton growth" is fueled by a promise. The same promise can be heard echoed throughout Milton's poem: "more hands." This haunting refrain points to a future in which the labor of desire will come to an end. It is a metonymy of the future represented by Adam and Eve's children. Not only does the promise of "more hands" open to the future, but it also hinges on the retroactive belief that something is missing. Milton reads the fall of man as the failure of this promise; it is only because Adam and Eve believe that something is missing that they are willing to sacrifice paradise for the dream of a better tomorrow.

Adam and Eve labor under the promise of finding something that does not exist: the complete and fully satisfying object—the end to their and their plants' diurnal work. *Paradise Lost* is, among other things, a poem about the failure of reading. Adam and Eve search for signs of the lost object that will satisfy their desires. However, each new object presents further limits to their success. What makes Milton's poem so important in this context is that it teaches us to read the secret of Adam and Eve's desire as the desire for *limits*.[13] Milton uses the space of the poem to draw out a radical insight: what satisfies Adam and Eve's desire is not the material object but its absence. Eve's repetition of "more hands" proves this point. The "hands" that might help bring about paradise do not, in fact, come, yet the repetition of the phrase secures their absence, and that, for Milton, is the point.

Unlike the object of ecocriticism, Milton's object fails to cohere; the garden in his poem is forever "Tending to wild."[14] Although we are invited to see paradise as something that Adam and Eve lost, this is only a fantasy. Milton's real point is that paradise exists only as missing. We desire it because it is missing.

I argue that Milton's lesson is just as pressing today, perhaps even more so, as the dream of human progress burns in the embers of capitalist ruins, and as the accelerations of the Capitalocene switch into hyperdrive, setting our house, the earth, ablaze. Because the new materialisms believe that matter must mean, they are ill-equipped to recognize failure as the true object of desire. Whereas the new materialisms seek to awaken readers to the structures that perpetuate ecological destruction, this commitment to wakefulness mimics the illusory coherence of the capitalist $ubject, who believes no less passionately that matter and meaning must cohere; they cohere as commodities. But this belief that matter must mean and that all things being equal exist on the single surface of sense, as sensibles, is an idealism, *not* a materialism.[15] It is precisely the sort of idealism that psychoanalysis resists by positing a subject who is unconscious to her desire. A subject who is unconscious to desire can never fully appear on the single surface of sense—ecocriticism's web. Or if she does appear, she can only appear as a gap or interruption to that web. When I say that the new materialisms are ill-equipped to resist ecological destruction, I mean that ecocriticism denies the subject's place in desire and so leaves the subject no place beyond the Other's (the web of life's) discourse. By denying the alterity of desire, the new materialisms make the subject of ecocriticism fully visible, and a subject who is fully visible lacks the freedom to enjoy loss.

This means that Eve was only partly wrong after all. The work of the garden is a waste. But wasting need not be thought of as a dark and hopeless activity. As plants know, the greatest luxury comes from the fact that the sun expends itself without wanting anything in return. Although this solar expenditure has inspired the darkest of energy extractions (from mining in Milton's time to deepwater drilling and fracking today) and fueled countless wars, it can also inspire us to think at the surface of things *with* plants, where losing and receiving are, as Satan briefly muses in his tirade against the sun, the same:

> to thee I call,
> But with no friendly voice, and add thy name
> O sun, to tell thee how I hate thy beams
> . . . .
> Ah wherefore!
> . . . .
> What could be less than to afford him praise,
> The easiest recompense. (4.35–37, 42, 46–47)

Here, in the absolute (albeit temporary) breakdown of Satan's logic of extraterritorial expansion, "less" proves more, and to give "praise" proves "easiest":

a grateful mind,
By owing owes not, but still pays, at once
Indebted and discharged; what burden then? (4.55–57)

So vertiginous, so self-canceling is Satan's thought that it no longer inhabits "its own place"; Satan's thought is, instead, a nonplace.
Milton compares Satan's thought to "a devilish engine": Satan "back
recoiles," serpent-like, "upon himself" (4.17–18). Just as a combustion
engine converts fuel into energy and energy into work, Satan's inge-
nuity ("engine") converts thought into action. Here, however, Satan's
"devilish engine" only works to unwork itself, converting energy into
inaction, thought into paradox. No doubt, this back recoiling horrifies Satan, as it does Adam and Eve, who both recoil at their own
misdeeds. Nevertheless, Milton himself delights in such coiled figures. The garden, we have seen, is "wanton" from the start; life-matter
is an original chaos or "abyss" (1.21). When it comes to plants, there is
no "wherefore," but only, *yes, more.*

Milton's question is not, as ecocriticism tends to posit it, how to
conserve nature, since this very framing reproduces the environment as a "resource" or "standing reserve" for human use. While a
sustainability politics may work to sustain one form of life, life is, as
Alan Stoekl argues in his reading of the energy politics of Georges
Bataille,[16] both unsustainable and unworkable. A primordial chaos
(or pure solar expenditure, in Bataille's language), the energy of life
is "Tending to wild," Milton writes. It only becomes usable through
forms of capture—from the smallest organism to the human body to
"renewable energies," such as batteries. But these forms of capture, no
matter how sustainable, depend on a boundary or margin of excess.
Something must be sacrificed or wasted for sustainability to be imagined. A sustainable ecology is built on a foundation of loss.

At the end of *Paradise Lost*, loss appears to us in yet another back
recoiled figure: Adam and Eve "looking back" at a world already "disappeared," as "torrid heat / And . . . air adust / Began to parch that
temperate clime," wasting "Of Paradise, so late their happy seat"
(12.641, 640, 634–36, 642). Reading *Paradise Lost* now, from the vantage of a world on fire, it is impossible not to look back with Adam
and Eve and to see, in the figure of chiasmus, our world.[17] Milton's

poem confronts us with the trauma of world loss, a loss we inhabit still. Paradise, I have argued, is, for Milton, a paradox. "Looking back" at paradise as they wander forward, "hand in hand," Adam and Eve keep that image firmly planted in their minds. It will, we imagine, guide their "wandering steps." Today, however, this image holds us captive. "Looking back" to nature in the form of the new materialisms, we move forward into increasing uncertainty, including mass extinctions, intolerable heat, and ecosystemic collapse. Although our reparative readings insist, we are not subjects outside of nature; we are nature; this language repeats the same egoistic logic that the environmental humanities seek to surpass. The turn to matter repeats the temporal structure of Descartes's "I think, therefore I am," retrofitted as: "I mesh, I assemble, I become ... therefore I am." Both ecocriticism and Descartes's *cogito* presume the "I am" as the object pole of desire. Both are a form of "looking back."

By installing us, the reader, in the perspective of Adam and Eve's backward look, Milton turns the look—the gaze—*back on us.* The poem confronts us with the impossibility of our desire—a desire that, if truly recognized, would enable us to see futures beyond the pyric future witnessed by Adam and Eve and replayed still, from Eden to Australia to Paradise, California. It would enable us to stop looking back *to* matter and see that the "thing" we want is already here, in the failure of the look. Like the skull in Hans Holbein the Younger's portrait of *The Ambassadors* (1533),[18] which one only sees at an oblique angle, and to the exclusion of the painting's human figures, Milton's back recoiled image of Adam and Eve "looking back" to paradise obscures the trauma at its center. Milton's image of "Paradise" is, consequently, an image in anamorphosis (from the Greek prefix *ana-*, meaning "back, again," and *morphe*, meaning "shape" or "image").[19] Lacan uses the word anamorphosis in *Seminar XI* to describe the distortional gap that shapes our vision. Although we take vision to be neutral, Lacan's point is that vision, including the geometric vision of Renaissance perspectivism, organizes itself around a blind spot. This blind spot is not something that can be improved or corrected; it isn't simply out of focus or "foreshortened," as in Lawrence Buell's definition of the environmental unconscious.[20] Rather, this blank spot is the point at which desire enters the image as object.

Lacan calls this special object the gaze. Although we typically think of the gaze as a subjective action, Lacan reverses this way of thinking by treating the gaze as something objective. It—the gaze—looks back at us. According to Todd McGowan, gaze marks the point at which "our desire manifests itself in what we see."[21] Although Adam and Eve "see" paradise, we can, from a Lacanian angle, see this image as anamorphic; Milton's paradise includes a blank spot or void, and this void is what gives the image its gravitational pull. Gaze, in this sense, triggers our desire and is thus an object-cause of desire for the precise reason that it enables us to enjoy loss without knowing it. In Lacan's use, gaze is not panoptic; it does not give the subject power over the visual field. Gaze disempowers subjects by revealing their unconscious investment in loss. We are obliged to say, then, with eco-criticism, that desire entangles us with our objects, since we are never more entangled than when the object as gaze summons us. Except that the version of entanglement that I call anamorphic is extimate to these relations, not intimate. Anamorphic ecocriticism entangles us with the nonrelation or gap *in* relationality itself, so that it is right to say, after Lacan, that there is no such thing as an ecological relationship where desire is concerned. Desire means that we are entangled with lack.

Because poetry is free to experiment with the distortions that structure the visual field, poetry can, Milton says, make "darkness visible" (1.63). Likewise, the reading practice I propose in this book works by the light of its own distortion. Against the logic of the turn, I insist on a reading practice that is anamorphic. Anamorphic ecocriticism has neither a from nor a to; it has no "matter" in sight. Instead, it turns around a hole in the visual field. Although we, with Adam and Eve, cannot help but look back at a world disappeared, since to deny that backward look would be to forbid the very act of poetic making ("turning," after all, is in the groundwork of the word "verse"), one thing remains constant in all this turning and looking, and that is the gaze that hollows out our look. Looking back to life, as Orpheus looked back to Eurydice, we risk forgetting what all this turning was about: not bodies-objects-things, which, reader, be assured, the biopolitics of capture will never stop churning out, but the dehiscence of things that eludes capture (from the Latin *dehiscere*, meaning "to gape, yawn," "to stand open"; "in *Botany* to burst open, as the seed-vessels of plants").[22] In bursting open our look, the gaze re-seeds an impossible future.

Let us consider a final example of this look, taken from natural history. In Charles Darwin's second-to-last book, *The Power of Movement in Plants*, Darwin ventured a rather seductive (and Miltonic) hypothesis about the dissatisfactory pleasures of plants—what Eve, in her prolegomenon to the theory of the environmental unconscious, called their "wanton growth." Darwin's theory states that "light [acts] on the tissue of plants almost in the same manner as it does on the nervous system of an animal."[23] Darwin adds: "It is impossible not to be struck with the resemblance between the . . . movements of plants and many of the actions performed unconsciously by the lower animals."[24] Darwin admits that a plant's ability to "transmit an influence" is not identical to the workings of nervous tissue, since "plants do not of course possess nerves or a central nervous system." Nevertheless, he infers that our nervous system is simply a "more perfect" form of what plants are already able to do: "We may infer that with animals such structures [i.e., the central and peripheral nervous systems] serve only for the more perfect transmission of impressions, and for the more complete intercommunication of the several parts."[25] In his book's final paragraph, Darwin returns to the idea that first seduced him, that of an affinity between plant movements, or "circumnutation" (the rotational movements of the plant's various parts toward a stimulus) and animal movements. He goes so far as to posit the existence of a thinking, feeling plant-brain. Darwin writes:

> It is hardly an exaggeration to say that the tip of the radicle thus endowed [with sensitivity], and having the power of directing the movements of the adjoining parts, acts like the brain of one of the lower animals; the brain being seated within the anterior end of the body, receiving impressions from the sense-organs, and directing the several movements.[26]

The Power of Movement in Plants takes painstaking measures to trace the "circumnutations" of plants. As one scientific study puts it: "Plants were revealed [by Darwin] to live in a veritable whirl of activities—but at their own slow pace—in which plant parts (leaves, roots, tendrils) continually made rhythmic, and even diurnal, nastic, tropic and nutational movements."[27] Darwin attached small instruments, "not thicker than a horsehair," to the leaves and stems of the plants he observed to demonstrate these movements. These instruments allowed the plants "to trace their own courses," their peripatetic dance: "The movements of various organs to the light, which are so general throughout the vegetable kingdom, . . . are all modified forms of circumnutation; as again are the equally prevalent movements of stems, etc., towards the zenith, and of roots towards the centre of the earth."[28] The various forms of plant tropology—including geotropism, phototropism, and hydrotropism—result in a wide range of plant movement, including ellipses, ovals, zigzag lines, loops, and triangles, depending on the position of the plants to the stimulus of light and, more importantly, the intervals of light and dark. Darwin shows that there is no one-to-one correlation between the quantity of a stimulus and the reflex movement of plants (x amount of sunlight does not necessarily trigger y movement). Rather, plant cells are "excited by a difference in the amount of light received."[29] We may hear in this "difference" an echo of Jacques Derrida's definition of mnemonic-writing in "Freud and the Scene of Writing," where Derrida defines writing as a differential notation, or, to echo Darwin, "nutation."[30] Writing differs and delays; it zigzags around an impossible difference. In the case of plants, this difference is, according to Darwin, written in the language of light, moisture, nutriment, and gravitational pressure.

The thinking-writing that I call environmental poetics and, more generally, the environmental unconscious is also an impossible work: the zigzag pattern of the plant's anamorphic movement ("circumnutation") never meets its mark. But the thinking-writing triggered by difference is the same for both animals and plants. Darwin's plant-brain teaches us to miss our target again and again. For the poets in this study, the pleasure is in missing.

ACKNOWLEDGMENTS

It gives me great pleasure to thank the many individuals who made this book possible.

Julian Yates read *The Environmental Unconscious* from start to finish and bestowed on it his characteristic brilliance. I see now that I have been writing in dialogue with Julian for several years. His sense of *poiesis* as a furtive imprint of countless unknowable others (human and nonhuman) furnishes my thinking on the environmental unconscious; it also gets at the truth of thinking with others. This book is richer and stranger for thinking with Julian.

Benjamin Parris helped me see that the Lucretius–Lacan connection was at the heart of this book's argument. I thank Ben for his vision and encouragement.

Jean-Thomas Tremblay has been a peerless support throughout the writing and rewriting of this book. I think of Jean-Thomas as my coconspirator in ecological antipedagogy; we have been learning and unlearning the ways of environmental thought for some years. Jean-Thomas worked through many of the ideas in this book with me. Co-thinking with Jean-Thomas through phone calls, emails, emails about emails, movie nights, and our shared writing has been a rare and enlivening activity, for which I am incredibly grateful.

Karen Raber's influence on this book exceeds citation. I thank Karen for years of intellectual stimulation and comradery. I am particularly grateful to Karen for reading early drafts of this manuscript and sharing her astute comments, suggestions, and criticisms.

My teachers—Richard Rambuss, Elizabeth Wilson, Karen New-
man, and James Kuzner—nurtured this book when it was still just
the seed of an idea. Rick was the most exacting of readers and the
warmest. I could not have asked for a better mentor. One of the best
decisions I ever made in graduate school was to take Elizabeth's fall
2009 seminar on affect theory and psychoanalysis. Suffice it to say
that I was transformed, even if it took me several years to get back to
Freud. If *Nachträglichkeit* is 20/20, I see now that much of my interest in an ecology of negativity began then. Elizabeth has remained a
guiding light over the years, and I am grateful beyond words for her
encouragement and support.

I began my graduate education at Emory University, where I had
the good fortune of making homes in the English and women's, gender, and sexuality studies departments. I look back fondly on my
seminars with Patricia Cahill, Lynne Huffer, Michael Moon, and
Benjamin Reiss. As an early modernist, I learned a great deal from
Jonathan Goldberg, whose fierce intellect and theoretical adventur-
ousness helped shape the scholar I am today.

At Brown University, I am grateful to Timothy Bewes, Stephen
Foley, Coppélia Kahn, Jacques Khalip, and Kevin McLaughlin for
their feedback and support. Brown's John Carter Library and John
Hay Library provided quiet spaces in which to think and write; my
thanks to the librarians who aided my earliest archival digs. Providence's Avon Cinema and Cable Car Cinema were treasured places
of refuge and thought for a cinephile like me. I would be remiss not to
mention how vitalizing it was to sit in their dark caverns.

Other fellow travelers who have left an imprint on this book include Benjamin Bertram, Liza Blake, Craig Dionne, Lowell Duckert,
Holly Dugan, Hillary Eklund, Stephen Guy-Bray, Eileen Joy, Steve
Mentz, Vin Nardizzi, and Karl Steel. Stephen has been an incredibly
thought-provoking interlocutor over the years; he also knows exactly
where to go for happy hour in the Netherlands. Karl voiced support
for this book and got the ball rolling at a critical time.

I began writing this book in earnest as a postdoctoral fellow in
English at Tulane University. I want to thank my colleagues at Tu-
lane, Rick Godden, Michelle Kohler, Laura Marks, Scott Oldenburg,
Anne-Marie Womack, and Karen Zumhagen-Yeklpé, for their

generosity and conversation. Scott and Michelle were exceptionally welcoming and became dear friends and reliable dinner companions. I smile to think of my year in New Orleans.

I wrote most of this book in the belly of the beast, New York City. Thanks to my colleagues at Baruch for creating a stimulating environment in which to write and think. I owe special thanks to my department chair, Timothy Aubry, for always lending an attentive ear to my muddled thoughts. John Brenkman, too, has been a model of intellectual generosity over the years; I thank him for taking me under his wing. Jessica Lang helped me find my footing at Baruch and has remained a supportive presence ever since. Laura Kolb and Mary McGlynn have been marvelous colleagues; I thank them for their spirit and grace. Other colleagues I would like to thank include Eva Chou, Christina Christoforatou, Allison Deutermann, Matt Eatough, Shelly Eversley, Stephanie Hershinow, Sean O'Toole, Brooke Schreiber, Lauren Silberman, and Michael Staub. I am grateful to be in their excellent company.

Working with the students at Baruch has been an absolute pleasure. Special thanks to Kezia Velista, a phenomenal reader of pretty much everything—from K-pop to John Donne—for helping me to track down essential materials for this book.

The City University of New York is a vital public institution, and I am proud to be a part of it. Thanks to my union, the PSC, for improving the lives of CUNY faculty, staff, and students.

This book would not be the same without the encouragement, support, and occasional tough love of the following individuals: Natalie Adler, Monique Allewaert, Elizabeth Bearden, Caralyn Bialo, Dan Brayton, Joshua Calhoun, Felicity Callard, Joseph Campana, Catherine Clifford, Brent Dawson, Rachele Dini, Sarah Ensor, Des Fitzgerald, Joseph Gamble, John Garrison, Perry Guevara, David Hershinow, Richie Hoffman, David Hollingshead, Sujata Iyengar, Shazia Jagot, Anna Klosowska, Gary Kuchar, Wai-Leung Kwok, Jacques Lezra, Lynsey McCulloch, Tobias Menely, J. Allan Mitchell, Feisal Mohamed, Jennifer Munroe, Aley O'Mara, Julie Orlemanski, David Orvis, Lakshmi Padmanabhan, Julie Paulson, Tessie Prakas, Ayesha Ramachandran, Sara Ritchey, Lauren Robertson, Simon Ryle, Melissa E. Sanchez, Debapriya Sarkar, Myra Seaman, Laurie

Shannon, Brandon Shaw, Alan Stewart, Kathryn Bond Stockton, Antoine Traisnel, Whitney Trettien, Christine Varnado, Tiffany Jo Werth, Tom White, Seth Stewart Williams, Laura Lehua Yim, and Nancy Yousef. I thank you all.

For funding my research, I am grateful to the Cogut Center for the Humanities, the Folger Shakespeare Library, and the CUNY Research Foundation.

Working with the University of Minnesota Press has been a dream come true. Doug Armato is a visionary editor and a champion of theory in the humanities. I thank him for seeing the potential in this book and for shepherding it and me through the publication process. Zenyse Miller was a phenomenal help throughout the production of this book. I also want to thank my copyeditor, Scott Mueller, for sharpening my rough-hewn sentences. Lastly, I thank my readers, Julian Yates and an anonymous reader, for the discernment of their reports. They helped me see my way back to this project with renewed energy and excitement.

Lee van Laer and Neal Harris have been exceedingly gracious in-laws. I thank them for their hospitality and care.

None of this would have been possible without the love and support of my parents, Gail Swarbrick and Robert Swarbrick. My mother inspired my passion for reading and writing. My father instilled my love for trees. I was in graduate school when my dad passed away. He'll never read this book, but his absence fills its pages.

Toby and Gus have been the very best feline companions through it all. There is no joy more inexhaustible than they are.

Finally, I thank my partner, Rebecca van Laer, who helped me make sense of this book when I was at a loss. For her intellect, daring, and steadfast love, I dedicate this book to her.

NOTES

INTRODUCTION

1. This loss owes to the epistemic ruptures of science and the resulting knower/known dyad that philosophers from Kant to Hegel to Meillassoux have tried in different ways to resolve. Alexandre Koyré's account of the early modern scientific revolution is canonical in this regard. See Koyré, *Infinite Universe*. Closer to my purposes here, Joanna Picciotto argues that the Copernican revolution in scientific thought meant that experimentalist poets like Marvell and Milton had to labor to represent the material world. Bacon's new science epitomized that intellectual labor, as did Marvell and Milton's poetics. See Picciotto, *Labors of Innocence*. Summarizing these arguments, Alfred North Whitehead claims that the early modern world witnessed a widespread "bifurcation of nature." Much modern thought is founded on the bifurcation between the poet's "red glow" and the scientist's "molecules and electrons." This bifurcation has its roots, Whitehead argues, in the writings of Francis Bacon. See Whitehead, *Concept of Nature*, 31.

2. Faced with the sixth mass extinction and widespread ecological fragility, the new materialisms fuse matter and meaning together to posit a world that is animate, object-oriented, and geared toward repair. See Diana Coole and Samantha Frost's introduction to *New Materialisms* for a representative account of the new materialisms.

3. Karl Marx theorizes the dawn of the Anthropocene in his chapter on "primitive accumulation," linking the emergence of capitalism to

the systematic plunder of human and geologic life. Marx writes: "The discovery of gold and silver in America, the extirpation, enslavement and entombment in mines of the indigenous population of that continent, the beginnings of the conquest and plunder of India, and the conversion of Africa into a preserve for the commercial hunting of blackskins, are all things which characterize the dawn of the era of capitalist production. . . . These different moments are systematically combined together at the end of the seventeenth century in England." See Marx, *Capital*, 915.

4. Jason W. Moore pinpoints the emergence of capitalism's environmental upheavals at the start of the early modern period and in England in particular, where the extraction of "Cheap Natures" such as coal increased rapidly in the "long sixteenth century." See Moore, *Capitalism*, 4, 12, 14, and 115. Moore's thesis elaborates on Marx's chapter on "primitive accumulation." See Marx, *Capital*, 873–76, 914–15. For expanded accounts of primitive accumulation focused on poetry, gender, and race, see Halpern, *Poetics of Primitive Accumulation*; Federici, *Caliban and the Witch*; and Yusoff, *Billion Black Anthropocenes or None*, respectively.

5. Jacques Derrida and Paul de Man both respond to the same problem of poetic form: a tropological excess in language that must be accounted for within a theory of language in general and poetry in particular. For Derrida, moments of excess are the text's affirmation of its status as "ash," as a will to communicate that is always self-effacing. For de Man, these moments reveal how language operates without human intention, as "inhuman." In both cases, poetry conditions loss and vice versa. Gilles Deleuze and Félix Guattari push these observations into a more ecological register. When, for example, they write of the bird's refrain as a way of making sense of the earth's chaos, they do so in a materialist nod to poetry. As a noun, the refrain stabilizes identity through repetition, such as the repetition of a poetic line; but as a verb, to refrain means to break off or desist in some action, as in a caesura or line break. From the birdsong to the work of art, matter invents ways to break up meaning and relive loss again and again. We call this failure to be "poetry." See Derrida, "Shibboleth: For Paul Celan," 1–64; de Man, "Conclusions," 73–105; and Deleuze and Guattari, *Thousand Plateaus*, 311–15.

6. See Shannon, *Accommodated Animal*; Brayton, *Shakespeare's Ocean*; Mentz, *Shipwreck Modernity*; Goldberg, *Seeds of Things*; Greenblatt, *Swerve*; Lezra and Blake, *Lucretius and Modernity*; Hock, *Erotics of Materialism*; and Usher, *Exterranean*.

7. On this point, see Swarbrick and Raber, "Introduction," 313–28. For a critical introduction to Renaissance posthumanism, see Raber, *Shakespeare and Posthumanist Theory*.

8. Passannante, *Catastrophizing*, 4.

9. Edelman, *No Future*, 35–36.

10. For more on this neologism, see Swarbrick, "Nature's Queer Negativity."

11. Lacan, *Sinthome*, 3.

12. The idiom of "weak" and "strong theory" gained prominence in the humanities after the publication of Eve Kosofsky Sedgwick's essay "Paranoid Reading and Reparative Reading," by way of affect theorist Silvan Tomkins. Sedgwick defines "strong theory" as *one* affective position among many, suggesting "there may also be benefit in exploring the extremely varied, dynamic, and historically contingent ways that strong theoretical constructs interact with weak ones in the ecology of knowing" (145). I confess I am paranoid about this "ecology of knowing," not because psychoanalysis is a "monopolistic program" (144), as Sedgwick proclaims, but because psychoanalysis is not a program of knowing. The unconscious knows nothing and has nothing to learn. It is, if anything, apedagogical. The rubric of "weak" and "strong theory" thus fails to account for the fact that psychoanalysis is not a theory of knowledge among others, nor is it a subset of the many affective positions one can hold. The theory of the unconscious cleaves the ecological subject from itself, weakening the subject's claim to mastery. If this is strong, then give me strong theory. By contrast, the plurality of the affects (not to mention the centrality of Tomkins's ego-psychology to Sedgwick's late work) screens the castrating force of the unconscious from sight. Just when theory thought it was becoming weak by embracing the multiplicity of affective positions, it strengthened its egoic drive. See Sedgwick, "Paranoid Reading and Reparative Reading," 133–36. For a galvanizing argument in defense of strong theory, see Kornbluh, "Extinct Critique."

13. Benjamin, "Theses," 263.

14. "Now, it is this notion of immanence," Copjec writes, "this conception of a cause that is immanent within the field of its effects, with which this book quarrels and repeatedly condemns as historicist" (6). "Historicism . . . wants to ground being in appearance and wants to have nothing to do with desire" (14).

15. See Jameson, *The Political Unconscious*, 9.

16. Tobias Menely, in the groundbreaking *Climate and the Making of Worlds*, argues for the importance of "symptomatic reading practices" and "advances a mode of reading and an interpretation of the history of English poetry concerned with the relation between the positivity of representation and the unconscious as an absence, break, or negation" (19).

17. This is, of course, homage to Slavoj Žižek's psychoanalytic classic *Enjoy Your Symptom!*, which begins with an illuminating preface on the importance of exemplarity to materialist reading: "A materialist . . . tends to repeat one and the same example, to return to it obsessively: it is the particular example which remains the same in all symbolic universes, while the universal notion it is supposed to exemplify continually changes its shape, so that we get a multitude of universal notions circulating, like flies around the light, around a single example. Is this not what Lacan is doing, returning to the same exemplary cases (the guessing-game with five hats, the dream of Irma's injection), each time providing a new interpretation? Such an example is the *universal Singular*: a singular entity which persists as the universal in the multitude of its interpretations" (xi–xii).

18. See Harris, *Untimely Matter*; Raber, *Animal Bodies, Renaissance Culture*; Steel, *How Not to Make a Human*; and Yates, *Of Sheep, Oranges, and Yeast*.

19. I borrow the term "surplus vitality" from Mari Ruti. See Ruti, *Singularity of Being*, 40–41. For early modern studies that engage psychoanalytic theory, see Menon, *Unhistorical Shakespeare*; and Varnado, *Shapes of Fancy*.

20. Meillassoux, *After Finitude*, 7.

21. See Barad, *Meeting the Universe Halfway*; Alaimo, *Bodily Natures*; Morton, *Hyperobjects*; and Latour, *Reassembling the Social*.

22. Latour, "Out of Steam?," 248.

23. See, for example, Felski, *Limits of Critique*.

24. Barad, *Meeting the Universe Halfway*, 3.

25. See Merchant, *The Death of Nature*. On the "extirpation of animism," see Horkheimer and Adorno, *Dialectic of Enlightenment*, 1.

26. Picciotto, "Reforming the Garden," 26.

27. Picciotto, 25.

28. Picciotto, 26.

29. Bono, *Word of God*, 129–30.

30. For an alternative account of Bacon's materialism, one that sees "carelessness" and nonchalance as the defining features of Baconian practice, see Simon, *Light without Heat*, 1.

31. Kant determined the thing-in-itself unknowable. Today's anti-Kantians, i.e., new materialists and speculative realists, try to undo post-Kantian "correlationism" (the idea that we only have access to the correlation between thinking and being) by asserting the mind-independent reality of things. Meillassoux's theory of the "arche-fossil" or "fossil-matter" is exemplary in this regard. See Meillassoux, *After Finitude*, 10. For a study that critiques speculative realism while staying within its orbit, see Shaviro, *Universe of Things*.

32. One could argue that what Bennett calls "vibrant assemblage," Latour calls "actor-network," and Graham Harman calls "object" are not, in fact, presences per se but rather *occasions* (I choose this Whiteheadian vocabulary deliberately). While I do not contest this point, the veritable comings and goings of matter, the insistence on matter's mobility only serves to accentuate my argument: that theory today—by which I mean the proliferation of new ontologies of matter—is incapable of reading matter disastrously, that is, outside the prism of life-vitality-movement-becoming. These terms—life-vitality-movement-becoming—thus serve as a surreptitious ground or cause in theories that otherwise claim to be groundless. See Bennett, *Vibrant Matter*; Latour, *Reassembling the Social*; and Harman, *Tool-Being*.

33. On the Adamic art of naming, see Bono, *Word of God*, 131–32; and Picciotto, *Labors of Innocence*, 3, 35.

34. Neyrat, *Atopias*, 7.

35. In Barad's words, "There is no outside of nature from which to act; there are only 'acts of nature'" ("Nature's Queer Performativity [The Authorized Version]," 47). Everything is brought inside nature by eco-deconstruction. By contrast, my eco-psychoanalytic approach holds

that there is an "outside"; I call it the environmental unconscious. For a critique of Barad's relational ontology, see Swarbrick, "Nature's Queer Negativity."

36. Coole and Frost, introduction to *New Materialisms*, 1–2.

37. Here I echo Lacan on the "not-all" (*pas-tout*) of sexual being in *Encore*, 7. What makes sex *sexual* in Lacan's reading is that it is always subtracted from the order of sense. Sex, for Lacan, is not just an incomplete meaning; it is the *failure* of meaning that makes sex not-all. The not-all is the bone in the throat of every materialism because it includes failure in its very structure—a point Lacan shares with Lucretius.

38. Lucretius, *Nature of the Universe*, 1.907–14. I have also consulted W. H. D. Rouse's translation. See Lucretius, *On the Nature of Things*, 1.887–912.

39. Lucretius, *Nature of the Universe*, 1.819–22.

40. Lucretius, 2.1016–17.

41. See Lezra, *Unspeakable Subjects*.

42. See, for example, Goldstein, *Sweet Science*; and Smailbegović, "From Code to Shape," 134–72.

43. It is as if Lucretius read Paul de Man. In de Man's words: "The letter is without meaning in relation to the word, it is *a-sēmos*, it is without meaning. When you spell a word you say a certain number of meaningless letters, which then come together in the word, but in each of the letters the word is not present. The two are absolutely independent of each other. What is being named here as the disjunction between grammar and meaning, *Wort* and *Satz*, is the materiality of the letter, the independence, or the way in which the letter can disrupt the ostensibly stable meaning of a sentence and introduce in it a slippage by means of which that meaning disappears, evanesces, and by means of which all control over that meaning is lost" ("Conclusions," 89).

44. Zupančič attributes this failure to "*one signifier 'gone missing'*" (*What Is Sex?*, 47). According to Zupančič, "The human (hi)story begins not with the emergence of the signifier, but with *one signifier 'gone missing.'* We could indeed say that nature is already full of signifiers (and at the same time indifferent to them); and that at some point one signifier 'falls out,' goes missing. And it is only from this that the 'logic of the signifier' in the strict [Lacanian] sense of the term is born (signifiers start to 'run,' and to relate to each other, across this gap)" (47). Is this not the

very crux of Lucretian materialism? Lucretius posits that all of nature "runs" and relates across a "gap." Matter is precisely nature's attempt to knit together, to suture the gap left by one signifier gone missing.

45. Lucretius, *On the Nature of Things*, 1.418–21.

46. Lucretius, 1.822–30.

47. Like Lucretius, Deleuze and Guattari install antiproduction at the center of their philosophical system. Their desiring-machines are essentially death drive machines. "Desiring-machines make us an organism," Deleuze and Guattari write, "but at the very heart of this production . . . the body suffers from being organized in this way. . . . The full body without organs belongs to the realm of antiproduction" (*Anti-Oedipus*, 8). For a detailed account of antiproduction pertaining to environmental ethics, see Neyrat, *Unconstructable Earth*, 180, 182–85.

48. On the eroticism of Lucretian materialism, see Goldberg, *Seeds of Things*; and Hock, *Erotics of Materialism*.

49. Hence Deleuze's fascination with the nonsense of Lewis Carroll's portmanteaus. It is not that they point to a future world of sense *in the making*, a world that, in performative terms, is *to come*; on the contrary, what Carroll's poetic portmanteaus show, according to Deleuze, is that language, the ground of sense, is groundless. Language-matter is a stutter. See Deleuze, *Logic of Sense*, 82–83.

50. Lacan, "Science and Truth," 734.

51. Lacan, 727.

52. Lacan, 727.

53. Despite the wholesale rejection of Descartes, the question remains for ecocriticism: *Which* Descartes? The many recent displacements of the human toward the posthuman or inhuman have not budged the Cartesian legacy one inch. They have, rather, retrenched the Cartesian subject as one who is, properly speaking, rooted in place. For Descartes, we know that place is the place of the "I think." For the environmental humanities, that place is the *oikeios*. But notice what happens when embodied cognition, watery relations, human–animal participation, and place-based ecology take center stage. The result is not anti-Cartesian, but rather Cartesian through and through, according to Claire Colebrook: "The very concept of 'the environment' (seen as that which environs, is vulnerable to our destruction and therefore worthy of concern) shares all those features and affective tendencies

that structured the self-enclosed Cartesian subject that feminism has always had in its sites" (*Sex after Life*, 10–11). "What remains out of play," Colebrook argues, "is a consideration of forces of life that are not discernible from within our milieu" (*Sex after Life*, 11).

54. Buell, *Writing for an Endangered World*, 22.

55. Freud, *Interpretation of Dreams*, 608.

56. I derive this formulation—"the real has no place"—from Joan Copjec's electrifying analysis of post-Foucauldian theory in *Read My Desire*, 39.

57. Freud, *Interpretation of Dreams*, 509.

58. Greta Thunberg, "'Our House Is on Fire': Greta Thunberg, 16, Urges Leaders to Act on Climate," *The Guardian*, January 25, 2019, https://www.theguardian.com/environment/2019/jan/25/our-house-is-on-fire-greta-thunberg16-urges-leaders-to-act-on-climate.

59. Moore, *Capitalism in the Web of Life*, 2–3.

60. Moore, 8.

61. Moore, 12.

62. This wager is clearly polemical since to be ecocritical today is to position oneself—in knee-jerk fashion—in direct opposition to the mind-body dualism of Descartes. My Lacanian reading of the Cartesian subversion of the subject suggests that an alternative reading of Descartes is possible. For representative accounts of early modern ecocriticism's negative relation to Descartes, see Boehrer, *Animal Characters*, 1–27; and Fudge, *Brutal Reasoning*. The classic deconstructive argument in defense of Descartes's method of radical doubt comes from Derrida's debate with Michel Foucault on the meaning of the *cogito*. See Derrida, "Cogito and the History of Madness," 31–63. For a related argument focused on the important difficulties of Descartes's poetics, see Gadberry, *Cartesian Poetics*. And for an ecocritical argument interested in the affordances of Descartes's nonrelational thinking, see Swarbrick, "Idiot Science for a Blue Humanities," 15–32.

63. Bennett, *Vibrant Matter*, 112.

64. The literature on the "affective turn" is now vast. See, for starters, Massumi, *Parables for the Virtual*, esp. chapter 1, "The Autonomy of Affect"; Clough's introduction to *The Affective Turn*; and Stewart, *Ordinary Affects*. For an illuminating critique of the affective turn focused on "radical formalism," see Brinkema, *Forms of the Affects*, 37.

65. Malabou, *Our Brain?*

66. Edelman, *No Future*, 2.

67. Yates's "multispecies impression," a language that plays host to count-less nonhuman actors, is exemplary in this regard (*Of Sheep, Oranges, and Yeast*, 12). See also Craig Dworkin on "linguistic materiality—the specific forms and configurations taken by the signifier" (*Radium of the Word*, 1). Both Yates and Dworkin align their respective readings with a theory of poetics. The de Manian thesis about the inhuman nature of poetic form hovers in the background. "The inhuman is," de Man argues, "linguistic structures, the play of linguistic tensions, linguistic events." Consequently, "if one speaks of the inhuman, the fundamental non-human character of language, one also speaks of the fundamental non-definition of the human as such" ("Conclusions," 96).

68. Bennett, *Vibrant Matter*, xi, 25.

69. Badiou, *Logics of Worlds*, 1.

70. Badiou, 1.

71. Badiou, 1–2.

72. Badiou, *Handbook of Inaesthetics*, 9.

73. See Bryant, *Democracy of Objects*. Despite Byrant's engagement with Lacanian psychoanalysis, Bryant's object-oriented ontology (o o o) forbids the nonobjects or special objects that Lacan makes the cornerstone of his return to Freud. These special objects are what Lacan calls *objet petit a* (gaze, voice, breast, and so on); they are what the subject separates from in order to become a subject. Moreover, these lost objects are special because they trigger the subject's desire; they are the "object-causes of desire" in Lacan's vocabulary. Because Bryant's ontology is a flat ontology, there is no subject of desire and no hierarchy of objects. A philosopher is an object like any other object in o o o; moreover, there is no real difference between a philosopher and a toaster; o o o eliminates desire from the relational field. In psychoanalysis, things are more complicated. The subject of psychoanalysis is not a transcendental subject in the sense that it imposes its will on objects. The subject of psychoanalysis is a *disempowered* subject; it is disempowered by the nonobjects that stir it. Without a robust theory of desire, which would include a robust theory of lack, o o o cannot account for unconscious objects and so offers objects that are merely shy or retiring, there but not there. By contrast, psychoanalysis theorizes objects that are not just shy but *split*. By sacrificing the latter,

ooo gives us a democracy of things; but it gives us no real reason to *want* those things. I still prefer Nietzsche to a toaster.

74. Truth, for Badiou, is always ex-ceptional. Truth does not add to knowledge; it pierces a hole in knowledge. For this reason, Badiou is fully in league with Lacan, who, like the TV show the *X-Files*, insists "the truth is out there." Lacan states: "I always speak the truth. Not the whole truth, because there's no way, to say it all. Saying it all is literally impossible: words fail. Yet it's through this very impossibility that the truth holds onto the real" (*Television*, 3). For an illuminating account of the Lacanian Real in political and popular discourse, see Žižek, *Plague of Fantasies*, 1–54.

75. Badiou, *Logics of Worlds*, 4.

76. Stewart, *Poetry*, 1–2.

77. Stewart, 2.

78. Tsing, *Mushroom*, 7.

79. Barad: "I see myself drawn to poetics as a mode of expression, not in order to move away from thinking rigorously but, on the contrary, to lure us toward the possibilities of engaging the force of imagination in its materiality" ("On Touching," 216).

80. Bersani, *Culture of Redemption*.

81. This is my critical play on Donna Haraway's well-known joining of "nature" and "culture" into a single, interrelated series called "natureculture" in *The Companion Species Manifesto*, 2.

82. Bersani, *Culture of Redemption*, 1.

83. McEleney, *Futile Pleasures*.

84. Bersani, *Culture of Redemption*, 45.

85. Carson, *Eros the Bittersweet*, 10–11.

86. Sappho, *If Not, Winter*, 3.

87. Laplanche, "Theory of Seduction," 661.

88. "What truly belongs to the order of the unconscious," Lacan writes, "is that it is neither being, nor non-being, but the unrealized" (*Four Fundamental Concepts of Psychoanalysis*, 29–30). Žižek compares the Lacanian theory of language to a torture house in *The Ticklish Subject*, xv.

89. In Copjec's precise words: "Sex is the stumbling block of sense" (*Read My Desire*, 204).

90. Laplanche, "Theory of Seduction," 661.

91. See Zupančič, *What Is Sex?*, 10–11.

92. See Morton, *Ecology without Nature*.

93. For a critical reading of eco-melancholia, see Tremblay and Swarbrick, "Destructive Environmentalism," 3–30.

94. Morton, *Ecology without Nature*, 143, 187.

95. See especially Mortimer-Sandilands and Erickson, *Queer Ecologies*; and Morton, "Queer Ecology," 273–82.

96. Laplanche, "Unfinished Copernican Revolution," 80–81.

97. Laplanche, 61–62.

98. Laplanche, 81.

99. Colebrook argues that the purported self-maintenance and dynamic coupling of self and world, linked to an implicit, if unspoken, notion of the earth as a nurturing, providing mother, repeats rather than disrupts the Cartesian reduction of environment to a single, unified space accessible to *our* thoughts and *our* symbolic control. This version of ecocriticism displaces the human only to recenter the human on a higher level. Colebrook writes, "The very notion of environment that encircles our range of living practice, and the very notion of 'woman' as tied to place and oriented to care, always figure the world as *our* world. To say, as eco-feminists do, that we are essentially world-oriented and placed in a relation of care and concern to a world that is always place rather than meaningless space is to repeat the (masculine) reduction of the world to its sense *for us*. The problem, despite our protestations, is that we do *not care*" (*Sex after Life*, 10–11).

100. As Eva Haifa Giraud argues in *What Comes after Entanglement?*, "It is important to more fully flesh out an ethics of exclusion, which pays attention to the entities, practices, and ways of being that are *foreclosed* when other entangled realities are materialized" (2). Giraud adds: "Although narratives of entanglement grasp something important about the world, they do not capture everything. Attention also needs to be paid to the frictions, foreclosures, and exclusions that play a constitutive role in the composition of lived reality" (3).

101. In this respect, ecocriticism trails not only poetry but also cinema. See Cahill's *Zoological Surrealism* for a natural history of cinema responsive to the Copernican decentering of human life vis-à-vis nonhuman life-forms (16–25).

102. Anthropologist Eduardo Kohn draws on the Deleuzian language of assemblages in *How Forests Think* to point to representational

capacities beyond the human. Attending ethnographically to a series
of Amazonian other-than-human encounters, Kohn reflects "on what
it might mean to say that forests think" and that "nonhuman life-forms
also represent the world" (7, 8). Let us not hesitate any further: forests
think. Where things go awry in Kohn's argument is in the following
statement: "This way of understanding semiosis can help us move
beyond a dualistic approach to anthropology, in which humans are
portrayed as separate from the worlds they represent, toward a monistic one" (9). "Separation" has become a dirty word in ecological studies
because it echoes the mind-body dualism of René Descartes. Nevertheless, a certain notion of separation remains necessary (see Neyrat,
Unconstructable Earth, 150). While it is possible, indeed right, to say
that forests think, it is impossible in Kohn's monistic model to say that
the *unconscious* thinks, that forests have a death drive and are therefore
self-divided. My counterclaim is this: all of nature thinks, *but it does
not know what it thinks.* If we accept the posthuman proposition that
nonhumans represent the world and regard humanity as part of the
web of life, we cannot grant ourselves the posthuman alibi of thinking
that the nonhuman is any less disturbed by signs. On the contrary, it
is because nature is a signifying machine that we must also say that
nature is cracked from within.

103. Already in *Difference and Repetition*, Deleuze was revising the Lacanian "mirror stage"—that mythopoetic stage in human development
when we are accommodated to our "own" image—to be not just a stage
in human history when the child begins to contemplate his own reflection, but an ontological structure of the material world. Echoing Ovid,
Deleuze proclaims: "We are all Narcissus in virtue of the pleasure
(auto-satisfaction) we experience in contemplating, even though we
contemplate things quite apart from ourselves" (75). Every organism,
says Deleuze, discovers its "I" function, its means of representation,
through contemplating things outside it. "I"/nature is an other.

104. One example is Žižek, who insists that "the fact that man is a speaking
being means precisely that he is, so to speak, constitutively 'derailed,'"
so that "all attempts to regain a new balance between man and nature" are doomed from the start (*Looking Awry*, 36–37). Žižek does
not consider that nature, too, is constitutively derailed. He addresses

"the thwarted character of reality itself" in later books like *Sex and the Failed Absolute* (8).

105. Although psychoanalysis thinks of the unconscious in sexual terms, it restricts the sexual relation to human–human contact. Thus, Leo Bersani can write the following sentence in *The Freudian Body*: "Animals make love; humans make sexuality" (39). The suggestion here is that animal sexuality comes preprogrammed. Whereas what throws matter awry and drives humans to create the mess of sexuality is the derailment of animality by the signifiers of the unconscious. I ask: Why not the environmental unconscious? Although Bersani (following Laplanche) calls human sexuality an "evolutionary conquest," he restricts this evolution to human chronology. In psychoanalysis, the unconscious comes from the other, but we have yet to think the unconscious of the other in nonhuman terms.

106. According to Todd McGowan, Hegel *does* allow space for the environmental unconscious, making Hegel the true enemy of speculative realism and new materialism, not Kant. As McGowan puts it: "Hegel's point is not that subjects shape substances through the act of knowing them but that substances are themselves already subjectivized. This is not to say that rocks or planets can speak. They don't have the capacity for language but their being attests to the same division that constitutes the speaking subject. The speaking subject can appear because being suffers from an internal division and cannot be self-identical." See McGowan, "On the Necessity of Contradiction," 105.

107. "Poets," Lacan writes, "don't know what they're saying, yet they still manage to say things before anyone else—*I is an other*" (*Ego in Freud's Theory*, 7). Both Freud and Lacan show great interest in what poets inadvertently say about their objects. Julia Kristeva calls this inadvertent element "chora," in *Revolution in Poetic Language*, referring to the semiotic dimension of language that she and Lacan both associate with the unconscious.

108. Kolbert, *Sixth Extinction*.

109. Andrea Long Chu writes in a similar psychoanalytic vein about the impossibility of feminism. Chu calls feminism a "fantasy" (78). Like feminism, however, ecocriticism is a fantasy that one cannot (and would not want to) do without. See Chu, "Impossibility of Feminism."

1. SEX OR MATTER? (MALABOU AFTER SPENSER)

1. All quotations from *The Faerie Queene* (book, canto, and stanza) are taken from Edmund Spenser, *The Faerie Queene*, ed. A. C. Hamilton, 2nd ed.

2. Spenser, "Letter to Raleigh," 718.

3. Spenser, 714.

4. OED, s.v. "plastic," n. and adj.

5. Spenser, "Letter to Raleigh," 714.

6. Malabou, *New Wounded*, xv.

7. Malabou, *Ontology of the Accident*, 7.

8. Malabou, 6.

9. Malabou, 6.

10. In Lacan's brief discussion of "lamella," he describes the "libido, *qua* pure life instinct" as "simplified, indestructible life" (*Four Fundamental Concepts of Psychoanalysis*, 197–98).

11. Malabou, *New Wounded*, 212.

12. Malabou, 213.

13. Derrida, *Dissemination*, 304.

14. Malabou, *New Wounded*, 211.

15. Deleuze, *Pure Immanence*, 31.

16. Spenser, "Letter to Raleigh," 716.

17. Tiffany, *Toy Medium*, 3.

18. Tiffany, 3.

19. Tiffany, 5. For a related discussion of framing technologies in Renaissance poetry, see Kalas, *Frame, Glass, Verse*.

20. Derrida, *Archive Fever*, 10.

21. On a related point, see François, *Open Secrets*. François poses the possibility of an "open secret" within the period of the Enlightenment, which for her stands as "nonemphatic revelation"—that is, revelation "that does not demand response but is there for the having, as readily taken up as it is set aside" (xvi). Identifying a kind of interzone between "revelation" and "annihilation," François locates the idea of an "open secret" in certain "minor" poems of Romanticism—minor in that they are "minimally expressive"—and argues that such poems run counter to "the Enlightenment allegiance to rationalism and unbound progress," along with the concomitant belief in the "development and realization of human powers" through work (xvii, xvi). These poems

short-circuit "the hermeneutics of suspicion" informing our post-Enlightenment reading habits, François argues, where the objective of both literary criticism and theory remains rigidly twofold: either to recuperate something lost and undervalued or to demystify something of its ideological work. Nevertheless, "neither of these critical models . . . is prepared to accept something that does not require either the work of disclosure or the effort of recovery" (xvi). François's version of the "open secret" or "nonemphatic revelation" is comparable to the kind of conceptual dampening I wish to perform in this chapter with respect to trauma, which stands neither for revelation nor annihilation but rather for a kind of "thereness" that exceeds human mastery or control.

22. Malabou, *Our Brain?*, 7.

23. Caruth, "After the End," 125.

24. Caruth, 121.

25. Thacker, *Dust of This Planet*, 4–5.

26. Deleuze, *Masochism*, 111.

27. Deleuze, 112.

28. Deleuze, *Difference and Repetition*, 131.

29. Deleuze, 129.

30. Deleuze, 130.

31. Deleuze, 130.

32. Deleuze, 130.

33. Deleuze, 131.

34. Deleuze, *Masochism*, 113.

35. Deleuze, 113.

36. Malabou, *New Wounded*, 8.

37. Malabou, xiii.

38. Malabou, 7.

39. Deleuze, *Masochism*, 111.

40. Malabou, *New Wounded*, 7.

41. On the Lacanian subject of the unconscious, see Fink: "Now this 'other' subject . . . is *not* something which or someone who has some sort of permanent existence: it only appears when a propitious occasion presents itself. . . . *This subject has no other being than as a breach in discourse*" (*The Lacanian Subject*, 41).

42. Malabou, *New Wounded*, 8.

43. Malabou, xiii.

44. Malabou, xiii.
45. Malabou, 5.
46. Malabou, 5.
47. Malabou, 5.
48. Malabou, 5. Here and elsewhere, Malabou's language of shocks and bombardments echoes Benjamin's description of modern warfare. "Was it not noticeable at the end of the war that men returned from the battlefield grown silent—not richer, but poorer in communicable experience?" Benjamin asks. "A generation that had gone to school on a horse-drawn streetcar now stood under the open sky in a countryside in which nothing remained unchanged but the clouds, and beneath these clouds, in a field of force of destructive torrents and explosions, was the tiny, fragile human body" ("Storyteller," 84). As we shall see, however, Benjamin is most insightful not when he succumbs to the immediacy of the shock event but when he theorizes the disjunctive mediation of allegory.
49. Malabou, xiv.
50. Deleuze, *Masochism*, 114.
51. Malabou, *New Wounded*, 7–8.
52. Malabou, 212, 215.
53. Malabou, 2.
54. Malabou, 17–18.
55. Malabou, *Ontology of the Accident*, 3.
56. Rose, *Sexuality in the Field of Vision*, 9.
57. Malabou, *New Wounded*, 8.
58. Malabou, 213.
59. Benjamin, *Origin of German Tragic Drama*, 164, 165.
60. Benjamin, 166.
61. Benjamin, 166.
62. Benjamin, 162.
63. Benjamin, 176.
64. Lacan, "Seminar on 'The Purloined Letter,'" 20–21.
65. See, for example, Kohn, *How Forests Think*; and Wohlleben, *Hidden Life of Trees*.
66. Quoted in Fink, *Lacan to the Letter*, 80.
67. Fink, 80.
68. Fink, 82.

69. Lacan, *Four Fundamental Concepts of Psychoanalysis*, 25.

70. Chu, *Females*, 12.

71. Chu, 22.

72. See Rose's gloss on Lacan's theory of sexuation. According to Rose, sexuation, for Lacan, is inherently mobile, inherently trans: "For Lacan, men and women are only ever in language ('Men and women are signifiers bound to the common usage of language'). All speaking beings must line themselves up on one side or the other of this division, but anyone can cross over and inscribe themselves on the opposite side from that to which they are anatomically destined. It is, we could say, an either/or situation, but one whose fantasmatic nature was endlessly reiterated by Lacan" (73).

2. TRAUMA IN THE AGE OF WOOD (SPENSER AFTER MALABOU)

1. See Parker, *Inescapable Romance*. I am indebted to Campana's reading of "suffering matter," suffering he calls "elemental," in *The Pain of Reformation*, esp. chapter 1: "For one must remember," Campana writes, "that the Greek for *wood, hyle*, is also the word for *matter*" (48). Campana translates Spenser's wood into "suffering matter" to think about the shared vulnerability among humans; for my part, I reverse the translation to think about the shared traumatism among humans and nonhumans, including trees.

2. Tasso, *Liberation of Jerusalem*.

3. This cross-pollination of humans and plants derives in part from Aristotle. In *De anima*, Aristotle divides living beings into three distinct types: nutritive, sensitive, and intellective. Plants belong to the first type; animals belong to the second, and humans belong to the third. However, all share a nutritive soul. See Aristotle, *On the Soul*. See also the discussion of the tripartite soul in Park, "Organic Soul," 464–84. For a generative reading of Aristotle's *De anima*, one that foregrounds "humankind's complex embeddedness among creaturely life on earth," see Feerick and Nardizzi's introduction to *The Indistinct Human in Renaissance Literature*, 2–3.

4. Ovid, *Metamorphoses*, 32.

5. Freud, *Beyond the Pleasure Principle*, 22.

6. Caruth, *Unclaimed Experience*, 2.

7. This is Laplanche's preferred translation of *Nachträglichkeit*. See Laplanche, "Notes on Afterwardsness," 260–65.

8. Caruth, *Unclaimed Experience*, 4.

9. Caruth, 2.

10. Caruth, 3.

11. Freud, *Beyond the Pleasure Principle*, 26, 27.

12. Derrida, "Freud," 202.

13. Derrida, 203.

14. As Elizabeth Wilson explains in *Psychosomatic*, this strategy of difference and delay is as much a part of the origins of psychoanalysis as it is a part of the history of psychic beginnings. "It has been usual to locate the beginnings of psychoanalysis in Freud's clinical encounters with hysterical patients in the 1880s and 1890s. It was from the strange aggregations of psyche and soma—paralysis, amnesias, strangulated affects, nervous tics, and infantile fantasies—that Freud was able to forge the foundations of psychoanalytic theory and method.... Yet perhaps the body in psychoanalysis has been understood in terms that are too narrow. There has been a tendency, especially in feminist writing, to disregard Freud's neuroscientific and prepsychoanalytic bodies" (1). Alighting on a letter exchanged between Freud and Karl Abraham in 1924, Wilson notes that the subject of the letter—an early publication of Freud's on the nervous system of the lamprey—taxes our familiar understanding of psychoanalytic beginnings by turning our attention to precisely those neuroscientific and prepsychoanalytic bodies that Freud, and many of Freud's readers, thought they had moved beyond.

15. Freud, *Beyond the Pleasure Principle*, 27–28.

16. Benjamin, *Origin of German Tragic Drama*, 166; and Benjamin, *Arcades Project*, 463.

17. Benjamin, *Origin of German Tragic Drama*, 178.

18. Benjamin, 177–78.

19. Marder, *Plant-Thinking*, 27.

20. Malabou, *New Wounded*, xiv.

21. Malabou, *Ontology of the Accident*, 11–12.

22. Marder, *Plant-Thinking*, 20.

23. Heidegger, "The Question concerning Technology," 309.

24. Marder, *Plant-Thinking*, 28.

25. Heidegger, "The Origin of the Work of Art," 188, 191, 197.
26. Marder, *Plant-Thinking*, 30.
27. Marder, 30.
28. Marder, 30.
29. Vin Nardizzi, "Wooden Slavery," 313–15. For a fuller development of Nardizzi's ecomaterialist account of Shakespeare's woods, see Nardizzi, *Wooden Os*.
30. Nardizzi, "Wooden Slavery," 313–14.
31. For a literary and environmental history of deforestation in Shakespeare's time, see Barton, *Shakespearean Forest*.
32. Marder, *Plant-Thinking*, 30–31. Joshua Calhoun shows that plant matter lived on in surprising ways in the textual ecologies of early modern print. See Calhoun, *Nature of the Page*.
33. Benjamin, *Origin of German Tragic Drama*, 224.
34. Spenser's "Yet" disjoins the living present much like Derrida's reading of "the future-to-come" in *Specters of Marx*: "Turned toward the future, going toward it, it also comes from it, it proceeds *from* [*provient de*] the future. It must therefore exceed any presence as presence to itself" (xix).
35. Spenser, "Letter to Raleigh," 717.
36. Quotations from *The Shepheardes Calender* are taken from Spenser, *Shorter Poems*.
37. Goldberg, *Sodometries*, 64.
38. "Both pype and Muse, shall sore the while abye. / So broke his oaten pype, and downe dyd lye" (*Shepheardes Calender*, "Januarye," 71–72).
39. OED, s.v. "clot," n. Variant of "clod," as in a "clod of earth" ("clod," n.).
40. For more on Spenser's Virgilian progression, see Cheney, "Spenser's Pastorals," 86.
41. Brought to Faery Land "unweeting" by a faery and left in a furrow of land, Redcrosse Knight derives his name, Saint George, from georgic roots:

> Thence she thee brought into this Faery lond,
>   And in an heaped furrow did thee hyde,
> Where thee a Ploughman all vnweeting fond,
>   As he his toylesome teme that way did guyde,
>   And brought thee vp in ploughmans state to byde,
> Whereof *Georgos* he thee gaue to name. (1.10.66)

42. Kuzner, *Open Subjects*, 41–44.

43. I use the term "castration" here in the Lacanian sense of a subject's (ontological) lack-in-being. On this point, see Chu, *Females*, 12, 22–25; and Ruti, *Penis Envy*, xx–xxii.

44. Lacan writes: "The *objet a* is something from which the subject, in order to constitute itself, has separated itself off as organ. This serves as a symbol of the lack, that is to say, of the phallus" (*Four Fundamental Concepts of Psychoanalysis*, 103).

45. Žižek, *Sublime Object of Ideology*, 59.

46. The classic accounts of "error" as a mode of *différance* in Spenser's romance are Parker's *Inescapable Romance*; and Goldberg's *Endlesse Worke*.

47. Žižek, *Sublime Object of Ideology*, 61–62.

48. Žižek, 62.

49. Derrida's concept of *pas* names both a step and the negation "not." The result is a composite term that weaves together affirmation and negation in one complex movement. See Derrida, "How to Avoid Speaking: Denials."

50. See Raber, "Equeer," 347–62.

51. G. W. F. Hegel, *Hegel and the Human Spirit*, 87.

52. I should note that despite long-standing philosophical, ecocritical, and feminist codings to the contrary, nature is not "feminine" in any essentialist sense. Dark ecology maintains that nature is, at bottom, queer. See Morton's use of "dark ecology" in *Ecological Thought*, 81. I use the term "feminine" to underscore the hyperbolic treatment of maternal substance, rendered monstrous, in Spenser's representation. For an alternative "masculine" account, consider, by way of Bersani, that the "darksom hole" may also represent the rectum, conjuring the masochistic threat (of gay men's jouissance) that Bersani links to anal sex in "Is the Rectum a Grave?," 197–222.

53. Gregerson, *Reformation of the Subject*, 96.

54. Rhu, "Romancing the Word," 101.

55. On this point, see Campana, *Pain of Reformation*, 90–91.

56. Gregerson, *Reformation of the Subject*; and Quilligan, *Language of Allegory*, 36.

57. Although it is now commonplace to read Spenser's epic in light of post-Reformation religious and political turmoil, Campana makes a

compelling case for reading Protestant poetics as an ineluctably melancholy endeavor. Rather than accept a landscape bereft of corporeal and affective experience, Campana argues that Renaissance poets satisfied their desires indirectly through unique and stylistically inventive speech acts whose beauty owes to the textures of pain and suffering they gave rise to. According to Campana, "Allegory became one location for the contentious materiality of the body of Christ in an age in which both the idea of the real presence of Christ and, by extension, the nature and efficacy of sacraments were hotly contested." See Campana, *Pain of Reformation*, 79. For a related argument, see Schwartz, *Sacramental Poetics at the Dawn of Secularism*.

58. Sartre compares ordinary consciousness to the experience of a voyeur staring through a keyhole. See Sartre, *Being and Nothingness*, 282–84.

59. OED, s.v. "brood," n.

60. Freud, *Three Essays*, 194.

61. Freud, 194–95.

62. See Arendt, *Human Condition*; Nancy, *Birth to Presence*; and Badiou, *Logics of Worlds*, especially the conclusion, "What Is It to Live?"

63. Freud, *Three Essays*, 196.

64. Freud, 196.

65. Derrida, *Animal That Therefore I Am*, 4.

66. Derrida, 41.

67. Derrida, 47.

68. Teskey, *Allegory and Violence*, 2.

69. Teskey, 15–16.

70. Berger, *Revisionary Play*, 216.

71. Campana, *Pain of Reformation*, 49.

72. Donne, "Hymn to Christ."

73. Lewis, *Allegory of Love*, 2.

74. Lewis, 44.

75. Lewis, 298.

76. Lewis, 345.

77. Freud, *Beyond the Pleasure Principle*, 35.

78. Freud, 35.

79. Fudge, *Perceiving Animals*, 15.

80. Fudge, 15.

81. Daniel, *Melancholy Assemblage*, 5.

82. See Gail Kern Paster's influential study of the humoral body's co-composition with the environment in *Humoring the Body*.

INTERLUDE

1. See OED, s.v. "blatant," adj. and n.

2. OED, s.v. "blatant," adj. and n.

3. Derrida, *Animal That Therefore I Am*: "Since time, since so long ago, hence since all of time and for what remains of it to come we would therefore be in passage toward surrendering to the promise of that animal at unease with itself" (3).

4. OED, s.v. "blatant," adj. and n.

5. See OED, s.v. "bleat," v.

6. See OED, s.v. "clamour | clamor," n.

7. Milton, *Paradise Lost*.

8. For a related argument focused on the animal voice in eighteenth-century poetry, see Menely, *Animal Claim*.

9. Bennett, *Vibrant Matter*, xiii.

10. See Yates on the lures and limits to posthuman tele-phono-centrism. Yates likens the "dropped" call of multispecies belonging to a trauma: "Traumatized by all the calls (*phone*) that we receive from other beings that we once thought were at a distance (*tele*) but that now resonate within us (*infra*), the 'human' might find itself . . . transformed into some imperfect but potential receiver." "There may, after all, be as many as twelve thousand years' worth of dropped or blocked calls from other forms of life" (*Of Sheep, Oranges, and Yeast*, 21–22).

11. Lacan, "Instance," 413.

12. Lacan, "Seminar on 'The Purloined Letter,'" 17.

13. Schuster, *Trouble with Pleasure*, 21–22.

14. A hinge between the literature of the hunt and the biopolitics of capture, Spenser's poem illustrates Antoine Traisnel's fascinating distinction, which is also an onto-epistemological distinction, between the spatiality of the hunt and the temporality of capture: "If we read capture's displacement of the animal's pursuit from spatiality onto temporality," Traisnel writes, "we see that [capture] . . . inaugurates a hunt without end" (13). Capture presupposes the fugacity of its object (17–18). And because that object is, in Traisnel's sense, already escaped ("the animal is assumed invisible, disappeared,

unknowable"—hauntological rather than huntological), it can be "re-cast as endlessly reproducible and thus eminently disposable" (15, 13).

3. THE OCEANIC FEELING (RALEGH)

1. Mbembe, "Necropolitics," 11–40; Agamben, *Homo Sacer.*
2. Ralegh, *History of the World,* 45.
3. Shannon, *Accommodated Animal,* 1–28, 127–73.
4. Ralegh, *History of the World,* 45.
5. Ralegh, 45.
6. For a detailed analysis of the intellectual, political, and theological motivations that prompted Ralegh to work on a universal world history, see Nicholas Popper's *Walter Ralegh's History of the World and the Historical Culture of the Late Renaissance.*
7. For more on the sea as a potential "plane of immanence," see Cesare Casarino's excellent study, *Modernity at Sea,* which asserts the centrality of the sea to the making and unmaking of Western modernity.
8. See Chen, *Animacies.*
9. Agamben, *Homo Sacer,* 9.
10. Agamben, 9.
11. Colebrook, "Not Symbiosis, Not Now," 185–209.
12. Agamben, *Homo Sacer,* 4–5.
13. Badiou, *Saint Paul,* 7, 5.
14. Badiou, 5.
15. Derrida makes this point in *The Beast and the Sovereign,* vol. 1: "What is difficult to sustain, in this [Agamben's] thesis, is the idea of an entry (a modern entry, then) into a zone of irreducible indifferentiation, when the differentiation [between *bios* and *zoē*] has never been secure; and, above all, what remains even more difficult to sustain is the idea that there is in this something modern or new; for Agamben himself . . . is keen to recall that it [the biopolitical] is as ancient as can be, immemorial and archaic" (316–17).
16. Foucault, *Order of Things,* 387.
17. I borrow the phrase "autoimmunitary process" from Derrida: "As we know, an autoimmunitary process is that strange behavior where a living being, in quasi-*suicidal* fashion, 'itself' works to destroy its own protection, to immunize itself *against* its 'own' immunity" (*Philosophy in a Time of Terror,* 94).

18. On the idea of "reproductive futurity," see Edelman, *No Future.*

19. Freud, *Civilization and Its Discontents,* 64–65.

20. See Bersani and Dutoit, *Forms of Being,* 124–78; Bersani and Adam Phillips, *Intimacies,* 57–87; and Silverman, *Flesh of My Flesh,* 17–36.

21. See Masten's chapter "'Sweet Persuasion,' the Taste of Letters, and Male Friendship," in *Queer Philologies,* 69–82.

22. "Sweete" also compels the senseless "lull" of sleep, or "slomber of delight." For an illuminating study of the early modern ethics of sleep, or careless self-care, see Parris, *Vital Strife.*

23. Masten, *Queer Philologies,* 78.

24. See Hall, "Culinary Spaces, Colonial Spaces," 168–90. On the intersection of sugar commodification, domestic consumption, gender, and power, see Greene's *Unrequited Conquests,* 185–87; and Wall's *Staging Domesticity.*

25. Irigaray, *Marine Lover of Friedrich Nietzsche.*

26. Greenblatt, *Sir Walter Ralegh;* Helgerson, *Forms of Nationhood;* Fuller, *Voyages in Print.*

27. My call for a more aqua-centric literary criticism follows Patricia Yaeger's analysis in "Sea Trash, Dark Pools, and the Tragedy of the Commons," 523–45. I also draw on the "oceanic turn" in early modern studies. See, for example, Brayton, *Shakespeare's Ocean;* Duckert, *For All Waters;* Mentz, *Shakespeare's Ocean;* and Mentz, *Shipwreck Modernity.*

28. My thinking on imbroglios of material agents that are human and nonhuman draws on the work of Allewaert, *Ariel's Ecology;* Cronon, *Changes in the Land;* Latour, *Politics of Nature;* Morton, *Ecology without Nature;* and Parrish, *American Curiosity.*

29. Mentz, *Shakespeare's Ocean,* 1.

30. All quotations from Ralegh's "Cynthia" poems are taken from *The Poems of Sir Walter Ralegh,* ed. Michael Rudick. I have also consulted *The Poems of Sir Walter Ralegh,* ed. Agnes M. C. Latham.

31. Greenblatt, *Sir Walter Ralegh,* 104.

32. *Poems of Sir Walter Ralegh,* ed. Latham, xiv.

33. Glissant, *Caribbean Discourse,* 134.

34. Glissant, 135.

35. Glissant, 135.

36. Glissant, 139.

37. On the topos of *ultima Britannia*, antiquity's idea of England as a remote island at the margins of the Mediterranean, and its persistence in the early modern English imaginary, see Bellamy, *Dire Straits*.

38. Glissant, *Caribbean Discourse*, 139.

39. Goldberg, *Tempest in the Caribbean*, 3–37.

40. Hakluyt, *Divers Voyages*, 1–2.

41. Hakluyt, 1–2.

42. Woolfson, "Renaissance of Bees," 283.

43. Aristotle, *Generation of Animals*, 1176.

44. Pliny the Elder, *Natural History*, 149–57.

45. Virgil, *Georgics*, book 4.

46. Woolfson, "Renaissance of Bees," 283.

47. Freedberg, *Eye of the Lynx*, 165.

48. Virgil, *Georgics*, 4.198–202.

49. See Foucault, *Security, Territory, Population*.

50. See Vickers, "Diana Described," 265–79; and "'Blazon,'" 95–115.

51. Parker, *Literary Fat Ladies*, 126–54; Donne, "Mistress."

52. Montrose, "Work of Gender," 13.

53. Certeau, *Writing of History*, xxvi.

54. Montrose, "Work of Gender," 6.

55. Canguilhem, *Vital Rationalist*, 163.

56. Canguilhem, 163.

57. Canguilhem, 176–77.

58. Freedberg, *Eye of the Lynx*, 175.

59. Freedberg, 175–76.

60. Citations from Ralegh, *Discoverie of the Large, Rich, and Bewtifvl Empyre of Gviana* are from Ralegh, *Discoverie of Guiana*, 211–13.

61. Ralegh, *Discoverie of Guiana*, 31.

62. Montrose, "Elizabethan Subject," 315.

63. Traub, *Renaissance of Lesbianism*, 131–32.

64. Ralegh, *Discoverie of Guiana*, 213.

65. See Fuller, "Ralegh's Fugitive Gold," 218–40.

66. Allewaert, *Ariel's Ecology*, 2.

67. Ralegh, *Discoverie of Guiana*, 2.

68. Ralegh, 4–5.

69. Ralegh, 5–6.

70. Ralegh, 13.

71. Derrida, *The Animal That Therefore I Am*, 66.

72. Ralegh, *Discoverie of Guiana*, 95.

73. My reference to "worlding" here and elsewhere in this chapter alludes to Heidegger's well-known thesis in *The Fundamental Concepts of Metaphysics*—namely, that "the stone is worldless [*weltlos*], the animal is poor in world [*weltarm*], man is world-forming [*weltbildend*]" (176). Heidegger defines "world" according to a being's capacity for active engagement with the environment. His theses concerning "the animal" have been discussed at great length by Derrida in *Of Spirit* and *The Animal That Therefore I Am* and by Agamben in *The Open*. However, less has been said about Heidegger's theses concerning the elements. By calling attention to the worlding power of oceans, my purpose is to counter critical myopia toward the water and to show that, indeed, oceans, rivers, and other sealike bodies *have world* and are world-forming to the extent that they not only relate to the environment but also actively transform it. Ralegh's term for this active engagement is "breach[ing]." Recall that, in Derrida's essay on Freud's "Note on the Mystic Writing Pad," Derrida defines writing as a palimpsestic economy of "breaching" (*Bahnung*) and argues that it is the difference between facilitations that is at the origin of memory and historicity: "We then must not say that breaching without difference is insufficient for memory; it must be stipulated that there is no pure breaching without difference. Trace as memory is not a pure breaching that might be reappropriated at any time as simple presence; it is rather the ungraspable and indivisible difference between breaches" (201). Ralegh's attention to river-crossings and alluvial traces accords with Derrida's sense of breaching as an "ungraspable and indivisible difference." While I follow Derrida's lead in using the metaphorics of writing to describe the worlding power of oceans, it is not my intention to reduce oceanic writing to the history and memory of the human, a maneuver that would once again make man the measure of all things; rather, my intention is to open the concept of writing to histories beyond the human. The question is not simply, *What is nature such that it becomes a form of writing?* But rather, *What is writing such that it belongs always already to nature?*

74. Derrida, *The Animal That Therefore I Am*, 66.

75. Greenblatt, *Sir Walter Ralegh*, 131.

76. Ralegh, *History of the World*, 88.

77. Ralegh, 90.

78. Ralegh, 91.

79. Derrida, *Truth in Painting*, 73.

80. Derrida, 57.

81. Derrida, 57.

82. Yaeger, "Sea Trash," 526–27.

83. Ralegh, *First Invention of Shipping*, 1–2.

84. See Puttenham, *Art of English Poesy*, 221–22.

85. Walcott, "Sea Is History," 364–67.

86. See, for example, Eisenstein, *Printing Press*; Eisenstein, *Printing Revolution*; Febvre and Martin, *Coming of the Book*; Johns, *Nature of the Book*; McLuhan, *Gutenberg Galaxy*; and Ong, *Orality and Literacy*.

87. Casanova, *World Republic of Letters*.

88. Moretti, *Graphs, Maps, Trees*, 1.

89. Helgerson, *Forms of Nationhood*, 153.

90. Helgerson, 153.

91. Quoted in Fuller, *Voyages in Print*, 1.

92. Fuller, 1.

93. Fuller, 1, 66.

94. Shannon, *Accommodated Animal*, 1. For more on the idea of "the modern constitution," see Latour, *We Have Never Been Modern*, 13.

95. Shannon, *Accommodated Animal*, 270.

96. Quoted in Shannon, 275.

97. Shannon, 281.

98. See Colebrook: "What is required is not a shift in extensity (including more, respecting more, furthering our historical imagination), but a shift in *intensity*" ("Not Symbiosis, Not Now," 188).

99. Deleuze and Guattari, *Thousand Plateaus*, 7.

100. Massumi, *Parables for the Virtual*, 5.

101. Deleuze and Guattari, *What Is Philosophy?*, 36.

102. Deleuze and Guattari, 36.

103. Ralegh, *History of the World*, 75.

104. Deleuze and Guattari, *Kafka*, 7.

105. Deleuze and Guattari, 13.

106. Ralegh, *History of the World*, 92.

107. Ralegh, 92.

108. Ralegh, 93.
109. Ralegh, 93.
110. Spivak, *Death of a Discipline*, 93.
111. Spivak, 72.
112. Sloterdijk, "Geometry in the Colossal," 33.
113. Genesis 1:2. This citation is from the Geneva Bible; see *The Bible*.
114. Foucault, *Order of Things*, 386.

4. ARCHITECTURAL ANTHROPOLOGIES (MARVELL)

1. Alberti, *Architecture of Leon Battista Alberti*, 1. I have also consulted the following modern translation: Alberti, *Art of Building* (1988).
2. Alberti, *Architecture of Leon Battista Alberti*, 1.
3. Alberti, 1.
4. Alberti, 1–2.
5. Alberti, 2.
6. Alberti, 37.
7. Alberti, *Architecture of Leon Battista Alberti*, 9–10.
8. OED, s.v. "design," n.
9. For Derrida, the supplementary logic of linearism is such that the sequence of units (speech and *then* writing, or spirit and *then* matter) is not only reversible but also discontinuous and fractal. In other words, there is not speech and *then* writing, no more than there is writing and *then* speech; the latter simply reverses the sequence of terms without changing their unitary logic. Instead, speech, the datum of sense-understanding and universal communicability for *Homo loquens*, is, according to Derrida, already a kind of writing, understood in the general sense as an open-ended system of differentiation. Every ideal figure, in other words, is "itself" traced by a system of differences without common measure; these differences are not exterior to the ideal object but are woven with/in it. Hence, for Derrida, human language continuously encrypts itself—that is, ciphers or entombs its "origin"—by decrypting mobile figures into stable units of meaning. See Derrida, *Of Grammatology*: "This linearism is undoubtedly inseparable from phonologism; it can raise its voice to the same extent that a linear writing can seem to submit to it" (72).
10. Auerbach, "Figura," 14.
11. Auerbach, 14–15.

12. See Althusser, "Underground Current," 163–207.

13. Auerbach, "Figura," 16.

14. Auerbach, 16.

15. Auerbach, 16–17.

16. Lucretius, *Way Things Are*, 120, 121.

17. Deleuze, "Simulacrum and Ancient Philosophy," 253.

18. Quoted in Lezra, *Unspeakable Subjects*, 3.

19. Auerbach, "Figura," 17.

20. For a philosophical history of the "incorporeal" as it travels from the Stoics to Spinoza to Deleuze and beyond, see Grosz, *Incorporeal*.

21. Auerbach, "Figura," 17. Whereas Auerbach chronicles its demise, Yates reawakens the Lucretian sense of *figura* and charts its underground movement from Shakespeare to the present: "Figures (*figurae*), as a category, still matter," Yates writes. "But they count for more than the bodying forth of absent things in media (representations) or even the effects of that bodying forth on a reader or viewer (a memory, an affective response). They designate privileged material-semiotic zones (*topoi*), scenes of writing or marking, from which forms of life issue" (13–14).

22. Vasari, *Lives of the Artists*, 3.

23. Vasari, 3.

24. Wittkower, *Architectural Principles*, 29.

25. Plato, *Timaeus*, 1238, 1256.

26. Alberti, *Art of Building*, 196.

27. Galilei, *Assayer*, 183.

28. Cassirer, *Individual and the Cosmos*: "Seen from the point of view of 'nature,' the world of freedom always remains a mystery, a kind of miracle. This miracle cannot be recognized without losing the specific *sense* of the concept of nature, as the Renaissance conceived of it. For this sense consists in nothing other than in the idea of the unity and the uniqueness of the explanation of nature" (109).

29. Deleuze highlights this humanist puzzle in his early essay "Mathesis, Science and Philosophy": "The knowing mind, as distinct as it might be in itself from the extension with which it appears to have strictly nothing in common, nonetheless deploys the order of things in thinking the order of its representations. At the very moment where unity is affirmed, this unity breaks apart and destroys itself" (142).

30. The philosophical axiom "mathematics *is* ontology" marks the high point of Badiou's mathematical formalism. See Badiou, *Being and Event*, 4. For a comprehensive discussion of the "mathematical turn" in Badiou's thought and its relation to premodern thinkers, see Hallward, *Badiou*, 49–78.

31. All quotations from *Upon Appleton House* are taken from *The Poems of Andrew Marvell*, ed. Nigel Smith.

32. Puttenham, *Art of English Poesy*, 189.

33. See, for example, Marcuse's classic, *One-Dimensional Man*.

34. On the early modern history of animal architecture, see Raber, *Animal Bodies, Renaissance Culture*, 127–50.

35. Grosz, *Chaos, Territory, Art*, 10.

36. Deleuze and Guattari, *What Is Philosophy?*, 213.

37. Deleuze and Guattari, 209.

38. Edelman, *Homographesis*, 10, 14.

39. Derrida: "It is offered by a mute mark, by a tacit monument, I would even say by a pyramid, thinking not only of the form of the letter when it is printed as a capital, but also of the text in Hegel's *Encyclopedia* in which the body of the sign is compared to the Egyptian Pyramid. The *a* of *différance*, thus, is not heard; it remains silent, secret and discreet as a tomb: *oikēsis*" ("Différance," 4).

40. For a related account that reads Marvell's lyric events alongside Deleuze and Badiou, see Netzley, *Lyric Apocalypse*. Netzley reads Marvell's lyric events in an apocalyptic manner—that is, as events without (revolutionary) future. Marvell's events, according to Netzley, reside in the immanent time of now.

41. See Williams, *Country and the City*, on the country-house genre and its ideological modes. For critical accounts of Marvell's country-house poem, see Acheson, "Military Illustration," 146–88; Hequembourg, "Dream of a Literal World," 83–113; Kadue, "Sustaining Fiction," 641–61; and Rogers, *Matter of Revolution*.

42. Rogers, *Matter of Revolution*, 61.

43. Rogers, 61, 40, 55, 42.

44. Rogers, 61–62.

45. Rogers, 69.

46. Hegel, *Lectures*, 257.

47. Hegel, 288.

48. Spinoza, *Ethics*, 278.
49. Sharp, *Spinoza*, 2.
50. Spinoza, *Ethics*, 277.
51. Sharp, *Spinoza*, 22.
52. Spinoza, *Ethics*, 240.
53. Sharp, *Spinoza*, 22.
54. Sharp, 22.
55. Daniel P. Jaeckle offers a related interpretation of Marvell's "holy mathematics" in "Marvell's Reformed Theory of Architecture," 49–67. There, Jaeckle argues, "Marvell overtly rejects Pythagorean mathematics as the basis of architecture" and upholds the "sober frame" as "a truly holy signifier because it mathematically equals the humility of Fairfax" (49).
56. Alexander, *Infinitesimal*, 219.
57. Euclid, *Thirteen Books of the Elements*, 155.
58. Deleuze, "The Fold," 230.
59. Boyer, *History of the Calculus*, 4.
60. Eliot, "Metaphysical Poets," 247.
61. Boyer, *History of the Calculus*, 6.
62. Massumi, *Parables for the Virtual*, 28.
63. Massumi, 29.
64. Massumi, 29.
65. Eliot, "Marvell," 256.
66. Eliot, 256.
67. Eliot, "Metaphysical Poets," 245.
68. Mazzio, "Three-Dimensional Self," 43–44.
69. Mazzio, 44.
70. Mazzio, 45.
71. Jonson, "To Penshurst," 98.
72. Deleuze and Guattari, *What Is Philosophy?*, 204.
73. While this mode of subtraction proves essential to both classical and Italian architecture's theory of "figure," it is noteworthy that this mathematization of matter subtends even the furthest reaches of philosophical speculation from Plato to Descartes to the present. Of particular importance in this discussion is the philosophy of Badiou. In his effort to equate mathematics with ontology, Badiou rests the possibility of historical rupture (what he calls the "event," in the manner of the most universal, hence *formalizable*, truth events) on

the *subtraction* of material, sensuous reality from the purity of mathematical figures. Such subtraction, Badiou wagers, "*induces* a subject" by establishing the subject as an agent of truth. See Badiou, *Ethics*, 43. Whereas Lucretius imagined there to be no place outside the "dance of figures," Badiou understands "the subject of truth" in terms similar to that of Alberti's artist, as an architect of pure "Form" who stands outside nature's figures. As Hallward, Badiou's translator, writes, "Subjects are both *carried by* a truth—they compose the 'finite' points of an always 'infinite' truth—and provide its literal, material 'support.' Every subject *is*," Hallward remarks, "only an 'objective' individual, an ordinary mortal, become 'immortal' through his or her affirmation of (or transfiguration by) a truth that coheres at a level entirely beyond this mortal objectivity" (Badiou, *Ethics*, x). The truth-event, in other words, dematerializes the act of figuration by breaking with sensory immediacy; disincarnated by number and transfigured by truth, the "subject," according to Badiou, is capable of thinking the truth of Being qua number, since number, for Badiou, is indistinguishable from thought itself.

74. Deleuze, *Difference and Repetition*, 131.
75. Manuel DeLanda characterizes Deleuze's philosophy of life as "morphogenetic" for this reason: "While an essentialist account may rely on factors that transcend the realm of matter and energy (eternal archetypes, for instance), a morphogenetic account gets rid of all *transcendent* factors using exclusively form-generating resources which are *immanent* to the material world" (*Intensive Science and Virtual Philosophy*, 2). Notably, Deleuze does not juxtapose form to matter, nor does he restrict the operations of sense to the sensibility of the human body (as in phenomenology). Instead, Deleuze proposes an abstract materialism with the power to create form, including the form of the human body, and above all, the power to *deviate from that form*.
76. Colebrook, *Deleuze*, 115.
77. Deleuze, *Difference and Repetition*, 132.
78. Deleuze, 142.
79. Deleuze, "Simulacrum and Ancient Philosophy," 253, 254.
80. Deleuze, *Difference and Repetition*, 138.
81. Deleuze, 138.
82. Deleuze, 147.

83. Vitruvius, *On Architecture*, 1:161.

84. Deleuze, "Simulacrum and Ancient Philosophy," 256.

85. See Lacan, "Instance of the Letter," 430; and "In Memory of Ernest Jones," 594.

86. Freud, *Three Essays*, 147–48.

87. Freud, 182.

88. Freud, 182.

89. Laplanche, *Life and Death in Psychoanalysis*, 22.

90. Freud, "Leonardo da Vinci," 80.

91. Freud, 77.

92. Empson, *Some Versions of Pastoral*, 119.

93. Empson, 119.

94. All quotations from "The Garden" are taken from *The Poems of Andrew Marvell*, ed. Nigel Smith.

95. See OED, s.v. "toil," n. 2.

96. See Benjamin, *Origin of German Tragic Drama*. For an exhaustive study of Renaissance allegory that builds on Benjamin's insights, see Martin, *Ruins of Allegory*.

97. Empson, *Some Versions of Pastoral*, 119.

98. Freud, *Interpretation of Dreams*, 536.

99. Freud, 537.

100. Teskey, *Poetry of John Milton*, 82.

101. Marvell, "Upon the Hill and Grove," in *The Poems of Andrew Marvell*, ed. Nigel Smith.

102. Deleuze and Guattari, *A Thousand Plateaus*, 171.

103. Deleuze and Guattari, 172.

104. Deleuze and Guattari, 172–73.

105. See Yusoff, *Billion Black Anthropocenes or None*, 4–5.

106. In his lectures on abnormality, Foucault pinpoints the birth of biopolitics in the topographic survey, first used in the seventeenth century not to confine abnormality but rather to track its rates of mutation, transformation, and migration. Foucault's biopolitical figures are *aleatory* in Lucretius's sense: they track bodily movements and flows.

107. My reading of Marvell's crip ecology draws on Elizabeth B. Bearden's *Monstrous Kinds*, especially chapter 2, where Bearden reads early modern disability as the diverse "endowment of nature" (79).

108. Vitruvius, *On Architecture*, 2:213.

109. Here, too, disability is the rule rather than the exception, for it is only by loosening nature's clockwork, its rectilinear design, that architecture turns its face to the outside, to what, according to Deleuze and Guattari, architecture is all along—inhuman. Architecture is linked to the fabrication of a frame, be it through birdsong or poetry. "In this respect," Deleuze and Guattari write, "art is continually haunted by the animal" (*What Is Philosophy?*, 184).

110. Shakespeare, *A Midsummer Night's Dream*.

111. Vitruvius, *On Architecture*, 1:207.

112. Vitruvius, 1:207.

113. On the botanical and biopolitical history of the Oedipus story, see Nardizzi, "Budding Oedipus," 347–66.

114. Vitruvius, *On Architecture*, 1:209.

115. Vitruvius, 1:209.

116. Katie Kadue draws our attention to such moments and the "straightness" they imply in "Sustaining Fiction," 641–61. The appearance of the "young Maria" underscores Kadue's point that Marvell's poem, if queer, is ambivalently queer at best and may reassert patriarchy as its operating telos. My reading of *Upon Appleton House* differs from Kadue's in asserting that Marvell's strange geometry invites alternatives to the domesticated sexualities that Kadue critiques. I build this argument in light of other queer analyses that trace Marvell's sexual ambivalence in nonprocreative and ecological directions. See, in particular, Garrison, "Eros and Objecthood," 1–27; Guy-Bray, "No Present," 38–52; and Sanchez, "'She Straightness," 81–96.

117. Freud, "Medusa's Head," 273–74.

118. On the queer history of early modern Christianity and seventeenth-century English poetry's representations of Christ, see Rambuss, *Closet Devotions*. Although Rambuss does not include Marvell in his compendium of "incarnational" poets, it would not be a stretch to say that Marvell's ecstatic speaker extends the sacred eroticism of Donne, Crashaw, and others to encompass tree and earth.

119. Traub, *Renaissance of Lesbianism*, 129–32.

120. OED, s.v. "billet," n. 2.

121. See Rob Nixon, "Defending Tomorrow Today," *Edge Effects*, August 6, 2020, https://edgeeffects.net/defend-environmental-defenders/.

122. Harney and Moten, *Undercommons*, 17.

123. Harney and Moten, 20.

124. Deleuze, *Francis Bacon*, 12.

5. QUEER LIFE, UNEARTHED (MILTON)

1. Atwood, *Oryx and Crake*, 214.

2. Atwood, 216.

3. On the importance of the Adamic art of naming in early modern contexts, see Bono, *Word of God*; and Picciotto, *Labors of Innocence*.

4. On agential assemblages, see Bennett, *Vibrant Matter*, 20–38.

5. See Deleuze and Guattari, *A Thousand Plateaus*, 3–25; Morton, *Hyperobjects*; Puar, *Terrorist Assemblages*; and Serres, *Parasite*.

6. Puar, *Terrorist Assemblages*, 211. Puar's book "rearticulates terrorist bodies . . . as an assemblage that resists queerness-as-sexual-identity" (205). For a specifically Miltonic rearticulation of terrorist bodies, grounded in a reading of the suicide bomber, see Mohamed, *Milton*.

7. On the relation of finitude and the name, see Derrida: "It seems to me that every case of naming involves announcing a death to come in the surviving of a ghost, the longevity of a name that survives whoever carries that name. . . . Being called, hearing oneself being named, receiving a name for the first time involves something like the knowledge of being mortal and even the feeling that one is dying" (*The Animal That Therefore I Am*, 20, 14–19).

8. Atwood, *Oryx and Crake*, 222.

9. Foucault, *History of Madness*, xxviii.

10. Foucault, xxix.

11. On the notion of "time's arrow," see Gould's canonical account in *Time's Arrow, Time's Cycle*.

12. Foucault, *Order of Things*, 155–56.

13. See Foucault, *Abnormal*.

14. This reading of earthly fundament as fundamentally mad suggests Foucault's own reworking of psychoanalysis from an archaeological perspective. Whereas Freud theorized the return to inorganic life (i.e., the death drive) as a principle of regression internal to the life of bourgeois subjects, Foucault theorizes life's undoing as a geological event on the scale of the earth. For a further elaboration of this argument

concerning the inorganic, see Huffer, "Foucault's Fossils." Huffer also proposes this Foucauldian rereading of the death drive as a queer ethics of "desubjectivation" in *Are the Lips a Grave?*, 27–49.

15. Milton, "On Shakespeare," 20.

16. De Man, "Autobiography as De-facement," 75–76.

17. John Ray, *Three Physico-Theological Discourses*, "The Preface" [a].

18. Rudwick, *Earth's Deep History*, 9.

19. Rudwick, 9–10.

20. Ray, *Three Physico-Theological Discourses*, 6.

21. Ray, 147.

22. Ray, 133.

23. On the metaphorics of "life" as futural form, see Edelman's classic revision of "life," symbolized by the Child, as a form *without* future in *No Future*. See also Colebrook's withering critique of the "posthuman," which, like the Child for Edelman, symbolizes humanity's devastating imperative to survive its own extinction in *Death of the Posthuman*.

24. See, for example, Crutzen and Stoemer, "Anthropocene," 17–18; and Crutzen, "Geology of Mankind." Stoemer pioneered the term "Anthropocene," and Crutzen popularized it. For further exploration and critique, see Dipesh Chakrabarty's groundbreaking essay, "The Climate of History: Four Theses," 197–222, as well as Bonneuil and Fressoz, *Shock of the Anthropocene*; Davies, *Birth of the Anthropocene*; and Mitchell, *Carbon Democracy*. See also Mentz, *Shipwreck Modernity*, especially the "Theoretical Preface," for a sharp reworking of Anthropocene periodization.

25. On the current extinction crisis, see Kolbert, *Sixth Extinction*.

26. On biopolitics and war, see Foucault, *History of Sexuality*, 1:133–59. For important reworkings of Foucault's argument vis-à-vis Marxism, vitalism, and theories of state violence, see Agamben, *Homo Sacer*; Esposito, *Bíos*; Hardt and Negri, *Empire*; and Virno, *Grammar of the Multitude*.

27. Povinelli, "Rhetorics of Recognition in Geontopower," 428–42, 429. For a fuller development of this argument, see Povinelli, *Geontologies*.

28. Foucault, *"Society Must Be Defended,"* 7.

29. Foucault, 7.

30. Foucault, "Theatrum Philosophicum," 171.

31. See Grosz, *Becoming Undone*, 26–39.

32. On "homonationalism," see Puar, *Terrorist Assemblages*.

33. Brooks, *Well Wrought Urn*, 96.

34. All quotations from *Paradise Lost* are taken from Milton, *Major Works*.

35. On *Paradise Lost* as an allegory of the events of the English Civil War, see Norbrook, *Writing the English Republic*, 433–95; and Rogers, *Matter of Revolution*. On the earth's deep history as discovered by early modern naturalists, see Rossi, *Dark Abyss of Time*; Rudwick, *Meaning of Fossils*; and Rudwick, *Earth's Deep History*.

36. I borrow the phrase "slow violence" from Nixon. See Nixon's important book, *Slow Violence and the Environmentalism of the Poor*. My exact reference builds on Andreas Malm's use of "slow violence" to describe the *longue durée* or asynchronicity of geological time. See Malm, *Fossil Capital*, 8–11.

37. Meillassoux, *After Finitude*, 10, 9.

38. Ken Hiltner makes a brief but important reference to coal mining as it pertains to the much broader discussion of Earth, soil, and "place" in his book *Milton and Ecology*, 2. For a discussion of "cheap energy" in early modern England linked to capital accumulation and the rise of the fossil-fuel economy, see Moore, *Capitalism*, 111–40. Moore writes: "Modernity's energy revolutions do not date—as sometimes supposed—from the eighteenth century, but rather from the long sixteenth century. England's astounding increase in coal production began in the 1530s. By 1660, coal covered more than a third of the country's energy output" (132).

39. One thinks here, longingly perhaps, of the twin attacks leveled against the pastoralization of sex by Lacan ("The domain of the pastoral," he writes, "is never absent from civilization; it never fails to offer itself as a solution to the latter's discontents" [*Ethics of Psychoanalysis*, 88]) and Lacan's queer disciple, Bersani, in "Is the Rectum a Grave?" To the extent that queer theory is undergoing a pastoral Renaissance in collaboration with the new materialisms, it is doing so largely in the absence of the negative as insisted on by Lacan and Bersani.

40. Braidotti, "Interview with Rosi Braidotti," 19–37, 36.

41. Or take Povinelli's provocative formulation: "*What should we make of concepts that seem to conserve the qualities of life while denying its impermanence? Life no longer needs to face its terror: the lifeless, the inert, and the void of being. In other words, solving the problem of how governance will be with rather than merely with regard to the nonhuman*

and nonlife by extending either those attributes that most define the human (language, semiosis) or by extending what we find most precious about life (birth, becoming, actualization) does not solve the horror of the inert and the indifferent but merely saturates it with familiar and reassuring qualities. *It solves the problem by reassuring us, persuading us, that we can remain the same, namely, entities that become, actualize, signify*" ("Rhetorics of Recognition in Geontopower," 44, emphasis added).

42. Edelman, *No Future*, 70.

43. See Deleuze's early essay, "Desert Islands": "An island doesn't stop being deserted simply because it is inhabited. . . . Those people who come to the island indeed occupy and populate it; but in reality, were they sufficiently separate, sufficiently creative, they would give the island only a dynamic image of itself, a consciousness of the movement which produced the island, such that through them the island would in the end become conscious of itself as deserted and unpeopled" (10).

44. "What then is madness," Foucault asks, "in its most general but most concrete form, for anyone who immediately challenges any hold that knowledge might have upon it? In all probability, nothing other than *the absence of an oeuvre*" (*History of Madness*, xxxi). I translate Foucault's provocative statement, "*the absence of an oeuvre*," in order to highlight the ontological *negativity* at work in Milton's poetry. For a related argument that treats extinction as "a speculative opportunity," see Brassier, *Nihil Unbound*, xi.

45. Hiltner, *Milton and Ecology*, viii.

46. Hiltner, viii.

47. Hiltner, ix, 14.

48. Hiltner, 14–15.

49. Hiltner, 15, 1.

50. Hiltner, 15–16.

51. Hiltner, 18.

52. Or, as Milton says later, concerning nature's "wanton growth," no amount of labor can stop nature's "Tending to wild" (9.211).

53. Deleuze, "Kant: Synthesis and Time."

54. Hiltner, *Milton and Ecology*, 26.

55. Hiltner, 27.

56. Hiltner, 27.

57. Hiltner, 25.

58. OED, s.v. "speculate," v.

59. Bersani, "Is the Rectum a Grave?," 197–222.

60. Quoted in Hiltner, *Milton and Ecology*, 48.

61. Hiltner, 49.

62. A similar doubling of birth and expulsion, or advent and annihilation, occurs in Davies's *Birth of the Anthropocene*, which is as much "about the terminal crisis of the Holocene as it is about the birth pangs of the Anthropocene, or rather, . . . those two things are one and the same" (5). The birth of a new geological epoch marks the terminus of the last and consequently the abortion of our (Holocene-dependent) future. The life-affirming language of advent and birth thus comes to a crisis.

63. Deleuze and Guattari, *What Is Philosophy?*, 164.

64. Quoted in Deleuze, *Logic of Sense*, 148.

65. Freud, *Civilization and Its Discontents*, 70.

66. Freud, 70–71.

67. Colebrook and Weinstein, "Preface," x.

68. Grosz offers a useful gloss to this Deleuzian and Stoic (and Miltonic!) ethics of the event: "Stoic ethics is less interested in the more conventional questions of morality—What is to be done? How do I act? What should I do?—than the question of how to live well, how to live up to one's fate, how to address, with one's nature, character, and knowledge, the complexities that others, and the universe itself, imply. . . . Ethics is the elaboration, in other words, of freedom, not a freedom from cause or constraint, but a freedom because of it. Freedom in and with necessity" (*The Incorporeal*, 44–45, 50).

69. Deleuze and Guattari, *Logic of Sense*, 149.

70. Deleuze, "Exhausted," 154.

71. Deleuze, 155.

72. See Kuzner's incisive essay on this subject, "Early Modern Ideas of Freedom," 140–51.

73. Moore, *Capitalism*, 118.

74. Moore, 115.

75. On capital as a form of the undead, see Tomšič, *Capitalist Unconscious*, 7.

76. Chakrabarty, "The Climate of History," 208.

77. Marder, *Energy Dreams*, 2.

CONCLUSION

1. On the terminological debates surrounding the word "Anthropocene," see Moore's introduction to *Anthropocene or Capitalocene?*, 1–11.

2. See, for example, Vicki Kirby's eco-deconstructionist translation of Derrida's *il n'y a pas de hors-texte*, "there is no outside of nature," in *Quantum Anthropologies*, x.

3. On this point, see Wilson, "Acts against Nature," 19–31.

4. See, for example, Ghosh: "The uncanny and improbable events that are beating at our doors seem to have stirred a sense of recognition, an awareness that humans were never alone, that we have always been surrounded by beings of all sorts who share the elements of that which we had thought to be most distinctively our own: the capacities of will, thought, and consciousness" (*The Great Derangement*, 30–31).

5. See McGowan, *The Real Gaze*, 5–8.

6. The split between *effect* and *realization* is central to Copjec's argument (contra Foucault) that power fails to *realize* desire in any straightforward sense. Rather, it is because power is unconscious to its desire, Copjec argues, that Lacan can posit the peculiar *objet a*: object-*cause* of desire, which not only makes desire enigmatic but also empties power's decree. See Copjec, *Read My Desire*, 24.

7. Hence Copjec's claim that "film theory"—I would add, ecotheory—"operated a kind of 'Foucauldization' of Lacanian theory; an early misreading of Lacan turned him into a 'spendthrift' Foucault—one who wasted a bit too much theoretical energy on such notions as the antithetical meaning of words, or repression, or the unconscious" (19).

8. The idea that the relation is primary and that there is no outside beyond our relations is now the reigning orthodoxy of environmental thought. In Morton's words, ecological politics becomes "claustrophobic precisely because what is *outside* it is now *included*" (*Ecology without Nature*, 197). In Barad's words, "There is no outside of nature from which to act; there are only 'acts of nature'" ("Nature's Queer Performativity," 47). This eco-deconstructionist argument, though similar in some ways to the argument of this book, has become dangerously monotonous because it leaves no room for the unconscious act. The environmental unconscious means that while there may only be "acts of nature," these acts are always self-external, and therefore self-defeating. It is no longer enough to deconstruct the margins of the

subject if all that results are better, friendlier versions of the subject; what we need are subjects who desire their own lack.

9. See Foucault, *The History of Sexuality*, 1:10; and Sedgwick, "Paranoid Reading and Reparative Reading," 123–51. Foucault turns to "bodies and their pleasures" (48), while Sedgwick turns to the surface pleasures of Silvan Tomkins's affect theory.

10. The Velvet Underground and Nico, "I'll Be Your Mirror."

11. Here and elsewhere, I am indebted to Todd McGowan's analysis of capitalism as a logic of accumulation that preys on the subject's unconscious investment in loss. See McGowan, *Capitalism and Desire*, especially chapter 1, "The Subject of Desire and the Subject of Capitalism."

12. Žižek points to this phantasmatic "something" in *The Plague of Fantasies*. In *Paradise Lost*, "Adam loses X by directly choosing it, aiming to retain it" (19). Herein lies the paradox of jouissance, according to Žižek: "What, precisely, is symbolic castration? It is the prohibition of incest in the precise sense of the loss of something which the subject never possessed in the first place. Let us imagine a situation in which the subject aims at X (say, a series of pleasurable experiences); the operation of castration does not consist in depriving him of any of these experiences, but adds to the series a purely potential, nonexistent X, with respect to which the actually accessible experiences appear all of a sudden as lacking, not wholly satisfying" (19). Henceforth, what Adam and Eve enjoy isn't paradise, but "paradise"; they enjoy the X-factor, the lack, that inheres in the garden.

13. In Milton's poem, the limit isn't simply a barrier to enjoyment. It is, more precisely, an "enabling constraint," to use McNulty's illuminating formula in *Wrestling with the Angel*. According to McNulty, "The pursuit of subjective freedom may be enabled—and not impeded—by the struggle with limits, obstacles, and constraints" (1). Just as the garden in *Paradise Lost* "grows / Luxurious by restraint," so we are tested with seeing the limit to accumulation as desire's true aim.

14. Although it is beyond the scope of this project to trace, there is a through line connecting Milton's "wild" and Halberstam's definition of wildness as "a form of disorder that will not submit to rule, a mode of unknowing, a resistant ontology, and a fantasy of life beyond the human" (8). One important distinction, however, is that in Milton's

poem, the garden "grows / Luxurious" (i.e., excessive, unruly, wanton, and wild) "*by* restraint" (emphasis added), that is, not only against and athwart (as in Halberstam's definition) but also *through* the order that Adam and Eve seek to impose. Thus, instead of an imperious human order superimposing itself on the wild, we see the garden grow wilder by constraint. The same is true of any poem, such as a sonnet, the limits of which enable poets to experiment. For a closer reading of Milton's queer garden, see Swarbrick, "Unworking Milton."

15. It is for this reason, let us recall, that Derrida distinguished his terms—gram, trace, interval, text—from sensible matter, not because of some crypto-idealism, but because "things are not so simple": "If I have not very often used the word 'matter,' it is not, as you know, because of some idealist or spiritualist kind of reservation. It is that in the logic of the phase of overturning this concept has been too often reinvested with 'logocentric' values, values associated with those of thing, reality, presence in general, sensible presence, for example, substantial plentitude, content, referent, etc. Realism or sensualism—'empiricism'—are modifications of logocentricism. . . . In short, the signifier 'matter' appears to me problematical only at the moment when its reinscription cannot avoid making of it a new fundamental principle which, by means of theoretical regression, would be reconstituted into a 'transcendental signified.' It is not only idealism in the narrow sense that falls back upon the transcendental signified. It can always come to reassure a metaphysical materialism" (*Positions*, 64–65).

16. See Stoekl, *Bataille's Peak.*

17. See, for example, Tobias Menely's luminous reading of the poem's final scene, "the enormity of the loss and the psychological impossibility of Adam and Eve, the first climate refugees, facing it," in *Climate and the Making of Worlds*, 82–83.

18. The canonical psychoanalytic interpretation of the gaze in Hans Holbein's portrait is Lacan's. See Lacan, *Four Fundamental Concepts of Psychoanalysis*, 88–89.

19. OED, s.v. "anamorphosis," n.

20. Buell, *Writing for an Endangered World*, 18–27.

21. McGowan, *The Real Gaze*, 6. For a fascinating account of the gaze as it pertains to feminist ecocriticism and film media, see Tremblay, *Breathing Aesthetics*, 42–43.

22. OED, s.v. "dehisce," v.

23. Darwin, *Power of Movement in Plants*.

24. Darwin.

25. Darwin.

26. Darwin.

27. Baluska et al., "'Root-Brain' Hypothesis," 1121.

28. Darwin, *Power of Movement in Plants*.

29. Darwin.

30. See Derrida, "Freud and the Scene of Writing," 196–231.

BIBLIOGRAPHY

Acheson, Katherine O. "Military Illustration, Garden Design, and Marvell's 'Upon Appleton House.'" *English Literary Renaissance* 41, no. 1 (2011): 146–88.

Agamben, Giorgio. *Homo Sacer: Sovereign Power and Bare Life.* Translated by Daniel Heller-Rozen. Stanford, Calif.: Stanford University Press, 1998.

Agamben, Giorgio. *The Open: Man and Animal.* Translated by Kevin Attell. Stanford, Calif.: Stanford University Press, 2004.

Alaimo, Stacy. *Bodily Natures: Science, Environment, and the Material Self.* Bloomington: Indiana University Press, 2010.

Alaimo, Stacy. *Exposed: Environmental Politics and Pleasures in Posthuman Times.* Minneapolis: University of Minnesota Press, 2016.

Alberti, Leon Battista. *The Architecture of Leon Battista Alberti in Ten Books.* Translated by James Leoni. London, 1726.

Alberti, Leon Battista. *On Painting.* Translated by Cecil Grayson. London: Penguin Books, 2004.

Alberti, Leon Battista. *On the Art of Building in Ten Books.* Translated by Joseph Rykwert, Neil Leach, and Robert Tavernor. Cambridge, Mass.: MIT Press, 1988.

Alexander, Amir. *Infinitesimal: How a Dangerous Mathematical Theory Shaped the Modern World.* New York: Farrar, Straus and Giroux, 2014.

Allewaert, Monique. *Ariel's Ecology: Plantations, Personhood, and Colonialism in the American Tropics.* Minneapolis: University of Minnesota Press, 2013.

Althusser, Louis. "The Underground Current of the Materialism of the Encounter." In *Philosophy of the Encounter: Later Writings, 1978–1987,* 163–207. Translated by G. M. Goshgarian. London: Verso, 2006.

Arendt, Hannah. *The Human Condition.* 2nd ed. Chicago: University of Chicago Press, 1998.

Aristotle. *Generation of Animals.* In *The Complete Works of Aristotle: Revised Oxford Translation.* Vol. 1. Edited by Jonathan Barnes, 1111–1218. Princeton, N.J.: Princeton University Press, 1984.

Aristotle. *On the Soul.* In *The Complete Works of Aristotle: Revised Oxford Translation.* Vol. 1. Edited by Jonathan Barnes, 641–92. Princeton, N.J.: Princeton University Press, 1984.

Atwood, Margaret. *Oryx and Crake.* New York: Anchor Books, 2004.

Auerbach, Erich. "Figura." In *Scenes from the Drama of European Literature,* 11–76. Translated by Ralph Manheim. Minneapolis: University of Minnesota Press, 1984.

Badiou, Alain. *Being and Event.* Translated by Oliver Feltham. London: Continuum, 2012.

Badiou, Alain. *Ethics: An Essay on the Understanding of Evil.* Translated by Peter Hallward. London: Verso, 2012.

Badiou, Alain. *Handbook of Inaesthetics.* Translated by Alberto Toscano. Stanford, Calif.: Stanford University Press, 2005.

Badiou, Alain. *Logics of Worlds: Being and Event 11.* Translated by Alberto Toscano. London: Bloomsbury, 2013.

Badiou, Alain. *Saint Paul: The Foundation of Universalism.* Translated by Ray Brassier. Stanford, Calif.: Stanford University Press, 2003.

Baluska, Frantisek, et al. "The 'Root-Brain' Hypothesis of Charles and Francis Darwin: Revival after More than 125 Years." *Plant Signaling and Behavior* 4, no. 12 (2009). doi:10.4161/psb.4.12.10574.

Barad, Karen. *Meeting the Universe Halfway: Quantum Physics and the Entanglement of Matter and Meaning.* Durham, N.C.: Duke University Press, 2007.

Barad, Karen. "Nature's Queer Performativity (The Authorized Version)." *Women, Gender and Research,* nos. 1–2 (2012): 25–53.

Barad, Karen. "On Touching—The Inhuman That Therefore I Am." *differences* 25, no. 3 (2012): 206–23.

Barton, Anne. *The Shakespearean Forest.* Cambridge: Cambridge University Press, 2017.

Bearden, Elizabeth B. *Monstrous Kinds: Body, Space, and Narrative in Renaissance Representations of Disability.* Ann Arbor: University of Michigan Press, 2019.

Bellamy, Elizabeth Jane. *Dire Straits: The Perils of Writing the Early Modern English Coastline from Leland to Milton.* Toronto: University of Toronto Press, 2013.

Benjamin, Walter. *The Arcades Project.* Translated by Howard Eiland and Kevin McLaughlin. Cambridge, Mass.: Belknap Press of Harvard University Press, 1999.

Benjamin, Walter. *The Origin of German Tragic Drama.* Translated by John Osborne. London: Verso, 2003.

Benjamin, Walter. "The Storyteller." In *Illuminations: Essays and Reflections,* edited by Hannah Arendt, 83–109. New York: Schocken Books, 1968.

Benjamin, Walter. "Theses on the Philosophy of History." In *Illuminations: Essays and Reflections,* edited by Hannah Arendt, 253–64. New York: Schocken Books, 1968.

Bennett, Jane. *Vibrant Matter: A Political Ecology of Things.* Durham, N.C.: Duke University Press, 2010.

Berger, Harry, Jr. *Revisionary Play: Studies in the Spenserian Dynamics.* Berkeley: University of California Press, 1988.

Bersani, Leo. *The Culture of Redemption.* Cambridge, Mass.: Harvard University Press, 1990.

Bersani, Leo. *The Freudian Body: Psychoanalysis and Art.* New York: Columbia University Press, 1986.

Bersani, Leo. "Is the Rectum a Grave?" *October* 43 (1987): 197–222.

Bersani, Leo, and Ulysse Dutoit. *Forms of Being: Cinema, Aesthetics, Subjectivity.* London: BFI, 2010.

Bersani, Leo, and Adam Phillips. *Intimacies.* Chicago: University of Chicago Press, 2008.

The Bible: That Is, the Holy Scriptvres Conteined in the Olde and New Testament. London, 1595.

Boehrer, Bruce Thomas. *Animal Characters: Nonhuman Beings in Early Modern Literature.* Philadelphia: University of Pennsylvania Press, 2010.

Bonneuil, Christophe, and Jean-Baptiste Fressoz. *The Shock of the Anthropocene.* Translated by David Fernbach. London: Verso, 2016.

Bono, James J. *The Word of God and the Languages of Man: Interpreting Nature in Early Modern Science and Medicine.* Madison: University of Wisconsin Press, 1995.

Boyer, Carl B. *The History of the Calculus and Its Conceptual Development.* New York: Dover, 1959.

Braidotti, Rosi. "Interview with Rosi Braidotti." In *New Materialism: Interviews & Cartography,* edited by Rick Dolphijn and Iris van der Tuin, 19–37. Ann Arbor, Mich.: Open Humanities Press, 2013.

Brassier, Ray. *Nihil Unbound: Enlightenment and Extinction.* Basingstoke, U.K.: Palgrave Macmillan, 2010.

Brayton, Dan. *Shakespeare's Ocean: An Ecocritical Exploration.* Charlottesville: University of Virginia Press, 2012.

Brinkema, Eugenie. *The Forms of the Affects.* Durham, N.C.: Duke University Press, 2014.

Brooks, Cleanth. *The Well Wrought Urn: Studies in the Structure of Poetry.* New York: Harcourt, Brace and World, 1975.

Browne, Sir Thomas. *Religio Medici and Hydriotaphia, or Urne-Buriall.* Edited by Stephen Greenblatt and Ramie Targoff. New York: New York Review of Books, 2012.

Bryant, Levi R. *The Democracy of Objects.* Ann Arbor, Mich.: Open Humanities Press, 2011.

Buell, Lawrence. *Writing for an Endangered World: Literature, Culture, and Environment in the U.S. and Beyond.* Cambridge, Mass.: Belknap Press of Harvard University Press, 2001.

Cahill, James Leo. *Zoological Surrealism: The Nonhuman Cinema of Jean Painlevé.* Minneapolis: University of Minnesota Press, 2019.

Calhoun, Joshua. *The Nature of the Page: Poetry, Papermaking, and the Ecology of Texts in Renaissance England.* Philadelphia: University of Pennsylvania Press, 2020.

Campana, Joseph. *The Pain of Reformation: Spenser, Vulnerability, and the Ethics of Masculinity.* New York: Fordham University Press, 2012.

Canguilhem, Georges. *A Vital Rationalist: Selected Writings from Georges Canguilhem.* Translated by Arthur Goldhammer. New York: Zone Books, 2000.

Carson, Anne. *Eros the Bittersweet.* Champaign, Ill.: Dalkey Archive Press, 2009.

Caruth, Cathy. "After the End: A Response." *Studies in the Literary Imagination* 41, no. 2 (2008): 121–29.

Caruth, Cathy. *Unclaimed Experience: Trauma, Narrative, and History.* Baltimore, Md.: Johns Hopkins University Press, 1996.

Casanova, Pascale. *The World Republic of Letters.* Translated by M. B. De-Bevoise. Cambridge, Mass.: Harvard University Press, 2004.

Casarino, Cesare. *Modernity at Sea: Melville, Marx, Conrad in Crisis.* Minneapolis: University of Minnesota Press, 2002.

Cassirer, Ernst. *The Individual and the Cosmos in Renaissance Philosophy.* Translated by Mario Domandi. Chicago: University of Chicago Press, 2010.

Certeau, Michel de. *The Writing of History.* Translated by Tom Conley. New York: Columbia University Press, 1988.

Chakrabarty, Dipesh. "The Climate of History: Four Theses." *Critical Inquiry* 35, no. 2 (2009): 197–222.

Chen, Mel Y. *Animacies: Biopolitics, Racial Mattering, and Queer Affect.* Durham, N.C.: Duke University Press, 2012.

Cheney, Patrick. "Spenser's Pastorals." In *The Cambridge Companion to Spenser,* edited by Andrew Hadfield, 79–105. Cambridge: Cambridge University Press, 2001.

Chu, Andrea Long. *Females.* London: Verso, 2019.

Chu, Andrea Long. "The Impossibility of Feminism." *differences* 30, no. 1 (2019): 63–81.

Clough, Patricia Ticineto. Introduction to *The Affective Turn: Theorizing the Social.* Edited by Patricia Ticineto Clough with Jean Halley. Durham, N.C.: Duke University Press, 2007.

Colebrook, Claire. *Death of the Posthuman: Essays on Extinction.* Vol. 1. Ann Arbor, Mich.: Open Humanities Press, 2014.

Colebrook, Claire. *Deleuze: A Guide for the Perplexed.* London: Continuum, 1996.

Colebrook, Claire. "Not Symbiosis, Not Now: Why Anthropogenic Change Is Not Really Human." *Oxford Literary Review* 34, no. 2 (2012): 185–209.

Colebrook, Claire. *Sex after Life: Essays on Extinction.* Vol. 2. Ann Arbor, Mich.: Open Humanities Press, 2014.

Colebrook, Claire, and Jami Weinstein. "Preface: Postscript on the Post-human." In *Posthumous Life: Theorizing beyond the Posthuman,* edited by

Claire Colebrook and Jami Weinstein, ix–xxix. New York: Columbia University Press, 2017.

Coole, Diana, and Samantha Frost. Introduction to *New Materialisms: Ontology, Agency, and Politics*. Durham, N.C.: Duke University Press, 2010.

Copjec, Joan. *Read My Desire: Lacan against the Historicists*. London: Verso, 2015.

Cronon, William. *Changes in the Land: Indians, Colonists, and the Ecology of New England*. New York: Hill and Wang, 1983.

Crutzen, Paul J. "Geology of Mankind." *Nature* 415, no. 23 (2002). doi.org/10.1038/415023a.

Crutzen, Paul J., and Eugene F. Stoermer. "The Anthropocene." *IGBP Global Change Newsletter* 41 (2001): 17–18.

Daniel, Drew. *The Melancholy Assemblage: Affect and Epistemology in the English Renaissance*. New York: Fordham University Press, 2013.

Darwin, Charles. *On the Origin of Species*. Edited by Gillian Beer. Oxford: Oxford University Press, 2008.

Darwin, Charles. *The Power of Movement in Plants*. Urbana, Ill.: Project Gutenberg, 2004. http://www.gutenberg.org/files/5605/5605-h/5605-h.htm.

Davies, Jeremy. *The Birth of the Anthropocene*. Oakland: University of California Press, 2016.

DeLanda, Manuel. *Intensive Science and Virtual Philosophy*. London: Bloomsbury, 2002.

Deleuze, Gilles. *Cinema 2: The Time-Image*. Translated by Hugh Tomlinson and Robert Galeta. Minneapolis: University of Minnesota Press, 1989.

Deleuze, Gilles. "Desert Islands." In *Desert Islands and Other Texts, 1953–1974*, edited by David Lapoujade, 9–14. Los Angeles: Semiotext(e), 2004.

Deleuze, Gilles. *Difference and Repetition*. Translated by Paul Patton. New York: Columbia University Press, 1994.

Deleuze, Gilles. "The Exhausted." In *Essays Critical and Clinical*, 152–74. Translated by Daniel W. Smith and Michael A. Greco. Minneapolis: University of Minnesota Press, 1997.

Deleuze, Gilles. "The Fold." Translated by Jonathan Strauss. *Yale French Studies* 80 (1991): 227–47.

Deleuze, Gilles. *Francis Bacon: The Logic of Sensation*. Translated by Daniel W. Smith. Minneapolis: University of Minnesota Press, 2003.

Deleuze, Gilles. "Kant: Synthesis and Time." Translated by Melissa McMahon. *The Deleuze Seminars* online. March 14, 1978. https:// deleuze.cla.purdue.edu/seminars/kant-synthesis-and-time/lecture-01.

Deleuze, Gilles. *The Logic of Sense.* Edited by Constantin V. Boundas. Translated by Mark Lester with Charles Stivale. New York: Columbia University Press, 1990.

Deleuze, Gilles. *Masochism: Coldness and Cruelty.* Translated by Jean McNeil. New York: Zone Books, 1991.

Deleuze, Gilles. "Mathesis, Science and Philosophy." In *Collapse: Philosophical Research and Development,* vol. 3, edited by Robin Mackay, 141–55. Falmouth, U.K.: Urbanomic, 2012.

Deleuze, Gilles. *Pure Immanence: Essays on A Life.* Translated by Anne Boyman. New York: Zone Books, 2001.

Deleuze, Gilles. "Simulacrum and Ancient Philosophy." In *The Logic of Sense.* Edited by Constantin V. Boundas, 253–79. Translated by Mark Lester with Charles Stivale. New York: Columbia University Press, 1990.

Deleuze, Gilles, and Félix Guattari. *Anti-Oedipus: Capitalism and Schizophrenia.* Translated by Robert Hurley et al. Minneapolis: University of Minnesota Press, 1983.

Deleuze, Gilles, and Félix Guattari. *Kafka: Toward a Minor Literature.* Translated by Dana Polan. Minneapolis: University of Minnesota Press, 1986.

Deleuze, Gilles, and Félix Guattari. *A Thousand Plateaus: Capitalism and Schizophrenia.* Translated by Brian Massumi. Minneapolis: University of Minnesota Press, 1987.

Deleuze, Gilles, and Félix Guattari. *What Is Philosophy?* Translated by Hugh Tomlinson and Graham Burchell. New York: Columbia University Press, 1994.

de Man, Paul. "Autobiography as De-facement." In *The Rhetoric of Romanticism,* 67–81. New York: Columbia University Press, 1984.

de Man, Paul. "Conclusions: Walter Benjamin's 'The Task of the Translator.'" In *The Resistance to Theory,* 73–105. Minneapolis: University of Minnesota Press, 1986.

Derrida, Jacques. *The Animal That Therefore I Am.* Translated by David Wills. New York: Fordham University Press, 2008.

Derrida, Jacques. *Archive Fever: A Freudian Impression.* Translated by Eric Prenowitz. Chicago: University of Chicago Press, 1995.

Derrida, Jacques. *The Beast and the Sovereign.* Vol. 1. Translated by Geoffrey
Bennington. Chicago: University of Chicago Press, 2009.

Derrida, Jacques. "Cogito and the History of Madness." In *Writing and
Difference,* 31–63. Translated by Alan Bass. Chicago: University of
Chicago Press, 1978.

Derrida, Jacques. "Différance." In *Margins of Philosophy,* 1–27. Translated by
Alan Bass. Chicago: University of Chicago Press, 1982.

Derrida, Jacques. *Dissemination.* Translated by Barbara Johnson. Chicago:
University of Chicago Press, 1981.

Derrida, Jacques. "Freud and the Scene of Writing." In *Writing and Difference,* 196–231. Translated by Alan Bass. Chicago: University of Chicago
Press, 1978.

Derrida, Jacques. "How to Avoid Speaking: Denials." In *Psyche: Inventions
of the Other.* Vol. 2. Edited by Peggy Kamuf and Elizabeth Rottenberg,
143–95. Stanford, Calif.: Stanford University Press, 2008.

Derrida, Jacques. *Of Grammatology.* Translated by Gayatri Chakravorty
Spivak. Baltimore, Md.: Johns Hopkins University Press, 1976.

Derrida, Jacques. *Of Spirit: Heidegger and the Question.* Translated by
Geoffrey Bennington and Rachel Bowlby. Chicago: University of
Chicago Press, 1991.

Derrida, Jacques. *Philosophy in a Time of Terror: Dialogues with Jürgen
Habermas and Jacques Derrida.* Edited by Giovanna Borradori. Chicago:
University of Chicago Press, 2003.

Derrida, Jacques. *Positions.* Translated by Alan Bass. Chicago: University of
Chicago Press, 1981.

Derrida, Jacques. "Shibboleth: For Paul Celan." In *Sovereignties in Question:
The Poetics of Paul Celan,* edited by Thomas Dutoit and Outi Pasanen,
1–64. New York: Fordham University Press, 2005.

Derrida, Jacques. *Specters of Marx: The State of Debt, the Work of Mourning, and the New International.* Translated by Peggy Kamuf. New York:
Routledge, 2006.

Derrida, Jacques. *The Truth in Painting.* Translated by Geoffrey Bennington
and Ian McLeod. Chicago: University of Chicago Press, 1987.

Descartes, René. *Discourse on Method.* Translated by Donald A. Cress. 4th
ed. Indianapolis: Hackett, 1988.

Donne, John. "A Hymn to Christ, at the Author's last going into Germany."
In *The Major Works,* edited by John Carey, 283–84. Oxford: Oxford
University Press, 2008.

Donne, John. "To his Mistress Going to Bed." In *The Major Works*, edited by John Carey, 12–13. Oxford: Oxford University Press, 2008.

Duckert, Lowell. *For All Waters: Finding Ourselves in Early Modern Wetscapes*. Minneapolis: University of Minnesota Press, 2017.

Dworkin, Craig. *Radium of the Word: A Poetics of Materiality*. Chicago: University of Chicago Press, 2020.

Edelman, Lee. *Homographesis: Essays in Gay Literary and Cultural Theory*. New York: Routledge, 1994.

Edelman, Lee. *No Future: Queer Theory and the Death Drive*. Durham, N.C.: Duke University Press, 2004.

Eisenstein, Elizabeth L. *The Printing Press as an Agent of Change*. Cambridge: Cambridge University Press, 1979.

Eisenstein, Elizabeth L. *The Printing Revolution in Early Modern Europe*. Cambridge: Cambridge University Press, 1983.

Eliot, T. S. "Marvell." In *Selected Essays, 1917–1932*, 251–63. New York: Harcourt, Brace, 1932.

Eliot, T. S. "The Metaphysical Poets." In *Selected Essays, 1917–1932*, 241–50. New York: Harcourt, Brace, 1932.

Empson, William. *Some Versions of Pastoral*. New York: New Directions, 1974.

Esposito, Roberto. *Bíos: Biopolitics and Philosophy*. Translated by Timothy Campbell. Minneapolis: University of Minnesota Press, 2008.

Euclid. *The Thirteen Books of the Elements*. Vol. 1. Translated by Sir Thomas L. Heath. 2nd ed. New York: Dover, 1956.

Febvre, Lucien, and Henri-Jean Martin. *The Coming of the Book: The Impact of Printing, 1450–1800*. London: Verso, 1976.

Federici, Silvia. *Caliban and the Witch: Women, the Body, and Primitive Accumulation*. New York: Autonomedia, 2004.

Feerick, Jean E., and Vin Nardizzi. Introduction to *The Indistinct Human in Renaissance Literature*. New York: Palgrave Macmillan, 2012.

Felski, Rita. *The Limits of Critique*. Chicago: University of Chicago Press, 2015.

Fink, Bruce. *Lacan to the Letter: Reading* Écrits *Closely*. Minneapolis: University of Minnesota Press, 2004.

Fink, Bruce. *The Lacanian Subject: Between Language and Jouissance*. Princeton, N.J.: Princeton University Press, 1995.

Foucault, Michel. *Abnormal: Lectures at the Collège de France, 1974–1975*. Edited by Valerio Marchetti and Antonella Salomoni. Translated by Graham Burchell. New York: Picador, 2003.

Foucault, Michel. *History of Madness.* Edited by Jean Khalfa. Translated by Jonathan Murphy and Jean Khalfa. New York: Routledge, 2006.

Foucault, Michel. *The History of Sexuality.* Vol. 1: *An Introduction.* Translated by Robert Hurley. New York: Vintage Books, 1990.

Foucault, Michel. *The Order of Things: An Archeology of the Human Sciences.* Translated by Alan Sheridan. New York: Vintage Books, 1994.

Foucault, Michel. *Security, Territory, Population: Lectures at the Collège de France, 1977–1978.* Edited by Michel Senellart. Translated by Graham Burchell. New York: Picador, 2007.

Foucault, Michel. *"Society Must Be Defended": Lectures at the Collège de France, 1975–1976.* Edited by Mauro Bertani and Alessandro Fontana. Translated by David Macey. New York: Picador, 2003.

Foucault, Michel. "Theatrum Philosophicum." In *Language, Counter-Memory, Practice: Selected Essays and Interviews,* edited by Donald F. Bouchard, 165–96. Translated by Donald F. Bouchard and Sherry Simon. Ithaca, N.Y.: Cornell University Press, 1977.

François, Anne-Lise. *Open Secrets: The Literature of Uncounted Experience.* Stanford, Calif.: Stanford University Press, 2008.

Freedberg, David. *The Eye of the Lynx: Galileo, His Friends, and the Beginnings of Modern Natural History.* Chicago: University of Chicago Press, 2002.

Freud, Sigmund. *Beyond the Pleasure Principle.* In *The Standard Edition of the Complete Psychological Works of Sigmund Freud,* vol. 18, edited and translated by James Strachey, 1–64. London: Hogarth Press, 1955. (Orig. pub. 1920)

Freud, Sigmund. *Civilization and Its Discontents.* In *The Standard Edition of the Complete Psychological Works of Sigmund Freud,* vol. 21, edited and translated by James Strachey, 57–146. London: Hogarth Press, 1961. (Orig. pub. 1930)

Freud, Sigmund. *The Interpretation of Dreams.* In *The Standard Edition of the Complete Psychological Works of Sigmund Freud,* vol. 4, edited and translated by James Strachey, ix–627. London: Hogarth Press, 1953. (Orig. pub. 1900)

Freud, Sigmund. "Leonardo da Vinci and a Memory of His Childhood." In *The Standard Edition of the Complete Psychological Works of Sigmund Freud,* vol. 11, edited and translated by James Strachey, 57–138. London: Hogarth Press, 1957. (Orig. pub. 1910)

Freud, Sigmund. "Medusa's Head." In *The Standard Edition of the Complete Psychological Works of Sigmund Freud*, vol. 18, edited and translated by James Strachey, 273–74. London: Hogarth Press, 1955. (Orig. pub. 1922)

Freud, Sigmund. "Negation." In *The Standard Edition of the Complete Psychological Works of Sigmund Freud*, vol. 19, edited and translated by James Strachey, 233–40. London: Hogarth Press, 1961. (Orig. pub. 1925)

Freud, Sigmund. *Three Essays on the Theory of Sexuality*. In *The Standard Edition of the Complete Psychological Works of Sigmund Freud*, vol. 7, edited and translated by James Strachey, 123–246. London: Hogarth Press, 1953. (Orig. pub. 1905)

Fudge, Erica. *Brutal Reasoning: Animals, Rationality, and Humanity in Early Modern England*. Ithaca, N.Y.: Cornell University Press, 2006.

Fudge, Erica. *Perceiving Animals: Humans and Beasts in Early Modern English Culture*. Urbana: University of Illinois Press, 2000.

Fuller, Mary. "Ralegh's Fugitive Gold: Reference and Deferral in *The Discoverie of Guiana*." In *New World Encounters*, edited by Stephen Greenblatt, 218–40. Berkeley: University of California Press, 1993.

Fuller, Mary. *Voyages in Print: English Travel to America, 1576–1624*. Cambridge: Cambridge University Press, 1995.

Gadberry, Andrea. *Cartesian Poetics: The Art of Thinking*. Chicago: University of Chicago Press, 2020.

Galilei, Galileo. *The Assayer*. In *The Essential Galileo*. Edited by Maurice A. Finocchiaro, 179–89. Indianapolis: Hackett, 2008.

Garrison, John S. "Eros and Objecthood in 'Upon Appleton House.'" *Marvell Studies* 4, no. 1 (2019): 1–27. http://doi.org/10.16995/ms.28.

Ghosh, Amitav. *The Great Derangement: Climate Change and the Unthinkable*. Chicago: University of Chicago Press, 2016.

Giraud, Eva Haifa. *What Comes after Entanglement? Activism, Anthropocentrism, and an Ethics of Exclusion*. Durham, N.C.: Duke University Press, 2019.

Glissant, Édouard. *Caribbean Discourse: Selected Essays*. Translated by J. Michael Dash. Charlottesville: University of Virginia Press, 1989.

Goldberg, Jonathan. *Endlesse Worke: Spenser and the Structures of Discourse*. Baltimore, Md.: Johns Hopkins University Press, 1981.

Goldberg, Jonathan. *The Seeds of Things: Theorizing Sexuality and Materiality in Renaissance Representations*. New York: Fordham University Press, 2009.

Goldberg, Jonathan. *Sodometries: Renaissance Texts, Modern Sexualities.* Stanford, Calif.: Stanford University Press, 1992.

Goldberg, Jonathan. *Tempest in the Caribbean.* Minneapolis: University of Minnesota Press, 2004.

Goldstein, Amanda Jo. *Sweet Science: Romantic Materialism and the New Logics of Life.* Chicago: University of Chicago Press, 2017.

Gould, Jay. *Time's Arrow, Time's Cycle: Myth and Metaphor in the Discovery of Geological Time.* Cambridge, Mass.: Harvard University Press, 1987.

Greenblatt, Stephen. *Sir Walter Ralegh: The Renaissance Man and His Roles.* New Haven, Conn.: Yale University Press, 1973.

Greenblatt, Stephen. *The Swerve: How the World Became Modern.* New York: Norton, 2011.

Greene, Roland. *Unrequited Conquests: Love and Empire in the Colonial Americas.* Chicago: University of Chicago Press, 1999.

Gregerson, Linda. *The Reformation of the Subject: Spenser, Milton, and the English Protestant Epic.* Cambridge: Cambridge University Press, 1995.

Gregg, Melissa, and Gregory J. Seigworth, eds. *The Affect Theory Reader.* Durham, N.C.: Duke University Press, 2010.

Grosz, Elizabeth. *Becoming Undone: Darwinian Reflections on Life, Politics, and Art.* Durham, N.C.: Duke University Press, 2011.

Grosz, Elizabeth. *Chaos, Territory, Art: Deleuze and the Framing of the Earth.* New York: Columbia University Press, 2008.

Grosz, Elizabeth. *The Incorporeal: Ontology, Ethics, and the Limits of Materialism.* New York: Columbia University Press, 2017.

Guattari, Félix. *The Three Ecologies.* Translated by Ian Pindar and Paul Sutton. London: Continuum, 2008.

Guy-Bray, Stephen. "No Present." In *Sex, Gender and Time in Fiction and Culture*, edited by Ben Davies and Jana Funke, 38–52. New York: Palgrave Macmillan, 2011.

Hakluyt, Richard. *Divers Voyages Touching the Discouerie of America, and the Ilands Adiacent vnto the fame, made first of all by our Englishmen, and afterward by the Frenchmen and Britons.* London, 1582.

Halberstam, Jack. *Wild Things: The Disorder of Desire.* Durham, N.C.: Duke University Press, 2020.

Hall, Kim F. "Culinary Spaces, Colonial Spaces: The Gendering of Sugar in the Seventeenth Century." In *Feminist Readings of Early Modern*

Culture: Emerging Subjects, edited by Valerie Traub, M. Lindsay Kaplan, and Dympna Callaghan, 168–90. Cambridge: Cambridge University Press, 1996.

Hallward, Peter. *Badiou: A Subject to Truth.* Minneapolis: University of Minnesota Press, 2003.

Halpern, Richard. *The Poetics of Primitive Accumulation: English Renaissance Culture and the Genealogy of Capital.* Ithaca, N.Y.: Cornell University Press, 1991.

Haraway, Donna J. *The Companion Species Manifesto: Dogs, People, and Significant Otherness.* Chicago: Prickly Paradigm Press, 2003.

Hardt, Michael, and Antonio Negri. *Empire.* Cambridge, Mass.: Harvard University Press, 2000.

Harman, Graham. *Tool-Being: Heidegger and the Metaphysics of Objects.* Chicago: Open Court, 2002.

Harney, Stefano, and Fred Moten. *The Undercommons: Fugitive Planning and Black Study.* New York: Minor Compositions, 2013.

Harris, Jonathan Gil. *Untimely Matter in the Time of Shakespeare.* Philadelphia: University of Pennsylvania Press, 2009.

Hegel, G. W. F. *Hegel and the Human Spirit: A Translation of the Jena Lectures on the Philosophy of Spirit (1805–6).* Translated by Leo Rauch. Detroit: Wayne State University Press, 1983.

Hegel, G. W. F. *Lectures on the History of Philosophy.* Vol. 3: *Medieval and Modern Philosophy.* Translated by E. S. Haldane and Frances H. Simson. Lincoln: University of Nebraska Press, 1995.

Hegel, G. W. F. *Phenomenology of Spirit.* Translated by A. V. Miller. Oxford: Oxford University Press, 1977.

Heidegger, Martin. *The Fundamental Concepts of Metaphysics: World, Finitude, Solitude.* Translated by William McNeill and Nicholas Walker. Bloomington: Indiana University Press, 2001.

Heidegger, Martin. "The Origin of the Work of Art." Translated by Albert Hofstadter. In *Basic Writings,* edited by David Farrell Krell, 143–206. New York: Harper Perennial, 2008.

Heidegger, Martin. "The Question concerning Technology." Translated by William Lovitt. In *Basic Writings,* edited by David Farrell Krell, 311–41. New York: Harper Perennial, 2008.

Helgerson, Richard. *Forms of Nationhood: The Elizabethan Writing of England.* Chicago: University of Chicago Press, 1992.

Hequembourg, Stephen. "The Dream of a Literal World: Wilkins, Hobbes, Marvell." ELH 81, no. 1 (2014): 83–113.

Hill, Christopher. *The World Turned Upside Down: Radical Ideas during the English Revolution.* New York: Penguin Books, 1972.

Hiltner, Ken. *Milton and Ecology.* Cambridge: Cambridge University Press, 2003.

Hock, Jessie. *The Erotics of Materialism: Lucretius and Early Modern Poetics.* Philadelphia: University of Pennsylvania Press, 2020.

Horkheimer, Max, and Theodor Adorno. *Dialectic of Enlightenment: Philosophical Fragments.* Translated by Edmund Jephcott. Stanford, Calif.: Stanford University Press, 2002.

Huffer, Lynne. *Are the Lips a Grave? A Queer Feminist on the Ethics of Sex.* New York: Columbia University Press, 2013.

Huffer, Lynne. "Foucault's Fossils: Life Itself and the Return to Nature in Feminist Philosophy." In *Anthropocene Feminism,* edited by Richard Grusin, 65–88. Minneapolis: University of Minnesota Press, 2017.

Irigaray, Luce. *Marine Lover of Friedrich Nietzsche.* Translated by Gillian C. Gill. New York: Columbia University Press, 1991.

Jaeckle, Daniel P. "Marvell's Reformed Theory of Architecture: *Upon Appleton House,* 1-x." *John Donne Journal* 4, no. 1 (1985): 49–67.

Jameson, Fredric. *The Political Unconscious: Narrative as a Socially Symbolic Act.* Ithaca, N.Y.: Cornell University Press, 1981.

Johns, Adrian. *The Nature of the Book: Print and Knowledge in the Making.* Chicago: University of Chicago Press, 1998.

Jonson, Ben. "To Penshurst." In *Ben Jonson: The Complete Poems,* edited by George Parfitt, 95–98. London: Penguin Books, 1996.

Kadue, Katie. "Sustaining Fiction: Preserving Patriarchy in Marvell's *Upon Appleton House.*" *Studies in Philology* 114, no. 3 (2017): 641–61.

Kalas, Rayna. *Frame, Glass, Verse: The Technology of Poetic Invention in the English Renaissance.* Ithaca, N.Y.: Cornell University Press, 2007.

Kirby, Vicki. *Quantum Anthropologies: Life at Large.* Durham, N.C.: Duke University Press, 2011.

Kohn, Eduardo. *How Forests Think: Toward an Anthropology beyond the Human.* Berkeley: University of California Press, 2013.

Kolbert, Elizabeth. *The Sixth Extinction: An Unnatural History.* New York: Henry Holt, 2014.

Kornbluh, Anna. "Extinct Critique." *South Atlantic Quarterly* 119, no. 4 (2020): 767–77.

Koyré, Alexandre. *From the Closed World to the Infinite Universe*. Baltimore, Md.: Johns Hopkins University Press, 1957.

Kristeva, Julia. *Revolution in Poetic Language*. Translated by Margaret Waller. New York: Columbia University Press, 1984.

Kuzner, James. "Early Modern Ideas of Freedom." *Modern Philology* 110, no. 1 (2012): 140–51.

Kuzner, James. *Open Subjects: English Renaissance Republicans, Modern Selfhoods, and the Virtue of Vulnerability*. Edinburgh: Edinburgh University Press, 2011.

Lacan, Jacques. "In Memory of Ernst Jones: On His Theory of Symbolism." In *Écrits: The First Complete Edition in English*, 585–601. Translated by Bruce Fink. New York: Norton, 2006.

Lacan, Jacques. "The Instance of the Letter in the Unconscious, or Reason since Freud." In *Écrits: The First Complete Edition in English*, 412–41. Translated by Bruce Fink. New York: Norton, 2006.

Lacan, Jacques. "Science and Truth." In *Écrits: The First Complete Edition in English*, 726–45. Translated by Bruce Fink. New York: Norton, 2006.

Lacan, Jacques. *The Seminar of Jacques Lacan, Book II: The Ego in Freud's Theory and in the Technique of Psychoanalysis, 1954–1955*. Edited by Jacques-Alain Miller. Translated by Sylvana Tomaselli. New York: Norton, 1991.

Lacan, Jacques. *The Seminar of Jacques Lacan, Book VII: The Ethics of Psychoanalysis, 1959–1960*. Edited by Jacques-Alain Miller. Translated by Dennis Porter. New York: Norton, 1997.

Lacan, Jacques. *The Seminar of Jacques Lacan, Book XI: The Four Fundamental Concepts of Psychoanalysis*. Edited by Jacques-Alain Miller. Translated by Alan Sheridan. New York: Norton, 1998.

Lacan, Jacques. *The Seminar of Jacques Lacan, Book XX: On Feminine Sexuality, the Limits of Love and Knowledge, 1972–1973 (Encore)*. Edited by Jacques-Alain Miller. Translated by Bruce Fink. New York: Norton, 1999.

Lacan, Jacques. "Seminar on 'The Purloined Letter.'" In *Écrits: The First Complete Edition in English*, 6–48. Translated by Bruce Fink. New York: Norton, 2006.

Lacan, Jacques. *The Sinthome: The Seminar of Jacques Lacan, Book XXIII*. Edited by Jacques-Alain Miller. Translated by A. R. Price. Cambridge: Polity Press, 2018.

Lacan, Jacques. *Television: A Challenge to the Psychoanalytic Establishment*. Edited by Joan Copjec. Translated by Denis Hollier, Rosalind Krauss, Annette Michelson, and Jeffrey Mehlman. New York: Norton, 1990.

Laplanche, Jean. *Life and Death in Psychoanalysis*. Translated by Jeffrey Mehlman. Baltimore, Md.: Johns Hopkins University Press, 1976.

Laplanche, Jean. "Notes on Afterwardsness." Translated by Luke Thurston. In *Essays on Otherness*, 260–65. New York: Routledge, 1999.

Laplanche, Jean. "A Short Treatise on the Unconscious." Translated by Luke Thurston. In *Essays on Otherness*, 84–116. New York: Routledge, 1999.

Laplanche, Jean. "The Theory of Seduction and the Problem of the Other." Translated by Luke Thurston. *International Journal of Psychoanalysis* 78 (1997): 653–66.

Laplanche, Jean. "The Unfinished Copernican Revolution." Translated by Luke Thurston. In *Essays on Otherness*, 52–83. New York: Routledge, 1999.

Latour, Bruno. *Politics of Nature: How to Bring the Sciences into Democracy*. Translated by Catherine Porter. Cambridge, Mass.: Harvard University Press, 2004.

Latour, Bruno. *Reassembling the Social: An Introduction to Actor-Network-Theory*. Oxford: Oxford University Press, 2007.

Latour, Bruno. *We Have Never Been Modern*. Translated by Catherine Porter. Cambridge, Mass.: Harvard University Press, 1993.

Latour, Bruno. "Why Has Critique Run Out of Steam? From Matters of Fact to Matters of Concern." *Critical Inquiry* 30, no. 2 (2004): 225–48.

Lévi-Strass, Claude. *Tristes Tropiques*. Translated by John Weightman and Doreen Weightman. New York: Penguin Books, 2012.

Lewalski, Barbara Kiefer. *Protestant Poetics and the Seventeenth-Century Religious Lyric*. Princeton, N.J.: Princeton University Press, 1979.

Lewis, C. S. *The Allegory of Love*. Oxford: Oxford University Press, 1971.

Lezra, Jacques. *On the Nature of Marx's Things: Translation as Necrophilology*. New York: Fordham University Press, 2018.

Lezra, Jacques. *Unspeakable Subjects: The Genealogy of the Event in Early Modern Europe*. Stanford, Calif.: Stanford University Press, 1997.

Lezra, Jacques, and Liza Blake, eds. *Lucretius and Modernity: Epicurean Encounters across Time and Disciplines*. New York: Palgrave Macmillan, 2016.

Lucretius. *On the Nature of the Universe.* Translated by R. E. Latham. Revised by John Godwin. London: Penguin Books, 1994.

Lucretius. *On the Nature of Things.* Translated by W. H. D. Rouse. Revised by Martin Ferguson Smith. Loeb Classical Library. Cambridge, Mass.: Harvard University Press, 1982.

Lucretius. *The Way Things Are: The De rerum natura of Titus Lucretius Carus.* Translated by Rolfe Humphries. Bloomington: Indiana University Press, 1968.

Malabou, Catherine. *The New Wounded: From Neurosis to Brain Damage.* Translated by Steven Miller. New York: Fordham University Press, 2012.

Malabou, Catherine. *Ontology of the Accident: An Essay on Destructive Plasticity.* Translated by Carolyn Shread. Cambridge: Polity Press, 2012.

Malabou, Catherine. *What Should We Do with Our Brain?* Translated by Sebastian Rand. New York: Fordham University Press, 2008.

Malm, Andreas. *Fossil Capital: The Rise of Steam Power and the Roots of Global Warming.* London: Verso, 2016.

Marcuse, Herbert. *One-Dimensional Man: Studies in the Ideology of Advanced Industrial Society.* New York: Routledge, 2002.

Marder, Michael. *Energy Dreams: Of Actuality.* New York: Columbia University Press, 2017.

Marder, Michael. *Plant-Thinking: A Philosophy of Vegetal Life.* New York: Columbia University Press, 2013.

Martin, Catherine Gimelli. *The Ruins of Allegory: Paradise Lost and the Metamorphosis of Epic Convention.* Durham, N.C.: Duke University Press, 1998.

Marvell, Andrew. *The Poems of Andrew Marvell.* Edited by Nigel Smith. New York: Routledge, 2006.

Marx, Karl. *Capital.* Vol. 1. Translated by Ben Fowkes. London: Penguin Books, 1990.

Massumi, Brian. *Parables for the Virtual: Movement, Affect, Sensation.* Durham, N.C.: Duke University Press, 2002.

Masten, Jeffrey. *Queer Philologies: Sex, Language, and Affect in Shakespeare's Time.* Philadelphia: University of Pennsylvania Press, 2016.

Mazzio, Carla. "The Three-Dimensional Self: Geometry, Melancholy, Drama." In *Arts of Calculation: Quantifying Thought in Early Modern Europe,* edited by David Glimp and Michelle R. Warren, 39–65. New York: Palgrave Macmillan, 2004.

Mbembe, Achille. "Necropolitics." *Public Culture* 15, no. 1 (2003): 11–40.

McEleney, Corey. *Futile Pleasures: Early Modern Literature and the Limits of Utility.* New York: Fordham University Press, 2017.

McGowan, Todd. *Capitalism and Desire: The Psychic Cost of Free Markets.* New York: Columbia University Press, 2016.

McGowan, Todd. "On the Necessity of Contradiction: Hegel with the Speculative Realists." *Umbr(a)* (2013): 101–25.

McGowan, Todd. *The Real Gaze: Film Theory after Lacan.* Albany: State University of New York Press, 2007.

McLuhan, Marshall. *The Gutenberg Galaxy.* Toronto: University of Toronto Press, 2011.

McNulty, Tracy. *Wrestling with the Angel: Experiments in Symbolic Life.* New York: Columbia University Press, 2014.

Meillassoux, Quentin. *After Finitude: An Essay on the Necessity of Contingency.* Translated by Ray Brassier. London: Continuum, 2008.

Menely, Tobias. *The Animal Claim: Sensibility and the Creaturely Voice.* Chicago: University of Chicago Press, 2015.

Menely, Tobias. *Climate and the Making of Worlds: Toward a Geohistorical Poetics.* Chicago: University of Chicago Press, 2021.

Menon, Madhavi. *Unhistorical Shakespeare: Queer Theory in Shakespearean Literature and Film.* New York: Palgrave Macmillan, 2008.

Mentz, Steve. *At the Bottom of Shakespeare's Ocean.* London: Continuum, 2009.

Mentz, Steve. *Shipwreck Modernity: Ecologies of Globalization, 1550–1719.* Minneapolis: University of Minnesota Press, 2015.

Merchant, Carolyn. *The Death of Nature: Women, Ecology, and the Scientific Revolution.* New York: Harper Collins, 1980.

Milton, John. *The Major Works.* Edited by Stephen Orgel and Jonathan Goldberg. Oxford: Oxford University Press, 2008.

Milton, John. "On Shakespeare. 1630." In *The Major Works.* Edited by Stephen Orgel and Jonathan Goldberg, 20. Oxford: Oxford University Press, 2008.

Mitchell, Timothy. *Carbon Democracy: Political Power in the Age of Oil.* London: Verso, 2013.

Mohamed, Feisal. *Milton and the Post-secular Present: Ethics, Politics, Terrorism.* Stanford, Calif.: Stanford University Press, 2011.

Montag, Warren. *Bodies, Masses, Power: Spinoza and His Contemporaries.* London: Verso, 1999.

Montrose, Louis. "The Elizabethan Subject and the Spenserian Text." In *Literary Theory/Renaissance Texts,* edited by Patricia Parker and David Quint, 303–40. Baltimore, Md.: Johns Hopkins University Press, 1986.

Montrose, Louis. "The Work of Gender in the Discourse of Discovery." *Representations* 33 (199): 1–41.

Moore, Jason W. *Capitalism in the Web of Life: Ecology and the Accumulation of Capital.* London: Verso, 2015.

Moore, Jason W. Introduction to *Anthropocene or Capitalocene? Nature, History, and the Crisis of Capitalism,* 1–11. Oakland, Calif.: PM Press, 2016.

Moretti, Franco. *Graphs, Maps, Trees: Abstract Models for a Literary History.* London: Verso, 2005.

Mortimer-Sandilands, Catriona, and Bruce Erickson, eds. *Queer Ecologies: Sex, Nature, Politics, Desire.* Bloomington: Indiana University Press, 2010.

Morton, Timothy. *The Ecological Thought.* Cambridge, Mass.: Harvard University Press, 2010.

Morton, Timothy. *Ecology without Nature: Rethinking Environmental Aesthetics.* Cambridge, Mass.: Harvard University Press, 2007.

Morton, Timothy. *Hyperobjects: Philosophy and Ecology after the End of the World.* Minneapolis: University of Minnesota Press, 2013.

Morton, Timothy. "Queer Ecology." *PMLA* 125, no. 2 (2010): 273–82.

Nancy, Jean-Luc. *The Birth to Presence.* Translated by Brian Holmes et al. Stanford, Calif.: Stanford University Press, 1993.

Nardizzi, Vin. "Budding Oedipus: The Oedipal Family Tree and *King Lear.*" *Criticism* 62, no. 3 (2020): 347–66.

Nardizzi, Vin. *Wooden Os: Shakespeare's Theatres and England's Trees.* Toronto: University of Toronto Press, 2013.

Nardizzi, Vin. "Wooden Slavery." *PMLA* 126, no. 2 (2011): 313–15.

Netzley, Ryan. *Lyric Apocalypse: Milton, Marvell, and the Nature of Events.* New York: Fordham University Press, 2015.

Neyrat, Frédéric. *Atopias: Manifesto for a Radical Existentialism.* Translated by Walt Hunter and Lindsay Turner. New York: Fordham University Press, 2018.

Neyrat, Frédéric. *The Unconstructable Earth: An Ecology of Separation.* Translated by Drew S. Burk. New York: Fordham University Press, 2019.

Nixon, Rob. *Slow Violence and the Environmentalism of the Poor.* Cambridge, Mass.: Harvard University Press, 2013.

Norbrook, David. *Writing the English Republic: Poetry, Rhetoric and Politics, 1627–1660.* Cambridge: Cambridge University Press, 1999.

Ong, Walter J. *Orality and Literacy: The Technologizing of the Word.* New York: Routledge, 2002.

Ovid. *Metamorphoses.* Translated by David Raeburn. New York: Penguin Books, 2004.

Oxford English Dictionary Online. 2nd ed. Oxford: Oxford University Press, 1989. www.oed.com.

Park, Katherine. "The Organic Soul." In *The Cambridge History of Renaissance Philosophy,* edited by Charles B. Schmitt and Quentin Skinner, 464–84. Cambridge: Cambridge University Press, 1988.

Parker, Patricia A. *Inescapable Romance: Studies in the Poetics of a Mode.* Princeton, N.J.: Princeton University Press, 1979.

Parker, Patricia A. *Literary Fat Ladies: Rhetoric, Gender, Property.* London: Methuen, 1987.

Parris, Benjamin. *Vital Strife: Sleep, Insomnia, and the Early Modern Ethics of Care.* Ithaca, N.Y.: Cornell University Press, 2022.

Parrish, Susan Scott. *American Curiosity: Cultures of Natural History in the Colonial British Atlantic World.* Chapel Hill: University of North Carolina Press, 2006.

Passannante, Gerard. *Catastrophizing: Materialism and the Making of Disaster.* Chicago: University of Chicago Press, 2019.

Paster, Gail Kern. *Humoring the Body: Emotion and the Shakespearean Stage.* Chicago: University of Chicago Press, 2004.

Picciotto, Joanna. *Labors of Innocence in Early Modern England.* Cambridge, Mass.: Harvard University Press, 2010.

Picciotto, Joanna. "Reforming the Garden: Experimentalist Eden and *Paradise Lost.*" ELH 72, no. 1 (2005): 23–78.

Plato. *Timaeus.* In *Plato: Complete Works,* edited by John M. Cooper, 1224–91. Translated by Donald J. Zeyl. Indianapolis: Hackett, 1997.

Pliny the Elder. *Natural History.* Translated by John F. Healy. New York: Penguin Books, 2004.

Popper, Nicholas. *Walter Ralegh's History of the World and the Historical Culture of the Late Renaissance.* Chicago: University of Chicago Press, 2012.

Povinelli, Elizabeth A. *Geontologies: A Requiem to Late Liberalism.* Durham, N.C.: Duke University Press, 2016.

Povinelli, Elizabeth A. "The Rhetorics of Recognition in Geontopower." *Philosophy and Rhetoric* 48, no. 4 (2015): 428–42.

Puar, Jasbir. *Terrorist Assemblages: Homonationalism in Queer Times.* Durham, N.C.: Duke University Press, 2007.

Puttenham, George. *The Art of English Poesy: A Critical Edition.* Edited by Frank Whigham and Wayne A. Rebhorn. Ithaca, N.Y.: Cornell University Press, 2007.

Quilligan, Maureen. *The Language of Allegory: Defining the Genre.* Ithaca, N.Y.: Cornell University Press, 1979.

Raber, Karen. *Animal Bodies, Renaissance Culture.* Philadelphia: University of Pennsylvania Press, 2013.

Raber, Karen. "Equeer: Human-Equine Erotics in *1 Henry IV*." In *The Oxford Handbook of Shakespeare and Embodiment: Gender, Sexuality, and Race,* edited by Valerie Traub, 347–62. Oxford: Oxford University Press, 2016.

Raber, Karen. *Shakespeare and Posthumanist Theory.* London: Arden Shakespeare, 2020.

Ralegh, Walter. *The History of the World.* Edited by C. A. Patrides. London: Macmillan, 1971.

Ralegh, Walter. *The Poems of Sir Walter Ralegh.* Edited by Agnes M. C. Latham. London: Routledge, 1951.

Ralegh, Walter. *The Poems of Sir Walter Ralegh: A Historical Edition.* Edited by Michael Rudick. Tempe: ACMRS Press, 1999.

Ralegh, Walter. *Sir Walter Ralegh's Discoverie of Guiana.* Edited by Joyce Lorimer. London: Ashgate, 2006.

Ralegh, Walter. *Upon the first Invention of Shipping.* London, 1650.

Rambuss, Richard. *Closet Devotions.* Durham, N.C.: Duke University Press, 1998.

Ray, John. *Three Physico-Theological Discourses, Concerning I. The Primitive Chaos, and Creation of the World. II. The General Deluge, Its Causes and Effects. III. The Dissolution of the World, and Future Conflagration.* London, 1693.

Rhu, Lawrence F. "Romancing the Word: Pre-Texts and Contexts for the Errour Episode." *Spenser Studies* 11 (1996): 101–9.

Rogers, John. *The Matter of Revolution: Science, Poetry, and Politics in the Age of Milton.* Ithaca, N.Y.: Cornell University Press, 1996.

Rose, Jacqueline. *Sexuality in the Field of Vision*. London: Verso, 2005.

Rossi, Paulo. *The Dark Abyss of Time: The History of the Earth and the History of Nations from Hooke to Vico*. Translated by Lydia G. Cochrane. Chicago: University of Chicago Press, 1984.

Rudwick, Martin J. S. *Earth's Deep History: How It Was Discovered and Why It Matters*. Chicago: University of Chicago Press, 2014.

Rudwick, Martin J. S. *The Meaning of Fossils: Episodes in the History of Paleontology*. 2nd ed. Chicago: University of Chicago Press, 1985.

Ruti, Mari. *Penis Envy and Other Bad Feelings: The Emotional Costs of Everyday Life*. New York: Columbia University Press, 2018.

Ruti, Mari. *The Singularity of Being: Lacan and the Immortal Within*. New York: Fordham University Press, 2012.

Sanchez, Melissa E. "'She Straightness on the Woods Bestows': Protestant Sexuality and English Empire in Marvell's 'Upon Appleton House.'" In *Atlantic Worlds in the Long Eighteenth Century: Seduction and Sentiment*, edited by Toni Bowers and Tita Chico, 81–96. New York: Palgrave Macmillan, 2012.

Sappho. *If Not, Winter: Fragments of Sappho*. Translated by Anne Carson. New York: Vintage Books, 2002.

Sartre, Jean-Paul. *Being and Nothingness: An Essay on Phenomenological Ontology*. Translated by Hazel E. Barnes. London: Routledge, 2003.

Schuster, Aaron. *The Trouble with Pleasure: Deleuze and Psychoanalysis*. Cambridge, Mass.: MIT Press, 2016.

Schwartz, Regina Mara. *Sacramental Poetics at the Dawn of Secularism: When God Left the World*. Stanford, Calif.: Stanford University Press, 2008.

Sedgwick, Eve Kosofsky. "Paranoid Reading and Reparative Reading, or, You're So Paranoid, You Probably Think This Essay Is about You." In *Touching Feeling: Affect, Pedagogy, Performativity*, 123–51. Durham, N.C.: Duke University Press, 2003.

Serres, Michel. *The Parasite*. Translated by Lawrence R. Schehr. Minneapolis: University of Minnesota Press, 2007.

Shakespeare, William. *A Midsummer Night's Dream*. In *The Norton Shakespeare*. Edited by Stephen Greenblatt et al. 3rd ed., 1037–95. New York: Norton, 2016.

Shannon, Laurie. *The Accommodated Animal: Cosmopolity in Shakespearean Locales*. Chicago: University of Chicago Press, 2013.

Sharp, Hasana. *Spinoza and the Politics of Renaturalization*. Chicago: University of Chicago Press, 2011.

Shaviro, Steven. *The Universe of Things: On Speculative Realism*. Minneapolis: University of Minnesota Press, 2014.

Silverman, Kaja. *Flesh of My Flesh*. Stanford, Calif.: Stanford University Press, 2009.

Simon, David Carroll. *Light without Heat: The Observational Mood from Bacon to Milton*. Ithaca, N.Y.: Cornell University Press, 2018.

Sloterdijk, Peter. "Geometry in the Colossal: The Project of Metaphysical Globalization." *Environment and Planning D: Society and Space* 27, no. 1 (2009): 29–40.

Smailbegović, Ada. "From Code to Shape: Material-Semiotic Imbrications in the 'Particle Zoo' of Molecular Poetics." *differences* 29, no. 1 (2018): 134–72.

Spenser, Edmund. *The Faerie Queene*. Edited by A. C. Hamilton. 2nd ed. London: Longman, 2007.

Spenser, Edmund. "Letter to Raleigh." In *The Faerie Queene*. 2nd ed. Edited by A. C. Hamilton, 713–18. London: Longman, 2007.

Spenser, Edmund. *The Shorter Poems*. Edited by Richard A. McCabe. New York: Penguin Books, 1999.

Spinoza, Baruch. *Ethics*. In *Spinoza: Complete Works*. Edited by Michael L. Morgan, 213–382. Translated by Samuel Shirley. Indianapolis: Hackett, 2002.

Spivak, Gayatri Chakravorty. *Death of a Discipline*. New York: Columbia University Press, 2003.

Steel, Karl. *How Not to Make a Human: Pets, Feral Children, Worms, Sky Burial, Oysters*. Minneapolis: University of Minnesota Press, 2019.

Stewart, Kathleen. *Ordinary Affects*. Durham, N.C.: Duke University Press, 2007.

Stewart, Susan. *Poetry and the Fate of the Senses*. Chicago: University of Chicago Press, 2002.

Stoekl, Allan. *Bataille's Peak: Energy, Religion, and Postsustainability*. Minneapolis: University of Minnesota Press, 2007.

Swarbrick, Steven. "Idiot Science for a Blue Humanities: Shakespeare's *The Comedy of Errors* and Deleuze's Mad Cogito." *Journal for Cultural Research* 23, no. 1 (2019): 15–32.

Swarbrick, Steven. "Nature's Queer Negativity: Between Barad and Deleuze." *Postmodern Culture* 29, no. 2 (2019). doi:10.1353/pmc.2019.0003.

Swarbrick, Steven. "Unworking Milton: Steps to a Georgics of the Mind." *postmedieval* 7, no. 1 (2016): 120–46.

Swarbrick, Steven, and Karen Raber. "Introduction: Renaissance Posthumanism and Its Afterlives." *Criticism* 62, no. 3 (2020): 313–28.

Tasso, Torquato. *The Liberation of Jerusalem (Gerusalemme liberata)*. Translated by Max Wickert. Oxford: Oxford University Press, 2009.

Teskey, Gordon. *Allegory and Violence*. Ithaca, N.Y.: Cornell University Press, 1996.

Teskey, Gordon. *Delirious Milton: The Fate of the Poet in Modernity*. Cambridge, Mass.: Harvard University Press, 2006.

Teskey, Gordon. *The Poetry of John Milton*. Cambridge, Mass.: Harvard University Press, 2015.

Thacker, Eugene. *In the Dust of This Planet: Horror of Philosophy*. Vol. 1. Washington, D.C.: Zero Books, 2011.

Tiffany, Daniel. *Toy Medium: Materialism and Modern Lyric*. Berkeley: University of California Press, 2000.

Tomšič, Samo. *The Capitalist Unconscious: Marx and Lacan*. London: Verso, 2015.

Traisnel, Antoine. *Capture: American Pursuits and the Making of a New Animal Condition*. Minneapolis: University of Minnesota Press, 2020.

Traub, Valerie. *The Renaissance of Lesbianism in Early Modern England*. Cambridge: Cambridge University Press, 2002.

Tremblay, Jean-Thomas. *Breathing Aesthetics*. Durham, N.C.: Duke University Press, 2022.

Tremblay, Jean-Thomas, and Steven Swarbrick. "Destructive Environmentalism: The Queer Impossibility of *First Reformed*." *Discourse* 43, no. 1 (2021): 3–30.

Tsing, Anna Lowenhaupt. *The Mushroom at the End of the World: On the Possibility of Life in Capitalist Ruins*. Princeton, N.J.: Princeton University Press, 2015.

Usher, Phillip John. *Exterranean: Extraction in the Humanist Anthropocene*. New York: Fordham University Press, 2019.

Varnado, Christine. *The Shapes of Fancy: Reading for Queer Desire in Early Modern Literature*. Minneapolis: University of Minnesota Press, 2020.

Vasari, Giorgio. *The Lives of the Artists*. Translated by Julia Conaway Bondanella and Peter Bondanella. Oxford: Oxford University Press, 2008.

The Velvet Underground. "I'll Be Your Mirror." Track 9 on *The Velvet Underground & Nico*. Recorded April 1966. Andy Warhol (producer), and Nico (vocalist). Verve, 1967.

Vickers, Nancy J. "'The Blazon of Sweet Beauty's Best': Shakespeare's *Lucrece*." In *Shakespeare and the Question of Theory*, edited by Patricia Parker and Geoffrey Hartman, 95–115. London: Methuen, 1985.

Vickers, Nancy J. "Diana Described: Scattered Woman and Scattered Rhyme." *Critical Inquiry* 8, no. 2 (1981): 265–79.

Virgil. *Georgics*. Translated by Peter Fallon. Oxford: Oxford University Press, 2006.

Virno, Paolo. *A Grammar of the Multitude: For an Analysis of Contemporary Forms of Life*. Translated by Isabella Bertoletti, James Cascaito, and Andrea Casson. Los Angeles: Semiotext(e), 2004.

Vitruvius. *On Architecture*. 2 vols. Loeb Classical Library. Translated by Frank Granger. Cambridge, Mass.: Harvard University Press, 1998.

Walcott, Derek. "The Sea Is History." In *Collected Poems, 1948–1984*. New York: Noonday Press, 1994.

Wall, Wendy. *Staging Domesticity: Household Work and English Identity in Early Modern Drama*. Cambridge: Cambridge University Press, 2002.

Whitehead, Alfred North. *The Concept of Nature*. New York: Dover, 2004.

Whitehead, Alfred North. *Modes of Thought*. New York: The Free Press, 1968.

Williams, Raymond. *The Country and the City*. Oxford: Oxford University Press, 1973.

Wilson, Elizabeth A. "Acts against Nature." *Angelaki* 23, no. 1 (2018): 19–31.

Wilson, Elizabeth A. *Psychosomatic: Feminism and the Neurological Body*. Durham, N.C.: Duke University Press, 2004.

Wittkower, Rudolf. *Architectural Principles in the Age of Humanism*. New York: Norton, 1971.

Wohlleben, Peter. *The Hidden Life of Trees: What They Feel, How They Communicate*. Translated by Jane Billinghurst. Vancouver: Greystone Books, 2015.

Woolfson, Jonathan. "The Renaissance of Bees." *Renaissance Studies* 24, no. 2 (2009): 281–300.

Yaeger, Patricia. "Sea Trash, Dark Pools, and the Tragedy of the Commons." *PMLA* 125, no. 3 (2010): 523–45.

Yates, Julian. *Of Sheep, Oranges, and Yeast: A Multispecies Impression.* Minneapolis: University of Minnesota Press, 2017.

Yusoff, Kathryn. *A Billion Black Anthropocenes or None.* Minneapolis: University of Minnesota Press, 2018.

Žižek, Slavoj. *Enjoy Your Symptom! Jacques Lacan in Hollywood and Out.* New York: Routledge, 2008.

Žižek, Slavoj. *Looking Awry: An Introduction to Jacques Lacan through Popular Culture.* Cambridge, Mass.: MIT Press, 1992.

Žižek, Slavoj. *The Plague of Fantasies.* London: Verso, 2008.

Žižek, Slavoj. *Sex and the Failed Absolute.* London: Bloomsbury, 2021.

Žižek, Slavoj. *The Sublime Object of Ideology.* London: Verso, 2008.

Žižek, Slavoj. *The Ticklish Subject: The Absent Centre of Political Ontology.* London: Verso, 2008.

Zupančič, Alenka. *What Is Sex?* Cambridge, Mass.: MIT Press, 2017.

INDEX

accidents, 36–39; and identity, 52–54; and matter, 151; and sexuality, 38–39, 47–49, 51–53; as wounds, 39–40, 51–52. *See also* events; Malabou, Catherine

accumulation. *See* capitalism

actions, 161–63, 224–26, 230–31, 239–44; deferred, 64–65; and nonaction, 79, 160–61; suspended, 132–33. *See also* agency

Adam, Adamic, 8, 201–8, 215–19, 237–42, 253n33. *See also* matter, materiality, materialism; Milton, John: *Paradise Lost*

aesthetics, 19–20, 174, 198–99

affect: and defacement, 118–20; and events, 219–20, 223–26, 229–31; and exhaustion, 226–31; inhuman, 219–22, 226–27, 229–31; and oceanic self, 115–16

affect theory, 5–6, 251n12, 256n64, 289n9. *See also* matter, materiality, materialism

Agamben, Giorgio, 111–14, 140–41. *See also* biopolitics, biopower

agency: distributed forms of, 201–3; and mathematics, 162–63; and nature, 229; nonhuman, 67, 117, 121; and politics, 160–62

Alaimo, Stacy, 5

Alberti, Leon Battista, *De re aedificatoria* (On the Art of Building), 147–49, 152–54

Alexander, Amir, 164

allegory: and abstract form, 87–89; and animality, 86–87; breaking, 76–77; and closure, 89–90, 92–96; and destructive plasticity, 40–41, 54–55, 68; and dialectical reversal, 68–69; and events, 60–61; and gender, 87–89; and language, 57–60; and love, 92; and materialism ("allegorical materialism"), 36–39, 55–57, 79–81, 92, 97; and meaning, 87–89; and nature, 55–56, 58, 180–81; and

matter or materialism, 42–43, 46–47; and misrecognition, 234–36; and pleasure, 235–36; and queer theory, 2–3; and semiosis, 22–23; and sexuality, 23, 43–49, 58–61, 84–85, 176–77; and temporality, 77–79; and trauma, 41–43; and unconscious, 12–15, 22–23, 27, 261n105. *See also* desire; matter, materiality, materialism; unconscious

Puar, Jasbir, 201–3

Puttenham, George, 137–38; *The Art of English Poesy*, 154–56, 158–59

queerness, 191–93; and assemblages, 201–3; and bondage, 196–97; and desire, 28–21; and ecology, 282n116; erasing, 195–96; and geontopower, 220–21; and nature, 268n52; and nonlife, 212, 221–22, 229–31; and space, 215–18; and time, 224–25, 229–31. *See also* sexuality

queer theory, 2–3, 201–4; and geology, 211; and inhuman, 210; and new materialism, 285n39; pastoral turn in, 211–12, 285n39; and *sinthome*, 2–3

Quilligan, Maureen, 81

Raber, Karen, 4–5

race, racialization, 140, 187–88

Ralegh, Walter, 1–2; and disability, 111–13, 135–36; *The Discoverie of Guiana*, 114–15, 127–28, 130–35; and ecological assemblages, 118–21, 133–35; *The History of the World*, 111–15, 135–38, 142–43; and human reason, 142–43; and life, 141–42; and loss, 131–32; and nation, 117; and Noah's ark, 140; and ocean, 144–45; *Ocean to Cynthia*, 114–15, 118–20; *Upon the first Invention of Shipping*, 137–38

Ray, John, 206–8, 210–11

reading: and allegory, 81; close, 4–5, 16–17; distant, 137–38; and ecocriticism, 16; and failure of meaning, 14–15, 103–4, 108; and matter, 103–5; and misrecognition, 77–79; and negativity, 252n16; and new materialisms, 5–9; and silence, 103

real, realism, 2–6, 105–6, 258n74, 290n15; and abstraction, 141–42, 152; and language, 18–19; as nonplace, 15; speculative, 7–8, 22, 253n31, 261n106. *See also* life, lifeworlds; matter, materiality, materialism

redemption, 15–17, 19–21, 113–15, 203–4, 229

relationality, 5, 22–23, 60–61, 99; and cross-cultural poetics, 120–21; cross-species, 140; and desire, 241–42; and ecocriticism, 288n8; and failure of full speech, 104–5; and nations, 117; and nonidentity, 224–25; and production, 235–36; as scene of writing, 133–34; and subjectivity, 77; technological, 137–38; and trauma, 77. *See also* care; entanglement; mutuality

46–49, 58–61; and queer desire, 220–21; of seas, 35–36; and trauma, 45–47; and unconscious, 14–15, 22–23, 26n105. *See also* desire; psychoanalysis

Shakespeare, William, *A Midsummer Night's Dream*, 188

Shannon, Laurie, 1–2, 111–13, 140

Sharp, Hasana, 162–63

Sidney, Sir Philip, 121–23

silence, 11–12, 14–17, 75–76, 102–3, 197, 203–5

Silverman, Kaja, 115–16

sinthome, 2–3

Sloterdijk, Peter, 144–45

space, spatiality, 123–24, 152–53; and history, 223–24; of inscription, 158–60; of interior, 182–83; and nature, 215–18; and ocean, 115–16; and place, 213–21; of politics, 197–98; queer, 215–18; suspension of, 132–33. *See also* architecture; time, temporality

Spenser, Edmund, 1–2; allegorical materialism of, 36–37, 40–41; "Bowre of Blisse," 218–19; and destructive plasticity, 39–40; and ecological subjectivity, 77; *The Faerie Queene*, 35–36, 39–41, 63–64, 71–83, 85–103, 106–8; on Ralegh, 116–17; and reading, 103–4; and sexuality, 39–40; *The Shepheardes Calender*, 76–77; and trauma, 71–72

Spinoza, Baruch, *Ethics*, 161–63

spirituality, 92–94

Spivak, Gayatri Chakravorty, 144

Steel, Karl, 4–5

Stewart, Susan, 19–20

subject, subjectivity: and brain, 53–54; and contemplation, 157–58; decentering human, 63–64, 67; and desire, 105–6, 238–42, 257n73; discordant, 171; dissolution of, 116–17; ecological, 2–3, 77; headless, 106–8, 194–97; and humanism, 6–7; and libidinalism, 2–3; and loss, 41–42; material, 52–53; and nature, 179–81, 233; and negativity, 2–3, 79–81; and otherness, 117; and perception, 98; and place, 213; as potential whole, 126–27; and relationality, 77; as self-divided, 13; and self-possession, 197–98; and sexuality, 176–77; split, 105–6; subtracting, 170; and suspension, 113–15; and trauma, 71–72, 77–79; and unconscious, 13. *See also* psychoanalysis; self; unconscious

survival, 16–17, 42–43, 115, 132–33, 211–12, 283n7

suspension, 113–15, 117, 120–21, 132–33, 141, 158, 224

sustainability, 207–8, 211–12, 224–25, 240

symbol, 54–57, 60–61. *See also* allegory

symptom, symptomology, 3–4, 11–12, 45–46, 75–79, 82, 211–12, 218–19, 252n16

Vicker, Nancy, 124–27
violence: against animals, 95–97,
224–25; colonial, 126–27; symbolic, 124–25
Virgil, *Georgics*, 121–23
vitalism, 7–8, 16–17, 103–4, 114–15,
123–24, 157–58, 160–61, 181–82,
211–12, 227–31
Vitruvius, Marcus, 174, 188, 190–91
voice, 10, 39–40, 65–66, 104–6,
205–6, 270n8. *See also*
complaints

Weinstein, Jami, 224–25
wild, wildness, 96–97, 215–18,
237–40, 289n14
Winstanley, Gerrard, 160–61
Wittkower, Rudolf, 152–54
wood (*hyle*), 43, 57, 63–65, 73–75,
88–89, 96–97, 188–200, 265n1.
See also Marvell, Andrew;
matter, materiality, materialism;
Spenser, Edmund
Woodward, John, 210–11
Woolfson, Jonathan, 121–23
world, worlding, 133–34, 137–38,
274n73; and creation, 137–38;

globalized, 139; and history,
137–38; and inhuman, 143;
and movement, 142–43; and
ocean, 141–45; as parergonal,
136–37; and technology, 136–38;
world-systems, 137–38. *See also*
globe, globalization; ocean
wound, 26–27, 39–40, 43–57, 64–
67, 71–72, 75–77, 88–90, 97–100,
105–6, 118–20, 219–22, 225–31.
See also Malabou, Catherine;
Spenser, Edmund; trauma
writing: and difference, 243–44; of
earth, 133–34, 157–58, 168–70,
182, 188; homographic, 159–60,
192–93; and movement, 142–43;
of nature, 274n73; and worlding,
274n73

Yaeger, Patricia, 137–38
Yates, Julian, 4–5, 257n67, 277n21
Yusoff, Kathryn, 187–88

Zeno, 164
Žižek, Slavoj, 77–79, 252n17,
260n104
Zupančič, Alenka, 254n44